FIFTY KEY THINKERS IN CRIMINOLOGY

D0077296

FIFTY KEY THINKERS IN CRIMINOLOGY

Edited by
Keith Hayward, Shadd Maruna
and Jayne Mooney

Routledge
Taylor & Francis Group

LONDON AND NEW YORK

First published 2010
by Routledge
2 Milton Park Square, Milton Park, Abingdon, Oxon, OX14 4RN

Simultaneously published in the USA and Canada
by Routledge
711 Third Avenue, New York, NY 10017

Routledge is an imprint of the Taylor & Francis Group, an informa business

Typeset in Bembo by
Taylor & Francis Books

British Library Cataloguing in Publication Data
A catalogue record for this book is available from the British Library

Library of Congress Cataloging in Publication Data
Fifty key thinkers in criminology / edited by Keith Hayward, Shadd Maruna and Jayne
Mooney.
p. cm.
[etc.]
1. Criminologists–Biography–Dictionaries. 2. Criminology. I. Hayward, Keith J. II.
Maruna, Shadd. III. Mooney, Jayne, 1964-
HV6023.F54 2009
364.092'2–dc22
2009021755

ISBN10: 0-415-42910-2 (hbk)
ISBN10: 0-415-42911-0 (pbk)
ISBN10: 0-203-86503-0 (ebk)

ISBN13: 978-0-415-42910-8 (hbk)
ISBN13: 978-0-415-42911-5 (pbk)
ISBN13: 978-0-203-86503-3 (ebk)

CONTENTS

CHRONOLOGICAL LIST OF
CONTENTS

ALPHABETICAL LIST OF CONTENTS

CONTRIBUTORS

Katja Franko Aas is Associate Professor at the Institute of Criminology and Sociology of Law, University of Oslo, Norway. She has written extensively on issues of globalisation, surveillance and uses of information and communication technologies in contemporary penal systems. Her recent publications include *Technologies of Insecurity* (co-edited with H. M. Lomell and H. O. Gundhus) (Routledge-Cavendish, 2009), *Globalization and Crime* (SAGE, 2007) and *Sentencing in the Age of Information: From Faust to Macintosh* (Routledge-Cavendish, 2005).

Anthony Amatrudo is Programme Leader for Criminology at the University of Sunderland, UK, and a Visiting Research Fellow at the Max Planck Institute for Foreign and International Criminal Law, Freiburg, Germany. He has previously held visiting research posts at the Central European University in Budapest and St Edmund's College, Cambridge. He publishes mainly in legal and political theory and is the author of *Criminology and Political Theory* (Sage, 2009).

Gregg Barak is Professor of Criminology and Criminal Justice at Eastern Michigan University, USA. He is the editor and/or author of 16 books, such as *Crimes By the Capitalist State: An Introduction to State Criminality* (SUNY Press, 1991), *Gimme Shelter: A Social History of Homelessness in Contemporary America* (Praeger, 1991), *Representing O.J.: Murder, Criminal Justice and Mass Culture* (Harrow & Heston, 1996), *Violence and Nonviolence: Pathways to Understanding* (Sage, 2003), *Class, Race, Gender, and Crime: The Social Realities of Justice in America* (Rowman & Littlefield, Second Edition, 2007), and *Criminology: An Integrated Approach* (Rowman and Littlefield, 2009).

Joanne Belknap is Professor of Sociology at the University of Colorado, USA. She has published widely in the area of gender and crime, including research on female offenders and violence against women. She is the author of *The Invisible Woman: Gender, Crime, and Justice* (Wadsworth, Third Edition, 2007).

Frank Bovenkerk, an anthropologist by training, is a retired Professor of Criminology at the University of Utrecht in The Netherlands. He now fulfils the Frank J. Buijs Chair for Studies of Radicalisation at the University of Amsterdam. He has researched and written on migration, race discrimination, ethnicity and crime, organised crime, urban studies and cultural criminology. Among the titles of his books are *The Turkish Mafia* (Milo Books, 2007, together with Yücel Yesilgöz) and *The Organized Crime Community*, edited together with Michael Levi (Springer, 2007).

Heather Boyd earned a BS degree in Sociology at Oregon State University, USA, in 2008. She is currently a graduate student in the Master of Public Policy programme and a teaching assistant for the Department of Sociology at Oregon State University.

Kate Bradley is a Lecturer in Social History and Social Policy at the University of Kent, UK. Her research interests lie in the history of twentieth-century British social policy, with particular reference to the historical development and social construction of urban youth, citizenship and delinquency. She is the author of *Poverty, Philanthropy and the State: Charities and the Working Classes in London, 1918–79* (Manchester University Press, 2009).

David Brotherton is Professor and Chair of Sociology at John Jay College of Criminal Justice, The City University of New York (CUNY), USA, and a member of the PhD faculties in Criminal Justice, Sociology and Urban Education at The Graduate Center. Professor Brotherton's research and teaching primarily focus on processes of social exclusion and resistance. He has published widely on street gangs, urban education, youth subcultures, immigration and deportation. Professor Brotherton is author, co-author or co-editor of several books including: *Back to the Homeland: Social Control, Dominican Deportees and Transnationalism* (forthcoming), *Keeping Out the Other: A Critical Introduction to Immigration Control Today* (2008), and *The Almighty Latin King and Queen Nation: Street Politics and the Transformation of a New York City Gang* (2004).

Phil Carney is a Lecturer at the University of Kent, UK, coordinates the Common Study Programme in Critical Criminology, and is Director of Studies for the MA in Criminology. He is in the process of publishing his PhD thesis, *The Punitive Gaze*, which uses photographic, critical and cultural theory to examine the photograph as an instrument of punishment and terror. Currently he is interested in the relationships between desire and power in the culture of crime, control and punishment.

Patrick Carr is Associate Professor of Sociology at Rutgers University, USA, and is an Associate Member of the MacArthur Foundation's Research Network on the Transitions to Adulthood and Public Policy. He has published widely in the areas of communities and crime, informal social control, youth violence, and transitions to adulthood. He is the author of *Clean Streets: Controlling Crime, Maintaining Order and Building Community Activism* (2005, NYU Press) and he is co-author along with Maria J. Kefalas of the forthcoming *Hollowing Out the Middle: The Rural Brain Drain and What it Means for America* (2009, Beacon Press).

Ben Crewe is a Senior Research Associate at the Institute of Criminology, University of Cambridge, UK. He has written on various issues relating to prisons and imprisonment, and is currently engaged in a study of values, practices and outcomes in public and private sector corrections. He is the author of *The Prisoner Society: Power, Adaptation and Social Life in an English Prison* (OUP, 2009).

Matt DeLisi is Coordinator of Criminal Justice Studies, Faculty Affiliate with the Center for the Study of Violence, and Associate Professor in the Department of Sociology at Iowa State University, USA. His most recent books are *American Corrections: Theory, Research, Policy and Practice* (with Peter J. Conis, Jones & Bartlett, 2009) and *Delinquency in Society, 8th edition* (with Robert Regoli and John D. Hewitt, Jones & Bartlett, 2010). Professor DeLisi has published more than 100 scholarly works, and his research has appeared in criminology, criminal justice, genetics, psychology, psychiatry, public health, and forensics journals.

Ashley Demyan is a graduate student in Criminology, Law and Society at the University of California, Irvine, USA. Her research interests include trends in imprisonment and the sociology of punishment. Her current research focuses on sites of agency, resistance, and rehumanisation within American prisons.

David P. Farrington is Professor of Psychological Criminology at Cambridge University, UK. He has published 70 books and monographs and over 480 articles and chapters on psychological and criminological topics, especially on developmental criminology and early prevention (see e.g. his 2007 book *Saving Children from a Life of Crime*).

Jeff Ferrell is Professor of Sociology at Texas Christian University, USA, and Visiting Professor of Criminology at the University of Kent, UK. His books include *Crimes of Style*, *Tearing Down the Streets*, *Empire of Scrounge*, and with Keith Hayward and Jock Young, *Cultural Criminology: An Invitation*. He is the founding and current editor of the New York University Press book series *Alternative Criminology*, and one of the founding and current editors of the journal *Crime, Media, Culture*, winner of the 2006 Association of Learned and Professional Society Publishers' Charlesworth Award for Best New Journal.

Mark Findlay is Professor of Criminal Justice and Deputy Director, Institute of Criminology, University of Sydney, Australia. He also holds a Chair in International Criminal Justice, Centre for Criminal Justice, University of Leeds, UK. Since 2004 Professor Findlay has been a Senior Associate Research Fellow, Institute of Advanced Legal Studies (IALS), University of London, and was twice awarded the Inns of Court Fellowship from the IALS. Professor Findlay has taught and researched in Senior Positions at Trinity College (Dublin), City University of Hong Kong, and the University of the South Pacific. Most recently he is author of *The Globalisation of Crime* (CUP, Cambridge, 1999) and (with Henham) *Transforming International Criminal Justice* (Willan, Collumpton, 2005) and *Governing through Globalised Crime* (Willan, Collumpton, 2008). Currently he is writing *Beyond Punishment? Achieving International Criminal Justice* (with Ralph Henham).

Joshua D. Freilich is Associate Professor in the Criminal Justice Department at John Jay College, CUNY, USA. He is a lead investigator for the National Consortium for the Study of Terrorism and Responses to Terrorism (START), a Center of Excellence of the US Department of Homeland Security (DHS). Freilich's research has been funded by DHS directly as well as through START. He is the Principal Investigator (with Dr Steven Chermak, Michigan State University) on the United States Extremist Crime Database (ECDB) study, a large-scale data collection effort that is building the first of its kind relational database of all crimes committed by far-right extremists in the USA from 1990 to the present reported in an open source.

Loraine Gelsthorpe is Reader in Criminology and Criminal Justice at the Institute of Criminology, University of Cambridge, UK and a Fellow at Pembroke College. Over time her research interests have taken her into police stations, courts, probation offices, and prisons but recent work has revolved around sentencing provision for women offenders in the community and resettlement issues. She is the author of many works on women and criminal justice and youth justice. Recent publications include: *Provision for Women Offenders in the Community* (with G. Sharpe and J. Roberts, 2007, Fawcett Society) and *The Handbook of Probation* (edited with Rod Morgan, 2007, Willan Publishing).

Phillip Hadfield is Senior Research Fellow in the Centre for Criminal Justice Studies, School of Law, University of Leeds, UK. His research interests encompass criminological and sociological aspects of urban civility, policing and regulation. His publications include *Bar Wars: Contesting the Night in Contemporary British Cities* (2006), *Bouncers: Violence and Governance in the Night-time Economy* (2003) (as co-author), and *Nightlife and Crime: Social Order and Governance in International Perspective* (2009) (as sole editor), all published by Oxford University Press.

Laura J. Hanson is a doctoral research student in Criminology at the University of Kent, UK. Her research uses a historical overview of crime mapping and geographies of transgression to propose a multidisciplinary approach to better our understanding of deviance and crime. She completed a dual-Bachelors degree in Criminology and Sociology at the University of Florida, USA, and a Master's degree in Criminology at the University of South Florida. Her key research interests include cultural criminology, urbanism, emotion and space.

James Hardie-Bick is Lecturer in the School of Sociology and Criminology at Keele University, UK. His main areas of interest include social theory, sociology of risk and voluntary risk-taking and ethnographic research.

Keith J. Hayward is Senior Lecturer in Criminology and Sociology at the University of Kent, UK. He has published widely in the areas of criminological theory, cultural criminology, social theory, and popular culture. He is the author of *City Limits: Crime, Consumer Culture and the Urban Experience* (Routledge-Cavendish, 2004), the co-author of *Cultural Criminology: An Invitation* (Sage, 2008), and the co-editor of *Cultural Criminology Unleashed* (Routledge-Cavendish, 2004), *Criminology* (Oxford, 2009) and *Framing Crime: Cultural Criminology and the Image* (forthcoming).

Patrick Hebberecht is Professor of Criminology and Sociology of Law at the University of Ghent in Belgium. He has published in the areas of crime prevention, ethnic minorities and the sociology of criminal law. He is the co-editor of *The Prevention and Security Policies in Europe* (VUBPress, Brussels, 2002). His latest book is *De 'Verpaarsing' van de Criminaliteitsbestrijding in België: Kritische opstellen over misdaad en misdaadcontrole in de laatmoderniteit* (The 'purpleization' of criminal policy in Belgium: Critical thoughts on crime and crime control in late modernity) (VUBPress, Brussels, 2008).

Michelle Inderbitzin is Associate Professor of Sociology at Oregon State University, USA. Her research centres around juvenile justice, prison culture, and prisoner reintegration, and her work has been published in *Punishment & Society, Journal of Offender Rehabilitation*, and *Journal of Adolescent Research*. She regularly teaches Inside-Out classes in state prisons and works with young women in a youth correctional facility.

Yvonne Jewkes is Professor of Criminology at the University of Leicester, UK. She has published many books in the areas of media and crime and imprisonment including, *Crime and Media 3-Volume Set* (2009, Sage), *Prisons and Punishment 3-Volume Set* (2008, Sage), *Handbook on Prisons* (2007, Willan), *Crime Online* (2007, Willan), *Media and Crime* (2004, Sage) and *Captive Audience: Media, Masculinity and Power in Prisons* (2002, Willan). She is Associate Editor of *Crime, Media, Culture: An International Journal*, and Series Editor of both the Sage *Key Approaches to Criminology* series and (with Katja Franko Aas) the Ashgate *Crime, Technology and Society* series.

Jan Jordan is Associate Professor at the Institute of Criminology, Victoria University of Wellington, New Zealand. She has over 20 years' experience teaching and researching in the area of women, crime and victimisation. She is the author of three books: *Working Girls: Women in the New Zealand Sex Industry*; *The Word of a Woman? Police, Rape and Belief*; and most recently *Serial Survivors: Women's Narratives of Surviving Rape* (The Federation Press, Sydney, 2008) in which she explores how women attacked by the same serial rapist survived the rape attack itself as well as their subsequent involvement in police, trial and counselling processes.

Lila Kazemian is Assistant Professor in the Department of Sociology at John Jay College of Criminal Justice, New York, USA. She completed her doctoral degree in Criminology at the

University of Cambridge, UK, in 2005. Her research interests include life-course and developmental research, desistance from crime, comparative criminology, and offender reintegration. Her work has been published in the *Journal of Quantitative Criminology*, the *Journal of Research in Crime and Delinquency*, the *Journal of Contemporary Criminal Justice*, the *Journal of Youth and Adolescence*, and the *Canadian Journal of Criminology and Criminal Justice*.

John Lea is Professor of Criminology at Middlesex University, UK. He is author (with Jock Young) of *What is to Be Done about Law and Order?* (Penguin 1984/Pluto 1993). His most recent book is *Crime and Modernity* (Sage 2002). He has published in the areas of criminological theory and race and policing. He is currently working on organised crime and the relation between crime and war.

Anthony J. Lemelle, Jr. is Professor of Sociology and Criminal Justice at John Jay College, City University of New York, USA. He has published widely in the areas of deviance, race relations, African American culture, and public health. His forthcoming book for Routledge is *Black Masculinity and Sexual Politics*. He is Editor of the *Journal of African American Studies*.

Anne Logan is Lecturer in Social History at the University of Kent, UK. She researches and publishes work on the first women magistrates in England and Wales and on women's involvement in the construction of criminal justice policy in the period c. 1920–70. Her first book, *Feminism and Criminal Justice: A Historical Perspective* was published by Palgrave in 2008.

Marilyn D. McShane is Professor of Criminal Justice at the University of Houston-Downtown, USA. Her published work includes journal articles, monographs, encyclopaedias, and books on a wide range of criminological and criminal justice subjects. Recent works she has authored or co-authored include *Prisons in America* (LFB Scholarly Publishing, 2008), *Criminological Theory, 5th Edition* (Prentice Hall, 2009), *A Thesis Resource Guide for Criminology and Criminal Justice* (Prentice Hall, 2008), the co-edited three-volume set *Youth Violence and Delinquency: Monsters and Myths* (Praeger, 2008), and the *Encyclopedia of Juvenile Justice* (Sage, 2003).

Shadd Maruna is Professor of Justice Studies and Human Development and the Director of the Institute of Criminology and Criminal Justice at Queen's University, Belfast. He is the author or editor of four books on ex-prisoner reintegration, including *Making Good: How Ex-Convicts Reform and Rebuild Their Lives* (APA Books, 2001) and *Rehabilitation: Beyond the Risk Paradigm* (Routledge, 2007). He is currently a Soros Justice Fellow and previously has been a Fulbright Scholar and an H. F. Guggenheim Fellow.

Dario Melossi has been teaching at the Universities of California, USA, and Bologna, Italy, where presently he is Professor of Criminology in the Law School. He has just published *Controlling Crime, Controlling Society: Thinking About Crime in Europe and America* (Polity Press). His previous publications include *The Prison and the Factory* (with Massimo Pavarini), and *The State of Social Control*. He is working on issues of migration and deviance, especially youth deviance, in the Italian Region of Emilia-Romagna (within the EU framework).

Jayne Mooney is Associate Professor of Sociology at John Jay College of Criminal Justice and the Graduate Center, City University of New York, USA. She has published widely in the areas of gender and crime, domestic violence, the family and crime, and crime and the inner city. She is the author of *Gender, Violence and the Social Order* (Palgrave/Macmillan, 2000) and is currently completing *Rediscovering Criminology* for Pearson/Longman, and a study on extreme forms of violence.

Wayne Morrison is Professor of Law, Queen Mary University of London, and Director of the external undergraduate law programmes of the University of London (the largest common law programme in the world). He has written a number of books in Criminology, Legal Theory and Modernity. In particular *Criminology, Civilisation and the New World Order* (2006, Routledge-Cavendish); *Theoretical Criminology: From Modernity to Postmodernism* (1995, Cavendish); *The Politics of the Common Law: Perspectives, Rights, Institutions, Processes* (2009, Routledge/Cavendish, with Adam Gearey and Robert Jago); *Jurisprudence: From the Greeks to Post-modernity* (1997, Cavendish).

Mangai Natarajan is a Professor at John Jay College of Criminal Justice (CUNY), USA, and Director of the College's International Criminal Justice Degree Programme. She is an active policy-oriented researcher who has published widely in three areas: drug trafficking, women police, and domestic violence. Her most recent book, *Women Police in a Changing Society: Back Door to Equality* was published in 2008 by Ashgate.

Pat O'Malley is currently University of Sydney Professorial Research Fellow in Law. His research has focused mostly on risk management techniques as they are used to govern such fields as criminal justice. His recent books on risk include *Risk, Uncertainty and Government* (2004), *Crime and Risk* (forthcoming, Sage) and, with Kelly Hannah Moffat, *Gendered Risks*. His current work is focused on the use of money in justice and is outlined in *The Currency of Justice: Fines and Damages in Consumer Societies* (Routledge 2009).

Charlotte Pagni is a Lecturer at Eastern Michigan University, USA, specialising in media, gender and sexuality, and diversity issues. She has published articles on Public Access Television regulation and the Kinsey Reports' influence on American cinema in *The Spectator Journal of Film and Television Studies*.

Alex R. Piquero is Professor in the Department of Criminology & Criminal Justice at the University of Maryland College Park, USA, Executive Counselor with the American Society of Criminology, and Co-Editor of the *Journal of Quantitative Criminology*. His research interests include criminal careers, criminological theory, and quantitative research methods. He has received several research, teaching, and service awards, and his research has appeared in criminology, psychology, and sociology journals, and in 2007 Cambridge University Press published his co-authored (with Alfred Blumstein and David Farrington) book, *Key Issues in Criminal Careers Research: New Analyses from the Cambridge Study in Delinquent Development*.

Stephen C. Richards is Professor of Criminal Justice at the University of Wisconsin-Oshkosh, USA. His work has appeared in numerous journals. He is co-author of *Behind Bars: Surviving Prison* (Alpha/ Penguin 2002), co-editor of *Convict Criminology* (Cengage/Wadsworth, 2003), and co-author of *Beyond Bars: Rejoining Society After Prison* (Alpha/Penguin, 2009). Richards is a Soros Senior Justice Fellow. He is lead organiser of the Convict Criminology Group.

Martin D. Schwartz is Professor of Sociology Emeritus at Ohio University, USA. He is the 2008 Fellow of the Academy of Criminal Justice Sciences, and has received distinguished scholar awards from two different divisions of the American Society of Criminology: Women and Crime, and Critical Criminology. At Ohio University he has been named Graduate Professor of the Year, Best Arts and Sciences Professor, and awarded the university's research achievement award, the title of Presidential Research Scholar. He has written or edited (often with Walter S. DeKeseredy) 21 editions of 12 books, 70 journal articles and another 65 book chapters, government reports, and essays. He has never been convicted of a serious felony.

James Sheptycki is Professor of Criminology at York University, Toronto, Canada. He has published widely in the areas of transnational and comparative criminology and policing. He is the author of *Innovations in Policing Domestic Violence* (Avebury, 1993) and *In Search of Transnational Policing* (Ashgate, 2002) which was published in French translation as *En quête de police transnationale* (De Boek & Larcier, 2005). He has edited three books: *Issues in Transnational Policing* (Routledge, 2000); *Transnational and Comparative Criminology* (with Ali Wardak, Routledge, 2005); and *Crafting Transnational Policing* (with Andrew Goldsmith, Hart, 2007).

Gregory J. Snyder joined the Department of Sociology and Anthropology at Baruch College, USA, in the Fall of 2007, where the classes he teaches include: Introduction to Sociology, Race and Ethnic Relations, Social Class in American Life and Urban Sociology. His first book, *Graffiti Lives: Beyond the Tag in New York's Urban Underground*, was published by NYU Press in 2009. Currently Professor Snyder is hard at work on his second book tentatively titled, *Against the Grind: Professional Skateboarders and the Critique of Urban Space*.

Richard Sparks is Professor of Criminology at the University of Edinburgh, UK, and Co-Director of the Scottish Centre for Crime and Justice Research (www.sccjr.ac.uk/). Richard's main research interests lie in prisons; penal politics; public responses to crime and punishment; and criminological theory. His publications include: *Criminal Justice and Political Cultures* (with Tim Newburn (eds), Willan, 2004), *Criminology and Social Theory* (with David Garland (eds), Oxford University Press, 2000), *Crime and Social Change in Middle England* (with Evi Girling and Ian Loader, Routledge, 2000) and *Prisons and the Problem of Order* (with Tony Bottoms and Will Hay, Oxford University Press, 1996).

Jacqueline Tombs is Professor of Criminology & Social Justice and Director of the Institute for Society & Social Justice at Glasgow Caledonian University, UK. She has published widely in the areas of criminal justice and penal policy. Her publications include *Reducing the Prison Population: Penal Policy and Social Choices* (2005);

A Unique Punishment: Sentencing and the Prison Population in Scotland (2004); *The Chance for Change* (2003); *Making Sense of Drugs and Crime* (2002); *Rethinking Criminal Justice* (2000); *Social Work and Criminal Justice: The Impact of Policy* (with F. Paterson) (1998); *The British Crime Survey: Scotland* (with G. Chambers) (1984); and *Prosecution in the Public Interest* (with S. Moody) (1982).

Henk van de Bunt is full Professor of Criminology at the Erasmus University, Rotterdam, The Netherlands. He has published in the areas of organised crime, corporate crime and the administration of criminal justice.

René van Swaaningen is a Professor of International and Comparative Criminology at the Erasmus University, Rotterdam, the Netherlands, and Scientific Director of the Dutch Inter-University Research School on Safety and Security OMV. He has widely published – mainly in Dutch, English and Spanish – on criminal justice politics, comparative criminology, penology and crime prevention, and criminological and criminal justice theory. His major work in English is *Critical Criminology – Visions from Europe* (Sage, 1997).

Véronique Voruz is Lecturer in Law and Criminology at the University of Leicester, UK, and guest lecturer in Criminology at the école de criminologie of the Université Catholique de Louvain-la-Neuve in Belgium. She publishes in the areas of Foucault studies, psychiatry and psychoanalysis. She is the author of *Foucault and Criminology* (forthcoming).

Sandra Walklate is currently Eleanor Rathbone Chair of Sociology at the University of Liverpool, UK. She has written extensively on policing, gender and crime, and criminal victimisation with her work latterly being focused on the impact of the fear of terrorism on people's everyday lives. Her most recent publications include an edited collection (with G. Mythen) entitled *Beyond the Risk Society: Critical Reflections on Risk and Human Security* (McGraw-Hill/Open University Press, 2006) and a single authored book entitled *Imagining the Victim of Crime* (McGraw-Hill/Open University Press, 2007).

Colin Webster is Reader in Criminology at Leeds Metropolitan University, UK. He has published widely in the areas of race, ethnicity and crime, criminal careers, youth transitions and social exclusion and racist violence. He is the author of *Understanding Race and Crime* (Open University Press, 2007) and the co-author of *Poor Transitions: Social Exclusion and Young Adults* (Policy Press, 2004).

Iain Wilkinson is Senior Lecturer in Sociology at the University of Kent, UK. His publications include *Anxiety in a Risk Society* (Routledge, 2001), *Suffering: A Sociological Introduction* (Polity, 2005) and *Risk, Vulnerability and Everyday Life* (Routledge, 2009).

Frank P. Williams III is Professor of Criminal Justice at the University of Houston-Downtown and Professor Emeritus, California State University-San Bernardino, both in the USA. He has published a number of articles, research monographs, encyclopaedias, and books in areas ranging from criminological theory to correctional management. His recent works include *Statistical Concepts for Criminal Justice and Criminology* (Prentice Hall, 2008) and *Imagining Criminology* (Taylor & Francis, 1999), and he is co-author of *Criminological Theory, 5th Edition* (Prentice Hall, 2009), *A Thesis Resource Guide for Criminology and Criminal Justice* (Prentice Hall, 2008), and the three-volume edited set *Youth Violence and Delinquency: Monsters and Myths* (Praeger, 2008).

Majid Yar is Professor of Sociology at the University of Hull, UK. He has published widely across the areas of criminology, media and cultural analysis, and social and political theory. He is the author of *Cybercrime and Society* (Sage, 2006) and *Community & Recognition* (VDM Verlag, 2009), co-author of *Criminology: The Key Concepts* (Routledge, 2008) and co-editor of *The Handbook on Internet Crime* (Willan, 2009).

Jock Young is Distinguished Professor at the Graduate Center, City University of New York, USA and Professor of Sociology at the University of Kent, UK. He is the author and co-author of various books including *The Drugtakers*, *The New Criminology* (with Ian Taylor and Paul Walton) and *What is to be Done about Law and Order?* (with John Lea). His present research is on patterns of social exclusion in Europe, the USA and Latin America. His most recent books are *The Exclusive Society*, *The Vertigo of Late Modernity* and *Cultural Criminology: An Invitation* (with Jeff Ferrell and Keith Hayward). He has just completed *The Criminological Imagination*, and a new project, *Merton's Dreams and Quetelet's Warning* is in first draft.

INTRODUCTION

The history of criminology is a fascinating one. It is a story of human-kind's attempts to systematically study and understand the human capacity for crime and transgression. It provides a moral account of modernity and as such offers insight into the core meaning and value of humanity in our times. It is strange, then, that the story of criminology that unfolds in so many textbooks is often a rather formulaic, almost soulless one. This being the case, the invitation to edit this book was a difficult one to refuse. Our goal is to help enliven and humanise the story of criminology through the power of intellectual biographies, mixing life-story detail with analytical reflection on the contributions of 50 of criminology's important thinkers. We hope that this alternative introduction to criminology is of value to new students of the subject, and those in cognate areas of study like sociology, psychology, social geography or history, seeking to grasp the 'lay of the land' in our somewhat exotic field of research. Equally, we hope the book will also inspire debate and discussion within criminology itself. The major works of those thinkers profiled herein will be largely familiar to those with expertise in criminology, but the stories behind the ideas may be less so. These profiles may change the way some of us think about our field of study and the ideas that have shaped it.

A reasonable criticism of our approach to the story of criminology is that it contributes to the unfortunate (and largely discredited) tendency for histories that lionise the 'great white men' (or occasionally 'great white women' and 'great non-white individuals' as well). In other words, it presents an individualistic picture of criminology as being shaped by a select group of geniuses rather than a messy, dynamic intel-lectual process characterised by collaboration and cross-fertilisation. After all, the social science of criminology is a necessarily collective enterprise. The French physician Claude Bernard framed this concisely in his famous quote, 'Art is I, science is we'. Bob Bursik might have put this argument even more eloquently in a soon-to-be-legendary Presidential Address to the American Society of Criminology in 2008. Bursik argued that, in our efforts to remember the great 'elephants' of criminology's circus, we need to also remember the many sweepers who followed the elephants' paths, as without the sweepers (the forgotten 'lesser' names of criminology) the elephants (or 'big names') would have been most unpleasant entertainment. Indeed, the sweepers must get their due. Increasingly, the research articles in criminology are co-authored by teams of three or more individuals in various divisions of labour; even some of the most insightful theoretical works in the field have been co-authored (think Cloward and Ohlin, Gottfredson and Hirschi, etc.). Rather than appearing as if from 'on high', the 'big ideas' that have shaped criminology typically emerge out of dialogues between a professor and her students, research collaborations involving various colleagues, or, perhaps most commonly, from snippets of wisdom gleaned from ex-prisoners, active delinquents or criminal justice personnel during criminological fieldwork. Indeed, histories of science suggest that too often we equate profound scientific discoveries with individual 'great figures' – Darwin's 'discovery' of evolution is an example – even when such 'discoveries' more often emerge more out of the zeitgeist of one's era, with 'great figures' more often than not simply finding themselves in the right place at the right time.

Although this critique is valid, it also involves a misunderstanding of the nature of biography as utilised in this book. The point of the profiles in our collection is to set the theories and ideas of these thinkers squarely against the historical, cultural and interpersonal backdrops in which they emerged. Despite the myth of the 'self-made man' (*sic*), no person is an island, and no good biography features only one character. The point of biography is to show how human lives develop and unfold through interactions with the social environment, how each of us creates and is created out of our circumstances, associations and attachments. Intellectual biographies like the 50 in this collection highlight the unique influences that contribute to the theories that have inspired criminologists over the last century or so.

The most obvious example of this cross-fertilisation can be found by following the cross-references between different entries in this collection. Although the chapters in this book feature only one thinker (or on the odd occasion a pair of thinkers), within the profile one can usually find references to half a dozen or more others inside and outside of criminology. When one of these cross-references involves a person profiled in this book, we have printed the name in bold for emphasis. As such, perhaps the most interesting way to read this book would be to proceed not alphabetically or even chronologically, but rather to follow these cross-references as if one were clicking on hyperlinks on a computer screen. So, for instance, if one started the book by reading a profile of one of the more contemporary criminologists featured in this collection, Robert Sampson (born in 1956), one will see a reference to the work of Travis Hirschi (born 1935). In reading Hirschi's profile, one finds a link to the profile of Emile Durkheim (born 1858). In reading Durkheim's entry, one sees a reference to the contemporary work of David Garland (born in 1955). So, one can get from Sampson to Garland in three steps. How many links does it take to get from W. E. B. Du Bois to Sheldon and Eleanor Glueck or from Frances Heidensohn to Jeremy Bentham? In following these sorts of loops, one gets a different picture of the linkages and the remarkably few degrees of separation between so many of the 50 thinkers profiled, and indeed the field as a whole.

Of course, there will inevitably be disagreements about some of the people included and especially excluded from this volume – after all, part of the fun of any book of lists is the discussion and debates the list generates. Note, however, that the title of this collection is *Fifty Key Thinkers in Criminology* – not *The Fifty Most Important Thinkers*, but simply 'fifty key thinkers' (the absence of that definite article is crucial here). Indeed, even the phrase 'fifty key thinkers' is something of a misnomer in that there are actually 53 individuals discussed – three entries involve pairs who worked so closely together that we decided not to separate them. Nonetheless, every sentient reader of criminological work will justifiably wonder why X is included instead of Y or Z (where Y = the person's mentor/hero/neighbour and Z = the person himself or herself, depending on one's ego strength). Indeed, we would be shocked and a little disappointed if there were not such disagreements.

Although about half of the names on this list might be thought of as automatic or obvious choices, there was considerable contestation regarding the remainder of the list among the three of us as co-editors. To help us resolve this task – and it has to be said, to put an end to healthy debates that were in danger of becoming feuds! – we turned to some rough, empirical research. This involved highly informal 'focus groups' and one-on-one 'interviews' with trusted fellow criminologists, as well as a small open-ended survey distributed to an unrepresentative sample of 100 or so fellow criminologists at two academic meetings and via email. Respondents ranged from former presidents of various societies of criminology to final-year PhD students, and their recommendations included a variety of interesting possibilities including names like Fyodor Dostoyevsky and Truman Capote, whom we had never previously considered. We tallied up the responses from all of these data collection efforts, of course, but this was not an effort at majority-rules democracy or some faux-objectivity. Again, we make no claims that our final 50 is somehow 'the' list of most influential thinkers in criminology as if such a thing was even possible to determine. Instead, we used the (frustratingly inconclusive) results to inform our own thinking, to better understand how others interpret the idea of 'key thinkers in criminology', and to settle some internal disputes among ourselves somewhat like a more sophisticated coin toss. Like every other reader of this book, all three of the editors have particular heroes, mentors and favourites who did not make the list. To those individuals and all the others left off this list, we apologise, but remember no ranking of your individual importance is implied.

Still, some clarification of the rationale for inclusion is needed. For instance, in taking on this task, we had to decide among ourselves what exactly is meant by a 'key thinker' and indeed a 'key thinker in criminology'. As this book is part of a wider series on 'fifty key thinkers' in various disciplines, we inherited this title, but were allowed to interpret it as we chose.

We decided upon a working definition of a 'key thinker' as someone whose ideas have influenced the shape of the field of study currently labelled 'criminology'. As such, we are equating 'thinkers' primarily with those who have made a substantial theoretical contribution. Of course, most of the individuals on our final list are more than 'just' theorists. Many of them are also first-rate researchers, methodologists, teachers, organisers, administrators, activists, and even practitioners. However, we decided not to include individuals in the book whose primary contributions to the field could be categorised under these other headings. This was a difficult decision. The field of criminology has been immensely improved by a number of remarkable methodologists and experts in both qualitative and quantitative research. These methodological insights (the development of new statistical tests or analytic techniques, for instance) are 'ideas' too, and we do not want to imply that such remarkable social scientists are not 'thinkers' or 'key'. In fact, arguably, empirical researchers contribute more to the field of criminology than do theoreticians. Still, we had to limit our definition in some ways, and we chose to equate 'thinkers' with 'theorists' for this reason only.

As a result, many of the most important and famous figures in the history of criminology as a discipline are not featured on these pages. For instance, none of the three European émigrés widely regarded to be the founders of modern criminology in the UK – Hermann Mannheim, Max Grünhut and Leon Radzinowicz – are profiled here.

Their contributions to the discipline were immense and incontrovertible, but the legacy they have left is not primarily in the area of criminological theory. Further, we have mostly defined 'criminology' as academic criminology, not applied criminological work or practice. As such, there are no entries on hugely influential penal or police reformers like John Howard, Alexander Maconochie or Robert Peel. Admittedly, the line between academic and applied criminology is a fine one and this distinction is somewhat arbitrary, but (again) we needed to draw lines somewhere.

The same is true in regards to the invisible barriers between criminology and so many academic disciplines, and this is where we ran into the most difficulties in trying to delimit our list. We were insistent that we do not constrict ourselves to individuals who work or worked in departments of criminology or who labelled themselves first and foremost as 'criminologists'. At the same time, we were asked to profile key thinkers in criminology, not in sociology or law or any of criminology's other cognate disciplines. This task was made more difficult by the fact that criminology is a 'rendezvous discipline' constituted from an array of competing theoretical, methodological and ideological paradigms. Criminology meetings tend to be populated by individuals who work in dozens of different academic departments and who have been trained in disciplines as disparate as history, law, biology, philosophy, psychology and gender studies (or some combination therein). Indeed, only recently have academic departments of criminology started to hire staff who primarily have been trained in criminology or criminal justice. Likewise, published literature reviews in criminology journals draw on a wide variety of scholarship from multiple disciplines. Our list of 50 key thinkers, then, logically reflects this diversity.

At the same time, we did feel obligated to draw some arbitrary distinctions and exclude whole groups of thinkers from the collection. For instance, the list of psychologists who have influenced criminology and could rightly be included here is long and daunting. One immediately thinks of names like Hans Eysenck, Albert Bandura, Philip Zimbardo, even Sigmund Freud. Yet, it seemed to us that including these hugely important figures would open the floodgates and somewhat threaten to overwhelm the criminological story that we wanted to tell. If we include Bandura and Freud, for instance, then what about all of the other psychological pioneers in areas such as aggression, antisocial behaviour, violence, addiction, psychopathology and so forth? Why not B. F. Skinner, Stanley Milgram, Leonard Berowitz or even William James? The list could easily turn into a 50 key thinkers in psychology list, and there are already a variety of books devoted to the different areas of that discipline – including one in this series. The same problem occurred in regards to legal scholars. Several of the individuals profiled in our collection currently teach or formerly taught in law schools, yet the biggest names in criminal law and law and society research are not on these pages – even those like Malcolm Feeley, Norval Morris, Franklin Zimring, who have so actively engaged with criminological work. Again, our only excuse is the sense that legal research is such a huge area and so much of it impacts on criminological research questions that it was difficult to know where to stop if we were to include pioneers in criminal procedure, evidence, sentencing, drug laws, capital punishment and so forth. The same can be said of fields like sociology, international studies, politics and so forth.

So, for the most part, we decided our 'rule' would be to stick to those individuals whose ideas have clearly shaped the contemporary debates and discussions in *criminology* as the field is understood today – at the same time, excluding from this definition those whose primary contributions are clearly contained in another discipline (law, psychology, etc.). How, then, do we justify the inclusion of figures like Marx and Engels who are clearly more appropriately considered economists or sociologists or historians than criminologists? Basically, we can't. Eventually we decided that it was impossible to delimit the field of possible entries in any perfect, systematic way, so the final list includes some completely biased, idiosyncratic choices based on our own prerogative as editors.

Finally, one could also, justifiably, question the over-representation of white North American men (n = 20) on our list of 50. Although we have tried to reflect the multicultural make-up of the discipline with profiles of individuals born in at least 17 different countries, we did limit our profiles to those whose work has been written or widely translated into English, as our audience for this book is primarily within English-speaking criminology. Readers will also, no doubt, notice the pronounced gender imbalance of the final list. These biases, we hope, have less to do with our own informed choices, and are more of a reflection of the white male-dominated nature of academic criminology since its inception in the mid nineteenth century.

While this preface is perhaps not the right vehicle for taking on the issue of continued gender, racial and ethnic disparities within the discipline, we have made an effort to invite a diverse, multicultural group of contributors to write the profiles in this collection. The contributors range from very new PhDs in criminology to some of the same criminological pioneers featured in the book's profiles (we have not asked any of them to write their *own* autobiographical profile, however). The outcome, we think, is a necessarily subjective, idiosyncratic collection of 50 perspectives on 50 key thinkers and their lives. It is not meant as a 'last word' on the history of the field, but we hope it is as messy, dynamic, complicated and interesting as criminology itself.

KEITH HAYWARD, SHADD MARUNA, JAYNE MOONEY

FIFTY KEY THINKERS IN
CRIMINOLOGY

CESARE BECCARIA (1738–94)

Beccaria's name is today inextricably associated with what is often dubbed the 'Classical School' of criminology. This is something of a misnomer, as Beccaria was neither a criminologist (the idea of a discipline focused upon the systematic study of crime did not emerge until a century or so after Beccaria's death), nor was he a part of any clearly defined 'school' that held to a consistent set of views. Nevertheless, *On Crimes and Punishments* (1764), Beccaria's major work, exerted a wide-ranging influence both upon reformers and academics, and continues to be seen justifiably as a landmark in modern scholarship and intellectual development where it comes to the understanding of crime, law and punishment.

Beccaria was born in 1738 in the province of Lombardy, which at the time was under Austrian rule. He was born into privilege, the eldest son of an aristocratic Milanese family. Beccaria studied first at the Jesuit school of Parma, and later completed a degree in Law at the University of Pavia (1758). His early education under the Jesuit brothers Beccaria later characterised as 'fanatical'. This can be seen as indicative of the steadfast scepticism he exhibited in his work where it came to the power of the church in shaping and dictating the order of society. Equally telling was his difficult relationship with his father, whose authority he defied in 1761 to marry a woman (Teresa di Blasco) deemed to be of a lower social standing than himself. It has been speculated that this experience contributed to his critical stance against the aristocratic ideals and privileges that held sway at the time.

At one level, Beccaria might be viewed as a minor provincial intellectual. Reportedly inhibited by a socially crippling sense of shyness, Beccaria barely ventured outside his native Lombardy (on one rare occasion he accepted an invitation to Paris following the success of *On Crimes and Punishments*, only to find himself unable to cope with the attention focused upon him, choosing instead to flee back to the security of his homeland). However, despite the provincial seclusion in which he lived, in another sense Beccaria can be seen as an archetypal Enlightenment thinker. In his early twenties Beccaria fell under the influence of an older Milanese aristocrat, Pietro Verri. Verri had travelled widely and studied extensively the writings of both British economic and political thinkers and the French *philosophes*. Upon his return to Milan, Verri was determined to disseminate the new ideas and ideals of European Enlightenment in Lombardy, and to harness these to a project of social, political, economic and legal reform. Verri was the pivotal figure in a circle of like-minded young academics who called themselves the 'Academy of Fists'. This group was 'dedicated to waging relentless war against economic disorder, bureaucratic petty tyranny, religious narrow-mindedness, and intellectual pedantry' (Paolucci 1963: xii). It was through Pietro Verri (along with his brother Aleesandro, another leading figure of the group) that Beccaria became familiar with the works of Thomas Hobbes, David Hume, Denis Diderot, Claude Adrien Helvétius and Charles-Louis de Secondat (better known as Montesquieu). His first published work was entitled *On Remedies for the Monetary Disorders of Milan in the Year 1762*. In his later life he wrote little, although his works include a posthumously published treatise on political economy as well as a treatise on style. However, it is *On Crimes and Punishments* for which Beccaria is remembered and celebrated.

The authorship of *On Crimes and Punishments* has attracted some controversy over the years. It is clear that Beccaria was encouraged to undertake the study by Verri and other members of the Academy, and that they played a significant role in shaping its content through their advice and discussions. Moreover, Beccaria's manuscript was subjected to pre-publication editing by Verri, in the course of which he reordered the text, removed some of Beccaria's material, and added some of his own. The initial publication of the book was anonymous, and only later when the book had been accepted by the authorities did Beccaria attach his name to it. Further complications arose when, in 1765, the Abbé André Morellet prepared a French translation of the book, during the course of which he significantly rearranged the original manuscript. Morellet's translation subsequently served as the basis of numerous editions, while Beccaria continued to see through the publication of six editions of his book in Italian that did not incorporate Morellet's changes. Thus there exist a number of versions of the text that bear the marks of various changes initiated by individuals other than Beccaria himself (it is a matter of opinion as to whether these interventions are viewed as legitimate editorial 'improvements' or illegitimate editorial 'interference'). A final controversy occurred later in Beccaria's life when, having fallen out of favour with Verri, the erstwhile mentor began to stress his own contribution to the book. However, despite these ambiguities, it is widely accepted today that Beccaria can be rightly accepted as the primary author of the text, and it is to him that the lion's share of the credit for its innovations and insights is given.

One of the most significant features of *On Crimes and Punishments* is its incorporation of wider social and political ideas that were in vogue amongst progressive European intellectuals during the eighteenth century. It is not a narrow technical treatise concerned with legal minutiae, but a wide-ranging reconsideration of law and punishment in light of the philosophical, moral and economic analysis of human nature and social order. While no revolutionary (unlike many of the French *philosophes* from whom he drew inspiration), Beccaria's work nevertheless contained a reformist vision including such features as the critique of aristocratic property rights, the limitation of church authority, the endorsement of religious pluralism and tolerance, formal equality before the law, and the abolition of judicial torture and the death penalty. Broadly speaking, Beccaria's position can be seen as an interesting synthesis of utilitarianism, social contract theory, and the doctrine of inalienable natural rights. For example, from Helvetius in particular, he takes the utilitarian idea that society should be rationally organised so as to benefit the greatest number and to avoid unnecessary pain or suffering, something that detracts from rather than contributes to the overall well-being and happiness of a society and its members. From Hobbes he took the idea that an ordered society must be established through a 'social contract' that bound its members together. Citizens agreed to give up some of their freedom to do as they pleased, and in exchange were protected from arbitrary impositions from others. Under such an arrangement, individuals agreed to respect the property and physical integrity of their fellow citizens, thereby ensuring that all were secure from the fear of theft and violence. For Beccaria, those who committed criminal acts stood in breach of this contract, and so punishment must inevitably follow. Only in this way could the contract, which worked in the ultimate interests of all, be maintained. Second, Beccaria took from Hobbes the view that human beings are basically 'hedonistic' in nature. They are driven by a search for pleasure and satisfaction and a corresponding desire to avoid pain and discomfort. Individuals will rationally assess possible courses of action, and will act in a way that they believe will maximise the satisfaction of their wants and desires. Bringing these two points together, Beccaria believed that in order to be socially effective, criminal justice must be organised so as to make the punishment of crime *inevitable, consistent, proportionate* and *swift*. The inevitability of punishment would serve to convince the potential offender that the pain of punishment would always follow any criminal act, serving therefore as a deterrent. Equally important was the principle of consistency. This would ensure that the same kind and severity of punishment would always follow a particular crime. In this way, potential offenders would be made certain that they could not count upon arbitrary leniency from judges – it would be clear beforehand what kind of punishment would follow any particular offence. The principle of proportionality maintained that in order to be effective punishments must be of a severity that reflected the seriousness of the offence and the harm caused. Finally, the swiftness of punishment was held to be essential if it were to have a proper deterrent effect. This idea Beccaria based upon the philosopher David Hume's theory of the 'association of ideas'. Hume held that particular phenomena and experiences became linked together in the human mind because one followed closely upon another (for example, we associate fire with pain because upon burning ourselves pain immediately follows). Consequently, Beccaria felt that crime and punishment could only become firmly associated in the public mind if the latter followed the former as swiftly as possible. On the basis of these principles, he criticised the organisation of criminal justice in that it was typically characterised by inconsistency, arbitrariness, disproportionality and delay. Such a system could not use punishment efficiently to secure pubic order, and so would have to be radically reformed.

Another significant feature of Beccaria's work is his repudiation of both judicial torture as a means of extracting confession from suspects, and of the use of the death penalty as a criminal sanction. Both of these positions can be attributed to the influence of natural rights theories, which hold that all individuals enjoy certain inalienable rights whose violation cannot be morally justified. In the case of torture, Beccaria sees the use of such instruments as contrary to an individual's right to preserve their own existence, as a confession extracted under torture would compel suspects to implicate themselves and lead them to further harm and suffering. In respect of the death penalty, he holds that all individuals have a fundamental right to life, and that this right cannot and should not be abrogated by others including the sovereign power of the state. Such arguments are as pertinent today as ever, dealing as we must with the continued use of the death penalty in many countries, or with the state-sponsored use of torture techniques that is justified by appeal to a 'war on terror' or some other such state of emergency.

Beccaria's influence has been wide ranging since *On Crimes and Punishments* was first published. In his later decades Beccaria took up the chair of political economy at the Palatine School of Milan, an institution that trained those destined for government service. He continued to promulgate his ideas through his lectures, and they can be seen to have influenced judicial and other reforms that were instituted in Lombardy at that time. More broadly, given that his work was widely read and praised not just in Europe but further afield in the United States, Beccaria's ideas played a significant role in the organisation of judicial systems and legal processes. For example, numerous principles outlined in *On Crimes and Punishments* were subsequently incorporated into the United States constitution. Beccaria also influenced subsequent thinkers, including the moral philosopher and legal reformer **Jeremy Bentham**, who acknowledged his debt to his predecessor. Beccaria's thought continues to impact upon criminology, not least in those so-called 'Neo-Classical' perspectives (see **Ron Clarke**) that have flourished in recent decades.

Major works

Beccaria, C. (1963) *On Crimes and Punishments*, trans. Henry Paolucci. Englewood Cliffs, New Jersey: Prentice Hall.
—— (1986) *On Crimes and Punishments*, trans. David Young. Indianapolis, Indiana: Hackett Publishing

Further reading

Beirne, P. (1993) 'Towards a Science of Homo Criminalis: Cesare Beccaria's *Dei Delitti e Delle Pene*', in *Inventing Criminology: Essays on the Rise of Homo Criminalis*. Albany, New York: SUNY Press.
Maestro, M. (1973) *Cesare Beccaria and the Origins of Penal Reform*. Philadelphia, Pennsylvania: Temple University Press.
Mannheim, H. (1972) *Pioneers in Criminology*. Montclair, New Jersey: Patterson Smith.
Phillipson, C. (1970) *Three Criminal Law Reformers: Beccaria, Bentham, Romilly*. Montclair, New Jersey: Patterson Smith.
Young, D.B. (1973) 'Cesare Beccaria: Utilitarian or retributivist?', *Journal of Criminal Justice*, 4: 317–26.

MAJID YAR

JEREMY BENTHAM (1748–1832)

Jeremy Bentham's name is inextricably tied to his brainchild the Panopticon. This model prison afforded guards' views of each individual prisoner's behaviour at all times, while the prisoners could see neither each other nor the guards. Applied also to the school, the hospital, the factory and other 'disciplinary' institutions, the Panopticon provides the prototype of a form of correction and training that constantly but gently works to create obedient subjects by the application of a minimum of physical coercion. The Panopticon was nevertheless a child of Bentham's middle years rather than his crowning achievement. Indeed, although Bentham had the support of the powerful Lord Shelburne, who funded much of his travel and study, he remained a comparatively obscure figure until the early 1800s. Much to Bentham's everlasting chagrin, various attempts to have the British and the French governments build his panoptic prison stalled and collapsed during the 1790s, and the Panopticon gradually drifted from his attention.

Uncharitable critics such as Gertrude Himmelfarb (1968) regard Bentham's promotion of the panoptic prison – and the workhouses designed along similar lines planned to operate under a National Charity Company – as tainted by the hope of personal gain. While it is certainly true that Bentham insisted that the panoptical institutions should be run for profit and tendered his own services as the prison operator, such criticisms miss most of the mainsprings of his thoughts and motivations.

To begin with, as a utilitarian liberal, he firmly believed that the principle of economy as a public good would be most efficiently and effectively served by the private sector. Competition would ensure low costs to the state. Prison standards would be set by contract and policed not only by government inspectors but also by extending the panoptic principle to include public inspection of the prison. Thus he expected that conditions would be neither wretched nor too comfortable. Like many of his British contemporaries such as John Howard, Patrick Colquhoun and Jonas Hanway, he sought to change prisons from noisome holding pens to hygienic and orderly places of correction. Also, if Bentham lost interest in the Panopticon, it was not simply because of the failure to translate it into profitable practice. After the turn of the nineteenth century, he came to see more promise in monetary penalties. 'Pecuniary sanctions', he argued, were preferable because they could be undone in the case of injustice, did not involve physical coercion and could be used to help compensate those harmed. Indeed, he proposed that revenue from fines could be fed into an insurance scheme to compensate victims of crime. More broadly he even foresaw, and in degree approved of, mechanisms of social insurance that were to become pivotal a century after.

Such progressive welfare thinking is often forgotten by those who regarded the Panopticon's emphasis on rigorous solitary confinement (which was in any case abandoned in his later plans) as soulless cruelty in the service of mass conformity. No doubt a critic of modernism can see in such practices the ruthless pursuit of scientific principles at the cost of humanitarian concern. And it is true that Bentham rejected **Cesare Beccaria's** humanism, proposing instead a criminology and reform agenda that was based on the 'scientific' view of people as rational choice actors. Nevertheless he was not amoral. Accepting that 'the greatest happiness for the greatest number ... is the measure of right and wrong', Bentham assumed morality could be liberated from religion and narrow prejudice and itself rendered scientific: good and evil could be calculated on the basis of the utilities of any action. As the intellectual founder of the 'Benthamite' movement in liberalism, to which belonged such prominent liberals as James Mill (the father of John Stuart Mill) and David Ricardo, Bentham was to profoundly influence nineteenth-century liberalism.

Bentham had come to his vision of utilitarian liberalism through extensive reading of Claude Adrien Helvetius in his university days. Born in 1748, Bentham's family had intended that he follow in his father's footsteps and become a leading lawyer or judge. Under pressure from a somewhat grim and highly ambitious father, he proved precocious, entered the Queen's College Oxford at the age of 12 and was called to the Bar in 1769. Ever ambitious, his father disapproved of a relationship Bentham developed with a woman of lower status – Bentham obediently acquiesced. He was never to develop another close relationship with a woman, and study and writing became his passions. But already he was heading in other directions than the legal career his father intended. He rejected the obscurantism, arbitrariness and unpredictability of the common law and regarded legal practice under its auspices with disdain. Strongly affected by Helvetius' vision of law as the principal tool for creating the good society, and by Beccaria's Enlightenment proposals for reform of penal order, Bentham set out to create a new vision of law as the scientific foundation of a prosperous and free society. To this end he promoted codification of laws, both because this would reduce the arbitrariness and chicanery of common law and because law could then be understood by ordinary people.

As this begins to suggest, Bentham was far more than a penal reformer, and was only tangentially a criminologist – no matter how influential his writings have become in these fields. Indeed, most of his penal proposals were ignored in his time. It is fair to say that Bentham did not become well known among his contemporaries until long after his Panopticon years, and hardly at all in relation to his theories and proposals for reform of penal law. Public and international recognition came, rather, through his work on codification of law and for his Radical and democratic critique of the prevailing judicial and parliamentary system. His proposals in these areas, including universal suffrage, secret ballots, annual elections and a form of impeachment procedure for elected officials, were already forming the backbone of reform efforts at the time of his death. Alas for Bentham, he died on the eve of the greatest democratic political reforms Britain had ever experienced, many of which bore the stamp of his political writings. In other countries too, his writings received a warm reception, especially on the Continent, in Russia and in the United States. Despite his focus on large-scale political reform, nevertheless Bentham always regarded penal law as crucial, in part because of his particular take on human psychology.

He drew from Beccaria and from contemporary theorists of political economy, such as Adam Smith, the vision of people as rational choice actors. In the felicity calculus, human actions were assumed to follow a mental calculation of the ratio of pain to pleasure delivered by projected courses of action. While this image was famously derided as a reduction of human nature to the mentality of the English shopkeeper, it underlay Bentham's entire vision of governance. Put simply, the delivery of pain could be rationally calculated and universally applied to prevent wrong. Penal law was thus to be the central tool of government. Applied with certainty, punishment would guide subjects away from harmful activities.

At the same time, Bentham stressed that all punishment was a necessary evil, a form of government coercion, and thus to be delivered minimally. To this end, he followed Beccaria in urging that punishments should be graduated according to the crime. They should follow the principal of economy in delivering as little pain as is necessary for crime *prevention* – for punishment in the form of retribution he regarded as irrational and oppressive. (More generally, his proposals for a modern government included the establishment of a Ministry for Preventative Services.) Penal law thus included all law that delivered pain in response to an offence. In this light, he regarded the distinction between civil and criminal law as a mere matter of procedure: the award of 'civil' damages, for example, fell under penal law in his view because like the fine it delivered pain in the name of prevention as well as compensation.

Because he saw punishment as an oppressive act in itself, to be delivered rationally, Bentham spent much time mapping out scientific principles for its application. Each form of punishment was evaluated in terms of twelve criteria relevant to prevention: *variability* in degree or duration; *equability* so that the punishment should fit the crime; *commensurability* so that the measurement of pain be knowable in advance; *characteristicalness* so that it is easily learned; *exemplarity* so that its 'message' is clear; *frugality* so that it produces no needless pain; *subserviency to reformation* in order that correction may occur; *efficacy with respect to disablement*, or the incapacitation of potential harm doers; *subserviency to compensation* so that harms may be undone; *popularity* in that people accept the law; *simplicity of description* in order to aid intelligibility to all; and *remissibility* so that injustice can be undone.

Each principle was applied to each of a number of categories of punishment including corporal punishment, capital punishment, imprisonment, 'moral sanctions' such as those affecting reputation, pecuniary forfeitures and laborious punishment. The result is a kind of analytic grid which Bentham applied to punishments, finding them wanting or advantageous in varying ways. If it makes for sometimes tedious reading with a plodding Polonius-like quality, this rigorous approach nevertheless indicates the extent to which rationalisation of penal law was a key focus.

Yet in all of this, the central aim of law does not emerge as 'justice'. Rather, Bentham took the view that the central object of law is *security*. Security may broadly be defined as that condition of society in which the future is known in key respects, in particular with respect to the protection of life and property. Only if security exists can people make plans, and Bentham regarded the generalisation of this capacity as what differentiated an Enlightened society from one populated by barbarous hordes. This capacity for 'foresight' was the central condition that reconciled the rational choice actor with the principle of the most happiness for all. Only by ensuring that wealth, health and reputation be defended by law, and predators punished with certainty, would rational choice actors labour rationally and prudently to produce abundance rather than simply parasite on others.

Of the four 'ends of law' – security, abundance, subsistence and equality – Bentham was only secondarily interested in the last two. Although initially a strong supporter of the French Revolution, Bentham like many others of his time was alarmed by the 'excesses' it ushered in, and was concerned with governments that aimed to produce liberty and equality. Were law to pursue equality too energetically, he felt, it would undermine the other ends. A law ensuring equality would have to take away wealth from the prosperous and thus would undermine security, thereby reducing the motivation to create abundance and subsistence. In his schema, subsistence referred to the need for law to sustain the indigent, but also to ensure that they were set right upon the course to self-maintenance. It is also in this respect that the Panopticon has to be understood. Whether in the prison, the school, the workhouse or the factory, Bentham's aim was to persuade all subjects to take on the 'yoke of foresight' and thus to plan and to govern their own futures.

Of course an easy criticism is that Bentham inherited wealth, had wealthy supporters, and was able to pursue his chosen course only as a result of this. Yet Bentham was true to his own principles. His extraordinary output resulted from intense and constant labour by a man who not only regarded drinking brandy as incomprehensible because of its effect on the mind and the passions, but even regarded lying in bed when awake as an evil that stole time and (especially as he was never married) led to perversions. In such ways Bentham is easy to caricature. Many regard as typically and preciously odd his wish to have his body mummified after death so that in place of a stone statue of himself he could be an 'auto-icon'. (This duly occurred and it is now stored in University College London.) Even odder, it was suggested that his friends and disciples meet in the presence of the auto-icon periodically to discuss utilitarianism.

For all that, he was a major contributor to shaping 'bourgeois' philosophy and nineteenth-century liberalism more generally. And with the resurgence of liberal individualism in the past thirty years, Bentham's thought once again has had a profound influence in fields such as crime prevention (see **Ron Clarke**), the law and economics movement and 'neo-classical' criminology.

Major works

Bentham, J. (1962) 'An Introduction to the Principles of Morals and Legislation', in John Bowring (ed.) *The Works of Jeremy Bentham Vol. I*, pp. 1–155. New York: Russell and Russell.
—— (1962) 'Principals of Penal Law', in John Bowring (ed.) *The Works of Jeremy Bentham Vol. I*, pp. 365–580. New York: Russell and Russell.
—— (1969) 'Panopticon Papers', in M. Mack. (ed.) *A Bentham Reader*, pp. 194–208. New York: Pegasus.

Further reading

Dinwiddy, J. (1989) *Bentham*. Oxford: Oxford University Press.
Himmelfarb, G. (1968) *Victorian Minds 'The haunted house of Jeremy Bentham'*, pp. 32–81. New York: Alfred Knopf.
Semple, J. (1993) *Bentham's Prison. A Study of the Panopticon Penitentiary*. Oxford: Clarendon Press.

PAT O'MALLEY

ADOLPHE QUETELET (1796–1874)

Adolphe Quetelet is often referred to as the progenitor of 'ecological crime analyses'. His interest in the location and instances of recorded criminal offences, as opposed to the technicalities of law (see **Cesare Beccaria** and **Jeremy Bentham**), mark him out as one of the key figures (along with his contemporary André-Michel Guerry) in the development of nineteenth-century cartographic criminology.

Quetelet was born to a liberal, middle-class family in the Belgian city of Ghent in 1796. He attended the Lycée, and later, the University of Ghent, where he obtained his doctorate in Mathematics in 1819. Quetelet was no grey statistician, though – rather he should be considered something of a renaissance man; well read both in the classics and the modern literature of the day. He also wrote poetry, studied painting, and even composed an opera and two plays with his friend and fellow mathematician and engineer, Germinal Pierre Dandelin (1794–1847). However, as history is told today, Quetelet is most remembered for three things: first, his aforementioned role as a pioneer of early ecological analyses of crime; second, his positivistic belief that human behaviour was governed by scientifically verifiable laws; and third, his reliance upon government-generated statistics backed up by an unstinting quest for methodological rigour. Certainly, from a methodological perspective Quetelet took his lead from the natural sciences and the observation that crime rates seemed to obey the same 'law-like' regularities that govern the natural world. While his conception that crime flows from specific social, areal and organisational structures and not from human wickedness established a basis for later social policy and criminological analysis, his positivistic account of human behaviour continues to divide criminologists today.

During the Napoleonic era, France initiated a new criminal code; an expanding system of prisons, asylums, hospitals and workhouses, all backed up by a newly professionalised police force (gendarmerie) and a burgeoning class of technocrats charged with the smooth operation of the new code. Napoleon's goal was simple: to *normalise* the 'dangerous classes' through moral rehabilitation. However, it soon became apparent, both to politicians and the general public, that the project was a failure. Theft and public order offences almost doubled between 1813 and 1820. More pressingly, there were huge numbers of poor people (*les misérables*) in the cities, notably Paris, who resorted to crime to make ends meet and who routinely rioted over the dreadful social conditions they were forced to endure. Increasing recidivism rates after Napoleon's defeat to the British at Waterloo in 1815 seemed to further prove that the rehabilitation of the dangerous classes was not working in practice. The initial response to this failure of rehabilitation policy was for the French state to commission a number of detailed studies that would build up a statistical picture of who constituted the dangerous classes and why they were committing crimes against their fellow citizens.

The apparent failure to *normalise* the dangerous classes through the Napoleonic system led directly to the so-called *scientific* route of managing the population through the application of statistical techniques in the fields of crime control and prison policy. This entailed analysing parish records for births, baptisms, marriages and deaths; collating data on poor relief, taxation, fire and general insurance claims; and consolidating the public health information (especially rates of venereal disease) held at local, regional and national level. Detailed records of the army on the background and general health of soldiers along with court records and the files of the gendarmerie were also scrutinised. The population was analysed as never before and particular note was made of 'mortality', age, occupation, disease and levels of intelligence. In terms of analysing the dangerous classes, the prisons were studied for the first time by a variety of researchers, including some drawn from outside the government service. Religious groups, for example, concerned themselves not just with prison incarceration rates but other variables such as diet and the particularities of specific prison regimes. In the spirit of the time, no variable was excluded and no question ruled out, including the issue of whether prison itself was a factor in recidivism and the 'moral degradation' of offenders. In 1827, the first ever French national statistical tables on crime were published, *Le Compte générale de l'administration de la justice criminelle en France*. The *Compte* itself, though, was restricted to the analysis of the various courts in the French system, generating data on age, sex, occupation and educational attainment level (in later years the *Compte* was extended to include other categories of information). The *Compte*, as Piers Beirne has argued in *Inventing Criminology* (1993), was a decisive factor in the early development of a positivistic criminology.

By 1820, Quetelet had been appointed a professor at the Brussels Athenaeum and was elected as an academician at the Royal Academy of Sciences in Brussels. In 1823 his astronomical research led him to Paris, and it was here that Quetelet met a number of intellectuals working in the emerging field of *mécanique sociale* (social mechanics). These encounters encouraged Quetelet to apply advanced astronomical mathematics to demography and he quickly emerged as a leading authority on social mechanics. On returning to Brussels in 1824, he commenced work on Belgian demographic information to construct insurance actuarial tables. This work led him to construct certain *faits sociaux* (social facts) that pertain to the aggregated nature of human conduct. From this work he derived his *homme moyen* (average man) which illustrated the utility and accuracy of the hypothesised average value over the larger number of empirical observations. The construction of the average man allowed for detailed comparison in predictive statistical work. From 1827 onwards, Quetelet increasingly used the *Compte* in his work.

It is important to note that Quetelet was not uncritical or unreflexive about his research. He was, for example, very concerned about the limitations of the data he worked with, which frequently were not standardised or collected in what he considered to be a *scientific* manner. He was especially taken with the total population question; put simply, understanding the *actual* number of offences and their ratio vis-à-vis the sum of recorded crimes. Drawing on the *Compte* data for 1833–39, Quetelet discerned a constant relationship between notified crimes and their prosecution. His subsequent statistical analyses of additional judicial and official data led him to infer a constancy between the total population of crime and recorded crime. Quetelet was struck by the recurring constancy of crime data within specific geographical areas, from the number of murders per year, to the number of property crimes, to the number of accused failing to appear in court. All of this suggested to Quetelet that, contrary to what had been assumed, and allowing for the vagaries of individual conduct, criminal behaviour, in an aggregate sense, was constant and seemed to obey certain general patterns, or laws. Hence his famous quote:

> one passes from one year to the other with the sad perspective of seeing the same crimes reproduced in the same order and bringing with them the same penalties in the same proportions. Sad condition of the human species! The share of prisons, chains, and the scaffold appears fixed with as much probability as the revenues of the state. We are able to enumerate in advance how many individuals will stain their hands with the blood of their fellow creatures, how many will be forgers, how many poisoners, pretty nearly as one can enumerate in advance the births and deaths which must take place.
>
> (Quetelet 1831 cited in Beirne 1993: 82)

Quetelet had a definite view of human nature and he assumed that crime was dependent upon an individual's willingness to commit it. Hitherto certain groups, such as the poor, young men, the unemployed and the ill-educated were said to commit a disproportionate number of crimes. However, Quetelet showed that this correlation did not always hold true and that some of France's poorest regions were the ones with the lowest crime rates. Quetelet further argued that *inequality* of wealth between persons was more important than sheer levels of poverty. Moreover, he claimed that crime levels had more to do with the propensity of individuals to commit it, which, in turn, was related to issues concerning moral instruction and opportunity. This analysis increasingly pushed Quetelet towards the determination of crime causation, something he initially had been reluctant to study. He came up with a tripartite typology of causation which included, *accidental causation, variable causation,* and *constant causation.* Quetelet believed that the last category was the most important factor in determining criminal causation. However, these three categories all relate to Quetelet's conception of *l'homme moyen,* and not to any particular sociology of causation. Moreover, and more problematically, Quetelet ascribed a fixed level of determination to all three types of causation which, especially when combined with the overwhelming influence of age, sex, occupation and religion, ensured constancy to crime rates.

In many ways *l'homme moyen* was the centrepiece of Quetelet's *cartes thématiques.* For Quetelet, the average man is also the moderate man who tends to the mean in statistical terms. The average man's moderate life owes more to Aristotle than any notion of a person found in modern philosophical or political thought. Moreover, the notion of the average man – who always chooses the moderate path and who always avoids excess – would appear to be a rare anthropological creature in the era of high capitalism. Quetelet also contrasted the average man to other groups, such as gypsies, who, Quetelet contended, had an increased propensity to commit crime; and here Quetelet fails to escape the racism of his age. Indeed, from the 1840s onwards, Quetelet was increasingly drawn to biological metaphors, notably around the supposed 'contagion of crime.' He even anticipated **Cesare Lombroso** by factoring in such variables as head measurements in his analysis. Quetelet made explicit reference to the fact that the scientifically measured proportions of the body related to crime rates and that both were social facts. (Interestingly, Quetelet is also well known for a statistical device known as 'the Quetelet index' or 'body mass index', a bio-mathematical tool used in the calculation of obesity.) In this way Quetelet was increasingly drawn into using the concept of deviation, although, as Colin Sumner (1994) has pointed out, this is a statistical deviation and not the sociological deviation which **Emile Durkheim** originated (and which would come to prominence in the twentieth century).

Quetelet's influence exceeded the narrow parameters of statistical analysis and he made a series of policy recommendations to central government in France. He argued that the state should rigorously apply the criminal code and focus police attention towards known criminal minorities, and this included consistent sentencing. He also argued that the state should focus upon the higher moral, intellectual and scientific elements of modern civilisation in a bid to promote social stability. He understood that crime was a constant feature of all societies but he also realised that the state could both exacerbate and ameliorate the conditions which gave rise to it. This social understanding of crime was a major departure from the notions of a freely acting, wicked criminal, which pervaded public discourse in France at the time.

In terms of his overall criminological legacy, although Quetelet was soon eclipsed by the giant figures of **Durkheim, Marx** and Weber, his contribution to the social sciences is still considerable. Despite being tainted by the twin shadows of unflinching statistical positivism and biological determinism, his work did still assert that crime was the result of social factors rather than the product of moral or evil considerations, and in identifying regularities in the statistical record he opened up the possibility of a modern sociological explanation of crime. In these ways his work was, for the time at least, extremely progressive. However, Durkheim, who praised Quetelet's focus upon the existence of certain regularities and observable statistical features of the social world, also criticised his use of the average man on the grounds that merely to point to a phenomenon is not to understand that phenomenon. Durkheim specifically cited the phenomenon of suicide as a case where a given suicide rate does not presuppose that persons in general are exposed to the likelihood of committing suicide: and that to argue otherwise is fallacious. Durkheim also took issue with Quetelet's conception of 'normal'. The sociologist Durkheim understood that what was normal always related to a given social institution and a given level of development, whereas the mathematician Quetelet derived what was normal from the abstraction of statistical analysis and the development of the average man. Despite this, Quetelet should still be considered as a progressive: he resisted the pathologising of wicked individuals and instead pointed towards socio-environmental explanations of crime. Moreover, his idea that crime can be scientifically understood through analysing statistics is (rightly or wrongly) still with us today. When, for example, contemporary criminologists explore the relationship between age and offending, the role of gender in criminalisation, and the demographic relationships between poverty and alcohol and crime, they are following in the footsteps of Quetelet.

Major works

Quetelet, M.A. (1842) *A Treatise on Man and the Development of His Faculties*. Scholars, Facsimiles & Reprints. Edinburgh: William and Robert Chambers.
—— (1869) *Physique sociale, ou essai sur développement des facultes*. Brussels: C. Murquardt.
—— (1871) *Anthropométrie, ou mesure des différentes facultes de l'homme*. Brussels: C. Murquardt.

Further reading

Beirne, P. (1987) 'Adolphe Quetelet and the Origins of Positivist Criminology', *American Journal of Sociology*, 92(5): 1140–69.
—— (1993) *Inventing Criminology: Essays on the Rise of Homo Criminalis*. Albany, New York: State University of New York Press.
Mosselmans, B. (2005) 'Adolphe Quetelet, the Average Man and the Development of Economic Methodology', *European Journal of Economic Thought*, 12(4): 565–82.
Sumner, C.S. (1994) *The Sociology of Deviance: An Obituary*. Part One. Milton Keynes: Open University Press.

ANTHONY AMATRUDO

KARL MARX (1818–83) (AND FREDERICK ENGELS (1820–95))

Born in Trier, Germany, educated in Bonn and Berlin, Karl Heinrich Marx spent his early years as a radical journalist in socialist circles in Cologne. Escape from repression by the authorities took him to Paris where he began a longstanding collaborative relationship with Frederick Engels. Active in the communist movement, Marx and Engels were chased from one European capital to another by police and censors. They finally settled in England in 1849 where Marx, financially supported by his family and Engels, devoted himself to his great work *Capital: A Critique of Political Economy* (for a useful introduction to Marx see McLellan 2000).

Marx is the towering figure of modern social theory. It is no exaggeration to claim that all subsequent social theory is a debate with his legacy. His influence extends far beyond the critique of politics, philosophy and political economy which is the foundation of Historical Materialism. Marx and his collaborator Engels were not Victorian philanthropists, seeking to ameliorate the worst excesses of capitalism in order to guarantee its survival; they were revolutionaries concerned to analyse the dynamics of nineteenth-century capitalism for the purpose of understanding how it was to be superseded by a communist society. We should therefore not be surprised to find no proposals for crime reduction or legal reform in the manner of **Bentham** or **Beccaria**. The study of crime was peripheral to their main project. Marx himself wrote relatively little on crime and certainly nothing systematic on a par with his critique of political economy. Engels wrote more elaborately, with some acute observations on crime in the Manchester slums of the 1840s.

Probably the best starting point for understanding the contribution of Marx and Engels is that of methodology. Marx followed the great early nineteenth-century philosopher G.W.F. Hegel in a critique of abstract ways of thinking. Hegel (in 1817) had written a remarkable little essay in which he chose the example of the murderer on the way to the guillotine, pointing out that the seemingly concrete label of 'the criminal' was in fact an abstraction obtained only by annulling 'all other human essence in him with this simple quality'. Hegel thus turned on its head the common sense idea of abstract and concrete thought showing that 'concrete facts' – in this case the criminal – are often abstractions based on the suppression of numerous other characteristics and perspectives. Only through an investigation of the latter can we begin to approach the concrete character of phenomena.

Marx and Engels then turned Hegel on his head, replacing 'reason' as the motor of history with the material processes of political economy and class conflict. But the methodological insight remained and, like Hegel, they referred to crime as an example of abstract thinking which remains only at the level of the immediate appearances of things. In an early critique of German idealist philosophy they wrote: 'The same visionaries who see in right and law the domination of some independently existing, general will can see in crime the mere violation of right and law' (Marx and Engels 1845: 358). This perspective is crucial for a Marxist approach to crime. First, the notion that the criminal law is a normative system independent of social forces and conflicts and crime simply its violation, is a case of abstract thinking: of remaining at the level of appearances and eliminating the social forces and conflicts which give crime and the criminal law their real content. By contrast the essential nature of a phenomenon is precisely something that can only be concluded as a *result* of a detailed understanding. In the case of crime this involves a study of how forms of criminal law emerge in specific historical situations, whose interests they serve, the relationships between various types of criminal offenders and the state, the victims and the various groups in the rest of the population and the power relations between them. Second, the most important of such relationships is the conflict between classes and in which 'the ideas of the ruling class are in every epoch the ruling ideas' (Marx and Engels 1845: 60).

Marx developed this approach to crime in early (1842) newspaper articles on the law on the theft of wood passed by the Rhineland parliament in 1842, turning what had once been a traditional right of forest dwellers to gather fallen wood into a criminal offence. He wrote that the law 'has reduced the legislative power, administrative authority, the person of the accused, the idea of the State, even the crime and its punishment, to the evil instruments of private interests' (Marx 1842). Thus the fixed abstractions of 'crime' and 'criminal' dissolve into the complexities of the class relations between, on the one hand, the aspirant Rhineland bourgeoisie in its attempts to extend the new capitalist relations of production to the forests and woodlands and, on the other, the peasants determined to exercise their traditional customary right to gather fallen wood. It can only then be fully understood how the relationship between the forest owners and the poor takes the particular form of crime and why certain activities should become criminalised.

As the historian Peter Linebaugh (1976) remarked, it was his investigation of the stolen wood episode that awakened the young Marx to his ignorance of political economy and it is of course in this direction that he moved. In *Capital* Marx developed his analysis of the accumulation of capital in which the latter appears on the surface in its monetary form as investment funds and profits but through increasingly detailed and concrete analysis (stretching to three volumes) he is able to show that what is at work is a complex social relation between capitalists and workers in which the source of the former's profit is the surplus labour of the latter.

This relationship of class conflict, sometimes overt and sometimes nascent, lies at the heart of the process of capital accumulation which is the motor of modern capitalist society. *Capital* was Marx's life's work and crime was certainly not its central focus. However, the role of crime does feature in various places and very much in terms of the methodology we have outlined. For example, in the treatment of the emergence of the historical preconditions for capitalism by the pillaging of feudal estates and the enforced commercialisation of common land

Marx includes a concrete analysis of the dynamics of the criminalisation of the poor.

> The proletariat created by the breaking up of the bands of feudal retainers and by the forcible expropriation of the people from the soil, this 'free' proletariat could not possibly be absorbed by the nascent manufactures as fast as it was thrown upon the world. On the other hand, these men, suddenly dragged from their wonted mode of life, could not as suddenly adapt themselves to the discipline of their new condition. They were turned *en masse* into beggars, robbers, vagabonds, partly from inclination, in most cases from stress of circumstances. Hence at the end of the 15th and during the whole of the 16th century, throughout Western Europe a bloody legislation against vagabondage. The fathers of the present working class were chastised for their enforced transformation into vagabonds and paupers. Legislation treated them as 'voluntary' criminals and assumed that it depended on their own good will to go on working under the old conditions that no longer existed.
>
> (Marx 1867: 915)

Thus the violence of those powerful groups who organised the plunder of landed property and common land is not recorded as 'crime' while, at the same time, those forced off the land were transformed into criminals and then treated as if it was their own responsibility and wilful criminality to continue attempting the exercise of traditional rights.

Crime therefore, like any other social or legal 'fact', has to be deconstructed into the detailed context within which it occurs. This is not to reduce criminality to the status of a distortion of reality but to rather provide a detailed perspective on how, in a specific context, particular social relations take the form of 'crime'. An important consequence of this methodology is the refusal of any general theory of the 'causes of crime'. Marx was interested in particular forms of criminality in specific historical contexts as a reflection of the socio-economic forces at work at the time.

In recent times one of the most important applications of this method was the emergence of the concept of 'social crime' in the work of the British Marxist historians Edward Thompson and his colleagues during the mid 1970s (Hay et al. 1975). Inspired by Marx's brief essay on the 'Theft of Wood', they showed how criminal activities such as poaching and pilfering in eighteenth-century rural England were forms of resistance to the advance of capitalist farming and the decline of traditional rights with the enclosure of common lands – very much as in the German forests about which Marx wrote. Critics argued this was simply legitimising crime (see Langbein 1983). But Thompson et al. argued that the blurred boundaries between 'good' and 'bad' crime reflected the context in which no clear alternative legal political method was available through which to resist the advance of capitalist property relations. As resistance to the determined suppression of traditional rights through criminal law 'social crime' was something quite distinct. The blurred boundaries, rather than showing an unwillingness to call a crime a crime, in fact reflected the complex and shifting social conditions of the time and the embeddedness of both criminal law and its violation in those conditions. It was not that what appeared as crime was 'really' political resistance. The point is that neither concept had yet clarified its boundaries in the context of the rural turbulence of eighteenth-century England (see Lea 1999).

The establishment of modern urban capitalist society brings with it the modern forms of criminality of the poor. Here Engels' famous study of working-class Manchester in the 1840s (Engels 1845) was a major contribution. He gives a sophisticated account of the various dimensions of criminality amongst a working class living an impoverished, precarious existence in the slums of the early industrial revolution with little means of political redress available. On the one hand much theft can be seen as a primitive form of pre-political rebellion, an expression of rage: 'The working-man lived in poverty and want, and saw that others were better off than he. It was not clear to his mind why he, who did more for society than the rich idler, should be the one to suffer under these conditions. Want conquered his inherited respect for the sacredness of property, and he stole. ... ' (Engels 1845: 502–3).

But Engels is careful not to fit all types of working-class crime into the straightjacket of rebellion. In particular he pays attention to prostitution, sexual harassment and domestic violence as features of working-class family and working life which he sees as forms of brutalisation resulting from the destruction of family life by the long hours of work and intolerable living conditions which characterised the early stages of industrialisation (see Lea 1996). Nevertheless overall it is capitalism itself that has produced the conditions for criminality in the form of a 'war of all against all':

> In this country, social war is under full headway, every one stands for himself, and fights for himself against all comers, and whether or not he shall injure all the others who are his declared foes, depends upon a cynical calculation as to what is most

advantageous for himself. It no longer occurs to any one to come to a peaceful understanding with his fellow-man; all differences are settled by threats, violence, or in a law court. ... This war of each against all, of the bourgeoisie against the proletariat, need cause us no surprise, for it is only the logical sequel of the principle involved in free competition.

(Engels 1845: 427)

From this perspective Engels also gives graphic accounts of white-collar crimes such as food adulteration, intolerable factory health and safety conditions and workplace rape of female employees by employers. What is important in Engels' analysis is that crime is not a result of the breakdown of social relations; it is rather one of the necessary forms they take in the circumstances of the time. As Steven Marcus, in his biography of Engels, wrote, crime is 'in the first place, much too intimately connected with the values and norms it violates to be considered as simply anomic in respect to them; and secondly, no behaviour that is both an inversion and a parody of another can be properly or fully understood as a deviant form of the latter' (Marcus 1974: 223). In short, the crime documented by Engels is an expression of the social relations of early capitalism, part of its normality. In recent years criminologists who conclude that crime has again become normalised can usefully refer back to Engels' treatment.

Most schools of Radical Criminology would claim some affinity with Marx and/or Engels (see Greenberg 1993). Often this amounts to a rather general orientation stressing the role of class conflict and the economic depredations of capitalism in the causation of crime. An early example is the Dutch criminologist **Willem Bonger** whose studies of capitalism and crime at the beginning of the twentieth century stressed the culture of egoism and self-interest in a similar way to Engels. Another theme has been the power of ruling classes and elites as a factor in the dynamics of criminalisation and the effective decriminalisation of criminal actions by the powerful, including the state. Examples would be the work of **William Chambliss** and Richard Quinney (1977).

However, probably the most important conclusion is that the general perspective on crime derived from the work of Marx and Engels has a particular salience for the present situation. One of the major features of global capitalism today is the progressive blurring of the boundaries between criminality, warfare, politics, legitimate business activity and other forms of human interaction. A similar process of blurring is evident in the relation between politics, law, state sovereignty and criminal responsibility. As far as criminology is concerned, all perspectives which start from an insistence on the unproblematic and fixed boundaries of crime and then proceed with the search for its general causes are increasingly unable to analyse these complexities and shifting boundaries. The Russian revolutionary Vladimir Illych Lenin summed up much of what has been said above about Marx's approach when he said that 'the soul of Marxism is the concrete analysis of a concrete situation'. Quite apart from the revolutionary associations of Marxism and its 'yet to be realised' aspirations, this approach is arguably more open to the fluid contours of twenty-first-century conflicts.

Major works

Engels, F. (1845/1975) 'The Condition of the Working Class in England', in Karl Marx and Frederick Engels (eds) *Collected Works* (volume 4). London: Lawrence and Wishart.

Marx, K. (1842/1975) 'Debates on the Law of the Theft of Wood', in Karl Marx and Frederick Engels *Collected Works* (volume 1). London: Lawrence and Wishart.

—— (1867/1976) *Capital: A Critique of Political Economy* (volume 1). Harmondsworth: Penguin Books.

Marx, K. and Engels, F. (1845/1965) *The German Ideology*. London: Lawrence and Wishart.

Further reading

Greenberg, D. ed. (1993) *Crime and Capitalism: Readings in Marxist Criminology*. Philadelphia, Pennsylvania: Temple University Press.

Hay, D., Linebaugh, P., Rule, J.G., Thompson, E.P. and Winslow, C. (1975) *Albion's Fatal Tree: Crime and Society in Eighteenth Century England*. New York: Pantheon Books.

Langbein, J.H. (1983) 'Albion's Fatal Flaws', *Past and Present*, 98: 96–120.

Lea, J. (1996) 'Poverty, Crime and Politics: Engels and the Crime Question', in J. Lea and G. Pilling (eds) *The Condition of Britain: Essays on Frederick Engels*. London: Pluto.

—— (1999) 'Social Crime Revisited', *Theoretical Criminology*, 3(5): 307–25.

Linebaugh, P. (1976) 'Karl Marx, The Theft of Wood and Working Class Composition', *Crime and Social Justice*, 6: 5–16.

Marcus, S. (1974) *Engels, Manchester, and the Working Class*. London: Weidenfeld and Nicholson.

McLellan, D. (2000) *Karl Marx: Selected Writings*. Oxford: Oxford University Press.

Quinney, Richard (1977) *Class, State, and Crime*. New York: David McKay.

JOHN LEA

CESARE LOMBROSO (1835–1909)

Cesare Lombroso was an Italian physician whose research into the bodily characteristics of soldiers, asylum inmates and prisoners led to the foundation of criminal anthropology at the end of the nineteenth century. He was also a leading figure in the development of a positivist criminology that looked to scientific measurements and the meticulous collection of data for the explanation of crime and criminal behaviour. Lombroso is known especially for his concept of the 'born criminal' and his development of an extensive classification of 'criminal types'. He is also closely associated with the theory of the 'atavism' of criminals, the view that criminal behaviours in modern society are an evolutionary throw-back to less civilised states of humanity.

Lombroso was born in 1835 to a Jewish family in Northern Italy, and trained as a medical doctor in Padua, Vienna and Pavia, graduating in 1858. In 1859, the wars of the Risorgimento, or Italian unification broke out, and Lombroso volunteered on the side of the unification movement. During the four years in which he served in the army, Lombroso undertook a study of 3,000 soldiers on top of his military duties, looking in particular at cases of pellagra, cretinism and epilepsy, which he assiduously recorded. Between 1863 and 1872, he worked as the director of various asylums in Pavia, Pesaro and Reggio Emilia in northern Italy, where he also developed an interest in studying and collecting artefacts relating to so-called 'primitive peoples'. In 1876, he took up the Chair of Legal Medicine and Public Hygiene at the University of Turin. Around the same time, Lombroso began working with the inmates of the prison in Turin, as well as beginning to formulate the ideas that would be developed in the five editions of *Criminal Man* that were published between 1876 and 1897. Lombroso married in 1869, and his two daughters, Gina and Paola, later became part of his research team and professional circle. Paola later married the criminologist Mario Carrara, whilst her sister Gina married Guglielmo Ferrero, with whom Lombroso would work closely on *The Female Offender*. In 1893 Lombroso became a member of the Italian Socialist Party, and stood as the Socialist representative on the city council of Turin between 1899 and 1905. Towards the end of his life, Lombroso also developed an interest in spiritualism after seeing a medium elevate a table at a séance in 1891.

Lombroso, like many other European intellectuals in the late nineteenth century, was influenced by the evolutionary theories of Charles Darwin and others, such as Ernst Haeckel (the German biologist), Franz Joseph Gall (the founder of craniometry), and Benedict-Augustin Morel (a Franco-Austrian psychiatrist who linked social deviancy with insanity). Lombroso took the evolutionary notion of progress and allied it with phrenology and 'craniometry' to infer that primitive criminal impulses were written into the bodies of offenders. He was also heavily influenced by the work of the French Positivist philosopher and early sociologist Auguste Comte, who argued that human behaviour followed natural, scientific laws. Comte believed that if these laws governing human behaviour could be uncovered, then solutions to social and moral problems could likewise be devised. Following this school of thought, Lombroso believed that the answers to the problem of crime and criminal behaviour lay in the bodies of criminals and the mentally ill; and that a predisposition towards criminal and deviant behaviour would be noted in atavistic bodily characteristics. Lombroso claimed that his epiphany came in 1871 when he was performing an autopsy on one Giuseppe Villella, a notorious criminal. Lombroso declared that when he examined Villella's skull, he found that it had much in common in terms of shape and size with the skulls of the non-Western peoples he had been studying. This suggested to Lombroso that criminals were atavistic throw-backs to less 'civilised' periods in human history. Lombroso painstakingly recorded, catalogued and classified data from prison inmates, identifying the 'stigmata' that differentiated criminals and the insane from 'normal', law-abiding citizens. Although Lombroso failed to find one distinctive or definitive characteristic common to all criminals, he nevertheless found a range of attributes that he believed were shared by offenders: criminals had smaller skulls, with marked deformities; they were physically taller and heavier, and had darker skin, eyes and hair, along with large ears, protruding jaws, impaired muscular strength and a lower sensitivity to pain, both physical and emotional. Lombroso also believed that criminals' tattoos, writings, art and use of slang were indicative of their primitive state, and he compared his findings from the bodies of prisoners with the tattooing practices of various cultures, including Maori and Australian Aborigine. Lombroso and his team took photographs, made drawings and collected artefacts detailing their researches. This extensive collection formed the basis of various exhibitions Lombroso held from the 1880s onwards and was later permanently housed at the Museum of Criminal Anthropology in Turin.

However, Lombroso's concept of the 'born criminal' did not emerge until the second edition of *Criminal Man* in 1878, by which time he had begun collaborating with Guglielmo Ferrero and **Enrico**

Ferri. Ferrero and Ferri both had an important impact upon the subsequent development of Lombroso's work: Ferrero contributed the notion of the born criminal whilst Ferri encouraged Lombroso to systematically refine his classifications of the criminal. By the time of the publication of the second edition of *Criminal Man*, Lombroso had begun to distinguish between habitual criminals and those occasional criminals who committed crimes of passion. This was an important departure, as Lombroso began to consider the factors which caused some people to become regular and persistent offenders, whilst others committed crimes during their adolescence and others again acted out of character in response to intense stress or need, or who were driven through political belief. Throughout the later editions of *Criminal Man* and *The Female Offender* (1893 and 1903, with Ferrero), Lombroso developed a wide-ranging classification of criminal types, which included such groups as alcoholics and 'hysterics', and which began to explore the environmental or social triggers of crime. Lombroso included in his classification the 'pseudocriminal' and the 'criminaloid', the former possessing few of the stigmata and the latter an occasional lawbreaker with some of the characteristics of the born criminal. Lombroso increasingly became influenced by the degeneration theories discussed in France, following criticism that his concept of atavism did not fully explain criminal behaviours, and he incorporated further environmental factors, such as foetal disease, into his later work. Although he failed to identify a trait common to all criminals, through attempting to find definitive characteristics, Lombroso pointed to the complexity of reasons or causes for delinquent behaviour.

Lombroso's work should be seen as part of the general shift in Italian legal and criminological thinking which broke with the predominant influences of the 'Classical School' and **Cesare Beccaria** (1738–94), especially over the manner in which criminals should be treated by society and the state. Although both classicists and positivists such as Lombroso believed in the 'social contract' and that those who transgressed this code should be removed from society in order to protect its law-abiding members, they diverged on the matter of punishment. Beccaria believed that humans possess free will, and thus choose whether to uphold the law. He further argued that punishment should be swift and severe in order to act as a deterrent to others who might be tempted to commit similar crimes. For Beccaria, it was important that the punishment reflected the crime committed. Lombroso, however, believed that his born criminals were compelled by biology and environment to behave in particular ways, and that society should punish them in a manner appropriate to their condition. For Lombroso, the punishment should fit the offender. To this end, he also included recommendations of punishments for the various types of criminals in his writings – but of course this was dependent upon the correct diagnosis of the offender's type. Lombroso was a proponent of punishments with a rehabilitative function – such as probation and parole – which were adopted in both the French and US penal codes during his lifetime.

Lombroso's theory of the criminal has become problematic in a post-Holocaust world, where his identification of criminal types has strong resonances with the subsequent development of eugenics in the course of the twentieth century. But Cesare Lombroso and his theories need to be seen within their historical context. For Lombroso, science was a means of bringing progress and optimism into Italy, a means of overcoming the generations of corrupt and inefficient rule by the old, undemocratic regimes. And his research offered both an explanation of and a means for tackling the problems of crime in the newly formed Italian state, at a time when contemporaries were afraid that it would be overwhelmed by a tide of criminality. Although Lombroso scrupulously catalogued and classified his cases with some use of controls, his findings were inevitably skewed by social and cultural inequalities in the new Italian state, namely in the antagonistic relationship between Northern and Southern Italy. The southern regions of Italy suffered from high levels of economic deprivation, and thus Southern Italians accounted for a high proportion of the prison population. There were also powerful cultural connotations of the South with crime and atavism that intersected with Lombroso's view of the criminal. The South was seen as backward and uncivilised; it was also geographically closer to the African continent and thus it was imbued with the 'savagery' that the European colonial imagination bestowed upon Africa. In addition to the association of the Italian South with a lesser degree of civilisation, Lombroso's atavistic stigmata may appear to be the fruits of bad science, but his work is nonetheless an attempt to explain the conjunction of physical, psychological and social/environmental factors in criminal behaviour. Ultimately, Lombroso saw his work as being beneficial to the poor, as he attempted to harness science to the greater good of humanity. Although many social Darwinists have been associated with right-wing politics, Lombroso was politically a figure of the Left, from his days of fighting with the Risorgimento to his later membership of the Italian Socialist Party. Lombroso was sympathetic to the plight of the poor, and believed that his scientific researches could have a positive impact on policies relating to deprived communities in Italy and elsewhere.

Lombroso had a significant international impact during his lifetime, being one of the founders of the International Congress on Criminal Anthropology in 1885, in addition to the adoption of some of his principles by the United States and France, as mentioned earlier. By the early twentieth century, Italian policemen were routinely introduced to Lombroso's theories as part of their training. Lombroso was also a well-respected author, writing over thirty books and over 1,000 articles for both popular and academic audiences on such diverse topics as genius or political crime. He also managed to have a powerful cultural impact, with references to his work being made in Tolstoy's *Resurrection* (1899) and Joseph Conrad's *The Secret Agent* (1907). Yet Lombroso was not without critics or challenges within his lifetime. Two of the most sustained challenges to his theory came from Jean-Gabriel Tarde (1843–1904) and Charles Goring (1870–1919). Tarde believed that Lombroso's findings were fundamentally wrong: criminals were not born but made, through the processes of 'imitation' or socialisation into particular behaviours. Tarde energetically attacked Lombroso and his followers, both at the International Congresses and through various major publications, including his *La criminalité comparée* (1886) and *La philosophie pénale* (1890). Tarde's work had a profound impact upon the reception of Lombroso's work in France, whilst further challenge came from Goring's studies of 3,000 English prisoners, published in 1913 as *The English Convict*. Goring compared his findings from the prisoners with control groups from the non-criminal population, and concluded that, apart from being somewhat lesser in height and weight than the non-criminal groups, there were no substantial differences between criminal and non-criminal populations. The challenges posed by both Tarde and Goring impacted significantly upon the ways in which Lombroso's work was received in France, Britain and the United States, shifting criminological discourse away from the notion of the 'born criminal'. Yet there were still important echoes of Lombroso and the positivists in early to mid-twentieth century research on the links between criminality and body shape, as in the case of Ernst Kretschmer, William Sheldon and **the Gluecks**; and many of the debates that Lombroso inspired in terms of the existence of free will and biological determinism endure today. Although criminology has long since moved on from purely positivist approaches – and certainly from atavistic stigmata – Lombroso's work continues to cast a shadow over any discussion of recidivism, adolescence-limited offending and evolutionary criminology.

Major works

Lombroso, C. (1896) 'The Savage Origin of Tattooing', *Popular Science Monthly*, 793–803.
—— (2006) *Criminal Man*, trans. Mary Gibson and Nicole Hahn Rafter. Durham, North Carolina: Duke University Press.

Further reading

Beirne, P. (1993) *Inventing Criminology: Essays on the Rise of 'Homo Criminalis'*. Albany, New York: State University of New York Press.
Gibson, M. (2002) *Born to Crime: Cesare Lombroso and the Origins of Biological Criminology*. Westport, Connecticut: Praeger.
—— (2006) 'Cesare Lombroso and Italian Criminology: Theory and Politics', in Becker, P. and R. Wetzell (eds) *Criminals and Their Scientists: The History of Criminology in International Perspective*, pp. 137–58. Cambridge: Cambridge University Press.
Gramsci, A. (1978). 'Some Aspects of the Southern Question', in Antonio Gramsci (ed.) *Selections from Political Writings (1921–1926)*, trans. Quentin Hoare, pp. 441–62. London: Lawrence and Wishart.
Kurella, H. (1911) *Cesare Lombroso: A Modern Man of Science*, trans. M. Eden Paul. London: Rebman.
Morrison, W. (2004) 'Lombroso and the Birth of Criminological Positivism: Scientific Mastery or Cultural Artifice?', in Jeff Ferrell, Keith Hayward, Wayne Morrison and Mike Presdee (eds) *Cultural Criminology Unleashed*, pp. 67–80. London: Glasshouse.
Pick, D. (1989) *Faces of Degeneration: A European Disorder, c.1848–c.1918*. Cambridge: Cambridge University Press.
Rafter, N. (2006) 'Cesare Lombroso and the Origins of Criminology: Rethinking Criminological Tradition', in Stuart Henry and Mark M. Lanier (eds) *The Essential Criminology Reader*, pp. 33–42. Boulder, Colorado: Westview.

KATE BRADLEY

PETER KROPOTKIN (1842–1921)

The life and writings of Peter Kropotkin arced across the social turmoil of the late nineteenth and early twentieth centuries. By turns honoured, exiled and imprisoned, Kropotkin helped shape the revolutionary changes that would bring about the transition to modernity. In all of this Kropotkin maintained, by all accounts, both a gentle humanism and a sharply anarchic critique of authoritarian domination. Kropotkin's interplay of compassion, critique and political activism produced a body of work essential in the development of contemporary anarchist and anti-authoritarian theory, and one that established many of the orientations still utilised by anarchist theorists and activists: mutual aid, decentralisation and direct action. More importantly for criminologists, Kropotkin developed from his life and work a rigorously social analysis of crime, law and punishment that anticipated many of criminology's subsequent understandings of crime and crime control.

Born to an aristocratic Russian family, 'Prince' Peter Kropotkin had renounced his title by age twelve, inspired by his reading of libertarian and republican writings. By this time he was also writing novels and reading French and Russian political theory (he would throughout his life write in Russian, French and English), and this formidable intellect led him to the study of mathematics and geography at the University of St. Petersburg. Early in his professional career, his reputation as a geographer was such that he was offered the Secretaryship of the Russian Geographical Society – which he declined in solidarity with the Russian peasantry and others outside the orbit of the educated. By age 30 he was travelling Europe, studying and participating in workers' movements, and finding affiliation especially with equalitarian movements influenced by the anarchist Michael Bakunin. He also now began to theorise that social revolutions were inevitable – but he also began to consider how they could be brought about with the least violence and fewest victims.

Two years later he was arrested for revolutionary activity – the day after presenting a paper to the Geographical Society and again being put forward to lead it. Imprisoned for the next two years, Kropotkin ultimately escaped from the prison hospital with the help of friends and made his way out of Russia to England. Relocating a year later to Switzerland, Kropotkin became embroiled in the battle between Marxist communists and Bakuninist anarchists –or as Kropotkin put it, the battle between the 'centralisation' and 'state's paternal rule' of the Marxists and the 'principles of federalism' and 'the free commune' of the anarchists. Out of this conflict Kropotkin also began to theorise anarchism as a way of life, a philosophy, more than just a simple political orientation.

Subsequently expelled from Switzerland, Kropotkin landed in France, where he was again arrested and tried for membership in a revolutionary association, and sentenced to five years in prison (ultimately serving three years with other political prisoners). Expelled from France upon his release, he returned to England, his home for the next thirty years. Having continued to publish widely in journals and scientific magazines (his only source of income), Kropotkin was during this time offered the Chair of Geography at Cambridge University, on the condition that he would temper his political activism. Not surprisingly, he declined. At age seventy-five, with the start of the 1917 Russian Revolution, he returned to Russia, aiding in revolutionary activities but refusing to support the Marxist Bolsheviks in their takeover (despite Lenin's professed admiration for him). Upon his death four years later, Lenin and the Soviet government proposed an official state funeral. His family refused, and the funeral procession was instead organised by Russian anarchist groups, with 20,000 mourners marching to the gravesite under the black flag of anarchism.

The personal characteristics and social contradictions that defined Kropotkin – gentle soul and ardent revolutionary, esteemed scientist and imprisoned activist – all contributed to his criminology. The foundation for this criminology is what we today might call Kropotkin's sociology of law. Kropotkin argued that, in a variety of ways, modern law serves as a 'mainstay of oppression'. Evolving hand in hand with capitalism, engineered by the capitalist class and its representatives, the bulk of law operates to protect the interests of private property. Other dimensions of the legal structure, Kropotkin added, are designed to protect the State itself, and so also function to perpetuate institutionalised privilege and power. But beyond these structural arrangements is the law's deleterious effect on social existence. Kropotkin saw that even seemingly benign laws encode existing understandings, creating static templates against which actions are measured, and so retard shared responsibility and human development. The injunction to 'obey the law' furthers this tendency, robbing citizens of initiative and critical thought. Anarchist and revolutionary, Kropotkin (1975a: 30) was willing to criticise 'the very foundations of society which have hitherto been held sacred' – and 'first and foremost among them', he found, was 'that fetish, law'.

Of course, as Kropotkin knew first-hand, that fetish and its enforcement had yet another effect: the imprisonment of those found guilty of breaking the law. As regards this issue, Kropotkin might well have simply recounted his own prison experiences, or condemned the brutality he found there. Instead, he utilised his critique of imprisonment to develop further a critical, sociological criminology. As conventionally constituted, Kropotkin argued, prisons *inevitably* fail, due to the very structure of their operations. A prison is a 'school of crime', as Kropotkin said, and not only because one prisoner learns illicit skills from another. The prison 'kills all the qualities in a man [*sic*] which make him best adapted to community life' (Kropotkin 1975b: 44–45): work initiative and 'will power', individual dignity and identity, social contacts with those outside prison, even the 'finer sentiments' that develop in response to a varied, creative environment. Prison guards likewise 'suffer the consequences' of their 'false positions'; as Kropotkin (1975b: 49, 56) noted, 'it is the institution which makes them what they are—petty, mean persecutors'. Consequently, the prison only promotes dehumanisation, criminality and recidivism – and so 'the first duty of the revolution will be to abolish prisons, those monuments of human hypocrisy and cowardice'.

In making this argument, Kropotkin directly addressed another criminologist of his time: **Cesare Lombroso**. Even if Lombroso was correct in claiming that most prisoners exhibit a 'mental defect' or 'diseased' brain, Kropotkin contended, this in no way justified Lombroso's case for taking aggressively punitive measures against such 'idiots'; if such people are suffering from a disease, they should be cured through care rather than punished through imprisonment. More importantly for Kropotkin, what is labelled 'criminal insanity' can be found throughout society, 'in palaces as well as insane asylums'. Anticipating differential association and labelling theories of a century later, Kropotkin therefore argued that the key to criminality is not individual pathology, as Lombroso would have it, but the sorts of definitions and reinforcements offered by the social environment. 'Everything depends on the circumstances in which the individual suffering from a mental disease is placed', he said. 'The great majority of us have some one of these maladies. But they do not lead a person to commit an anti-social act unless external circumstances give them a morbid turn'. So important were these 'social causes' to Kropotkin that, in summarising them, he produced an early, elegant statement of sociological criminology. 'Society as a whole is responsible for every anti-social act committed,' he wrote. 'We have our part in the glory of our heroes and geniuses; we also share in the acts of our assassins. It is we who have made them what they are—the one as well as the other' (1975b: 52–53).

Focusing this social analysis on capitalism, Kropotkin also anticipated **Robert K. Merton's** strain theory, with its notion of the tension between societal means and social goals, and the resultant adaptations to this tension. In discussing the inequities of imprisonment, Kropotkin (1975b: 46, emphasis in original) first noted that 'the thirst for riches, acquired by every possible means, is the very essence of *bourgeois* society' – and yet it is petty thieves, not the 'great robbers' of 'high finance and commerce', that populate the prison. Broadening his analysis, he added that in the world's great cities, the poor suffer not only from their own impoverishment, but from seeing all around them the material excesses of high finance, wealth and luxury. His conclusion – that in this way, by promoting material wealth while denying legitimate access to it, 'society itself daily creates these people incapable of leading a life of honest labor, and filled with anti-social desires' (Kropotkin 1975b: 53) – foreshadowed Merton's sense of modern society's anomic tendencies. It also anticipated the later notion of *relative deprivation* – as utilised by **Jock Young** and others, the understanding that it is not so much impoverishment, but the discontent of impoverishment in a context of privilege, that spawns criminality.

Underlying each of Kropotkin's criminological insights and arguments – the social construction of criminality, the harms of institutionalised law, the need for prison abolition – was a deeper analysis of human society. In what remains his best-known intellectual formulation, Kropotkin (1902) argued – and attempted to demonstrate through extensive research – that human beings and their social evolution were defined in large part by *mutual aid*. Tracing this tendency from particular animal species through early human societies and into the present, Kropotkin showed that mutual cooperation has remained the social dynamic essential for survival and progress. If oppressive social institutions could be changed, then, this human tendency could once again flourish – and the prevalence of criminality could be greatly diminished. Freed from the shackles of law, groups of people could find ways to cooperatively solve problems; *sans* the brutalising effects of prison, the number of habitual criminals would drop dramatically; in a society organised around common good rather than predatory profit, crimes of property and of interpersonal violence might all but disappear.

Kropotkin argued that this was no utopian dream – that this 'social sense' was instead a part of human history, from early tribal affiliations to later rural communes and contemporary industrial unions. He also made this case for mutual aid directly in opposition to the 'survival of the fittest' models popular at the time among the followers of Charles Darwin and Thomas Huxley. Given that Darwin, Huxley and their followers founded their claims on their scientific research – and given Kropotkin's own training and professional stature as a geographer and scientist – Kropotkin grounded his alternative model in his own and others' extensive historical and scientific research as well. As Stephen Jay Gould (1997) has shown, he also drew on a well-developed school of Russian evolutionary thought that had emerged in response to Darwin. Interestingly, the Russian school that Kropotkin exemplified offered yet another sociological perspective; this time on science itself, arguing that Darwin's findings might well reflect the competitive values of his own British society more than the observable dynamics of the natural world.

In this debate and others, Kropotkin readily drew on his own scientific training, and on the period's popular belief in science as an engine of social and intellectual progress. Consequently, his use of the scientific paradigm remained relatively uncritical – or by today's standards, naïve – as he often conflated social and scientific analysis, made recourse to totalising natural 'laws', and argued unproblematically that 'statistics prove it' (Kropotkin 1970, 1975a: 42). In this sense, while Kropotkin offered a progressive, perhaps even visionary, alternative to the work of other early criminologists like Lombroso, he continued to share with them a common intellectual terrain. In his sociological understanding of law, crime and punishment, though, and in his commitment to humanitarian social change, Kropotkin began to find new terrain, and to frame many of the criminological perspectives that would emerge over the following century. In addition, his distinctively anarchic analysis of legal authority and its criminogenic effects has continued to echo in the work of contemporary criminologists like Larry Tifft, Dennis Sullivan, **Stanley Cohen**, Jeff Ferrell, Randall Amster, Bruce DiCristina and Hal Pepinsky.

Then again, given his politics and personality, Kropotkin might prefer a different sort of commemoration – perhaps that offered by the 20,000 who marched with his funeral cortege, carrying signs saying 'where there is authority, there is no freedom', and filing past Moscow's Butyrki prison as 'the inmates shook the bars on their windows and sang an anarchist hymn to the dead' (Avrich 1978: 227).

Major works

Kropotkin, P. (1902) *Mutual Aid*. London: Heinemann.
—— (1906) *The Conquest of Bread*. London: Chapman and Hall.
—— (1968) [1899] *Fields, Factories and Workshops*. New York: Greenwood.
—— (1975a) [1886] 'Law and Authority', in E. Capouya and K. Tompkins (eds) *The Essential Kropotkin*, pp. 27–43. New York: Liveright.
—— (1975b) [1877] 'Prisons and Their Moral Influence on Prisoners', in E. Capouya and K. Tompkins (eds) *The Essential Kropotkin*, pp. 44–56. New York: Liveright.

Further reading

Avrich, P. (1978) *The Russian Anarchists*. New York: Norton.
Gould, S.J. (1997) 'Kropotkin was no crackpot', *Natural History*, 106 (June): 12–21.
Kropotkin, P. (1970) [1901] 'Modern Science and Anarchism', in Roger Baldwin (ed.) *Kropotkin's Revolutionary Pamphlets*, pp. 146–94. New York: Dover.
——— (1975c) [1910] 'Anarchism', in Emile Capouya and Keitha Tompkins (eds) *The Essential Kropotkin*, pp. 108–20. New York: Liveright.

JEFF FERRELL

ENRICO FERRI (1856–1929)

On 7 April 1926 the Hon. Violet Albina Gibson, sister of the second Baron Ashbourne, broke through a crowd on the Piazza del Campidoglio in Rome. Carrying a gun in one hand and a stone in the other, she shot at Benito Mussolini, catching him on the tip of his nose. Previously detained in asylums in England, the fifty-year-old Miss Gibson was examined for the military tribunal by Enrico Ferri, Professor of Criminal Law and Procedure at the University of Rome. Shortly after the attempted assassination, Ferri, who was to defend her, presented his report to the Italian dictator, a diminutive figure behind an oversize desk. In the defence memorandum Ferri was gladdened by Mussolini's recovery, and made great effort to praise the *Duce*. Calling the deed 'nefarious' he also extolled Mussolini's 'untiring devotion to work', which had raised his country to 'a high and sure destiny'. Ferri also found time to conclude that Gibson was an insane person with tendencies to suicide and criminality, considering her dangerous enough to be 'deprived of her personal liberty'.

After listening carefully, Mussolini assented and replied that he knew Gibson would be defended with 'all the serene calm that science can afford her'. Ferri had met him before and, feeling he could read character from a face, was impressed with the tranquillity, benevolence and 'noble attitude' of the dictator. In all this flattery he put to one side a little fact he must surely have known: in the Paris police criminal archives was filed a mug shot, taken some years before, of an ill-kempt anarchist by the name of Benito Mussolini, the same man who was now the leader of Fascist Italy.

Ferri's fulsome praise for the dictator was neither passing sycophancy nor convenient politesse, for it reflected his sincere political views at this juncture, as his books *Fascism in Italy: The Works of B. Mussolini* and *Mussolini Statesman*, which appeared a year later, testify. Such was his status in the *Duce's* eyes that he was nominated to the Senate but died in 1929 before he could take up the position. Yet only a year before Mussolini came to power, Ferri had been sufficiently socialist to be 'chased from his classroom', according to Sorel, by fascist students. Certainly Ferri had come a long way from his 'intransigent revolutionary', Marxist days in the Socialist Party to his support of fascism. It is arguable, however, that one set of highly influential criminological ideas held both political positions together: his doctrines of 'social defence' anchored by positive criminology and sociology. This theorisation was already evident in his most famous work *Criminal Sociology*. Here he described – in a vocabulary that would have resonated with the social Darwinism inhabiting the contemporary radical politics of both the left and right at the time – 'a continuous struggle between society and criminals'.

Alongside **Lombroso** and Garofalo, Ferri was one of the 'holy trinity' of the Italian Positive School. He had risen to fame in the late nineteenth and early twentieth century as a campaigning socialist, gifted orator, skilled legal advocate, distinguished parliamentarian and academic champion of positive criminology. Without Ferri's charisma, international prominence and tireless writing, positive criminology might have remained what it was under the early Lombroso: a photographic cabinet of criminal curiosities. The history of ideas has taught us not to attribute to particular individuals the invention of concepts and ways of thinking. But if the Italian Positive School was the culmination and relay of a host of scattered writings and practices cultivated over the previous century, Enrico Ferri's personal contribution to criminology is more than just a synthesiser of ideas and spokesman for a mood and way of thinking of a period. His elastic 'criminal sociology' and his theory of social defence would exert a key influence on both progressive and reactionary versions of positive criminology, whether they took the form of Chicago School social disorganisation theory or Bell-Curve biologism. They were also instrumental in conveying through fascism to our criminological present the dark doctrine that respectable society is at war with the dangerous criminal.

Born in 1856 in San Benedetto Po, Mantua, the son of a salt and tobacco shopkeeper, Enrico Ferri was taught at school by Roberto Ardigò, a priest who gave up his vocation and faith to write the materialist *Psychology as a Positive Science,* which argued that psychology was a natural science, a branch of biology with its models of observable cause and effect. The young Ferri would also encounter

Herbert Spencer's positivist *The Study of Sociology* and *The Principles of Sociology*. Important to wider European social thought in the second half of the nineteenth century, it conveyed metaphors of the 'social body', the 'body politic', 'organisation', the 'organic' and 'social pathology' to social science.

In 1878 he went to the Sorbonne in Paris to study the crime statistics of the *Compte générale*, the most long standing and comprehensive in Europe at the time. In the 1830s **Adolphe Quetelet** had used them in his ecological theories to deduce a stable propensity to crime. Ferri's longitudinal study, a considerable labour that examined them from 1826 to 1878, found significant variations in the statistics that could only be attributable to social and economic change. He emerged from his Paris experience as a thoroughgoing positivist, already believing that a complex combination of individual, local and social factors, researched by the methods of the natural sciences, accounted for crime and its variation.

Ever since his student days he had been a staunch opponent of the armchair speculation and metaphysics of the classical school, and his Paris research confirmed his conviction. The factors in the causation of crime should be investigated scientifically and the study and careful analysis of statistics was the privileged route to positive knowledge. His own study had shown that, though anthropological and 'telluric' (or physical) factors had been stable over time, there was considerable variation in social factors which accounted for the changes in crime rates. Armed with his Sorbonne study he went in 1879–80 to work with Lombroso, the Professor of Legal Medicine at the University of Turin. While he is often regarded as an intellectual son of Lombroso, he was, in fact, the principle architect of the *scuola positiva* and influenced its future direction, particularly in the study of sociological factors.

Before he reached the age of 25, Ferri was appointed in 1880 to the Chair in Criminal Law at Bologna, moving via Siena, to the University of Pisa in 1890. Whilst in Siena he famously defended peasant leaders in Mantua who, subject to harsh exploitation, were in dispute with their wealthy landowners. The state had accused them of insurrection and Ferri ably argued, perhaps even in a positivistic way, that their economic circumstances had given them no choice but to act in this manner. At this time arbitrary police action and the aggressive use of courts and prison to support employers and repress strikes, trade unions and worker protest was a common experience of the activist left in Europe and America. When Ferri unexpectedly won the case he found himself in common cause with socialists of the time. Describing himself in his inaugural speech as an 'evolutionary sociologist', he was elected as a deputy to the national parliament in 1886 and soon moved from a radical-liberal syndicalism to embrace Marxism.

By the time he joined the newly formed Italian Socialist Party in 1892, his politics had become too much for the university authorities and he was dismissed from his Chair at Pisa. He threw himself into political activity but never abandoned the intellectual life, delivering public lectures, developing an international reputation and continuing his support for the positive school in lectures, articles, pamphlets and books. A year after his expulsion from academia he published his *Socialism and Positive Science (Darwin, Spencer, Marx).* Spencer had recruited the science of evolution to defend the liberal argument for competition in market society. But for Ferri and other socialists, society would evolve beyond competitive individualism in the direction of social solidarity. Darwin and Spencer's 'struggle for existence' would become the struggle to build cooperation and to defend solidarity. Furthermore, a socialist society would ensure that the physically and morally healthy would thrive.

This viewpoint was no mere eccentricity. A whole swathe of socialist opinion, motivated by a combination of anti-clericalism, opposition to conservative tradition, and a myth of progress through struggle, was attracted to the scientific models found in social Darwinism and contemporary scientific Marxism. Such strands of thought are discernible not only in the thoughts of the more revolutionary radicals of the time but also among British Fabians and the founders of the London School of Economics who, as scientific socialists, were campaigners for social hygiene and eugenics. Indeed the problems of society were seen by many on the left at this time as curable social pathology so that a 'therapeutic' approach to social policy should seek to ameliorate poverty, improve health and welfare, as well as confront the problem of crime. We might be tempted to see a contemporary figure such as the Marxist, **Willem Bonger**, as far removed from the *scuola positiva*, but he also used a familiar set of metaphors from biology and pathology, when he wrote about crime as a 'deeply-rooted social disease' threatening the 'body' of society with its economic and moral harms.

Despite attempts to disown him by socialists such as Kautsky in Germany, Ferri was a prominent figure in this broad intellectual movement, with many of his pamphlets and books translated into English for the leftist and labour groupings thriving in the early years of the twentieth century. On the other side of the Atlantic in 1901 the Chicago *International Socialist Review* regarded Ferri's *Socialism and Modern Science* as second only to **Karl Marx**'s *Capital* in its contribution to 'the socialist movement of the English-speaking world'.

In this period Ferri faced imprisonment having lost a libel case brought by the navy after he denounced them for corruption. But the scandal could not be suppressed and his stand won widespread public admiration when damning evidence became public. Now, after thirteen years of banishment from the academy, he could not be stopped from taking up the prestigious Chair in Law at the University of Rome in 1906. In the ensuing years he continued his socialist campaigning and promulgation of the doctrines of positive criminology, setting up, along the way, the Institute of Criminology at Rome at which the young students Leon Radzinowicz and **Thorsten Sellin** would come to study during the years of fascism.

Ferri's positive criminology compared the impulsiveness and improvidence of criminals to 'children and savages'. He was not only appealing to Lombrosian theories of atavism but reflecting new anxieties that brought together concerns about the 'dangerous classes' in the slums, unruly children on the streets, and rebellious subjects in the colonies. Indeed, like Lombroso, Ferri incorporated into his criminology the widespread racist notion associated with colonial anthropology that the natives were more cerebrally immature, intellectually inferior, impulsive and thus crime-prone, an idea revived within our time by the neo-positivism of the American right to describe the underclass.

More influential was his doctrine of 'social defence', which was also evident from these early years. Though the metaphors of war against the enemies of society were pervasive in the intellectual life of the second half of the nineteenth century, Ferri brought them together in a coherent doctrine of social defence against crime, describing the natural 'struggle' of the body of honest citizens against the criminal. He argued that it was the central purpose of the institutions of government and criminal justice to protect society (conceived as natural organism) against the disease of crime, without being distracted by the metaphysically concocted arguments of classical theory with all its talk of rights, the social contract and the rule of law. A substantial proportion of crime (perhaps up to half) was the product of 'born criminals' (a phrase Ferri claimed to have coined), who, through discretionary and indeterminate sentencing, should be contained and treated.

In later life he was directly responsible for the substantial positivist influence on the new criminal code presented to parliament in 1921. But it never made the statute book as Italy was overtaken by the social and economic turmoil in the midst of which fascism came to power. After Mussolini's accession, Ferri moved rapidly towards fascism in the course of 1922. There was later influence on Mussolini's criminal code, but, in many respects, positivism had already taken over what **Michel**

Foucault would later call the 'infra-penality' of governmental and social policy in a myriad of scattered practices. In any case, it was clear that Ferri's critique of classical rights and his advocacy of discretionary state authority in social policy was most congenial to the mind of Mussolini.

We cannot afford to treat Ferri as a historical curiosity: under his leadership, the therapeutic discourse of criminology became a respectable social science in the early years of the twentieth century. The dark, old dreads and fears of slum-stuck primitives in the heart of our cities were supplemented and legitimised by bright new technologies of welfare policy that nonetheless continued to construct and produce classes 'below' the 'social' who still haunt politics today. In his writings we can trace the lineaments of a criminology that has not only survived post-war scepticism but is in revival today, from the Bell Curve hypothesis to underclass theories, from the renewal of incapacitation to the renaissance of dangerousness, from our various 'wars' on crime to the foundationalist dogma that natural scientific methods, particularly those based on statistical analysis, provide the only route to criminological knowledge and policy. Reading Ferri in social and historical context is also to read a history of the present.

Major works

Ferri, E. (1881) *Studi sulla criminalità in Francia dal 1825 al 1878*. Roma: Eredi Botta.
—— (1895) [1884] *Criminal Sociology*. London: T. Fisher Unwin.
—— (1901) *The Positive School of Criminology: Three Lectures Given at the University of Naples, Italy on April 22nd, 23rd, and 24th*. Chicago, Illinois: Charles H. Kerr.
—— (1905) [1894] *Socialism and Positive Science (Darwin, Spencer, Marx)*. London: Independent Labour Party.

Further reading

Beck, N. (2005) 'Enrico Ferri's Scientific Socialism: A Marxist Interpretation of Herbert Spencer's Organic Analogy', *Journal of the History of Biology*, 38: 301–25.
Ferri, E. (1927a) *Il fascismo in Italia e l'opera di B. Mussolini*. Mantova: Paladino.
—— (1927b) *Mussolini, uomo di stato*. Mantova: Paladino.
—— (1928–1929) 'A Character Study and Life History of Violet Gibson Who Attempted the Life of Benito Mussolini, on the 7th April, 1926', *American Institute of Criminal Law and Criminology*, 19: 211–19.

Jenkins, P. (1982) 'The Radicals and the Rehabilitative Ideal, 1890–1930', *Criminology*, 20: 347–72.

Radzinowicz, L. (1999) *Adventures in Criminology*. London: Routledge.

Sellin, T. (1958) 'Pioneers in Criminology XV: Enrico Ferri', *Journal of Criminal Law, Criminology and Police Science*, 48: 481–93.

PHIL CARNEY

EMILE DURKHEIM (1858–1917)

Emile Durkheim is one of the most influential figures in Western sociology. Arguably, he is more responsible than anybody else for validating 'society' as a legitimate focus of study and for institutionalising sociology as an academic discipline dedicated to this purpose. Although he is primarily known for his innovative work in sociological theory, Durkheim took an active interest in criminology and in the early part of his career taught a two-year course on 'criminal sociology'. His work is still a source of inspiration for theoretical criminology (e.g. DiCristina 2004, 2006).

For Durkheim, society is far more than a product of social interactions between individuals; rather, it is a reality that exists over and above individuals. He conceptualises society as a moral force which is experienced both internally as part of our emotional–psychological make-up and as an external pressure upon our conscience and behaviour. He argues that modern society is undergoing a profound process of change that involves a reordering of the moral rules that govern our lives as well as a fundamental recasting of our social psychology. His sociology is devoted to understanding the social and cultural conditions by which society acquires its moral character and force. In this he makes known the social pathologies that dispose modern individuals to 'egoistic' impulses coupled with painful experiences of 'anomie'. A large portion of his work is also committed to the task of outlining the institutional arrangements, cultural values and political processes whereby society might attain a new state of moral solidarity in which individuals would be able to maximise their sense of social and personal well-being. His sociological ambition calls for nothing less than a moral reformation of epochal proportions.

Durkheim was born on 15 April 1858 in the town of Epinal in France. His family were Ashkenazic Jews, but while at secondary school he stopped practising Judaism and for most of his adult life pronounced himself agnostic in relation to metaphysical concerns. Despite his lack of religiosity, his Jewish ancestry had a profound impact on his life. In the aftermath of France's defeat in the 1870 Franco-Prussian war, for instance, he faced anti-Semitism when the Jews were accused by the French establishment of betraying the nation to the Germans. Durkheim understood this vicious outbreak of racism as a symptom of moral pathology and along with figures such as the novelist Emile Zola and artist Claude Monet, committed himself to a human rights campaign on behalf of a Jewish artillery officer, Albert Dreyfus, who was falsely convicted of treason in a closed trial. The political pressure brought by the 'Dreyfusards' (as they came to be known) upon the military courts was such that senior officers eventually confessed to fabricating evidence and Dreyfus was granted a presidential pardon. Following the arguments raised in his famous essay on *Individualism and the Intellectuals* (1898), commentators are inclined to regard Durkheim's involvement in the Dreyfus campaign as not just a product of his social networks, but also, as a practical outcome of his sociological theory.

Aside from this excursion into politics, the main events in Durkheim's life take place around his university career. Following his graduation from the prestigious *Ecole Normale Superieure* in 1882, he pursued a scholarly life as a working academic. He was based at the University of Bordeaux from 1887 to 1902, and from there he moved to the Sorbonne to take up the Chair of Education. This was re-named the Chair of Education and Sociology in 1913; and by this time his courses had become an obligatory part of the curriculum for all those studying degrees in philosophy, history, literature and language. He died on 15 November 1917, grief stricken and in the midst of a bout of severe depression following the death of this son, Andre Durkheim, in World War I.

When compared to other thinkers in so-called 'classical' sociological theory, Durkheim provides us with one of the most systematic and sustained projects of work. His first book, *The Division of Labour in Society* (1893) is a sociological study of the origins and effects of processes of individualisation on society and in this he outlines some of the key theoretical problems that occupy his career. He observes that at the same time as a society embarks on the process of industrialisation, it also grows in size and acquires more varied and complex institutional arrangements. With more specialisation in the division of labour, people develop a more pronounced sense of their own individuality. He argues that this process marks the breakdown of older 'mechanical' forms of social solidarity and underlines a requirement for the development of new 'organic' solidarities; the moral rules that govern social relationships need to become more adaptable to the task of moderating individual behaviours in multiple and varied social circumstances.

The negative social consequences of this transition are manifested at an individual level in more pronounced experiences of *egoism* and *anomie*. Egoistic individuals are characterised by a lack of social attachments that incline them to be self-preoccupied to a point that is socially corrosive, while the experience of anomie resides in a profound sense of moral disorientation that leaves individuals feeling ill-equipped to direct the course of their lives. When pointing to possible solutions to this predicament, Durkheim holds that whatever form they take, these must be disciplined by the understanding that social conditions now dispose people to be sentimentally involved in 'the cult of the individual'. Durkheim argues that if modern societies are to attain states of moral solidarity, then new social institutions, legal systems and cultural practices need to be established that are guided by an ethic of 'moral individualism'. The possibility for our moral unity lies in nurturing of a broader sympathy for all human sufferings and in upholding the social well-being of 'the individual' as a sacred value.

In other works, Durkheim elaborates upon his analyses and arguments and also moves to present sociology as a discipline ideally suited for studying the social arrangements that provide the basis for moral solidarity. *The Rules of Sociological Method* (1895) lays down methodological principles for studying society. Durkheim argues that, even though the life of the social world in its entirety lies beyond the grasp of our senses, we can still move to indirectly diagnose and measure its impact upon us through a combination of historical, statistical and ethnographic data. In *Suicide* (1897), he demonstrates a portion of his sociological methodology by surveying suicide statistics and arguing that the primary cause of increased rates of suicide is located in changes in the social structure of society. In *The Elementary Forms of the Religious Life* (1912), he takes a greater interest in the project of cultivating moral individualism, and draws on ethnographic research in order to explore the social arrangements that give rise to religious sentiments and the role played by religious rituals in the maintenance of social solidarities. There are also a number of publications that document his interventions within various philosophical, political and policy disputes. The most important of these include his lectures on *Moral Education* (1902–3), *Professional Ethics and Civic Morals* (1890–1912), *Socialism* (1895–96) and *Sociology and Philosophy* (1898–1911).

The importance of Durkheim's work for criminology lies in the challenge he brings to any attempt to reduce the explanation of criminal behaviour to either components of individual psychology or purely economic factors. He offers a level of analysis that explores the bearing of relative conditions of moral solidarity upon individual attitudes and behaviours. He focuses on the quality of the moral ties that bind individuals to society as a means to explain pathological behaviours and movements of social reform (see **Travis Hirschi**'s later adaptation of this view in the study of delinquency). On this view, criminal behaviour can be explained as a result of anomie or egoism and as a phenomenon that serves to highlight the relative strengths of processes of moral regulation and social integration (see **Robert Merton**). Durkheim encourages us to understand changes in definitions of crime, rates of criminal activity and approaches to punishment as all heavily moderated by the social organisation of moral life.

Criminological readers may well find that his essay on *Two Laws of Penal Evolution* (1900) provides a useful point of entry into his work, for here Durkheim explores the implications of his theory for analysing the social evolution of punishment. Here he argues that the modern preference for imprisonment as the primary response to criminal behaviour is rooted in the extent to which processes of individualisation have re-shaped the moral outlook of society; and in particular, the social credence that is lent to the view that individuals should be morally responsible for their behaviours. Beyond this, Durkheim contends that the force of moral individualism within the modern criminal justice system is manifested in the liberalisation of law, and that this social phenomenon is also implicated in the extent to which people now recoil from the use of violence as punishment. Commentators also commend this essay on the grounds that it provides a useful context for analysing Durkheim's notion of the *conscience collective*; that is, the idea that individuals partake in a unified mental and emotional orientation to the world and that this is moderated according to the moral needs of society.

Students should be wary of the popular portrayal of Durkheim as the founder of structural functionalism; particularly where this is coupled with the argument that he was a conservative patriarch whose affiliations to positivism are displayed in an anti-individualistic and overly deterministic account of human behaviour. In criminological textbooks, Durkheim is often featured as a theorist whose interests lie in the 'positive functions' of crime for the maintenance of social order. There is a tendency to focus exclusively on his analysis of the contribution of crime to 'the normal evolution of morality and law' (Durkheim [1895] (1938: 67–75)). Durkheim's many sociological insights are hereby reduced to the argument that crime is an inevitable and normal part of the process in which a society adapts to the moral conditions of its existence. Students learn that Durkheim understood criminal acts and the social sanctions that they carry to function either as a means to challenge or to affirm boundaries between shared understandings of good and bad behaviour; but they are provided with no wider knowledge of his social theory or the contexts in which it was written.

Arguably, the representation of Durkheim as a structural functionalist is a product of the ways in which his work was taken up and adapted by the American social theorist, Talcott Parsons. It is Parsons rather than Durkheim who is chiefly responsible for championing structural functionalism within Western sociological theory. Many textbook accounts of Durkheim are essentially involved with analysing his work through the lens of debates surrounding the legacy of Talcott Parsons; they do not appear to be based on a first-hand reading of Durkheim's books and articles. Certainly, there are some functionalist strains in Durkheim thinking, but these never feature as the headline topic of concern in his work. Students of criminology who encounter Durkheim as a flag-waving functionalist or who find him featured as a mere 'stepping stone' en route to an exploration of **Robert Merton**'s and **Albert Cohen**'s adaptation of his writings on anomie, should understand that there is far more to his legacy than that which tends to be noted in most introductory textbooks.

Following the seminal interventions of Alvin Gouldner (1962) and Steven Lukes (1973), contemporary Durkheimian scholarship is concerned to highlight his support for socialism, his radical humanism, and in particular, the extent to which his earlier interest in the social determinants of 'conscious strategic action' gives way in his later 'religious sociology' to a greater emphasis upon the ways in which social interactions take place as 'motivated expressive behaviour'. He is represented as having socialist sympathies, but also, as labouring to make clear the extent to which human flourishing depends on social arrangements and moral factors that cannot be addressed as mere products of our material relations (Pearce 1989). Durkheim is identified as providing the groundwork for the development of sociological thinking towards an appreciation of the force of bodily experience and emotional feeling within the dynamics of human behaviour (Shilling and Mellor 1998). He is also celebrated for providing sociological insight into the sociocultural conditions through which the ideal of human rights acquires its popular appeal and powers of influence over the institutional organisation of society (Wilkinson 2005). On these terms it may well be the case that we are only now beginning to re-discover the full provocation of his conception of the moral condition of humanity in the age of industrial modernity (Meštrović 1991).

Major works

Durkheim, E. [1890–1912] (1957) *Professional Ethics and Civic Morals*. London: Routledge & Kegan Paul.

—— [1893] (1964) *The Division of Labour in Society*. New York: The Free Press.

—— [1895] (1938) *The Rules of Sociological Method*. New York: Free Press.

—— [1895–96] (1962) *Socialism*. New York: Collier Books.

—— [1896] (1973c) 'Two Laws of Penal Evolution', *Economy and Society*, 2(3): 285–308.

—— [1896–1911] (1974) *Sociology and Philosophy*. New York: Free Press.

—— [1897] (1952) *Suicide: A Study in Sociology*. London: Routledge & Kegan Paul.

——[1898] (1973a) 'Individualism and the Intellectuals', in Bellah, R. (ed.) *Emile Durkheim on Morality and Society*. Chicago, Illinois: University of Chicago Press.

—— [1902–3] (1973b) *Moral Education: A Study in the Theory and Application of the Sociology of Education*. New York: Free Press.

—— [1912] (1915) *The Elementary Forms of the Religious Life*. London: Allen & Unwin.

Further reading

DiCristina, B. (2004) 'Durkheim's Theory of Homicide and the Confusion of the Empirical Literature', *Theoretical Criminology*, 8(1): 57–91.

—— (2006) 'Durkheim's Latent Theory of Gender and Homicide', *British Journal of Criminology*, 46(2): 212–33.

Gouldner, A. (1962) 'Introduction', to Durkheim, E. *Socialism*. New York: Collier Books.

Lukes, S. (1973) *Emile Durkheim: His Life and Work: A Historical and Critical Study*. Harmondsworth: Penguin

Meštrović, S.G. (1991) *The Coming Fin De Siècle: An Application of Durkheim's Sociology to Modernity and Postmodernism*. London: Routledge.

Pearce, F. (1989) *The Radical Durkheim*. London: Unwyn Hyman.

Shilling, C. and Mellor, P.A. (1998) 'Durkheim, Morality and Modernity: Collective Effervescence, Homo Duplex and the Sources of Moral Action', *British Journal of Sociology*, 49(2): 193–209.

Wilkinson, I. (2005) *Suffering: A Sociological Introduction*. Cambridge: Polity.

IAIN WILKINSON

ROBERT EZRA PARK (1864–1944)

Robert Ezra Park, urban explorer and champion of rich, descriptive criminology, was the leading light of the Chicago School of sociology during the 1920s and early 1930s (see **Edwin Sutherland** and **Clifford Shaw**). The Chicago School was responsible for the first large-scale study of crime in America and, according to most accounts, directly set the tone for the majority of subsequent American criminology. Using the burgeoning metropolis of Chicago as their 'natural laboratory', Park and his fellow Chicagoans identified and defined social problems and then set about studying them empirically using a theoretical/geographical framework inspired by plant ecology. While Park himself wrote comparatively little, he stimulated a generation of students to undertake fieldwork in the urban micro-worlds of Chicago, urging them to pepper their analyses with naturalistic description and ethnographic detail. His primary contribution to criminology, though, was the notion that neither crime nor delinquency can be reduced to individual or ethnic predispositions. Instead they need to be explained by general social processes such as group disorganisation in specific urban locations.

Park's life was as cosmopolitan as his work. Born in Harveyville, Pennsylvania in 1864, he was raised in Minnesota, the son of a prosperous businessman. He commenced his studies at the University of Michigan, graduating with a philosophy degree in 1887. After graduation, Park spent eleven years as a newspaper journalist in various cities in the United States. As a city and police reporter he became well versed in the seamier side of urban America, writing muckraking articles on city corruption, political scandal and the squalid conditions of immigrant neighbourhoods and the criminal activities that took place therein. In 1894 he married the painter Clara Cahill, the daughter of a prominent Michigan lawyer. They had four children together.

In 1898 Park changed tack and returned to academic life. He enrolled first as a Master's student at Harvard and then, a year later, moved with his family to Berlin to continue his philosophical studies at the Friedrich Wilhelm University. It was here that he attended lectures by the sociologist Georg Simmel, whose insights into communication and interaction theory were to exert a lasting influence on Park's work. From Berlin, Park moved first to Strasbourg and then to Heidelberg where he studied philosophy and the social sciences with the neo-Kantian scholar Wilhelm Windelband. Under Windelband's tutelage, Park defended his doctoral thesis (in German) on crowd behaviour in 1903. Park was forty years old.

In 1903 Park changed course once again and embarked on a nine-year period of activism. He went to colonial Africa as the editorial secretary for the Congo Reform Association against Belgian Misadministration. He also worked as a ghost writer for the Black American civil rights leader Booker T. Washington in Tuskegee, Alabama. It was during this period that Park became acquainted with the Black community in the South, interviewing hundreds of African Americans about their lives and concerns. He developed a strong interest in the internal contradictions of the status of the Free Negro and wrote about the Negro as a 'marginal man' (a term that others would later develop into a famous sociological concept). Washington and Park toured Europe in 1910 to compare the conditions of black tenant farmers in Alabama with those of the poor in Europe. The resulting *Outlook Magazine* article, 'The Man Farthest Down' (co-authored with Washington), was, for the time, extremely progressive. However, it did not sit well with some African American leaders, who saw their fight as being against racism rather than class oppression (see **W.E.B. Du Bois**). However, Park's work was recognised by the leading sociologist, William I. Thomas, who invited Park to join the staff of the new and rapidly expanding Sociology Department of the Rockefeller-funded University of Chicago.

Academically speaking, Park was a late developer. He came to Chicago at the age of 50 and did not become full professor until 1923 at the age of fifty-nine. It may have been because the clock was ticking that Park was so dynamic. He quickly established a relationship with his junior colleague, Ernest Burgess, and together they would become the driving force of the Chicago School of Sociology. For years their *Introduction to the Science of Sociology* (1951), a comprehensive text of over 1,000 pages containing 196 readings, was the most important sociology textbook in the United States. As a well-established scholar, Park also served as president of the American Sociological Association (1925), the editor of many academic journals, and as a member of various learned societies such as the Social Science Research Council.

Robert Park was a colourful man in any number of ways. He would enter the lecture hall as a casually dressed absent-minded professor, but as soon as he opened his mouth, he captured his students' attention. In the thriller *Organised Crimes*, set at the University of Chicago Sociology Department, the author Nicholas von Hoffman later described the atmosphere as follows: 'Mr. Park was in a mood to tell stories and rhapsodize about the city he was teaching a new generation of students to go out and study firsthand. He was the first sociologist who said that theory was nothing, library work less, that what must be done is to venture forth and see how people live.' After retiring from his teaching career in Chicago in 1936, Park continued to share his knowledge with students at Fisk University and the universities of Hawaii. His travels also took him to China, India, South Africa and Brazil. In an autobiographical note added to his Collected Papers called *Race and Culture*, he boldly claimed, 'I have actually covered more ground, tramping about in cities in different parts of the world, than any other living man.'

Park's contribution to the social sciences started from Georg Simmel's notion that interaction between individuals is the basis of society. Collective behaviour (Park's Ph.D. dissertation subject) is governed by a body of traditions and norms that arise in the interaction process itself. This leads to a form of consensus in which social control is essential. 'Society is everywhere a control organization. Its function is to organize, integrate, and direct the energies resident in the individuals which compose it' (Park 1952: 157). Rather than being static, society is conceived as a process and antagonism is the normal state of affairs. Park distinguished four major social processes: competition, conflict, accommodation, and assimilation. Accordingly, disruptions and crises should be studied as normal phases in social development. Social change and development follow a patterned order and develop in cycles of predictable sequence. When races or ethnic groups live together (as in an immigrant community), their relationships go through a *natural history* of conflict and accommodation that Park termed the *race relations cycle*.

This view of society was applied in a programmatic paper on urban life in industrial America entitled 'The City: Suggestions for the Investigation of Human Behavior in the Urban Environment' (1923). As the 'natural habitat of civilized man', Park asserted that cities provide the perfect testing ground for sociological research. This article greatly influenced the thinking of his colleague Burgess, whose ecological zonal model of the expansion of Chicago would go on to become arguably the most famous diagram in sociology. Drawing on Park's ideas, Burgess argued that the settlement of new immigrant groups can be studied by following the movements of successive immigrant generations via the city model. Each 'natural area' undergoes a natural history of conflict and accommodation. It begins with the resident population creating *social distance* to the newcomers and is then followed by open resistance. Once the newcomers get established, the old group moves on to the next more prosperous area of the city. They now defend their neighbourhood against the next immigrant invasion. In this ongoing social process, phenomena such as racial prejudice and ethnic violence are viewed as logical and predictable rather than abnormal.

Importantly, Park encouraged his students to venture into the mosaic of social worlds and study them via direct observation. **David Matza** later wrote in his classic text, *Becoming Deviant,* 'It was as if an anthropologist let loose in Chicago had discovered urban America in its full diversity'. Park's students, though, quickly moved beyond simply studying the social ecology of Chicago's expansion (the most famous example being, of course, Zorbaugh's *Goldcoast and the Slum*). Enthusiastically supported by Park, they began to focus on particular social problem areas, ultimately engaging in what became known as 'D-sociology' – the study of drugs, drinking, disease, delinquency and disorganisation.

Park's pupils considered crime a logical product of community disorganisation rather than a manifestation of individual pathology, demonstrating time and again that crime rates were higher in the *urban zone in transition*, that is, the low-rent area immediately surrounding the city centre. Here first-generation American immigrants grew up under criminogenic conditions. It was the *neighbourhood* that produced the high juvenile crime rates rather than the particular ethnic or racial group that happened to live there at any given moment. Park's line of reasoning was clear in the first academic book on American youth gangs published in 1927 by his student Frederic Thrasher.

Park's most important legacy, though, was his promotion of naturalistic, highly descriptive research methods. We learn very little about the criminal in the laboratory, he noted. Instead sociologists should study people in real-life situations. As a newspaperman, Park had sent his cub reporters out into the city, and as a professor he did the same with his students; ordering them to study life in the streets, bars and homeless shelters – indeed anyplace where criminals gathered. Here they were to employ the noble research arts of *looking and hearing*, the very same *nosing around* skills that he himself had relied upon as a reporter (Lindner 1996).

For Park, all sorts of empirical material can be useful, from life histories and interviews, to case studies and newspaper articles – he even had his students read novels by the likes of Emile Zola. His goal was to ensure that his students present their findings in an engaging and accessible style that could be read by everyone, not just professionally trained fellow sociologists. Because of this approach, Chicago sociology of the 1920s is sometimes considered by some critics as little more than *sociological journalism*. Park, though, would have reacted harshly to such criticisms. His goal was to make sociology more *scientific*, not less. He argued that the still fledgling discipline of sociology needed to dissociate itself from social work, the missions and reform politics. The social world, he declared, should be described objectively as it is and not as 'do-gooders' would have it.

Reflecting on Park's work today, it is impossible not to note the absence of a more critical perspective on American politics and society. Likewise, it is difficult not to notice that the Chicago sociologists of the 1920s also failed to analyse the relationship between organised crime and Prohibition, nor did they take a political position on the matter (see **the Schwendingers**). In Park's defence, though, he always stressed that what he was searching for was an understanding of the dynamic rhythms and everyday vagaries of urban life and its related public institutions, rather than the structural inequalities of capitalist society.

In conclusion, few would argue that Park's contributions to the field of collective behaviour are less relevant today. While he is rightly remembered for theoretical concepts like the 'marginal man' and 'social distance', the ecological model of the city and its predictions on crime are utilised more in the field of geography than in social science – and even there they are employed with some hesitation. At the same time, his ideas on the race relations cycle still inspire scientists seeking to understand the logic of prejudice and succession, and his preference for naturalistic description and urban ethnography are key features of today's cultural criminology. Without question, his clarion call to criminological researchers to 'go get the seat of your pants dirty in *real* research' is as timely today as it ever was.

Major works

Park, R.E. (1915) '"The City": Suggestions for the Investigation of Human Behavior in the Urban Environment', *American Journal of Sociology*, 20: 577–612.

—— (1921) *Old World Traits Transplanted*. New York: Harper and Row.

—— (1950) *Race and Culture, Vol. 1, Collected Papers of Robert E. Park*. New York: The Free Press.

—— (1952) *Human Communities*. New York: The Free Press.

Further reading

Ballis Lal, B. (1990) *The Romance of Culture in an Urban Civilization. Robert E. Park on Race and Ethnic Relations in Cities*. London: Routledge.

Coser, L.A. (1971) *Masters of Sociological Thought: Ideas in Historical and Social Context.* New York: Harcourt Brace Jovanovich, Inc.

Lindner, R. (1996) *The Reportage of Urban Culture: Robert Park and the Chicago School.* Cambridge: Cambridge University Press.

Rauschenbush, W. (1979) *Robert E. Park: Biography of a Sociologist.* Durham, North Carolina: Duke University Press.

FRANK BOVENKERK

W.E.B. DU BOIS (1868–1963)

William Edward Burghardt (W.E.B.) Du Bois is now regarded as one of the founders of modern sociology. A prolific civil rights activist and scholar of race in America and beyond, Du Bois was also a progenitor of major criminological developments such as conflict theory and socio-ecological criminology. His talents were manifold and his outcome prodigious, but whether working as a historian or educator, political agitator or poet, his goal was always to stress how one of the central problems of the twentieth century was the problem of the colour line. His early texts addressed the barriers to racial progress and equality in post-Civil War America and in particular how these problems impacted on the rise of black urbanisation. A committed researcher, he employed the best social scientific methods available in his day to investigate racism and its effect on black culture. For Du Bois, understanding social problems, such as crime and discriminatory policing, meant considering the socio-historic factors of capital growth, materialism and the exclusion of Black folks from a mainstream white society. He dedicated his life to the pursuit of social justice before dying in Ghana in 1963.

Born in 1868, Du Bois was raised by his mother in Great Barrington, Massachusetts, a small, and by most accounts, friendly town with relatively few black residents and minimal overt displays of racism. His mother received employment opportunities and assistance from the affluent members of the community, affording Du Bois the opportunity to mix with the white social elite and gain exposure to privileged life. As a gifted student, Du Bois aspired to attend Harvard University but lacked the substantial financial resources required. Instead, he moved to Nashville, Tennessee and attended Fisk College (University) from 1885 until 1888. This move to the American South proved to be a life-changing experience. For the first time in his life the issues of systematic segregation and explicit racism confronted him on an everyday basis. More committed than ever to help ameliorate the fault lines of colour in American society, he persevered with his studies and won a small scholarship to attend Harvard, where he completed a second bachelor's degree in 1890. Five years later he famously became the first African American to be awarded a PhD from Harvard. Du Bois' doctoral research was a critical investigation of slavery and Negro emancipation in America during the nineteenth century. He published his thesis, *The Suppression of the African Slave Trade to the United States of America*, in 1896 as the first volume in Harvard's Historical Studies series. It was an important and timely text that proffered a number of interlinked ideas.

Of the propositions put forth in his doctoral thesis, two key issues greatly contributed to the foundations of criminological thought. First, Du Bois' examination of the African slave trade uncovered the contribution of emancipation to the rise in crime amongst the black population in America. He cited the magnitude of social injustices against the black population as a strain on the moral lassitude of society which in turn encouraged crime and lawlessness from the black population. Inequitable and brutal forms of punishment, such as the convict lease system or the threat of lynching, instigated rebellion amongst those blacks at risk of being accused of crimes. This transgressive response was in turn the catalyst for even harsher social control and criminal justice measures. This historic critique of the spiralling relationship between the black criminal response to social injustice, and the discriminatory practices of the American legal system, provided one of the foundation stones for subsequent US conflict theories.

Second, Du Bois contributed to criminology's awareness of the impacts of global injustice and capitalism on crime. During the course of his PhD, Du Bois spent two years in Germany studying at the University of Berlin. It was during this time that he was further exposed to the racial struggles experienced by Negroes outside of America, in Europe and elsewhere. This exposure contributed to Du Bois' contention that the illicit trafficking of slaves during the nineteenth century was a problem that emphasised international moral indolence in favour of financial gain. He formulated a hypothesis concerning the illicit trafficking of people as goods, exposing the connection between global markets and the crimes of the powerful. Additionally, this corrosive situation sowed the seeds for a critical theory of race, in America and beyond, by extending the platform for the discussion of racial identity and discrimination.

Upon his return from Germany and after the submission of his thesis, Du Bois sought an academic position to continue examining racial disparity in stratified societies. Du Bois taught for two years at Wilberforce in Ohio, later accepting a fellowship at the University of Pennsylvania, where he studied the social life of the Negro in Philadelphia's Seventh Slum. He published his findings in the monograph *The Philadelphia Negro* (1899), an impressive and inspiring ethnographic investigation that mixed first-hand observation with personal accounts and statistics. Du Bois also plotted the geographic distribution of his findings, and was thus an early (if frequently not credited) progenitor of the type of socio-ecological criminology that would later become the stock in trade of Chicago School protagonists such as **Robert Park** and **Clifford Shaw**.

Importantly, Du Bois' research also produced conclusions that undermined the then popular theories of eugenics as the underlying causes of crime and social deviance. Countering the pseudo scientific racism of eugenics, Du Bois insisted that the problem of crime within the black community was the by-product of the discriminatory social conditions that were the legacy of slavery and racial prejudice. Not only were Negro men in Philadelphia forced to deal with the day-to-day inequalities associated with their skin colour, but they also lacked the necessary skills and education needed to function effectively in a competitive industrial job market. The Negro man in the American social system was thus doubly disadvantaged with little chance of assimilating and achieving middle-class status. Du Bois argued that the 'submerged tenth' of Negroes turned to criminal and transgressive behaviours as a rebellious response to the inequitable social environment, which in turn created a different set of problems for the Negro community. Additionally, he acknowledged that disparity in social environments was not the only factor responsible for the varying levels of perceived criminal offending between the races. Du Bois pointed to the influence of public opinion and the social construction of crime for the high rates of black offending. He notes in his analysis how white-collar crimes, such as embezzlement or fraud, were often treated with leniency due to the offenders' social position and influence. On the other hand, the petty street crimes of the black population were treated as direct threats to the commercial community, thus requiring diligence in apprehension and severity in punishment. *The Philadelphia Negro* anticipated social exclusion, exposed environmental factors in the commission of crime, and created a foundation for early conflict theory to emerge. Perhaps most importantly, his sociological observations about the gaping disparity between white and Black groups in American society created a platform for future discussions surrounding equality and social inclusion for the Black community.

After concluding his research in Philadelphia, Du Bois accepted a position at Atlanta University, where he continued his research on Negro society, crime, and morality. His subsequent work continued the theme of what it means to be Black and thus a 'problem' in America. Switching from the empirical methodological approach that characterised *The Philadelphia Negro*, Du Bois' next major work, *The Souls of Black Folk*, was more theoretical in nature; a lyrical and auto-biographical exposé that addressed the question: 'How does it *feel* to be a problem?' In *The Souls of Black People*, Du Bois describes the dichotomy or 'double-consciousness' of Negro Americans who, whilst exposed to the great prizes and dreams of capitalist America, are also denied them simply for being Black. As a result, life in White society for Black Americans was always one of negotiation, and thus the double-consciousness also reflects the sense of always having to gauge oneself through the responses of others.

Du Bois applied a symbolic expression, 'the Veil', to explain the obstacles and hardships of racial division and the degradation faced by the Black man, creating a social theory of a specific population that was at once accessible to an academic and a popular audience. Offering disempowered and oppressed narratives from the other side of 'the veil' also demonstrated how racial prejudice is detrimental to both the Black and White communities. For Du Bois, the assimilation of the Negro population in society could only be accomplished through the assertion of Black voting rights, civic equality and the equitable education of youth. These initiatives would, in turn, reduce the seduction of oppositional street culture as a rebellious response to a mainstream society that marginalised and excluded Black people.

Du Bois' work also served as a touchstone of strength for the developing African American civil rights movement. *The Souls of Black Folk* and other subsequent publications set forth the argument that true liberation and equality had to be an all or nothing cause. He rejected the premise that arbitrary or occasional advances were the way forward for the civil rights movement. At the turn of the century, Booker T. Washington became the spokesperson for the African American community, serving as a powerful representative and compromiser for the Negro population amongst the white power elite. Washington beseeched Black men to forgo political struggle and implored Black youths to concentrate instead on industrial training over education in higher institutions. Du Bois took issue with Washington's stance, and argued instead that piecemeal compliance to white norms and expectations would result in an inferior political and civil status, further disfranchising the Negro. From a more personal perspective, Du Bois had seen for himself the value of higher education, and he was not about to block the chances of other Black men and women to follow in his stead.

It would be remiss not to comment briefly on the marginalisation of Du Bois within American sociology. While his work has recently experienced something of a revival (see Zuckerman 2004; Blum 2007; Gabbidon 2007), it is fair to say that for much of the twentieth century, it was largely a footnote to the work of the Chicagoans. It has been argued that this may well stem from **Robert Park**'s close relationship with Booker T. Washington. Park, a towering institutional figure in American Sociology, shared Washington's 'integrationist' position on race, and was thus perhaps disinclined to champion the more radical views espoused by Du Bois. Ironically, then, Du Bois' commitment to racial justice may well have been politically damaging to his academic career.

Throughout his life, Du Bois never relented in his advocacy for equality for all men in the United States. In 1906, an assembly of fellow advocates joined Du Bois to form the 'Niagara Movement' to promote social justice, freedom and the eradication of racial discrimination everywhere. A group of liberal whites joined the Niagara Movement three years later to form the National Association for the Advancement of Colored People (NAACP), an organisation that remains influential today. Du Bois served as the Director of Publications and Research for the organisation, and was the editor in chief of their journal, *Crisis*, for twenty-five years. The continual promotion of African American rights took Du Bois to France in 1919 for a Peace Conference as a representative of the NAACP. This trip inspired him to organise a Pan-African conference to once again emphasise the inequality and problems of Africans worldwide, again stressing that the problem of the colour-line was not limited to America.

Du Bois had devoted his life to educating the world about racial degradation and its corrosive social consequences. Yet, despite his many accomplishments, he never rested on his laurels. Indeed, towards the end of his life he became increasingly disheartened and frustrated about the slow pace of change surrounding racial equality in the United States. Following an invitation from President Kwame Nkrumah, Du Bois relocated to Ghana in the early 1960s, where he took up citizenship and lived out his last days as an expatriate and official member of the Communist Party USA. He died on 27 August 1963, the day before the *March on Washington for Jobs and Freedom* that saw approximately a quarter million supporters descend on the American capital to rally for equality. While Du Bois was ultimately frustrated by his inability to further dissolve the colour-line that plagued twentieth-century American society, his legacy remains an inspiration for scholars attempting to understand the plight of oppressed people the world over.

Major works

Du Bois, W.E.B. (1972 [1935]) *Black Reconstruction in America*. New York: Athenum.

—— (1994 [1903]) *The Souls of Black Folk*. New York: Dover Publications.

—— (1996 [1899]) *The Philadelphia Negro: A Social Study*. Philadelphia, Pennsylvania: University of Pennsylvania Press.

—— (1999 [1896]) *The Suppression of the African Slave Trade to the United States of America, 1638–1870*. Mineola, New York: Harvard University Press.

Further reading

Blum, E. (2007) *W.E.B. Du Bois, American Prophet*. Philadelphia, Pennsylvania: University of Pennsylvania Press.

Gabbidon, S. (2007) *W.E.B. Du Bois on Crime and Justice: Laying the Foundations of Sociological Criminology*. Hampshire, England: Ashgate Publishing.

Lewis, D. (1994) *W.E.B. Du Bois, 1868–1919: A Biography of Race*. New York: Holt Publication.

—— (2003) *W.E.B. Du Bois, 1919–1963: The Fight for Equality and the American Century*. New York: Holt Publication.

Zuckerman, P. (ed.) (2004) *The Social Theory of W.E.B. Du Bois*. Thousand Oaks, California: Pine Forge Press.

LAURA J. HANSON

WILLEM BONGER (1876–1940)

Willem Adriaan Bonger was born in Amsterdam on 6 September 1876, the youngest of ten children in a rather liberal middle-class family. As a law student at the University of Amsterdam he developed an interest in the pressing social problems of the time and became a socialist and a member of the Sociaal-Democratische Arbeiderspartij (the Social Democratic Workers Party). Shortly after completing his law studies in 1900, he entered an academic contest organised by his Law Faculty. The subject was the influence of economic conditions on criminality. Although he failed to win the prize – his paper was honourably mentioned – the experience fired his interest in the problem of crime and was to be a key moment in his academic development. The paper also formed the basis of a subsequent doctoral thesis in law – 'Criminalité et conditions économiques' ('Criminality and economic conditions') – which he defended in 1905 at the University of Amsterdam.

His doctoral thesis consisted of two main parts. The first part was a critique of the way nineteenth-century authors had previously understood the influence of economic conditions on criminality. According to Bonger, these authors had largely ignored the wider economic system and how it served to organise society and in turn influence an individual's involvement in crime. Bonger was also highly critical of the 'individual positivist' criminology (see **Cesare Lombroso** and **Enrico Ferri**) of the second half of the nineteenth century. For Bonger, biological and psychological defects could only account for a very small minority of (pathological) criminals. In contrast, he asserted that economic and social circumstances were the key factors that determined an individual's involvement in crime. Importantly, Bonger was not intrinsically opposed to other modes of positivist analysis. For example, he was less critical of the social positivism of the likes of André-Michel Guerry and **Adolphe Quetelet**, and some have even argued that Bonger's own particular interpretation of Marxism was itself rather positivistic.

The second part of his doctoral thesis was a historical analysis of the dynamic relationships between the capitalist regime of production, 'social organisation' (Bonger's term), and crime. Greatly influenced by **Friedrich Engels** and Karl Kautsky's (the theoretician and political leader of the German Social Democrats) respective interpretations of **Karl Marx**'s work, Bonger stresses the unequal power relations between social classes and sexes, highlighting in particular the changing role of the family under the capitalist mode of production. Bonger also developed – what was for the time at least – an extremely innovative sociological concept of crime. He argued that what determined whether an act was classified as criminal, rather than simply immoral or anti-social, was the act's relationship to the economically determined social order. For example, in a society divided into a dominant and subordinate class, the penal law is determined by the will of the dominant class.

Central to Bonger's analysis of the effects of the capitalist system of production on society and crime were the concepts of 'altruism' and 'egoism'. In contrast to the Social Darwinists who defined egoism as a fundamental human characteristic, Bonger subscribed to Karl Kautsky's view that levels of altruism within society are determined by strong

social instincts and sentiments. The capitalist production regime weakened this altruism, undermining the moral strength of people and
ultimately making it more likely that 'criminal ideas' will be converted
into criminal acts. Conversely, under these same economic conditions,
egoism is (directly and indirectly) rewarded. Importantly, Bonger stressed that egoism will be experienced differently by different classes. The
more unfavourable the economic and social circumstances with which a
social class is confronted, the more likely egoism will lead to a 'criminal
idea', which in turn – because of weakened altruism – will be realised in
the commitment of a criminal act. In contrast, because the bourgeoisie
have legal means to become rich, egoism will give rise to fewer 'criminal ideas' among this class. (That said, Bonger did not discount the
crimes of the wealthy. In fact he was one of the first criminologists to
actually study fraudulent bankruptcy, consumer fraud and other crimes
committed by the capitalist bourgeoisie.)

In sum, Bonger's goal in his thesis was to stress the importance of
economic and social circumstances in the aetiology of crime. His
message was straightforward and absolute: only when economic and
social conditions have been transformed and society made more
equable will crime be effectively prevented.

After completing his PhD in 1905, Bonger started work at an insurance company in Amsterdam, a position he would occupy until 1920.
Whilst working in insurance Bonger continued to develop the ideas set
out in his thesis – indeed such was the significance of his doctoral work
it continued to serve as the foundation stone of his research until his
death in 1940 (see e.g. Bonger 1913, 1916, 1936, 1943). Central concerns for Bonger included the relationship between religion and crime,
the evolution of morality, the history of criminological theories, and
questions about race and crime. In 1913 he published *Geloof en misdaad:
Een criminologische studie (Religion and Crime: a Criminological Study)*, a
thoroughgoing analysis of the relationship between religious denomi-
nation and crime in the Netherlands. Put simply, he contested the thesis
that non-belief caused crime. In contrast he asserted that economic and
social circumstances determined levels of crime equally among *both*
'believers' and 'non-believing' groups.

In 1922, at the age of 46, Bonger became the first professor of
sociology and criminology in the Netherlands at the University of
Amsterdam. (The title of his inaugural speech was 'Over de evolutie
van de moraliteit' ('About the Evolution of Morality') in which he
argued that moral prescriptions were relative and changeable according to place and time). By this time, Bonger's fame was growing. The
original French version of his thesis – which included his controversial

critique of the criminalisation of homosexuality – ensured that his progressive ideas had found a wide audience throughout continental Europe. His growing reputation as a scholar was further enhanced by the publication of his thesis in English in 1916 (*Criminality and Economic Conditions*) under the auspices of the American Institute of Criminal Law and Criminology. (Interestingly his critique of the criminalisation of homosexuality was excluded from the English translation.) Building on this growing reputation, in 1932 he published *Inleiding tot de criminologie*, a work oriented to a large public and conceived as a historical overview of different criminological schools and theories (an English translation with the title *An Introduction to Criminology* was published in 1936).

Because of the growing popularity of race theories within criminology (especially over the Dutch border in Nazi Germany), Bonger felt the need to scientifically debunk the thesis that race influenced criminal behaviour. In 1939 he published the book *Ras en Misdaad* (*Race and Crime*) (translated into English in 1943 shortly after his death). In this work, Bonger dismissed the existence of so-called 'criminal races' as pure nonsense, arguing that physical differences between races (the colour of the skin, the body length, the form of the skull, etc.) were all totally irrelevant to criminology. Likewise, he was similarly scathing of the body of work that suggested that there were also 'psychological differences in temperament' between races.

As this review of his work has hopefully made clear, for Bonger criminology and sociology were inseparable social scientific disciplines. As a sociologist he drafted scientific contributions on suicide, prostitution, morality, disability, demography, war, democracy and religion. He also wrote important statistical studies about property and income and about belief and disbelief in the Netherlands. In 1936 he was one of the founders of the Dutch Sociological Association, serving as its first president until 1940. However, Bonger was not just an academic sociologist and criminologist – he was also a passionate political activist. As one of the theoretical and intellectual driving forces behind the Social-Democratic Workers Party, he defended many worthy public causes and was an emotional political orator when he needed to be. This thoroughgoing political engagement co-existed with his more empirical sociological work, and he published in different Dutch socialist publications about such subjects as World War I, democracy and dictatorship, extremism in the left movement and intellectuals and socialism. Whilst he presented himself as a democratic and internationalist socialist, and was happy to call himself a Marxist, he was acutely opposed to both political left extremism (e.g. anarchism and Leninism) and to dogmatism in the Marxist movement. He also steadfastly despised Fascism and National Socialism – indeed his total rejection of its values and totality were embodied in his final act. Five days after the German army crossed the Dutch-German frontier on 15 May 1940, Bonger and his wife committed suicide. It was a well-considered act as is made clear in his suicide note: 'I don't see any future for myself and I cannot bow to this scum which will now overmaster us'.

Bonger's intellectual legacy has been framed in a number of conflicting ways and as a result his popularity and influence within the discipline have vacillated. In the immediate post-war period Bonger was fairly faithfully represented as a scientific Marxist (see Valkhoff 1950). However, during the 1950s, a subtle rereading of his work took place which resulted in less emphasis being placed on his more basic Marxist assumptions. Instead he was depicted and came to be understood more as a general, if still highly influential, sociological criminologist (see Van Bemmelen 1960).

Likewise, Bonger's oppositional stance towards rigid communist ideology ensured his work as a Marxist social theorist was largely ignored by the intellectual communist movement. Indeed, during the 1960s, Bonger was frequently reduced to a so-called 'conflict criminologist' (see Turk 1969). However, with the emergence of the New Left movement of the 1970s, Bonger was once again championed as an important Marxist criminologist – only then to be marginalised once more, this time for being too positivistic and economically deterministic (see Mike 1976; and especially Taylor et al. 1973: 209–36). Bonger's work then fell foul both of the political crisis of Marxism in Eastern Europe and the Soviet Union during the 1980s (see Van Heerikhuizen 1987), and the rise of neo-liberalism and its associated discourses within criminology during the 1990s.

Despite these vacillations in popularity and disciplinary status, the writings of Willem Bonger remain an essential critical buffer against individual positivism – something which, once again, appears on the rise in contemporary criminology. Indeed, as we today face the deleterious social effects brought about by the restructuring of the global capitalist production regime, his analysis of the relationship between capitalism and crime can greatly contribute to our critical understanding of late modern developments in crime and crime control.

Major works

Bonger, W. (1905) *Criminalité et conditions économiques*. Amsterdam: G.P. Tierie.

—— (1913) *Geloof en misdaad. Een criminologische studie.* Leiden: Brill.
—— (1916) *Criminality and Economic Conditions.* Boston, Massachusetts: Little, Brown and Company (Translation of *Criminalité et conditions économiques* 1905).
—— (1936) *An Introduction to Criminology.* London: Methuen (Translation of *Inleiding tot de criminologie*, 1932, Haarlem: Bohn).
—— (1943) *Race and Crime.* New York: Columbia University Press (Translation of *Ras en misdaad* 1939, Haarlem: Tjeenk Willink).
—— (1950) *Verspreide Geschriften. Deel I & II* (Collected writings. Part I & II). Amsterdam: De Arbeiderspers.

Further reading

Mike, B. (1976) 'Willem Adriaan Bonger's *Criminality and Economic Conditions*: a Critical Appraisal', *International Journal of Criminology and Penology*, 4: 211–38.

Taylor, I., Walton, P. and Young, J. (1973) 'Marx, Engels and Bonger on Crime and Social Control', in *The New Criminology*, pp. 209–36. London: Routledge & Kegan Paul.

Turk, A. (1969) 'Introduction', in *Willem Bonger, Criminology and Economic Conditions* (Abridged), pp. 3–20. Bloomington, Indiana: Indiana University Press.

Valkhoff, J. (1950) 'Bongers werken' (Bonger's writings), in *Prof. Mr W.A. Bonger. Verspreide Geschriften. Deel I* (Collected writings. Part I), pp. xxvi–lxxxviii. Amsterdam: De Arbeiderspers.

Van Bemmelen, J.M. (1960) 'Willem Adriaan Bonger', in Mannheim, Hermann (ed.) *Pioneers in Criminology*, pp. 349–63. London: Stevens and Sons Limited.

Van Heerikhuizen, B. (1987) *W.A. Bonger. Socioloog en socialist* (W.A. Bonger. Sociologist and socialist). Groningen: Wolters-Noordhoff / Forsten.

PATRICK HEBBERECHT

EDWIN SUTHERLAND (1883–1950)

No understanding of modern criminology is complete without recognition of the enduring contributions of Edwin Sutherland. His early life, upbringing and education might not suggest a person who would eventually become regarded as the 'Dean of American criminology'. Born 13 August 1883 in Gibbon, Nebraska he grew up in rural Nebraska and Kansas where his father was a Baptist Minister and his mother was active in Christian service. He received a classical education after which he briefly taught Latin, Greek, history, and shorthand at Sioux Falls College in South Dakota. His subsequent career remained secular and sociological in orientation, but it also reveals fundamental values like compassion, empathy and an underlying concern for social justice. In 1906 he entered Graduate School at the University of Chicago. He completed his PhD on labour relations and conflict in 1913 after which he went on to a successful career moving between several universities in the American Midwest, ultimately ending up as Head of the Department of Sociology at Indiana University from 1935 to 1949.

Sutherland is known for his work as a sociological criminologist and it is largely due to him that this perspective came to dominate American criminology. In 1921 he was invited to write a criminology textbook by Edward C. Hayes, the chair of his department and general editor of sociology books for the publisher J.B. Lippincott. The result was *Criminology* (1924). Subsequent editions after 1934 were titled *Principles of Criminology*, each showing the further evolution of his ideas. The first edition reflected contemporary scholarship concerning crime. At that point, the existing literature represented the view that the multiple 'causes' of criminal behaviour were to be found in poverty, slum conditions, 'feeblemindedness', and other characteristics held to be highly associated with low-class status. True to his sociological predilections Sutherland largely rejected the claim that criminals were simpleminded but endorsed the view that criminal behaviours were the result of the multiple influences of various geographic, economic, political and sociological factors. Sutherland is perhaps most remembered for *The Professional Thief* (1937) and *White Collar Crime* (1949), but he also published more than fifty articles in scholarly journals and a number of other books (see Gaylord and Galliher 1988).

It is worth considering the backdrop to Sutherland's work. At the time the most influential platform for expounding criminological ideas to the general public was via the John D. Rockefeller Jr.-funded Bureau of Social Hygiene. In common with virtually all of the anti-vice-and-crime campaigners of the time, Rockefeller subscribed to the social eugenics view which advocated sterilisation (breeding out) as one technique for controlling deviance. Of course, the eugenic idea was not the only one then prevalent in control discourse. American society was, from the mid-nineteenth century onwards, becoming a policed society with an ever-growing penal establishment; a trend that was set to continue throughout the Great Depression and World War II years. In sum, the political background conditions for the emergence of academic criminology were driven by the articulations of a social, economic and political elite which advocated that the control apparatus of government should be improved in order to ensure their own particular vision of social order.

What was lacking was a relevant knowledge base for making this a reality. In 1932 the Bureau of Social Hygiene published what became known as the Michael-Adler Report which aimed at establishing a national institute to train criminological researchers. The report was highly critical of existing research in the field characterising it as 'raw empiricism ... [with] an exclusive emphasis upon observation to the total neglect of the abstractions of analysis'. Its authors recommended the establishment of an institute of criminology and of criminal justice. The institute was to be staffed by 'a logician, a mathematician, a statistician, a theoretical physicist, an experimental physicist, a mathematical economist, a psychometrician', and 'a criminologist who has a wide acquaintance with the literature of criminology, preferably one who has not himself engaged in criminological research!' (Laub 2006: 236–37). Although its precise recommendations were not realised in the initial instance (partly due to the criticisms of Sutherland himself), the blueprint envisaged by Jerome Michael and Mortimer Alder may well have influenced the subsequent founding of other criminological institutes around the world.

While Sutherland was interested to put academic criminology on a more secure intellectual footing (in particular, he had internalised the criticism that, up to that point, criminologists had not attended to the development of an abstract theoretical orientation capable of giving the enterprise an overall intellectual coherence), he was critical of the recommendations put forward in the report. His assessment is revealing:

> My general reaction to the Report is that its condemnation of criminology as a science that has failed in its early years to produce the results that have been achieved in the mature sciences is unwarranted and that an attempt is being made to reinstate an extreme rationalism which has already been tried in all the social sciences and has been found to be unproductive. The authors are in effect recommending that we abandon an infant which is showing a healthy growth and adopt a mummy which has been dead for more than a century.
>
> (Quoted in Laub 2006: 238)

This is a sentiment that is as true now as it was then, even though the campaign to make criminology 'scientifically credible' continues to the present.

This kind of criminology might more aptly be called 'controlology'. It is interesting to note that over the course of Sutherland's career, there was also the slow genesis and consolidation of what was to become the American Society of Criminology. This institutional formation was driven initially by the reforming doyen of American police professionalism August Vollmer and other similarly placed individuals. They defined criminology as the study of the causes, treatment and prevention of crime. Sutherland's vision was rather different and, largely because of him, the control impulse in academic criminology was somewhat blunted. However, as can be seen, criminology was intended to have a specific trajectory in the service of the state and powerful interests. Understanding this helps us make sense of **Sheldon Glueck**'s need to rubbish what is often considered to be Sutherland's main intellectual achievement some six years after his death. According to Glueck: 'the theory of differential association ... fails to organize and integrate the findings of respectable research and is, at best, so general and puerile as to add little or nothing to the explanation, treatment, and prevention of delinquency' (Glueck 1956). Glueck, professor and researcher in criminology at Harvard, is known for contributions which bear all the hallmarks of the type of pseudo scientific criminology that Sutherland sought to curtail.

Sutherland's principal contributions to academic criminology lie in his theoretical notions of differential association and differential (dis) organisation and two books: *The Professional Thief* and *White Collar Crime*. Looking first at his theories, it is notable that Sutherland was keeping intellectual company with sociologists, many of whom were associated with the Chicago School of Sociology. A key idea was that of 'culture conflict' which suggested that in complex, heterogeneous societies, the beliefs of the 'dominant culture' and subordinate cultures may clash. According to this perspective, behaviour that is considered obedient in one group may be unorthodox and even criminal in the eyes of others. One implication is that what is officially defined as criminal behaviour may actually conform to some subcultural standards. It is also obvious that what counts as criminal is neither universal nor can it be reduced to the inadequacies of the so-called born criminal.

It was around this time that Sutherland first met Broadway Jones (*alias* Chic Conwell). A boastful, fast-talking and articulate Chicago-area confidence man, Jones' stories about his many criminal exploits eventually became *The Professional Thief*, which was published in 1937. It was during this period that Sutherland became convinced that criminals, whether professional or otherwise, essentially learn the necessary techniques and attitudes of criminality in the context of close relationships with other people. The 1934 edition of *Principles of Criminology* contained a single paragraph suggesting that crime occurs when behaviours learned within different cultures and groups come into conflict. It was not until the publication of the fourth edition in 1947 that Sutherland presented differential association theory as a set of nine formalised and abstract principles. These principles suggested that behaviour is learned through a process of communication in intimate personal groups. These groups teach 'definitions' (including skills, motivations, attitudes and rationalisations) either favourable or unfavourable to the violation of the law. The theory suggests that criminal behaviour results when one is exposed to an excess of definitions favourable to the violation of the law over definitions that are unfavourable. Exposure to such definitions varies in frequency, intensity, duration and priority. In this framework, crime is a deviant action that is learned by essentially normal persons who have been influenced through processes of learning by specific cultural processes. This explanation is vulnerable to the criticism that it is a *tabula rasa* theory of human behaviour. *Tabula rasa* is a Latin phrase which means 'blank slate' and it is used to denote a family of theories which suggest that individual human beings are born with no innate or built-in mental content and that their resource of knowledge and personality is gradually built up from experiences and sensory perceptions from the outside world. If biological explanations err too far on one side of the nature–nurture debate, then presumably Sutherland's theory goes too far the other way.

Sutherland was aware that individuals differed in their responses to social setting and that social psychological elements need to be included in the understanding of crime and, indeed, any other social act. He also knew that it was one thing to explain why some individuals commit crime, but that it was quite another to answer the knotty problem as to why some social groups appear to have higher or lower overall crime rates than others. His answers to these problems were socio-historical in nature. He argued that modern American society had moved quickly from the simple to the complex, partly because of the speed of the industrial revolution. Showing Durkheimian influence, he observed that, simultaneous with this process, there had been a diminution in the uniformity of social control. He noted that traditional social controls such as those exercised by the family, religion and community, were coming under increasing challenge by the rise of political-economic individualism, its associated material acquisitiveness and increased social and geographic mobility. A feature which was particular to North

America was that successive waves of immigration had exacerbated this process of social disorganisation through intercultural conflict.

Most assessments of Sutherland's contributions stress his neologism 'white-collar crime', a concept which forever changed the perceptual parameters of criminology. He took the view that police statistics were biased when they showed that most crimes occurred in lower-class neighborhoods and in order to bolster this proposition in 1928 he began a study of law violations among large corporations. After years of painstaking documentary research, Sutherland finally made his findings public but, fearing lawsuits, neither his publisher, Dryden Press, nor his university would permit the publication of the actual names of the convicted corporations when the book was published in 1949. A complete and unexpurgated version of *White Collar Crime* did not appear until 1983! (Geis and Goff 1983.)

The concept of white-collar crime was immensely important prompting the eminent British criminologist Hermann Mannheim to suggest that, if there were a Nobel prize in criminology, Sutherland would have received it for this contribution. His presidential address on the topic given to the American Sociological Society in 1939 (Sutherland 1940) was a rarity in that it received front-page publicity in the daily newspapers. The book itself received favourable, or at least sympathetically critical, reviews and it inspired much related research. However, after the initial enthusiasm, American criminology drifted back to more traditional concerns. It was not until the 1970s and the emergence of the new and critical criminologies that 'crimes of the powerful' again became important (see **William Chambliss** and **the Schwendingers**).

Sutherland studied 'white-collar crime' at least partly in order to augment his hypotheses attributing the causes of crime to social phenomena rather than to individual biological and emotional characteristics. But his motivations were probably more complicated than that. In the opening sentence of the book he observed that 'criminal statistics show unequivocally that crime, as popularly understood and officially measured, has a high incidence in the lower socioeconomic class and a low incidence in the upper socioeconomic class'. After defining the term 'white-collar crime' as 'a crime committed by a person of respectability and high social status in the course of his occupation' he went on to assert that 'the financial cost of white-collar crime is probably several times as great as the financial cost of all the crimes which are customarily regarded as the 'crime problem''' (Sutherland 1949). His writings reveal that he considered white-collar crime a greater threat to society than street crime because it promotes cynicism and distrust of basic social institutions. In insisting that the many professionals who commit crimes should also be brought within the scope of the theories of criminal behaviour, and showing that they mostly evaded the rigours of criminal punishment, Sutherland displayed some of his personal values.

These values were also in evidence in *The Professional Thief*. In befriending Broadway Jones, aka Chic Conwell, and taking time to understand the world from his point of view, Sutherland did much more than skillfully report the language, attitudes, and lifestyles of con artists and 'grifters'. The book allowed a picture to emerge of the thief as a human being with real human qualities, a far cry from the verminisation evident in the discourses concerning the pathologies of 'born criminals'. In recent years speculation has arisen that Jones/Conwell may have been a drug-taker and that Sutherland downplayed this fact out of fear that readers might interpret that as an indication of mental illness (Wright 2004). The fact is that he could just as easily have shown Jones' drug use to be a learned behaviour, as **Howard Becker** later famously argued. If the professional thief was also a drug addict, and if Sutherland chose to downplay this aspect of the narrative, it might just as easily be explained as the effect of compassion, empathy and understanding for a friend struggling with a difficult burden. It is not inconsistent with what is known of the man to suggest that, by writing this aspect out of the narrative, Sutherland may well have been allowing Jones/Conwell to maintain an aspect of his dignity and self-worth. However, it has to be admitted that this is speculation because it has never been shown that the protagonist in the *Professional Thief* was a serious drug-taker, nor do we know what motivations Sutherland may have had when drafting his version of the man.

Sutherland was the preeminent American criminologist of the twentieth century who helped to ensure that criminology was sociological, exploratory and insightful. His tireless efforts to defend criminology against the notion of the 'criminal mind' were crucial. In two important articles, 'Mental Deficiency and Crime', published in 1931 and 'The Sexual Psychopath Laws', published in 1950, he attacked psychological explanations of criminal behaviour. In the former he disputed the idea that 'feeblemindedness' could offer a general explanation for crime, given the superior intelligence of some offenders. In the latter he criticised laws that defined child molesters and rapists in terms of mental illness, rejecting the general claim that these offenders were simply sexual psychopaths with no impulse control. He also defended academic criminology against the claims of legalists who argued that crime was defined by the criminal law and that criminologists should only study those acts which have been so defined and those persons who have actually been convicted of said crimes. Such a view was contrary to his interest in crimes of the powerful, many of which frequently escape such definition. He maintained that, while conviction is important in the study of responses to crime, criminology should not be reduced to the parameters of criminal law (Sutherland 1945). He argued that criminology must explain all forms of law-violating (not just criminal law-violating) and take account of harmful behaviour. This expanded definition of crime was important for academic criminology, making possible, for example, the emergence of green criminology which operates at the very edges of what is defined by criminal law.

Sutherland's keenest attacks were directed against bio-psychological explanations of criminal behaviour. In a number of book reviews published over the course of his career he harshly criticised scholars who attributed criminal behaviour to the physical inferiority of offenders, or to its opposite 'mesomorphy', or to multi-factoral approaches that included bio-physiological factors. Given recent advances in bio-psychology and brain science this combative rejection might seem misguided. However, in attacking such theorisations, he was not merely defending academic criminology as a process of producing sociological *understanding*; he was also, by implication, defending it against controlology. In so doing he revealed underlying values of compassion, empathy and concern for social justice that he learned in early childhood and as a young adult. Given that his own theories suggested that behaviour is learned, that makes a certain amount of sense.

Edwin Sutherland was a seminal thinker who contributed immensely to academic criminology. His ideas of differential association and differential social (dis)organisation, seem as relevant today as they did in the mid-twentieth century. Likewise, the neologism of white-collar crime, coined in the middle of the last century, is especially relevant in a world dominated by global corporations. Above all, his insistence that the job of the academic criminologist is to produce better understanding of the social and cultural context that makes crime possible reflects a humanising impulse that is sorely needed in an era when criminological discourse is dominated as never before by the unreflective impulse to control.

Major works

Sutherland, E.H. (1924) *Principles of Criminology*, Chicago, Illinois: J. P. Lippincott (see also any other extensively revised editions).

—— (1937) *The Professional Thief; by a Professional Thief.* Chicago, Illinois: University of Chicago Press
—— (1940) 'White Collar Criminality', *American Sociological Review*, 5(1): 1–12.
—— (1945) 'Is "White-Collar Crime" Crime?' *American Sociological Review*, 10: 132–39.
—— (1949) *White Collar Crime.* New York: Dryden Press.

Further reading

Gaylord, M. and Galliher, J.F. (1988) *The Criminology of Edwin Sutherland.* London: Transaction Publishers.
Geis, G. and Goff, C. (1983) 'Introduction', in Edwin Sutherland (ed.) *White Collar Crime; the Uncut Version*, pp. ix–xxxiii. New Haven, Connecticut: Yale University Press.
Glueck, S. (1956) 'Theory and Fact in Criminology', *British Journal of Delinquency*, 7: 92–109.
Laub, J.H. (2006) 'Edwin Sutherland and the Michael-Adler Report: Searching for the Soul of Criminology Seventy Years Later', *Criminology*, 44(2): 235–57.
Sutherland, E.H. (1956) *The Sutherland Papers*, in Albert Cohen, Alfred Lindsmith and Karl Schuessler (eds) Bloomington, Indiana: Indiana University Press.
Wright, R.A. (2004) 'Edwin H, Sutherland', in Richard A. Wright and J. Mitchell Miller (eds) *The Encyclopedia of Criminology*. London: Routledge.

JAMES SHEPTYCKI

CLIFFORD SHAW (1895–1957)

Clifford Shaw was a central figure within the Chicago School of Sociology at the University of Chicago during the 1930s and 1940s. He is rightly considered one of the grandees of American criminology, having made seminal contributions both to criminological understandings of pathways into crime and to sociological methodology more generally.

The Chicago School was essentially a new school of sociological enquiry which emerged out of the dynamic social character of the city of Chicago at the start of the twentieth century (see **Robert Park** and **Edwin Sutherland**). The city had grown from a somewhat obscure trading post to a city of over three million inhabitants within only a couple of generations. By 1930 Chicago had become home to disparate social and ethnic groups constituted both from European immigrants and migrating African Americans seeking refuge from the rural poverty and repression of the American South. This tremendous social turbulence lent itself to innovative sociological analyses. Alongside fellow Chicago School sociologists, Shaw and his colleague Henry McKay set about the task of studying Chicago's rapid urban expansion, statistically testing the assumption that crime was greater in disorganised areas than elsewhere in the city (Shaw and McKay 1942). By carefully documenting juvenile court statistics they showed that juvenile delinquency was consistently highest in the run-down, inner city zones. Such findings marked a major development in criminology since they facilitated a move away from theories which simplistically located the cause of crime in the individual to an understanding of crime as the product of social factors (the neighbourhood and 'culturally transmitted' values included). But Shaw's contribution was also distinctive in other ways as a notable sociologist, methodologist *and* reformer.

Shaw was born in August 1895 in the rural Midwest, the fifth of ten children. He was brought up on a farm in Luray, Indiana, a town of little more than a collection of a dozen or so houses grouped around an intersection of roads. His parents also owned a local general store and his father often worked as a harness-maker and shoemaker (as well as being active in county politics). However, Shaw's own accounts of his childhood suggest a slight reworking of history. In a hand-written biography which formed part of his university application form he represents his family as 'poor dirt farmers' and states that his 'parents' financial status has had a very marked influence upon the course and thought of my life' (Snodgrass 1976: 3). Whatever the case, Shaw's upbringing was fairly typical of a child in the rural Midwest at this period, and he was well versed both in conservative Christian values and the demands of farming life. When Shaw was fifteen he heard a Methodist minister from Adrian College, Michigan, speaking in the Luray Church and was encouraged to study for the ministry. He subsequently went on to attend Adrian College. However, in his junior year, Shaw quickly became disillusioned with institutional Christianity, and subsequently joined the navy submarine corps as a pharmacist's mate in 1917 (Bennett 1981). He undertook pharmacy training at John Hopkins University; however the war ended before he could see active service. Thus in the autumn of 1918 Shaw returned to Adrian College to complete his undergraduate degree. The very next year, Shaw enrolled in the graduate programme in sociology at the University of Chicago, a move which confirms C. Wright Mills' perceptive observation that many 'social pathologists' were 'fathered' by the rural, protestant ministry.

Whilst studying sociology, Shaw lived in a settlement in Chicago called 'The House of Happiness' in an Eastern European neighbour-hood near the inner city. Shaw's role as a residential settlement-house worker in a Polish neighbourhood is thought to have had a profound effect on him (Snodgrass 1976: 4). From 1921 to 1923, Shaw worked part-time as a parole officer for the Illinois State Training School for Boys at St. Charles. This work included home visits and finding employment for parolees. Between 1924 and 1926 Shaw was employed as a probation officer at the Cook County Juvenile Court. This role involved the investigation of cases, home visits and the presentation of cases within the court. However, whilst Shaw completed coursework at the University of Chicago in 1924, he did not complete his PhD – either because he did not have a foreign language (which, at the time, was a requirement for successful completion of a doctorate) or because he saw no need for it once he had identified what was to be his life's work (Bennett 1981). (Shaw was subsequently awarded an honorary Doctor of Laws from Adrian College in 1939.)

Shaw came close to accepting an academic position at McGill University towards the end of his graduate studies in the mid-1920s, partly because he wanted to be near his prospective wife, a social worker who had practised in Chicago but who by then had returned to Boston. But in the event, she agreed to marry Shaw and returned to Chicago to be with him. Shaw taught at the George Williams College and then at the Central YMCA College as well as being Director of the Institute for Juvenile Research from 1926 – set up by the Behavior Research Fund. (The Institute was formerly known as the Chicago Juvenile Psychopathic Institute which had been headed by the esteemed psychoanalyst William Healy.) Henry McKay, Shaw's erst-while fellow graduate student, was also employed at the Institute for Juvenile Research from 1927. It was perhaps this working relationship at the Institute which spawned their professional association. Snodgrass depicts the two men in this way: 'McKay was the *professional* scholar and gentleman – polite, kind, thoughtful – an academic out to prove his position with empirical evidence. Shaw was the emotional practitioner, a professional administrator and organizer – talkative, friendly, person-able, persuasive, energetic, and quixotic – out to make his case through action and participation' (1976: 3). Later, after 1941, Shaw taught at the downtown Centre (that is, campus) of the University of Chicago. He died in 1957 after a lengthy period of illness.

As indicated earlier, as well as introducing the concept of 'social disorganisation' to explain crime, Shaw was also an innovator in regard to methodology. Most notably, he was a chief collector of life histories of juvenile delinquents at the Institute for Juvenile Research (IJR) in Chicago in the 1920s and 1930s. At that time, life history became a significant sociological and methodological tool. Amongst other things, life history 'illuminated urban institutions and other aspects of behaviour' (Burgess and Brogue 1964; Bennett 1981: 221), providing a clear depiction of urban pathology, and, critically, contributing to an understanding of the development of delinquency. Shaw's customary procedure was to persuade a boy in a correctional institution to write his own biography. The boys were typically those drawn from the highly disorganised urban slums. This fuelled his belief (subsequently proved through statistical analysis) that social environment was all important in explaining delinquency, and that psychological factors were not the sole causal influence. Shaw recognised the role of groups and small gangs in the onset of delinquency but likewise attributed this to disorganisation of the community in slum areas. The most famous exemplar of the life history method in practice was Shaw's groundbreaking story of the 'Jack Roller' (the term referring to someone involved in the practice of 'rolling' – that is, the robbery of drunks). *The Jack Roller: A Delinquent Boy's Own Story* (Shaw 1930) was an account of the life of 'Stanley', one of the sixteen-year-old boys Shaw had met during the course of his work (see also the fifty-year follow-up, Snodgrass 1982).

Shaw's lead in the new methodological technique of life histories also encouraged colleagues to engage in focused interviews and direct observation on the streets. Indeed, Shaw's work spawned a whole series of rich qualitative studies that went some way towards establishing a theorised methodology for studying social action.

Having accumulated a mass of evidence pointing towards neighbourhood disorganisation, Shaw and McKay and colleagues then set out to establish measures to rebuild communities and to test whether this made a difference to patterns of delinquency. This research became known as the Chicago Area Project (CAP). As 'action research' the project involved the setting up of clubs and sports leagues and other such practical measures in attempts to improve area conditions and combat crime. It is also something that Bennett (1981), amongst others, has described as 'the city as laboratory'. In time, the life history approach was used to promote the importance of sociological understandings of pathways into crime and to balance the psychological approaches which had dominated within the IJR. There were also evident 'splits' amongst the Institute's researchers in terms of the choices of political activity to address the powerlessness and injustices which such life stories served to expose. For instance, some of those attached to the IJR became political activists fighting against the political power of the period (Bennett 1981). Shaw's own practical 'social reform' approach remained steadfastly one of empowering local communities to organise themselves; working co-operatively with government institutions to facilitate this. As testament to the importance of this, the CAP has survived in modified form to the present (DuCAP 2007).

The significance of Shaw's work and its implications for practical reform is encapsulated by Burgess and Brogue when they write:

> Because of the daily contacts ... with a wide variety of delin-quents and with judges, probation officers, court social workers, and civic leaders throughout the community, his research was able to bring a realism to criminology and especially the study of juvenile delinquency which had been conspicuously scarce in American sociology before 1920. In fact, empirical American sociology was perhaps popularized and transmitted to all corners of the world by the Shaw monographs more than by any other examples of this brand of social research.
>
> (1964: 591)

The Chicago School of Sociology is renowned for other work relating to the 'theory of human ecology', 'concentric zone theory' and 'differential association', all of which draws attention to environmental and social factors, but arguably it is the empirical work of Shaw and McKay and the CAP which has had the greatest impact on the trajectory of criminological thinking (Faris 1967). Shaw's innovative research methods and focus on the life-worlds of delinquents established a firm foundation for subsequent reflexive qualitative analysis. His work also challenged the dominant assumptions that crime was a product of innate biological or pathological factors. This said, how far individual action can be explained by the social environment in which someone lives remains open to question. This critical question has become known as the 'ecological fallacy'. Moreover, critics have suggested that Shaw and McKay failed to recognise that criminal statistics are themselves 'socially constructed'; indeed, the 'delinquency areas' identified and charted were not necessarily where the delinquents committed crimes, but where they lived.

Importantly, however, the collective action prompted by Shaw and his collaborator McKay in the settlements under scrutiny brought social change in the form of the New Deal. Shaw was a key protagonist for community action and the years in which he was developing the

CAP should be set against the background of the depression and the role of community cohesion in heralding change.

Major works

Shaw, C. (1930) *The Jack-Roller: A Delinquent Boy's Own Story.* Chicago, Illinois: University of Chicago Press.
—— (1952) *Brothers in Crime.* Philadelphia, Pennsylvania: Albert Saifer.
Shaw, C. and McKay, H.D. (1942) *Juvenile Delinquency and Urban Areas.* Chicago, Illinois: University of Chicago Press.

Further reading

Bennett, J. (1981) *Oral History and Delinquency. The Rhetoric of Criminology.* Chicago, Illinois: University of Chicago Press.
Burgess, E.W. and Brogue, D.J. (1964) *Contributions to Urban Sociology.* Chicago, Illinois: University of Chicago Press.
DuCAP (2007) DuPage Count Area Project, Illinois. Available online at: www.ducap.org/ (accessed March 2007).
Faris, R.E.L. (1967) *Chicago Sociology 1920–1932.* San Francisco, California: Chandler Publishing Company.
Snodgrass, J. (1976) 'Clifford R. Shaw and Henry D. McKay: Chicago Criminologists', *British Journal of Criminology,* 16(1): 1–19.
—— (1982) *The Jack-Roller at Seventy: A Fifty-Year Follow-Up.* Lexington, Massachusetts: Lexington Books.

LORAINE GELSTHORPE

THORSTEN SELLIN (1896–1994)

No sociologist better represents the development of American sociologically oriented criminology during the course of the twentieth century than Thorsten Sellin. His work spans the 1920s to the last decade of the twentieth century and touches on practically every aspect of the criminological enterprise – from the sociology of punishment to the sociology of criminal behaviour, from methodological issues having to do with measurement of crime to normative issues such as the death penalty. Outside this longevity, there is also something else that marks Sellin's career out from most others; something connected to his immigrant origins. While during the early years of American sociology it was not uncommon to be a second-generation immigrant, in Sellin's case, he migrated to the United States when he was already seventeen – something which probably accounted for his life-long interest in attitudes and matters European. This attachment to European intellectual traditions meant he was deeply interested in history and especially the history of penality, or what he preferred to call *penology*. He was also very interested in ideas, and in the ways in which the administration of justice and punishment has ethical, social and economic connections with the rest of society. This internationalist, or cosmopolitan, element would never desert Sellin. His career was characterised by a continuous attention for (and participation in) international enterprises, some of which also involved his native country. He was also a very generous host, especially to young scholars and overseas visitors. Indeed, this was something I witnessed first hand when I was honoured to be his guest in his beautiful study/barn in New England, many years ago. But more on this later.

To understand Sellin's particular theoretical orientation it is essential to understand his biography. Thorsten Sellin was born on 26 October 1896, in Örnsköldsvik, northern Sweden, to a working-class family. He spent his high school and early college years in Sweden, and then migrated with his family to Canada in 1913. His Bachelor Degree was completed at Augustana College, Rock Island, Illinois. His early research interests turned around labour problems, a subject which would inform much of his subsequent research. At this point he was also a committed Socialist (Laub 1983). This interest in social reform was not unusual for the period. Indeed many early American sociologists shared such concerns, especially if their roots lay in Europe which, at the time, was traversed by a huge Socialist movement, particularly powerful among the working masses (from whose ranks migrants were of course generally recruited). More specifically, however, his interest in 'labour problems' and 'labour economics' coloured many aspects of his intellectual activity and especially his penological studies.

When his father moved to Philadelphia for work, Sellin followed and enrolled in the graduate school of the University of Pennsylvania where he completed his MA in Sociology (with education and economics) in 1916. Returning to his 'home town' of Minneapolis, Sellin made a living for a while teaching German and Swedish at Minnesota College and in the Central High School. In 1920, he married Amy J. Anderson, who would be his life-long companion. The newly married couple returned to Philadelphia where Thorsten once again enrolled at the University of Pennsylvania, this time on the doctoral programme in Sociology. In 1921 he began teaching a course at Penn on 'Social Problems'. The course covered areas such as immigration, race relations, and delinquency, and thus for the first time in his career he was forced to engage with the discipline of criminology (his 1922 dissertation would be on marriage and divorce legislation in Sweden).

In an interview with John Laub (1983), Sellin explained that criminology at that point was far more developed both institutionally and intellectually in Europe than in the United States. Furthermore, the books of prominent European criminologists, such as **Lombroso**, **Ferri** and Garofalo, had just been translated and published in the United States. Europe was therefore the place to go and in 1924 the Sellins decided to head for Paris – a not unusual destination for American intellectuals in the 1920s, given that *la ville lumière* was a popular retreat for the likes of Ernest Hemingway, Gertrude Stein and other famous Americans. Altogether they stayed in Europe for two years; the first year in Paris and part of the second year in Italy, in Florence and Rome.

One night in early October 1925, Sellin and his wife were strolling through central Florence when they happened upon the sort of violent encounter that typified this particular period of Italian history – a time when Italian Fascists and their leader Mussolini were completing their take-over of the Italian State. As retaliation for the killing of a prominent Fascist, groups of young black-shirted thugs started to loot and burn down shops and institutions somehow connected with Socialists and Freemasons (the killer of the Fascist was publicly lynched and two prominent local Socialist leaders were also assassinated). Sellin was so shocked by what he had witnessed he decided to write an article for *The Nation* that was subsequently published (on 4 November 1925) under the telling title 'Fascism at Work'. Shortly afterward, in Rome, his interest in labour history and law brought him together with D'Aragona and Buozzi, the leaders of the free Italian unions that by now had been officially banned by the Fascists.

During his sojourn in Europe, Sellin also discovered historical documentation about early correctional institutions in Florence and Rome, as well as relevant information about France and other European countries. He would later publish a series of articles based on this documentation. These articles heralded Sellin's enduring interest in early forms of punitive policies, or 'penology' – an interest that later culminated in the publication of *Pioneering in Penology* (1944), a book on the Amsterdam houses of corrections (circa 1600) that would go on to become one of the classic works in the genealogy of punishment studies. Once again, Sellin's European roots would shine through. Not only did he rely on his knowledge of European languages, especially German, in order to reconstruct a historical turn of events that lie at the roots of the modern correctional experience both in Europe and the United States, but the initial idea for the book came during his Parisian trip when by chance he happened upon a book published in 1898 by the German scholar Robert von Hippel.

Sellin returned to the United States in 1926 and once again began teaching and researching at the University of Pennsylvania. It was to be a period of immense productivity. In 1931 he published an article on crime statistics which led to collaboration with the newly created Bureau of Criminal Statistics (which at that point had just begun collecting uniform crime and criminal justice statistics throughout the United States). He also arranged the collection of Federal statistics on capital executions, a process that would trigger a life-long interest in the issue of the death penalty. In 1934 he joined the Board of Directors of the Social Science Research Council. This was the midst of the Depression and Sellin was tasked with writing a *Report on Crime in the Depression* (1937). It was his first book and also one of the very first attempts, at least within American criminology, to look into the relationship between changing economic conditions and changing crime patterns.

Also in 1934, Sellin was approached by Julian Gumperz, who was in the United States representing the famous German Institute for Social Research in Frankfurt. Gumperz was scouting around for a suitable site to relocate the Institute, a move that would later enable its members to escape persecution by the Nazis in Germany. In order to promote itself to the American public, the Institute wanted to publish a book on punishment from a social-structural perspective based on the manuscript of a certain Georg Rusche. The Institute's key figures were keen to have the opinion of foremost American sociologists and criminologists and thus Gumperz approached both Sellin and **Edwin Sutherland** to read the manuscript. It would have been hard to think of anybody in the United States better placed to read Rusche's work than Sellin. Not only was he deeply conversant with the history of punishment, but (as mentioned earlier) he also had considerable expertise in labour economics, something that was extremely useful given the nature of Rusche's analysis. Sellin liked the manuscript and made a number of thoughtful observations, especially with regard to the last section on the depression in the United States. Both Sellin and Sutherland were of the opinion that this section was sensationalist in its description of the harsh conditions of American prisons and should be extensively corrected. Despite this concern, both men were generally positive about the manuscript, Sellin even volunteering to work extensively on it as an editor. However, as it later turned out, pre-existing problems between the Institute and Rusche ensured that it was not until over a year later that the Institute would finally give the publication the green light, and then only after bringing in a fellow émigré, Otto Kirchheimer, to finish the work. The result was *Punishment and Social Structure* by Georg Rusche and Otto Kirchheimer, published by Columbia University Press in 1939, with a Foreword by Thorsten Sellin and a Preface by Max Horkheimer, the then Director of the Institute (recently republished in 2003).

In 1938 Sellin completed *Culture Conflict and Crime* (1938), his *magnum opus* and one of the cornerstone texts in American criminology. Central to the book was Sellin's concept of 'culture conflict', basically derived from a reflection on Chicagoan motifs that were fundamental to both Sellin and Edwin Sutherland (according to Sellin, the inspiration for the idea of 'culture conflict' had come originally from a work by Louis Wirth). In this essay, Sellin emphasised the clash between 'legal conduct norms' and 'non-legal conduct norms' as one of the basic mechanisms that trigger what a legal system officially designs as 'crime'. As **Donald Cressey** would later assert (see Cressey's contribution in Wolfgang (1968)), in many ways Sellin's work on cultural conflict was a close cognate of Edwin Sutherland's 'differential association theory'. However, in spite of the similarity of the two theorisations, Sellin's particular emphasis on 'culture' made it so that his theory was eventually applied especially to the issue of migration and crime. In particular, Sellin was concerned with the so-called 'divided self' of second-generation Americans; the goal being to try and understand why second-generation immigrants appeared to have higher rates of criminal behaviour than other sectors of society. Cressey would later offer a distinction between Sellin's idea of a 'cultural conflict' and Sutherland's construct of 'normative conflict' (the theory of differential association).

From 1945 to 1959 Sellin was Chair of the Sociology Department at Penn and in 1956 he became President of the International Society of Criminology (until 1965). In the 1950s he wrote several pieces intended to show the lack of deterrence of the death penalty, culminating in a report that was published in 1959. Further, together with Marvin Wolfgang, who was his main adherent and successor at Penn, he published *The Measurement of Delinquency* in 1964. Sellin's name became so linked with the discussion of how to measure crime and delinquency that in their benchmark textbook Sutherland and Cressey would make reference to the so-called 'Sellin principle'; the idea, that is, that '[t]he value of criminal statistics as a basis for measurement of criminality in geographic areas decreases as the procedure takes us farther away from the offence itself' (Sutherland and Cressey

1978: 30). Together with Wolfgang and Robert Figlio he also authored the famous cohort study, *Delinquency in a Birth Cohort*, published in 1972. In 1968, he retired and was appointed Professor Emeritus.

In 1976, he published his last and most comprehensive contribution to the history and sociology of punishment, *Slavery and Penal System*. Moving from the text of another famous German legal theorist, Gustav Radbruch, who had postulated a historical causal relationship between the institution of slavery and penal servitude (see relatedly **W.E.B. Du Bois**), he basically reconstructed the evolution of the punishment of imprisonment. The other major influence on this work was of course Rusche and Kirchheimer's book. In October 1978 I had the great privilege of meeting Sellin at his home in New Hampshire (the goal of the meeting being to discuss Rusche's life and work). Greg Shank had just reviewed *Pioneering in Penology* and *Slavery and the Penal System* in *Crime and Social Justice* and Sellin had become a point of reference for so-called 'critical criminologists'. When John Laub later asked him about this in an interview, Sellin scoffed at the idea. However, I think it fair to say he was actually rather pleased to be, at his age, an appealing figure to the 'young Turks of criminology' (as Donald Cressey liked to call 'critical criminologists'). Besides, as we have seen, Sellin knew more than most what it meant to be 'a Socialist'.

I last met Sellin when he was aged 91 at the meetings of the American Society of Criminology in Montreal in 1987. I remember him sitting in a chair at a late-night party after a full day of meetings (it had become clear to me from our previous meeting in Gilmanton that he was a true 'night owl'!). He was trying to protect himself from the slightly too excited and somewhat overbearing homage of an up and coming criminological 'quant', mostly intent on self-praise. Sellin remained silent but his expression was quite eloquent. That image stuck in my mind as a sort of metaphor for the state of American criminology at that point in time. Thorsten Sellin died a few years later, in Gilmanton, New Hampshire, on 17 September 1994, at the age of 97.

Major works

Sellin, T. (1937) *Research Memorandum on Crime in the Depression*. New York: Social Science Research Council.

—— (1938) *Culture Conflict and Crime*. New York: Social Science Research Council.

—— (1944) *Pioneering in Penology: The Amsterdam Houses of Correction in the Sixteenth and Seventeenth Centuries*. Philadelphia, Pennsylvania: University of Pennsylvania Press.
—— (1976) *Slavery and the Penal System*. New York: Elsevier.
Sellin, T. and Wolfgang, M.E. (1964) *The Measurement of Delinquency*. New York: John Wiley and Sons.
Sellin, T., Wolfgang, M.E. and Figlio, M. (1972) *Delinquency in a Birth Cohort*. Chicago, Illinois: University of Chicago Press.

Further reading

Laub, J.H. (1983) 'Interview with Thorsten Sellin', in J.H. Laub (ed.) *Criminology in the Making: An Oral History*, pp. 166–81. Boston, Massachusetts: Northeastern University Press.
Rusche, G. and Kirchheimer, O. (1939) *Punishment and Social Structure*. New Brunswick, New Jersey: Transaction Publishers, 2003.
Sutherland, E.H. and Cressey, D.R.(1978) *Criminology* (tenth edition). Philadelphia, Pennsylvania: J.B. Lippincott.
Wolfgang, M.E. (ed.) 1968 *Crime and Culture: Essays in Honor of Thorsten Sellin*. New York: John Wiley and Sons.

DARIO MELOSSI

ELEANOR TOUROFF GLUECK (1898–1972) AND SHELDON GLUECK (1896–1980)

It is often said that criminology is an eclectic area of study that draws on a wide range of intellectual traditions. If this is the case, then Eleanor Glueck and her husband Sheldon were surely the quintessential criminologists. The Gluecks drew on their early training in cognate disciplines and a range of different intellectual influences to fashion a distinctive approach to understanding the causes of crime. Over more than forty years they produced a series of empirical studies of adult and juvenile delinquents which located the aetiology of crime within the individual. In common with many researchers of their day, they perceived crime as a social disease or 'pathology' and drew heavily upon medical metaphors and analogies in their analysis. However, they also considered the influence of social factors on the 'delinquent', and thus did not limit their approach to physical and psychological matters. By following up their studies of ex-offenders with further investigations they hoped to assess the effectiveness of various forms of 'treatment' and intervention thereby informing and influencing future policy and practice. For the Gluecks, then, criminology was essentially a practical enterprise of applied social science rather than purely a theoretical pursuit, an attitude that must have sprung in large part from Eleanor's background in social work.

The Gluecks both grew up in immigrant families. Eleanor's family was the more prosperous of the two. Her father, Bernard Touroff, came from Russia and had studied law before a successful career in real estate. He valued education, and after Eleanor graduated high school in 1916 he funded her English degree at the liberal arts school, Barnard College. At the time of Eleanor's graduation in 1920, educated women had few employment opportunities open to them: teaching was regarded as the most suitable career for female graduates, but social work was also developing as a professional occupation. Eleanor chose the latter and enrolled at the New York School of Social Work where she was taught by the forensic psychiatrist Bernard Glueck, Sheldon's older brother. After two years of training in New York she took a job as head social worker in a Boston community settlement.

Born in Poland in 1896, one of seven children, Sheldon's childhood was tougher. His father, Charles, had been the unsuccessful owner of a small steel shop before emigrating to Milwaukee, Wisconsin. On arrival in America, the family continued to struggle, and at one point Charles was even forced to work as a street peddler. Despite this tough upbringing, Sheldon prospered and won a university scholarship. However, due to his parents' ill health, he was forced to decline the offer, and instead take up a job with the US government. While working for the government he gained Bachelor's and Master's degrees in law at night school, his studies only interrupted by the two years he served with the army during World War I. He later moved to New York (where his brother Bernard was based) and continued to study part-time, this time for the Bar examination. After meeting Eleanor, he abandoned plans to practise law and moved instead to Massachusetts where the newly married couple both enrolled as graduate students at Harvard in 1922.

Within three years Eleanor had gained a Master's degree in education, given birth to their only child, Joyce, and finished her doctorate in the School of Education (the only Harvard department which at that time admitted women). Sheldon meanwhile had completed his PhD in the Department of Social Ethics in 1924. Thereafter the couple spent their entire academic careers at Harvard. However, their standing at perhaps America's finest university was by no means assured. Eleanor was a woman working in one of the most anti-co-education establishments in the country, the Harvard Law

School; an institution that only deemed to admit women as students in 1950, and even then, according to Laub and Sampson (1991: 1406) treated them as 'an alien species'. Despite beginning their joint research projects in the mid-1920s, Eleanor only achieved 'promotion' from research assistant to research associate in 1953. After thirty years at Harvard, her 'social position [was] akin to what many PhD candidates today face *before* graduation' (ibid.). Furthermore, the vast proportion of the Gluecks' research was not funded by the University, but by private foundations. Eleanor was obliged to spend considerable time seeking research grants to support the activities of their growing team of researchers, which by the 1940s consisted of over thirty people.

Sheldon also faced a degree of prejudice and discrimination. When he first arrived at Harvard he was refused admission to the Law School (in which he would later become professor) because graduates of evening schools were ineligible for acceptance as postgraduate students. Instead he joined the Department of Social Ethics, a move that undoubtedly contributed to the interdisciplinary flavour of the couple's subsequent work, since he was able to take the department's courses in sociology and psychology as well as studying criminal law.

The Gluecks' joint researches began with *500 Criminal Careers* (1930), a project on 510 young male 'graduates' of the Massachusetts Reformatory at Concord. Sheldon later acknowledged the importance of Eleanor's social case-work background and her studies in education in the construction of their research methodology: 'She had a special knack of reaching for the relevant in a tangled web of fact and hearsay ... She had an extraordinary, orderly mentality and was of great aid in arranging data in a way to bring out their true significance' (Glueck 1977: 15). Indeed, it is interesting that their joint endeavours contradicted gender stereotypes. While Eleanor concentrated on statistical and 'scientific' matters, Sheldon (whose hobby was writing plays) was more involved in the literary and legal perspectives.

Their first collaboration set the template for further studies in several respects: the use of a large statistical sample of individual case studies, the collation of material on the subjects' histories, backgrounds, penological treatment and subsequent 'careers', and the inclusion of prediction tables that weighted the significance of certain criminogenic factors. This mixture of quantification and case-study detail was repeated in both *500 Delinquent Women* and *1000 Juvenile Delinquents* (both published in 1934). Like their predecessor, these studies (based respectively on women at the Framingham Reformatory, Massachusetts and boys seen by the Judge Baker Foundation child guidance clinic in Boston) attempted to evaluate the effectiveness of some of the paradigmatic institutions of penal welfarism, which was then in vogue with progressives both in the United States and in Western Europe. Significantly, the Gluecks' approach was initially influenced by medical research methodology utilised in following up diagnoses of heart disease: penology was perceived as the 'treatment' of the individual, the effectiveness of which could be assessed through the study of aggregates, which could then in turn be used to make predictions about the efficacy of the treatment. Their intent was to influence policy and improve sentencing practices through the application of the prediction tables.

Yet the 'scientific' basis of the research can be questioned in that the data from the case studies were infused with morality and loaded with value judgements. For example, the *500 Delinquent Women* were found to be 'a sorry lot', their marriages 'casual' and 'irresponsible' ('most of them married "pick-ups" – often vicious and criminal wasters and irregular, inefficient workers') while their 'conjugal relations' were poor (Glueck and Glueck 1934a: 301–2). Such a moralising tone inevitably gives their work a rather dated tone that no doubt contributed to its unpopularity during the 1960s and 1970s. The subjective nature of the judgements that underpinned the Gluecks' empiricism can also be illustrated by their contribution to the topical post-World War II debate concerning the relationship between working mothers and juvenile delinquency. Investigators were charged with evaluating whether a mother's supervision of her son was 'suitable', 'fair' or 'unsuitable' (Glueck and Glueck 1964). Both the delinquents and a control group of non-delinquents who were also deemed to have been 'unsuitably' supervised were then correlated against their mothers' employment status. While care was taken to define terms such as 'regular' and 'occasional' worker, no explanation regarding 'suitability' was ever offered.

Later research projects by the Gluecks followed a similar pattern. They did several 'follow-up' studies, returning again to the same individuals they had previously investigated, thus creating longitudinal studies of delinquency and initiating the notion of the 'criminal career'. In the 1940s they embarked on their most ambitious project, investigating 1,000 delinquents and a similarly sized, matched group of non-delinquents. Their results were published in 1950 in *Unraveling Juvenile Delinquency*. Probably their most famous work, this book examined multiple factors in the aetiology of crime including education, club membership, personality and body structure, as well as influences within the family. The correlation between body type (somatotyping, the controversial categorisation of human physique as

developed by the Harvard psychologist William Sheldon) and propensity for crime was then further expanded in *Physique and
Delinquency* (1956). Despite this interest in physiological factors, the
Gluecks continued to regard the family as the most important factor
in determining involvement in crime. In 1962 they returned to their
favourite theme in *Family Environment and Delinquency*. Here sixty-six
personal traits were related to forty-four social factors in the production of 2,904 tables. While the Gluecks' research process was always
organic, one idea logically following the other, the cornerstone of
their work was always the production of tabulated prediction tables.

Despite their somewhat discouraging initial findings (*500 Criminal
Careers* found that nearly 79 per cent of the traceable ex-reformatory
men had re-offended over a five-year period) the Gluecks were strong
supporters of 'modern', welfare-orientated penal policies. This can be
seen in Eleanor's involvement with the Judge Baker Foundation in
Boston, where she served as a trustee for forty years. Founded by
William Healy, a neurologist formerly based in Chicago, and the clinical psychologist Augusta Bronner, and backed by Boston philanthropists, the Foundation was dedicated to providing psycho-therapy
for delinquent children and became the model for child guidance clinics
elsewhere in the USA and abroad. Indeed, Healy's *The Individual
Delinquent* (1915) was a major influence on the Gluecks' own style of
research. Eleanor's longstanding involvement with the clinic underlines
the extent to which she retained links with the world of voluntary
social agencies even after she had formally left the social work profession.

These connections may also have accounted for the Gluecks' continued preference for individualised, psychological explanations of
criminal behaviour. Certainly, their lack of interest in sociological
factors earned them a good deal of criticism, both during their day
and subsequently. Most famously, the Chicago School heavyweight,
Edwin Sutherland, was scathing in his critique of the Gluecks;
deriding their hypothesis concerning 'criminal careers' (Laub and
Sampson 1991: 1413) and dismissing their work on crime and body
types as an affront to sociological perspectives within criminology. He
was also highly critical of the Gluecks' 'multi-factoral' approach to
crime causation, regarding it as atheoretical and too constrained by
legal definitions of criminal behaviour.

Although their eclecticism might be assumed to have been more
popular in mid-twentieth-century England than in the United States
(given British criminology's similar lack of adherence to any single
disciplinary approach), there was no shortage of Glueck critics on the
other side of the Atlantic either. While making use of prediction

methods himself, the British criminologist Leslie Wilkins pointed to methodological problems in *500 Criminal Careers*, while a *Howard Journal* reviewer questioned the reliability of prediction tables and offered the opinion that they were 'somewhat terrifying if a person's life is to be settled by them' (VII, 1, 1945–46). The Gluecks' most strenuous British critic, though, was Barbara Wootton, who chided *Unraveling Juvenile Delinquency* in particular for its over-concentration upon individual, rather than social factors. Wootton, herself a strong advocate of sociological perspectives on crime and another deep sceptic where psychological discourses were concerned, criticised the Gluecks' reliance on value judgements (or 'soft data') and claimed that their investigation into the relationship between neurosis and delinquency was 'tautological'. Like Sutherland, Wootton was also unimpressed by the Gluecks' theory concerning criminality and maturation.

More recently, however, the Gluecks' work has been reappraised with their reputation undergoing something of a revival. In particular, because of their interest in 'control perspectives' they are seen by some commentators as progenitors of Gottfredson and **Hirschi**'s (1990) influential control theory. There has also been a revival of interest in longitudinal research or 'life course criminology' (the term 'criminal career' is now seldom used). In the 1990s **Robert Sampson** and John Laub emerged as the Gluecks' champions, refocusing attention on social control and the family and their hypotheses concerning crime and the life course. They even went as far as to argue that the Gluecks' research agenda was 'currently dominating criminology' (1991: 1433). In 1993, Sampson and Laub developed an 'age graded theory of informal social control' by reanalysing the Gluecks' original data from the *Unraveling Juvenile Delinquency* project.

More broadly, 'control criminology' has informed many of the crime reduction programmes adopted since the early 1990s, for example, the 'project on human development in Chicago neighborhoods' headed by Felton Earls, Robert Sampson and Stephen Raudenbush with a total budget of $51 million. Also in the United States the Office of Juvenile Justice and Delinquency Prevention has expressed interest in the forty-year-old High/Scope Perry Pre-school Project, claiming that it demonstrates 'the value of prevention and early intervention efforts in promoting protective factors that reduce delinquency'. The relevance to these schemes of the Gluecks' work seems obvious: indeed their positivist conception of criminology as a practical, empirical and eclectic discipline, capable of informing policy and planning the development of successful strategies of crime reduction, seems to have been largely rehabilitated. Thus the recent emergence of projects such as 'Headstart' in the United States and 'Surestart' in the UK, which seek to combine pre-school education with parenting support, undoubtedly owe at least something to Eleanor and Sheldon Glueck's approach to the problems of crime and delinquency.

Major writings

Glueck, E. and Glueck, S. (1930) *500 Criminal Careers*. New York: A. A. Knopf.
—— (1934a) *500 Delinquent Women*. New York: A. A. Knopf.
—— (1934b) *1000 Juvenile Delinquents: Their Treatment by Court and Clinic*. Cambridge, Massachusetts: Harvard University Press.
—— (1950) *Unraveling Juvenile Delinquency*. New York: The Commonwealth Fund.
—— (1964) *Ventures in Criminology: Selected Recent Papers*. London: Tavistock Publications.

Further reading

Glueck, S. (1977) *Lives of Labor, Lives of Love: Fragments of Friendly Autobiographies*. Hicksville, New York: Exposition Press.
Laub, J.H. and Sampson, R.J. (1991) 'The Sutherland-Glueck Debate: On the Sociology of Criminological Knowledge', *The American Journal of Sociology*, 96(6): 1402–40.
Sampson, R.J. and Laub, J.H. (1993) *Crime in the Making: Pathways and Turning Points Through Life*. Cambridge, Massachusetts: Harvard University Press.
Book Review of Glueck, S. and Glueck, E.T., *The After Conduct of Discharged Offenders*, Howard Journal of Criminal Justice, July 1946, Vol. 7, No. 1, pp. 61–2.

ANNE LOGAN

ROBERT MERTON (1910–2003)

Robert King Merton, one of the most eminent American sociologists of the twentieth century, certainly would not have considered himself a criminologist but his work has had a profound influence on criminological theory. In particular the article 'Social Structure and Anomie' ('SSA') published in 1938 which, as a twenty-seven-year-old teaching assistant, he presented to his undergraduate class at Harvard (including **Albert Cohen**), has become part of the repertoire of every criminology student and is in all probability the most cited article in sociology.

Great thinkers are inevitably the subject of textbooks and revision. The patina of the time leads to an accumulation of representations, some pursued with such energy as to have a life of their own. So has it been with Merton, so that anomie has become 'strain' theory, parts of 'SSA' have become bowdlerised to represent the whole and writers of both the left and the right have spun the work out of recognition. Thus Merton has been characterised unjustly as a conservative, as making a fundamental break with Durkheim, as a leading sociological positivist – all of which are wildly off the mark at least as far as his early writings are concerned.

Robert Merton was born Meyer Schkolnick, the son of poor Jewish immigrants, in the slums of South Philadelphia: a place, as he put it, 'almost at the bottom of the social structure'. The family's uninsured dairy shop was accidently burned down and his father became a carpenter's assistant at the Philadelphia Navy Yard. Merton, himself, did not feel 'relatively deprived', but held 'the unquestioned promise that things would somehow get better [and] surely so for the children' (Merton 1997: 78). He relished the cultural resources of Philadelphia; the wonderful library bestowed on the neighbourhood by 'the robber baron' Andrew Carnegie; the twenty-five cent seats at the Academy of Music; and the resource-strapped free education at the local school. He was undoubtedly an ambitious boy, committed to upward mobility and the American Dream and as he later surmised: 'the opportunity structure' for mobility was there.

He was intrigued by magic and by fourteen he was earning modest fees acting as a magician at children's parties and Sunday schools. He fleetingly gave himself the stage name Robert K. Merlin but this quickly metamorphosised into Merton, a less hackneyed moniker. Thus, just as Merton's boyhood hero, Houdini, had Americanised his name from Ehrich Weiss, son of Rabbi Mayer Samuel Weiss, Merton transformed his identity in the same sort of magical escape.

Merton was intensely aware of anti-Semitism and this change of name was part of his 'strategy for upward mobility', as David Greenberg once put it. Thus Cullen and Messner (2007: 33) in their revealing interview with Merton write: 'Merton might have seen his own local environment as benign, but also may have been aware that ascending in the cosmopolitan world beyond his neighborhood would require the more "innovative adaptation" of hiding his Jewish heritage.'

Merton would have been aware of the passage of the 1924 Johnson-Reed Act, which drastically reduced Eastern European immigration into the United States whilst favouring German, British and Irish immigration, just as he would have known of the Ivy League college quota system (including Harvard) which restricted Jewish entry. Even the local Quaker-inspired University of Pennsylvania had a virtual caste system with separate fraternity houses, social events and lodging for Jews and non-Jews.

As it was, his family could not afford the fees to Pennsylvania University and instead at seventeen, on a scholarship, he entered the local Temple College (not yet accredited as a university), an institution set up for 'the poor boys and girls of Philadelphia'. The choice was fortuitous. For here Merton describes stumbling upon sociology and being befriended by George E. Simpson as 'serendipitous' – a favourite word of his, which he was to use subsequently to describe his meeting with Pitirim Sorokin at the annual meeting of the American Sociological Association and hence, ultimately, his route to Harvard. But serendipity was only a small part of the matter for surely the attraction of sociology was that it held out an explanation or at the very least posed the questions of the crisis of the world which befell him: 'the Great Depression' on the one hand and the social stigmatisation of anti-Semitism on the other. It was an exciting discipline for a young man who was working class, Jewish and upwardly mobile at a time of world crisis.

Simpson, who later became well known as a Durkheimian scholar, saw the potential in the young student who became his research assistant, his drinking partner and his protégé. Simpson was working on his doctoral dissertation *The Negro in the Philadelphia Press* and Merton's first sociological investigation was on media representations of Philadelphia's black community. Through Simpson he was introduced to a range of black intellectuals, including Ralph Bunche (later to become a Nobel Peace Prize winner) and Franklin Frazier (famous for *The Black Bourgeosie* and other works) who were instructors at Temple. There is no doubt that he would have read at that time **W. E. B. Du Bois**' great work *The Philadelphia Negro* (1899), which he repeatedly extolled in later life. Its themes of crime and social exclusion and the self-fulfilling nature of prejudice greatly influenced his work. Indeed if 'SSA,' his most famous article, was written at Harvard, its core themes of the American Dream and the limits of opportunities for mobility were forged out of personal experience and the intellectual ideas gleaned at Temple during the Depression.

It was while at Temple that he attended the annual meeting of the American Sociological Association and was introduced by Simpson to Sorokin. He was duly impressed:

... Plainly he was the teacher I was looking for. Moreover, it was evident that Sorokin was not your ordinary academic sociologist. Imprisoned three times by czarists and then three times by the Bolsheviks, he ... had had a death sentence commuted into exile by the normally unsparing Lenin. That too was bound to matter to me since, like many other Temple College students during the Great Depression, I was a dedicated Socialist.
(Merton 1997: 286)

Merton's socialism was grounded in Marxism learnt, first of all, from the 'shoemaker intellectual' at the street corner where he grew up. The influence was strong certainly in his early work. During his interview with Cullen and Messner he reaches out to a book shelf in his study and picks up a battered copy of *Das Kapital, Volume I* with a private index of 100 pages. And in a letter to his lifelong friend (and one-time student) the brilliant, if somewhat maverick, Marxist Alvin Gouldner, he describes himself as being perplexed by those who see Marxism as either totally valid or invalid: 'I have taken all that I find good in Marxian thought – and that is a considerable amount – and neglected conceptions which do not seem to me to meet tests of validity. For that reason I am in thorough agreement with your distinction between Marxism and Marxists' (Merton 1982: 917–18).

Sorokin was Merton's entry into Harvard. With Sorokin's encouragement, he applied for graduate studies, obtained a scholarship and was appointed to work as Sorokin's teaching assistant. His first surprise was what was expected of him. Sorokin announced that he had 'stupidly' agreed to present a paper on recent French sociology and commandeered Merton to read up the vast body of work from **Emile Durkheim** onwards. This massive task turned Merton into what he called 'a transatlantic Durkheim' and 'laid the groundwork for what would become [his] own mode of structural and functional analysis' (Merton 1997: 286).

Such functionalism was nurtured at Harvard by Talcott Parsons. Merton was clear about the influence of Parsons on his work but forthright about their differences. The contrast between the biographies of the two men could not be greater. Parsons, brought up in the small town of Colorado Springs in a middle-class Protestant family, majoring in biology at Amherst, his life experience largely in the sheltered world of the academy. This is a formula for a conceptually circular functionalism caught up in the metaphor of the organism, the model for the Grand Theory so roundly satirised by C. Wright Mills in *The Sociological Imagination* and 'The Professional Ideology of Social Pathologists'.

Inevitably, given the task set by Sorokin, Merton's first articles were on Durkheim and French sociology. It was here, as he put it later, he 'dared satirize the enlightened Boojum of Positivism' (1997: 291) – a positivism of which he was to remain critical throughout his early career. Of great significance for the sociology of deviance was his 1936 article, 'The Unanticipated Consequences of Purposive Social Action', the precursor of his more famous paper published in *The Antioch Review* in 1948, which introduced the celebrated phrase 'the self-fulfilling prophecy'. This is illustrated by the way that the panic about insolvency during the Depression forced otherwise solvent banks into ruin and by the way in which racist stereotypes of blacks engenders social exclusion which, in turn, results in crime and thus reinforces stereotypes. It embodies the keen sense of irony which Merton brought to his analysis of society. For although influenced by Parsons, Merton's version of structural functionalism is more of a useful metaphor than a literal portrayal and must be seen in this light. His functionalism is imbued with irony: it is scarcely a functionalism pinned to the metaphor of the organism. (For biology, although sometimes tragic and frequently banal, is rarely ironic.) Merton's is a functionalism of alternatives, not of fixity and stasis.

Furthermore the use of such a free-form, fluid functionalism, as **David Matza** argued, dismisses conventional notions of deviancy as a pathology involving patterns of behaviour which lack meaning and are simple products of disorganisation. If a pattern of deviant behaviour exists on any large scale, it is not a simple problem of system failure or a 'leakage', as Kai Erikson famously castigated positivism. Instead, it is a product of the system itself, and has some function and meaning for some section of the population.

With his firm intellectual background in Marx and Durkheim and keen awareness of anti-semitism and racial prejudice from his background growing up in a 'benign slum', Merton was fully aware of the inequalities and unintended consequences of US society. Yet, surprisingly it is a world which hangs together, which 'functions' against all odds. He is a young man with his foot on the ladder at one of America's most prestigious universities and it is there, at the age of 27, that he writes 'SSA'.

'SSA' is a firecracker of an article abuzz with ideas and displaying a conceptual flair which grabs the reader's attention, moving from normality to deviance, from culture to transgression, from the social structure to the actor and back again from action to the social structure. It has all the characteristics which C. Wright Mills was to extol in *The Sociological Imagination* – perhaps somewhat strangely as Merton was later to be seen as the leading exemplar of the sociology of the 'middle range'. It has a rush of illustrations from conspicuous consumption to competitive athletics, from Al Capone to the bombing of civilian populations, from revolution to ritualism to retreatism. It involves first of all a critique of method and second, a critique of the system itself.

It begins with a dismissal of biological positivism, the notion that non-conformity is rooted in original nature and that social order is simply a device for the 'impulse management' of 'imperious social drives'. In this he follows closely – contrary to many critics – Durkheim's insistence that whereas biological drives are limited and easily satiated, culturally induced desires are incessant and potentially infinite (especially under the regimen of capitalism). Indeed he reverses positivism – for Merton, crime is a meaningful, creative response to a situation; it is a product not of lack of socialisation but a socialisation into a culture which involves the pursuit of incessant goals and constant frustration. Crime is thus not a pathological but a 'normal response' of people to 'abnormal conditions'. The system 'calls forth' deviance. If he retains the concept of pathology, then, it is American society as a whole which he views as metaphorically sick. His position could hardly be more radical: he turns on its head what C. Wright Mills scathingly called 'the professional ideology of social pathologists'. We do not have a healthy organic society where deviance is confined to a pathological fringe but a dysfunctional society where crime is normalised.

Merton's analysis in SSA involves a comprehensive critique of market societies, the unrestrained capitalism of which he sees the United States as an extreme example. It involves six elements: (1) an overwhelming emphasis on monetary success; (2) a notion of success which involves incessant ends; (3) an emphasis on the priority of ends over means; (4) a notion that means have little satisfaction in themselves; (5) a situation where opportunities to success are blocked particularly to those who are low in the class structure; and (6) a strong undercurrent of individualism where both success and failure are seen as primarily the province of the individual. These six components provide us with an extraordinary indictment of a market society which is in every respect the mirror image of social democracy. Such a society is, as he sees it, a society in disequilibrium, a formula for disenchantment with the social order, a subtle equation of motivations and frustration which engenders anti-social behaviour.

If Merton rejects individual positivism, he is also resolutely critical of social positivism. For example, he is adamant that poverty does not lead ineluctably to crime. He takes note of Sorokin's observation that many poorer countries have less crime than richer countries and that the economic improvements of the second half of the nineteenth century and the beginning of the twentieth did not give rise to a decrease in crime. He reflects on the fact that poverty is less highly correlated with crime in southeastern Europe than in the United States. Neither poverty nor limited opportunities *per se* would seem to lead to crime. His conclusion, famously, is that the explanation lies with the American Dream – an ideology which insists that any one can be successful whatever one's background, that social mobility is merely a matter of effort. The meaning of poverty in the American Dream is transformed. Poverty becomes an indication of individual failure. Yet the fact of the matter is that individual mobility is considerably restricted, that there is a contradiction between culture and structure, between meritocratic ideals and opportunities which are highly structured by class. Other societies may have even less mobility such as those structured by caste or the rigid class societies of southern Europe, but they do not have the emblematic promise that success is within every citizen's grasp. It is this frustration together with the prioritisation of pecuniary success and ends over means, which gives rise to anti-social behaviour. Thus Merton (1938: 680) writes:

> It is only when a system of cultural values extols, virtually above all else, certain *common* symbols of success *for the population at large* while its social structure restricts or eliminates access to approved modes of acquiring these symbols *for a considerable part of the same population*, that anti-social behavior ensues on a considerable scale ... These goals are seen to *transcend class lines*, not be bounded by them.

Such a systematic and trenchant critique of the economic and cultural conditions prevalent in the United States remains relevant, some would say even more relevant, today. Its core theme of a crisis of legitimation is social democratic in its politics and radical in its tone. In 1973, Gouldner wrote:

> Unlike Parsons, Merton always knew his Marx and knew thoroughly the nuances of controversy in living Marxist culture. Merton developed his generalized analysis of the various forms of deviant behavior by locating them within a systematic formalization of Durkheim's theory of anomie, from which he gained analytic distance by tacitly grounding himself in a Marxian ontology of social contradiction. It is perhaps this Hegelian

dimension of Marxism that has had the most enduring effect on Merton's *analytic rules*, and which disposed him to view anomie as the unanticipated outcome of social institutions that thwarted men in their effort to acquire the very goods and values that these same institutions had encouraged them to pursue.

(1973: x–xi)

A contemporary re-reading of Merton suggests that Gouldner was spot on. As David Downes (1998: 107–8) put it more recently:

With hindsight, Merton has taken one component of Marx's analysis of capitalist political economy and distilled a theory of deviance from its implications. Despite his borrowing of the term *anomie* from Durkheim, he is more Marxist than Durkheimian in its analysis though it is a secularized and filleted Marxism, not the full-blown thesis.

Downes notes that it is this process of 'filleting' which has made the theory unattractive to Marxists and one might add has made it so easy for Merton to be interpreted as a more conservative thinker by a host of contemporary criminologists whilst, at the same time, allowing the most anodyne portrayal of his theory in the vast majority of criminological textbooks.

But why was Merton's relationship to Marxism so 'tacit', to borrow Alvin Gouldner's term? In retrospect it is hardly surprising. This was a young man who was pursuing 'a strategy for upward mobility'; he had changed his name and got a foothold in an Ivy League university. His analysis followed his background, his circumspectness matched his foreground: his metamorphosis into the professional scholar, and his immersion into the ivory tower of scholarly caution. Furthermore, worries about what, in the United States, would be perceived as political extremism must have crossed his mind. Certainly by the publication of the first edition of *Social Theory and Social Structure* in 1949, the McCarthyite witch hunts were in full swing. He would have been only too aware of the persecution of DuBois, Mills, Bunche and Frazier, amongst many others. What he probably did not know was that he was himself a suspect Communist in the eyes of the FBI as revealed in Mike Keen's remarkable book *Stalking the American Dream* (1999/2004), based on research made possible by the Freedom of Information Act. The FBI investigation had a Monty Python-esque quality about it and centred on the full-scale investigation between 1952 and 1954 of Talcott Parsons as the suspected leader of a communist cell in Harvard. (Seemingly, Merton was supposed to have been placed at Colombia University by members of the Harvard cell!) This lengthy investigation culminated in an interrogation of Parsons at the American Embassy in London in 1954.

In truth, the reasons behind Merton's move from Harvard are more mundane. After teaching for four years, Merton's Harvard contract ran out. The 'dismal 1930s' as he put it, left few opportunities for the non-tenured and there was a zero-growth policy at Harvard. He felt lucky therefore to gain a post at the Tulane University in New Orleans in 1939 where he stayed until 1941. Whilst at Tulane, he published perhaps the only article he wrote directly on the subject of criminology – 'Crime and the Anthropologist' (1940) co-authored with M.F. Ashley-Montagu. This is a wonderful satire of the work of Earnest Hooton, the well-known biological positivist, who developed the theory of the relationship between criminality and body types.

In 1941, Merton moved to Columbia as Assistant Professor where he stayed for the rest of his life, as a full professor in 1963 and Emeritus in 1979. Most of his later work moved away from criminological concerns, and instead he became pre-eminent in the sociology of science. There is a point, however, where both these intellectual paths cross. Indeed, Merton was extremely pleased with his 1957 paper in *The American Sociological Review* entitled 'Priorities in Scientific Discovery' where he applied his concept of anomie to the deviance of scientists with its implications for white-collar crime in general. Here he points to the fashion by which the high emphasis on discovery and original scientific work can lead to sharp practices ranging from fraud and forgery to the concocting of false data. One particular example of this is the claiming of priority in scientific discoveries. But note here that he, once again, emphasises both culture and opportunity structures.

> Scientists do not all occupy similar positions in the social structure; there are, consequently, differentials in access to *opportunity* for scientific achievement (and, of course, differences of individual capacity for achievement). The theory of the relations of social structure to anomie requires us to explore differential pressures upon those scientists variously located in the social structure. Contrast only the disputatious Robert Hooke, a socially mobile man whose rise in status resulted wholly from his scientific achievements, and the singularly undisputatious Henry Cavendish, high-born and very rich.
>
> (Merton 1957: 69 n51)

Of course, Merton's own achievements have had an immense and continuing influence on deviancy theory and on criminology. His conception of the self-fulfilling prophecy became a major component of labelling theory, taken up particularly by Kai Erikson and **Howard Becker**, whilst the openness of his functionalism to the idea of deviance as meaningful helped greatly in the new deviance theorists' demolition of ideas centring around pathology and disorganisation. Yet, it is of course subcultural theory where his work has left the most obvious mark. In particular, his two remarkable students **Albert Cohen** and **Richard Cloward** developed and elaborated Merton's original theory. Cohen added energy, anger and transgressiveness to Merton's deviant actors who seemed somewhat utilitarian in their adaptations, and pinpointed the high school as a prime site of meritocratic disappointment. Cloward expanded the notion of illegitimate opportunity structures alongside the legitimate avenues of mobility. Most importantly, together with his co-worker Lloyd Ohlin, Cloward was instrumental in turning the basic Mertonian theory of anomie into practical policy on a grand scale through Mobilization for Youth. This multi-million dollar funded project was launched in the Lower East Side of Manhattan in the early 1960s, and aimed to directly reduce delinquency by expanding job opportunities. It is noteworthy that it soon ran awry: *The New York Daily News* denounced the project as a tool of 'commies', the FBI raided their offices and seized files. But 'what could be more American', Stephen Pfohl asks 'than trying to incorporate all people into the opportunity structure as a whole?' (1994: 279). The answer, Pfohl, gives lies in the ideological nature of the Dream, its promises of mobility and the resistance to any concerted action by the poor to changes in the status quo. The echoes of the radical nature of Merton's original formulation deserve consideration here: the mythic nature of the Dream, its use as sop to conceal the rigid structures of class, as does its resonance with its constant invocation in the recent presidential election, the trope of a dream lost that must be reclaimed, the simple words HOPE on the Obama tee-shirts.

What is troublesome in practice is also bothersome in theory. Downes talked of the 'filleted' Marxism of SSA, but such a process of filleting is more evident in later interpretations than in the original work itself. Some of Merton's commentators have filleted with great *finesse*, many others have thrown out most of the fish to suit the palates of late twentieth-century criminology and some, alas, have thrown out the fillets all together. It is difficult, for example, to work out the extraordinary rendition of Mertonian anomie theory which occurs in so many of the textbooks. The students emerge remembering the five adaptations by heart yet somehow believing that it is a quiescent theory set way back in the 1930s in the last Great Depression – before this one. It is difficult to puzzle out what possible relationship Robert Agnew's 'strain theory' has to the original formulation although it lays claim to be the heir apparent. Yet, Merton's idea of anomie flourishes, at the heart of Philippe Bourgois' *In Search of Respect* (1995), Steven Messner and Richard Rosenfeld's *Crime and the American Dream* (2001), and my own works *The Exclusive Society* (1999) and *The Vertigo of Late Modernity* (2007). We are a long way from Philadelphia's Depression-era slums of Merton's youth, yet Merton's theories can claim great purchase today when confronting the present excesses of a market economy which he so brilliantly criticised.

Major works

Merton, R.K. (1936) 'The Unanticipated Consequences of Purposive Social Action', *American Sociological Review*, 1(6): 894–904.

—— (1938) 'Social Structure and Anomie', *American Sociological Review*, 3: 672–82.

—— (1948) 'The Self-Fulfilling Prophecy', *The Antioch Review*, 8: 193–210.

—— (1949) *Social Theory and Social Structure*. New York: Free Press.

—— (1957) 'Priorities in Scientific Discovery', *American Sociological Review*, 22: 635–59.

Merton, Robert K. and M.F. Ashley-Montagu (1939) 'Crime and the Anthropologist', *American Anthropologist*, 42(3): 338–408.

Further reading

Agnew, R. (1985) 'Strain Theory Revisited', *Social Forces*, 64: 151–67.

Cullen, F.T. and Messner, S.F. (2007) 'The Making of Criminology Revisited: An Oral History of Merton's Anomie Paradigm', *Theoretical Criminology*, 11: 5–37.

Downes, D. (1998) 'Back to the Future: The Predictive Value of Social Theories of Delinquency', in S. Holdaway and P. Rock (eds) *Thinking about Criminology*. London: UCL Press.

Gouldner, A.W. (1973) 'Preface' to I. Taylor, P. Walton and J. Young (eds) *The New Criminology*. London: Routledge and Kegan Paul

Keen, M. (1999/2004) *Stalking the American Dream*. New Brunswick, New Jersey: Transaction Publishers.

Merton, R.K. (1982) 'Alvin W. Gouldner: Genesis and Growth of a Friendship', *Theory & Society*, 11(6): 915–38.

—— (1997) 'A Life of Learning', in K. Erikson (ed.) *Sociological Visions*. Lanham, Massachusetts: Rowman & Littlefield.

Pfohl, Stephen (1994) *Images of Deviance and Social Control* (2nd edition). New York: McGraw Hill.

JOCK YOUNG

EDWIN M. LEMERT (1912–96)

As a new sociologist in the 1940s, Edwin M. Lemert was asked to teach a course on social pathology, but found himself rather baffled by the then-existing textbooks on the subject. The texts, he felt, failed to delimit the notion of behavioural pathology in a sociologically meaningful way. In a systematic review of the ten most widely adopted social pathology textbooks, detailing no fewer than thirty-three pathologies, Lemert derived the conservative estimate that approximately 104,020,324 out of 127,250,232 American citizens could be considered 'sociopaths' by these standards. The purpose of this exercise for Lemert was to raise the question of 'whether the time has not come to break abruptly with the traditions of older social pathologists and abandon once and for all the archaic and medicinal idea that human beings can be divided into normal and pathological' (Lemert 2000: 20–21). Although written over half a century ago, Lemert's critical question is more urgent today than ever (when no doubt all of us qualify for at least one of the endless pathologies listed in the latest *Diagnostic and Statistical Manual of Mental Disorders*). As the sociologist Charles C. Lemert, the late sociologist's nephew, writes: 'In a time when public thinking on crime has the odor of vacuous rot, one could hardly do better than to read or reread Edwin Lemert' (Lemert 2000: 4).

Like other great social scientists, Lemert was a consummate listener – fascinated by the stories of others, he frequently went into 'the field' with no expectations of what he might find, guided only by a 'yen for rustic islands' (Winter 2000: 283). In one of his best-known articles, Lemert (1974: 457) quotes James Branch Cabell as saying, 'We should write beautifully of things as they are'. It is clear that Lemert took this advice to heart. Besides being a great writer, Lemert was also a champion of empirical data, and disdained armchair theorising. He argued that social scientists 'should develop or derive theoretical concepts from bodies of data and be careful not to generalize beyond our data' (Laub 1983: 127). To a large extent, his research reflects this insistence, with his innovative ethnographic work ranging from explorations of the social world of the check forger to the use of alcohol among Native American groups.

Somewhat ironically, though, his most enduring contributions to criminology are theoretical rather than empirical in nature – most notably his work on societal reaction theory. Developed in his book *Social Pathology* (1951), a foundational textbook for the emerging field of deviance studies, Lemert's societal reaction theory turned the study of sociopathology on its head. Emerging in an era of 'Red scares' and McCarthyite witch hunts in Hollywood and elsewhere (among the targets was the Provost of the University of California at Los Angeles where Lemert was teaching), the theory starts from the assumption that understanding deviants required, first, an understanding of reactions to deviance.

At the centre of the theory was the distinction between *primary deviation* and *secondary deviation*. Primary deviation involves the initial flirtation and experimentation with deviant behaviours. Secondary deviation, on the other hand, is deviance that becomes 'incorporated as part of the "me" of the individual' (Lemert 1951: 76). Primary deviation can arise out of a variety of 'causes'. In the case of alcoholism, for instance, he suggests these triggers might include the death of loved ones, exposure to death in battle, the strain of business competition, family role ambivalence, inferiority feelings and the like (reflecting the Freudian tenor of the times, Lemert also lists 'nipple fixation'). Secondary deviation, on the other hand, could be said to take place when the person begins to employ his or her deviant behaviour or a role based upon it 'as a means of defense, attack, or adjustment to the overt and covert problems created by the societal reaction to it' (Lemert 1951: 76). In other words, 'A person who began to drink heavily because of anxieties over his [or her] professional competence now drinks heavily because of the failures due to his drinking and corresponding sense of guilt and introjected self-definitions' (ibid: 28).

This two-pronged understanding of deviance allowed Lemert (1951: 75) to avoid 'the fallacy of confusing original causes with effective causes'. Freed from what he saw as a 'burdensome' debate around initial aetiology, Lemert focused on why some primary deviants underwent a symbolic reorganisation at the level of their self-identity and others did not. Lemert's story for how this process works is, of course, his most enduring legacy to criminology. Lemert argued that secondary deviance was largely a product of societal reaction. Drawing on the symbolic interactionist notion of the 'looking-glass self-concept', the theory suggests that a stigmatised individual will come to view himself based upon what he believes other people think he is. 'The escalation to secondary deviance rests heavily on the subjective effects of being labeled; that is, the labeling experience serves to recast individuals *in their own eyes* as well as in the eyes of others' (Paternoster and Iovanni 1989: 378).

A favourite illustration of this pattern for Lemert (1951, 1967) was stuttering. In one of his first academic jobs, Lemert worked closely with the clinical psychologist Charles Van Riper, who introduced him to research on speech pathology and helped shape his ideas in regard to societal reaction:

> The young child who has trouble with certain speech sounds, for a number of reasons, hardly even notices the problem. ... But in time, with the help of the reactions of parents and teachers, and the negative attention of peers, the problem becomes so magnified that the child hesitates, stammers, gets red in the face, and produces a whole new set of secondary characteristics, complicating the original problem beyond recognition.
>
> (Winter 2000: 277)

It was a short leap from these 'Golem effects' to a theory of criminal development that suggested efforts to 'correct' young offenders might have the reverse effect. Lemert consequently became a powerful critic of the juvenile court system, and an early champion of 'judicious nonintervention' in the name of reducing stigma and recidivism.

In doing so, he laid the foundation for what became known as the 'labelling perspective' in criminology, although this was not a term that Lemert used to describe his own work. At the time he wrote *Social Pathology*, he had not been aware of earlier work by Frank Tannenbaum (1938) that some see as the first actual discussion of the labelling perspective (Petrunik 1980). Likewise, despite the parallels in their work, Lemert had little interaction with the best-known proponent of labelling theory, **Howard Becker**, beyond his editorial work at the journal *Social Problems*. For the most part, their theoretical work grew up independently of one another and Lemert sought to distance himself from Becker's better-known work (e.g. Lemert 1974). As most of these differences between the two traditions are fairly technical, it seemed that Lemert's primary qualm was simply being saddled with the label of 'labelling theorist'. As a natural iconoclast, he would chafe at this sort of pigeon-holing.

This resistance to conformity can be seen throughout his life. With his boots and a bolo tie, Lemert looked the part of the California cowboy, but actually had strong roots in the Midwest. Raised in a middle-class but non-academic family (his father was a self-made businessman with limited education) in Ohio, Lemert's career path in sociology was barely comprehensible to his family (and his fondness for amateur boxing, exotic travel, boat building and organic farming did little to salvage his reputation as an odd ball). Like most social scientists, Lemert had not planned to go down the road he took (he was supposed to go to law school), but he became hugely influenced by the sociologist William F. Cottrell when doing an undergraduate degree at Miami University of Ohio. Lemert went on to work briefly in social work, but soon returned to academia to pursue a PhD in sociology at Ohio State University. There, he became intrigued by the work of anthropologist John Gillin, and eventually changed his PhD focus to 'sociology and anthropology' to take on board this interdisciplinary interest. His thesis, *Technology and Social Controls in Soviet Russia*, was supervised by F.E. Lumley, but clearly demonstrated Cottrell's influences on his thinking.

Upon his graduation in 1939, Lemert stayed close to home and taught briefly at a couple of small Midwestern universities (Kent State, Western Michigan University) before moving to Los Angeles in 1944, where he would help turn UCLA's Department of Sociology into one of the world's leading centres for sociological and criminological research. He joined as one of only three sociologists in the department, which soon attracted the likes of **Donald Cressey**, Ralph Turner and Phillip Selznick, and students such as Aaron Cicourel, John Kitsuse and Sheldon Messinger.

Yet, just as he was about to be named Chair of this elite group, Lemert chose instead to leave UCLA for what was, in 1953, California's agricultural hinterland at the University of California Davis (known then as the 'University Farm') (Winter 2000). Rather than commuting to the campus from Berkeley like other Davis academics, Lemert embraced the northern California lifestyle, taking up cattle ranching and taking his meals 'with other regulars at the Buckhorn Café' (Lemert 2000: 12). At Davis, even more so than previous jobs, Lemert was essentially on his own as a sociologist in a university unfamiliar with the discipline. This allowed him the freedom that comes with building a department from scratch. Unlike Los Angeles, UC-Davis became a home for Lemert, and he stayed there until his retirement and beyond, working with colleagues such as James Austin and **Travis Hirschi**. (Lemert and Hirschi 'got on like cats and dogs', Hirschi recalled in an interview with John Laub.)

In retrospect, it seems clear that Lemert's work is very much a product of the radically transforming culture of California in the middle part of the twentieth century with its uprooted inhabitants making a new life for themselves in the sunshine. In fact, the Ohio-born Lemert would became a founding figure of what is sometimes referred to as the 'West Coast School of Sociology' – a Mead/Cooley-influenced symbolic interactionist movement including Lemert as well as **Erving Goffman** (with whom Lemert was particularly close), **David Matza**, Fred Davis, Alfred Lindesmith and others (see Petrunik 1980). Lemert also was a core member of the so-called 'Pacific Seminar' organised at Berkeley and involving such soon-to-be luminaries as Irving Piliavin, Ruth Kornhauser, Anthony Platt, Jerome Skolnick and **Nils Christie**, among others.

Appropriately for one of the founders of the sociology of deviance, though, Lemert was a committed and lifelong contrarian. His career choices estranged him from his conservative Midwestern family, and his societal reaction theory made him a radical figure in the McCarthyite early 1950s. Yet, his curmudgeonly tendencies to go against the grain also extended to his violations of the liberal 'political correctness' of his West Coast academic colleagues in the 1960s and beyond. Lemert was notorious for engaging in a sort of 'trickster conservatism' (including voting for Barry Goldwater in 1964) that 'drove colleagues in the department he founded in Davis to such distraction that eventually they voted to exclude him (late in his retirement) from participation in its meetings' (Lemert 2000: 10).

This contrarian spirit could also be seen in his relationship with the theoretical tradition he is credited with founding. Just as labelling theory had risen to the peak of its prominence in American sociology, Lemert publicly broke ties with the theory in his Presidential Address to the Society for the Study of Social Problems in 1973, titled 'Beyond Mead' (Lemert 1974). Fearing that the sociological theory was becoming too 'subjective and psychological', Lemert urged labelling theorists to contend with the 'reciprocal effects of those who are labeled on the labelers' (Laub 1983: 126).

Yet, Lemert's balanced, systematic assessment of the state of labelling theory preceded a more hostile broadside against the theory in the years that followed (see especially Gove 1975), and Lemert did seek to defend the theory from these attacks.

Today, Lemert's work – most especially Lemert 1951 – continues to be routinely cited as the founding text for what became 'labeling theory' or 'societal reaction theory' in the study of deviance. Yet, it is unclear just how often his original work is still actually read and digested in criminology or the field now referred to (largely thanks to Lemert's influence) as deviance studies. Much of Lemert's contribution to the field has been either lost or distorted because of the unfortunate and highly premature burial of the labelling perspective in criminology in the late 1970s – a reactionary episode in the sociology of ideas that Petrunik (1980) refers to as 'the construction and deconstruction of a sociological straw man' (see also Paternoster and Iovanni 1989).

Although his contributions to criminology have been well recognised – he was the recipient of the American Society of Criminology's most coveted prize, the Edwin H. Sutherland Award in 1974, and was invited in 1967 to serve on Lyndon Johnson's highly influential presidential commission on Law Enforcement and the Administration of Justice – Lemert felt that his work might be 'better known abroad than at home' (Laub 1983: 129). Moreover, later in his career, he turned away from criminology to focus more on socio-legal studies and sociological jurisprudence.

Still, even though many of Lemert's essays will be unfamiliar to contemporary readers, the content often seems eerily contemporary. This is mostly because so many of the taken-for-granted language and concepts in deviance research today were anticipated by Lemert. Shades of his still widely used concept of primary/secondary deviance can be seen in Terrie Moffitt's highly influential offender typology. And, Lemert's urging to 'begin the (criminological) analysis with the societal reaction, more particularly social control, rather than with etiology', is now paradigmatic for a whole new field of research, sometimes called 'punishment and society' (see e.g. **John Braithwaite**'s reintegrative shaming theory).

New scholars discovering Lemert after his death will be too young to remember the heady debates of Berkeley's 'Pacific Seminar' between positivists and constructivists, but perhaps this is actually a good thing. In the conclusion to his 1973 Presidential Address, Lemert argues that the labelling perspective may yet be saved, but it might not happen until the paradigm wars of the 1970s had cooled out:

> [Labeling theorists] obviously 'can't go home again' to old style structural, positivist sociology any more than conservative sociologists can stomach the extremes of labeling theory. But there may be a less pretentious midground on which to meet – if not they, then a less committed generation of sociologists yet to come.
>
> (Lemert 1974: 467)

As the 1960s–1970s generation of criminologists slowly moves into retirement, then, the time for revisiting Lemert may now be upon us.

Major works

Gove, W. (1975) 'The Labeling Perspective: An Overview', in W. Gove (ed.) *The Labeling of Deviance: Evaluating a Perspective*, pp. 3–20. Beverly Hills, California: Sage.

Lemert, E.M. (1948) 'Some Aspects of a General Theory of Sociopathic Behavior', *Proceedings of the Pacific Sociological Society. Research Studies, State College of Washington*, 16: 23–29.

—— (1951) *Social Pathology: Systematic Approaches to the Study of Sociopathic Behavior*. New York: McGraw-Hill.

—— (1967) *Human Deviance, Social Problems and Social Control*. Upper Saddle River, New Jersey: Prentice Hall.

—— (1974) 'Beyond Mead: The Societal Reaction to Deviance', *Social Problems*, 21: 457–68.

Further reading

Laub, J. (1983) 'Interview with Edwin M. Lemert', in J. Laub (ed.) *Criminology in the Making: An Oral History*, Boston, Massachusetts: Northeastern.

Lemert, C.C. (2000) 'Whatever Happened to the Criminal?: Edwin Lemert's Societal Reaction', in Lemert, C.C. and Winter, M.F. (eds) *Crime and Deviance: Essays and Innovations of Edwin M. Lemert*, pp. 1–15. Lanham, Maryland: Rowman & Littlefield.

Paternoster, R. and Iovanni, L. (1989) 'The Labeling Perspective and Delinquency: An Elaboration of the Theory and an Assessment of the Evidence', *Justice Quarterly*, 6: 359–94.

Petrunik, M. (1980) 'The Rise and Fall of "Labeling Theory": The Construction and Deconstruction of a Sociological Straw Man', *Canadian Journal of Sociology*, 5(3): 213–33.

Tannenbaum, F. (1938) *Crime and the Community*, Boston, Massachusetts: Ginn.

Winter, Michael F. (2000) 'Edwin M. Lemert: An Intellectual Portrait', in Lemert, C.C. and Winter, M.F. (eds) *Crime and Deviance: Essays and Innovations of Edwin M. Lemert*, pp. 273–94. Lanham, Maryland: Rowman & Littlefield.

SHADD MARUNA

ALBERT COHEN (1918–)

Albert Cohen was born in a Jewish neighbourhood on the outskirts of Boston. The son of immigrants, his father was a tailor and his family although not poor was of modest means. Roxbury at the time was a working-class neighbourhood with little crime. He later attended nearby Harvard University, partially because he was an outstanding student, but also because he could not afford to leave home. Cohen's parents saved up enough to pay for his initial tuition, and, thereafter, he earned scholarships to pay his way. He recollects taking the railway every day with the peanut butter and jelly sandwiches that his mother had prepared for him, his books stuffed in a big green bag and studying until ten or eleven at night clandestinely eating his sandwiches in the library stacks when the weather was bad. In his second year he attended an introductory course in sociology taught by Pitirim Sorokin. The drama and historical sweep of Sorokin, a man exiled by Lenin, and now the head of the first sociology department at Harvard, entranced Cohen. The need to study society as a total system set in history remained with him and was reinforced by being taught by Talcott Parsons – at that time an up-and-coming young professor. Finally, in terms of intellectual mentors, **Robert K. Merton**, himself a student of Sorokin, began teaching a course which Cohen attended in his senior year. It was from this course that Merton's pivotal article 'Social Structure and Anomie' emerged.

Out of this extraordinary intellectual environment Cohen developed what he termed his 'infatuation' with sociology. But he still had no interest, indeed, no knowledge of criminology. That change in focus would result from completely unintended circumstances. Cohen graduated from Harvard in 1939 and began applying for graduate assistantships at over a dozen universities. Although he had references from Parsons, Merton and Timasheff and a stellar academic record, he received refusal after refusal. One Harvard faculty member explained that this was because Cohen was Jewish, and that he had better be prepared to face similar anti-Semitism throughout his academic career. One must remember that quotas limiting Jewish entry were commonplace in the American academy at that time. In fact, one department head sent a personal letter to Cohen saying that although he would recommend him 'it was against the policy of the university to hire Jews'. In desperation Cohen applied for almost any job; then out of the blue came a telegram from Indiana University – a school he had forgotten he had applied to. It was from **Edwin Sutherland** offering him an assistantship.

Edwin Sutherland, by far the most famous criminologist of his day, had an enormous impact on the sociology department at Indiana. It was, as Cohen jokes, 'a department of differential association'. Yet, this was Cohen's first encounter with criminology. For Cohen, Indiana was also personally liberating; up to that time he had rarely been anywhere he could not reach on the Boston subway or streetcar system. Here he was in an intense graduate community, who partied together and talked sociology incessantly. He lived in a rooming house; it was the first time he had ever spent more than ten days away from his family. He described the department as being like a family, with Sutherland almost a guru figure, a revered and warm father: 'I was comfortable with him; I could drop by his house on the way home from the University. We would chat ... on first name terms' (Cohen in Lavender 1993: 158).

At Indiana, Cohen also met a wide range of faculty and fellow students who would become famous in later life. This included Lloyd Ohlin, Lester Hewitt and most importantly Alfred Lindesmith. It was the latter's notion of analytic induction (which he evolved from his desire to develop a general theory of addiction) that was of great influence on Sutherland's theory of differential association.

Cohen melded the Harvard tradition which talked of total systems and their rise and fall, with the origins of deviant behaviour (and especially cultural transmission) descended from the Chicago school. The question that he asked a rather nonplussed Sutherland at his first seminar was 'Where did these cultures come from that were transmitted by differential association?' It was the answer to this question posed as early as 1939 that was to fundamentally shape his theoretical development.

Cohen's Master's dissertation on 'The Differential Implementation of Criminal Law' grew out of Sutherland's concept of 'white-collar crime'. Cohen focused imaginatively on the laws of the Anglo-Saxon kings, of interest because there was a schedule of fines and punishments dependent on what social status you had in society (a serf, a lord, a churl, for example). Here one would expect given the implication of the concept of white-collar crime that penalties were inversely related to status – 'That the poor get shat on' (Cohen in Laub 1983: 191) as Cohen put it. But, and here one can detect a flicker of Cohen's dissidence, the opposite was true: the higher the rank of the offender, the greater the punishment.

Cohen then worked full time for a year at the Indiana Boys School, a juvenile correctional institute, where he was Director of Orientation, interviewing each boy on arrival about his family, background and delinquency. During World War II, he served as an officer in a chemical mortar unit in the Philippines. He returned to Harvard for his doctorate, where he again read 'furiously'. He was particularly struck by William Foote Whyte's *Street Corner Society*. By the end of the semester he felt he had to answer the question he had asked as a first-year graduate student, bolstered as it was by his experience working at the boys' correctional institute and his reading of *Street Corner Society*.

In 1947, he returned to Indiana University, now as part of the faculty. A revealing early publication was a short commentary he wrote in the *American Sociological Review* in 1948 as part of a discussion on an article by Francis Merrill on the nature of social problems. He launches into a spirited attack on the notion of social problems occurring as somehow autonomous from the wider social system. He points to how our 'most honored and cherished values may produce unanticipated and unintended consequences' (259) sometimes of a deplorable nature (a clear reference to Merton's work at the time). Moreover, that these same 'sacred' institutions may produce for some people strains and tensions which give rise to subcultures and that these deviant value systems may be 'the price or precondition. ... for the stability and preservation of the existing order' (ibid.). Thus Cohen states clearly the notion embraced by the functionalists and then the new deviancy theorists, that good can cause evil, rather than the conventional 'evil causes evil' equation – a position which would bring forth much ill-deserved scorn from **Travis Hirschi** two decades later. He also made an even more controversial point: namely, that because of this systemic interconnectedness, 'seemingly localized and uncomplicated problems may really be incapable of solution within the framework of the existing institutional order' (ibid.). Finally, he rounds upon the concept of 'disorganisation' as an explanation of crime, indeed that disorganisation and crime are one and the same thing. It is, Cohen remarks, one of the 'fuzziest' concepts in sociology utilised frequently because of some terminological predilection for symmetry with 'organisation'. Instead, he argues, that in a closely linked social system many social problems are 'normal and chronic incidents of highly organized systems' (ibid.: 260).

He finished his PhD thesis *Juvenile Delinquency and the Social Structure* in 1951. It was an exceptional piece of work in two volumes: the first part, which Cohen now sees as the most important, was a general theory of subcultures; the second applied these principles to the specific problem of delinquency. His tour de force *Delinquent Boys: The Culture of the Gang* appeared in 1955. It provided a theory of subcultures which fits C. Wright Mills' sociological imagination in that it shuttles from the total society to the psychology of the individual and back again. It does not rule out the influence of a psychological level of analysis. Indeed with his concept of *reaction formation* he makes a great deal of this level. Yet, he is unwilling to countenance reductionism. The psychological problems of adjustment which visit the individual boy are the result of social contradictions experienced collectively on the level of the wider society – not just his personal problems nor that of his family, but of the social structure as a whole.

First of all, the book is an attempt to solve the problem Cohen posed back in 1939 at that first Indiana seminar. The book contains both a theory of the transmission and of the cultural origins of delinquency, and in this it attempts to bring together Sutherland's rendering of the Chicago School and the sociological insights of Harvard. It attempts to explain both working-class and middle-class delinquency and the differentials between boys and girls and the relationship of masculinity to crime. It is prescient in its use of reference group theory; it has, to my knowledge, the first mention of subterranean values; it has an emphasis on the foreground and background of crime; and a notion of energy and transgression which is the precursor of present-day 'cultural criminology'. It is above all lively yet methodical: it is the book that every student of criminology should read at the beginning of their studies.

The book pivots around the elaboration of a general theory of subcultures as solutions to problems (as perceived from the cultural perspective of the participants). They are not necessarily tenable solutions but they must be understood as creative, meaningful endeavours: they are not just agencies of transmission but sites of constant change and innovation. His examples of subcultures range from medical doctors, through jazz musicians to juvenile delinquents. Behind this, one can detect the influence of social anthropology, particularly the work of Malinowski whose lectures at the London School of Economics so impressed Parsons and whose work had a great impact on William Foote Whyte. The book is also greatly shaped by social movements research, especially as an explanation of such diverse phenomena as the rise of revivalist religious movements amongst American Indians, political movements such as the Nazis, and cults such as The Oxford Group and Father Divine's Kingdom. Here we can see an approach which makes meaningful that which is often conventionally thought of as inchoate or meaningless, which places such events in the context of wider society and which explains them as *collective* adaptations to the problems facing the group concerned. This is particularly evidenced by his illustration of the 'mass psychoneurosis' of conscript soldiers during World War I as a collective adaptation by the men to the indescribable and unbearable conditions of the frontline.

He commences *Delinquent Boys* by asking what facts a theory of delinquency must fit, focusing on three aspects: the *content* of the delinquent subculture, its *class distribution* and the *differentials of sex*. His depiction of the content of the subculture is the antithesis of the utilitarian, means-ends model of Merton in 'Social Structure and Anomie'. Its characteristic, he claims, is non-utilitarian, malicious and negativistic. A stolen dollar is a dollar valued more than a dollar earned; a stolen sweet tastes all the sweeter. Moreover, much delinquency has no utilitarian end; rather its aim is to cause trouble, disturbance, to get a laugh out of a boring situation, to ridicule rules and authority. In contrast, Merton's 'innovators', denied access to legitimate opportunities, merely find the easiest route to material gain; they are creatures of rational choice. Cohen characterises the subculture precisely as an act of transgression, constituted by the *inversion* of middle-class values. The working-class boy, ill-suited for competition in the middle-class world of the school, reacts to this humiliation by a process of *reaction formation*, reacting against values which, although he can acknowledge their legitimacy and authority, he finds threatening.

At the same time Cohen is fiercely critical of those who would view delinquency as a manifestation of the irrational, where deviant impulses supposedly burst boundaries in situations of social disorganisation. Such deficit arguments, so common today, in for example, the work of Gottfredson and Hirschi, are 'wholly negative' in Cohen's opinion; they do not explain *either* the origins of such delinquencies *or* indeed their content.

Although Cohen's general theory of subcultures was a great breakthrough, the actual description of the delinquent subculture is ultimately flawed as Cohen himself acknowledges. For having given his actors creativity and consciousness, he then takes it away. It is as if he has taken the ball all the way across the field and dropped it just before the goal line. The contrast between Whyte's depiction of the Italian neighbourhood of Boston, where there is a rich leisure culture of bonhomie and support as well as a modicum of delinquency and a dash of political skullduggery, stands in contrast with the 'negativism', 'maliciousness' and rather inconsequential 'non-utilitarianism' of his delinquent boys. Indeed, Cohen's own initial depiction of the differences between working- and middle-class culture dwells on the individualism, ambition and normative rigidity of middle-class life which he compares rather unfavourably with the warmer more relaxed lifestyle of the working class. Indeed if Whyte views his cornerboys as individuals in the round, from a *sociological* point of view, Cohen in his depiction of the culture of the boys sees, from a *criminological* perspective, nothing but delinquency. It is surely this contradiction with his own commitment to a sociological understanding of the world – so apparent in his interest in social movements – that makes Cohen in later life so unsure of this aspect of his theory: 'the thing that causes me the greatest concern, or shakes my confidence in the theory, the most, is the notion of negativism' (Cohen in Laub 1983: 191). In fact, he completely reversed his negativistic assessment of delinquent subcultures as a spiteful inversion of middle-class values in later work. For example, in his review of Ruth Horowitz' *Honor and the American Dream,* written in 1985, he describes the *piece de resistance* of the book as the depiction of the core members of the gang. They are, he writes: 'not psychopathic or unstable, they are not marked by social disability, and their relationships to one another are not precarious but warm, strong intimate and enduring'. And he adds: 'This conclusion is at variance with much of the scholarship on the subject.'

It is important to situate Cohen's theory in terms of his own personal experience. He is the archetypical scholarship boy whose mobility is financed by his academic success. He is between cultures, leaving one and feeling the tug of the other. It is no coincidence that the book that influenced him the most was *Street Corner Society*. Set in an Italian section of Boston, the North End, it was scarcely the disorganised slums depicted by the early Chicago School, each with their own strong cultures based on class and ethnicity. *Street Corner Society* is of course famous for its depiction of corner boys and college boys. The corner boys, the homeboys of those days, hung around the street corners and the bars fiercely loyal to their Italian working-class culture and to each other. The college boys set their sights on upward mobility, their decisions were more individualistic, their loyalty to their friends fragile, their break with working-class culture necessary if they were to move on up. Such a situation must have been precisely that of Cohen's. Indeed when he writes of 'reaction formation' it is easy to see the *mirror image* of his own life and the costs of social mobility.

It is also useful to compare Merton and Cohen. Although similar in familial and educational background, Merton wrote of anomie during the Great Depression, Cohen wrote at the time of America's post-war affluence. Merton was influenced by Durkheim and Marx, whereas Cohen was influenced by Sutherland, Parsons and, ironically, Merton. For Merton (1938) there is a legitimation crisis of the system; for Cohen (1955) it is a problem occurring in an otherwise successful system. It is the problem of why those at the very bottom do not realise the American Dream, not why the Dream fails many or why, indeed, the Dream acts as a mystification supportive of the *status quo*. For Merton there is a contradiction between culture (the dream of a meritocratic society) and structure (a class structure which is too rigid and inhibits mobility). For Cohen, it is a contradiction between cultures. It is a clash between middle-class and working-class cultures, an inability of kids equipped with working class culture to measure up to schools' standards grounded in the culture of the middle class.

In 1962, Cohen published a stringent attack on multifactor approaches to the explanation of crime derived significantly from the first volume of his 1951 thesis. This attack was largely directed at the work of Cyril Burt and **Eleanor and Sheldon Glueck** with their ragbag of factors ranging from body shape to church attendance, amassed inductively from what were poorly representative and, in Burt's case, sometimes fabricated samples. For Cohen, as for most, sociologists, theories are underlying principles which explain a body of facts. This is in stark contrast to multifactor 'theory' where a host of factors are correlated with crime from somatypes to socioeconomic situations and these are deemed to impinge upon people and propel them into crime. The meaning of these factors is obviated. It is a very 'thin narrative' in Jack Katz's terms, or in Cohen's words: simply the 'intuition of the author', 'implicit, inarticulate, preconscious'.

Yet, although Cohen's subcultural theory is dismissive of multifactor analysis, is it not irreconcilable with Sutherland and Lindesmith's notion of analytic induction? Cohen's question about the origin of deviant values which so 'non-plussed' Sutherland at that first seminar held within it a critique of differential association theory itself. It was perhaps because of Cohen's loyalty to Sutherland that it took him fifteen years and a return to Harvard, to find a satisfactory answer. The general laws, which Sutherland and Lindesmith sought, which could apply to all crimes at all times, lead to abstractions, which it has to be said, are often of a remarkably mundane nature. They take the myriad of social meanings out of the picture whilst subcultural theory does the opposite. Thus, for example the heroin addiction of the physician and the street addict are miles apart because of the differences in subculture and predicament of the actors involved. A general theory of addiction which lumps the two together and looks only to what they have in common forgets the meanings which dramatically set them apart. Likewise general theories of crime whether of Sutherland or, indeed Hirschi, tend to degenerate into cliché or tautology.

In 1964, after seventeen happy years at Indiana, Cohen decided that 'new experiences were not happening any more' and that he didn't want to spend the rest of his career 'resting on his oars', so he moved on to the University of Connecticut. His first publication there, in 1965, was the hugely innovative 'The Sociology of the

Deviant Act: Anomie Theory and Beyond'. Its significance is in its attempt to bring together the two strands of the New Deviancy Theory which had emerged in the immensely creative period 1955 to 1965. The 'first wave' was a series of classic subcultural texts including **Gresham Sykes'** *Society of Captives* (1959) and **Cloward** and Ohlin's *Delinquency and Opportunity* (1960); the 'second wave' was what one might call updated works of labelling theory such as Kai Erikson's 'Notes in the Sociology of Deviance', John Kitsuse's 'Societal Reactions to Deviant Behavior', and the immensely influential *Outsiders* by **Howard Becker** (1963). The second wave was critical of the first because it did not problematise deviance; it did not capture the existential nature of the human experience; it accepted the definitions of the *status quo*, and it did not ask 'whose side are we on?' Most importantly, the social constructionist current which labelling theory was a part of, was buoyed up by the rise of the counterculture; for the 1960s were upon us and the talk was not just who and why people were excluded from the American Dream but the sanctity of the Dream itself. Now was the time for new experiences, now was the time to take up the oars again. And this Cohen did with gusto. Thus he talked about the expressive nature of much deviance, that it was often part of identity rather than a route to identity; he talked of the 'discontinuous' nature of human behaviour, the interplay between agency and structure, the interaction between action and reaction. He even developed sophisticated notions of 'othering' before the idea became fashionable.

In particular Cohen explores the situation where punitive and vindictive behaviour occurs towards the deviant although there is no seeming conflict of interest. In doing this he draws upon the concept of *ressentiment*, an idea with a fascinating genealogy in Nietzsche, Scheler and Sombart. This is 1965, remember; the old disciplines of work and sacrifice are vanishing in the immediacy of the consumer society, a hedonistic youth culture is burgeoning, the new bohemia is emerging, and intergenerational moral indignation is widespread. Note how moral indignation parallels reaction formation: one is anger from above, one anger from below – both involve a psychodynamics of energy and emotion, both involve attraction and repulsion, yet moral indignation has the more critical edge and reaction formation is the less insightful and progressive.

In December 1972 Cohen gave a lecture at Oxford University entitled 'The Elasticity of Evil' which was published in pamphlet form by the Penal Research Unit two years later. It is an elegant study of the changing definitions of good and evil and the way in which both the wicked and the saintly allow us to fix bearing on our identity. It also gives us a clear insight into his own sense of moral change and challenges to his own perspectives and identity drawing on the My Lai massacre and the crash of a U2 spy plane in May 1960 among other incidents.

On 12 January 1973, presumably as part of his British visit, he also gave a paper to the National Deviancy Conference entitled 'The Policy and Ideological Implications of the New Deviancy Theory' to a large and appreciative audience. It is difficult to imagine what he made of this encounter with British radical criminology with its heady mixture of Marxism and anarchism. The generational gap which he was so aware of must have been palpably evident. In a later interview in 1979, he reflected on Marxist criminology saying that, although he was not enamored by their solutions, 'who else really is talking about the relationship between structure of systems as a whole and the kind of phenomena that we are talking about?' (Laub 1983: 200). But it was the vision of anarchism that he found 'immensely attractive'. It is easy to imagine this heir of Sorokin taking nurture from the sophistication and sensitivity of the libertarian analysis stemming out of the new deviancy theory and its countercultural backdrop.

In 1988, at age 70, Cohen retired from Connecticut as an Emeritus Professor, in part to spend time looking after his ailing wife. In a 1993 interview he talks with pride, but in the past tense, about his work and his achievements. And of course there are many. His influence on subcultural theory in all its manifestations from liberal to Marxist to postmodernist has been profound if often unacknowledged. He was a core source for moral panic theory; his work – whether about moral indignation or reaction formation – is a key precursor of cultural criminology. His attempt to knit together the contradictions of the social with the pychodynamics of the personal is exemplary, and his indictment of multifactoral 'theory' is as relevant today as ever. Above all he has held to his commitment to a cultural understanding of deviance and has constantly been ahead of the stream.

Major works

Cohen, A.K. (1948) 'The Study of Social Problems: Discussion', *American Sociological Review*, 13(3): 259–60.
—— (1955) *Delinquent Boys: The Culture of the Gang*. Glencoe, Illinois: Free Press.
—— (1962) 'Multiple Factor Approaches', in M. Wolfgang, L. Savitz and N. Johnston (eds) *The Sociology of Crime and Delinquency*. New York: Wiley.

—— (1965) 'The Sociology of the Deviant Act: Anomie Theory and Beyond', *American Sociological Review*, 30: 5–14.

—— (1966) *Deviance and Control*. Englewood Cliffs, New Jersey: Prentice-Hall.

Merton, R.K. (1938) 'Social Structure and Anomie', *American Sociological Review*, 3: 672–82.

Further reading

Cohen, A.K. (1974) *The Elasticity of Evil: Changes in the Social Definition of Deviance*. Oxford: Blackwell for the Oxford University Penal Research Unit.

—— (1985) Review, *Honor and the American Dream: Culture and Identity in a Chicano Community* by Ruth Horowitz, *The American Journal of Sociology*, 90(5): 1146–7.

Laub, J. (1983) 'Interview with Albert Cohen, June 1st, 1979', in J. Laub (ed.) *Criminology in the Making*. Boston, Massachusetts: North Eastern University Press.

Lavender, A. (1993) 'Doing Theory: An Interview with Albert K. Cohen', *American Journal of Criminal Justice*, 18(1): 153–67.

JOCK YOUNG

DONALD RAY CRESSEY (1919–87)

Although perhaps best known for carrying on the tradition of **Edwin Sutherland**'s differential association theory, Donald Cressey was in his own right one of the great American criminologists of the twentieth century. Following Sutherland's death, Cressey took responsibility for revising five new editions of *Principles of Criminology*, Sutherland's seminal criminological textbook. However, his reputation as a key criminological thinker was based on a host of other original achievements: he was an expert on organisational and organised crime and also published widely on prisons, penology and the administration of criminal justice. His book *Theft of the Nation* (1969), about the structure of the Sicilian Mafia (the Cosa Nostra) in America, became a bestseller and classic of the discipline.

Cressey was a versatile and diligent academic. His working day started at 5 am and continued late into the evening. Despite this obsession with work, he always found time for his students and co-workers. He was described as a 'superlative storyteller' with a repertoire of anecdotes running into the hundreds, many of which he used to enliven his lectures and academic papers. He was an exemplary teacher, a capable administrator, and a creative and highly productive researcher, publishing ten books and nearly 100 articles and chapters. He also operated outside the walls of academia, acting as a private and public consultant on *inter alia* the President's Commission on Law Enforcement and Administration of Justice, and various state commissions and international advisory boards on crime and criminal justice. However, whether working as a consultant or university scholar, Cressey was driven by a burning desire for justice – a concern that owed much to his early childhood in the American Midwest.

Cressey was born into a working-class family in a small Minnesota town, growing up in the deplorable economic conditions of the Great Depression. The family's plight was not helped when Cressey's alcoholic father lost his job following an arrest for drunk driving in 1932. Times were extremely tough and so to help make ends meet the young Cressey took a job as a paperboy to earn some extra money for his family. One night his father asked to borrow $2.50 of his earnings to buy food, but that same evening Cressey saw his father singing and drinking in a pool room: 'It was obvious that he was boozing it up with my money' (Cressey 1990: 244). Cressey mentioned this incident as one of the many injustices he experienced in his childhood: 'I simply learned early on that some people are unfair and then learned how to cope with this fact of life. Injustices I experienced as a boy are reflected in my criminological writings' (ibid: 240).

After earning a Bachelor's Degree in Sociology at Iowa State College, Cressey served in the armed forces during World War II. He then became the last of Sutherland's PhD students at Indiana University. Cressey was determined to make the best of his educational opportunities, even though at first he had doubts about his own competence. However, in April 1946 an incident occurred that gave him the confidence and security he was lacking: 'I heard a terrible paper on housing in Cleveland, whose punch line was "Why, in many houses the rats run in and out freely". The paper changed my life. If such crap was sociology, I concluded, then, I was surely capable of becoming a competent sociologist. I thought I had it made. I was right. I made it' (Cressey 1990: 259). This quote is typical of the way in which Cressey approached academic life. He had little patience with ideas that he considered 'crap' or 'dumb' and he was more than happy to dish out criticism when he felt it was necessary (Akers and Matsueda 1989: 423–24). That said, he was also more than happy to accept and reflect on criticism when it came his way – which it did following the publication of *Theft of the Nation,* a text which, although widely admired, was also heavily criticised in some quarters for its (then) controversial ideas and method of research (see below).

Cressey started his academic career in 1949 as a lecturer in Sociology at the University of California, Los Angeles (he became full professor there in 1959). In 1962 he moved to UC Santa Barbara as Dean of the College of Letters and Science; a post he retained until 1967. After that he served as Professor of Sociology until his retirement in 1986. During his long academic career, Cressey carried out research in a number of different areas, but is most remembered for his contribution to Sutherland's differential association theory and his book *Theft of the Nation* on the existence of the Cosa Nostra in America.

The theory of differential association attempted to identify universal mechanisms that explain the genesis of crime regardless of the macro- or micro-conditions involved. Simply stated, Sutherland's differential association theory asserts that criminal behaviour is learned by the same process as non-criminal behaviour. The theory rejects psychological learning theories which locate the causes of criminal behaviour in socialisation processes gone wrong. The theory also opposes the idea that criminal behaviour can be explained by poverty or social class. At the core of the theory is the assertion that, in principle, every person can develop delinquent behaviour. The decisive factor lies in the interactions with others, particularly the 'associations' with criminal and anti-criminal definitions and attitudes. The principle of differential association is that a person becomes delinquent because of an excess of definitions favourable to violation of the law over definitions unfavourable to violation of the law.

Cressey's first involvement with the theory was his study of the process by which people come to embezzle. For this study he conducted lengthy interviews with 133 prison inmates who had been convicted of embezzlement. In *Other People's Money* (1953) he concluded that embezzlers learn and apply rationalisations or verbalisations such as 'The money is really mine' or 'I'm just borrowing the money'. They learn these definitions not only in associations with other embezzlers, but also from general cultural rationalisations. In plain terms, if individuals do not learn and apply these types of definitions, they will not go on to act as embezzlers. Cressey's concept of rationalisation or verbalisation became the foundation for **Gresham Sykes** and **David Matza**'s subsequent 'techniques of neutralization'. In addition to applying differential association theory to embezzlement, Cressey's other major contribution in this area was to respond to the various criticisms of differential association, further clarifying and consolidating the theory within American sociology (see e.g. Sutherland and Cressey 1966).

In 1967 Cressey became one of the consultants for the President's Task Force Commission on Organized Crime. When the Commission commenced its work, Cressey was not an acknowledged specialist in the area of organised crime. However, such was his ability to consume a subject that, only two years later, Cressey had turned research undertaken for the President's Commission into his landmark text *Theft of the Nation*. Here, Cressey described the structure of organised crime as a bureaucratic organisation, with a hierarchy of ranks, a code of conduct for its members, and a set of internal dynamics that allowed it to function as an effective and highly ordered secret society. Cressey asserted that the Cosa Nostra consisted of 24 families located in various large cities across the United States. He considered the Cosa Nostra to be the most rational type of organised crime in terms of the division of labour, the number of participants, role descriptions of its members, and the existence of a so-called 'Commission'. This Commission, he maintained, functioned primarily to settle disputes amongst the families, but also served as a combination board of business directors, legislature, Supreme Court and arbitration board (Cressey 1969: 111). According to Cressey, this bureaucratic structure made organised illegal activities profitable and relatively safe.

Such revelations caused a mixture of shock and disbelief, but Cressey was sure of his ground. Albini (1988: 339) refers to conversations he had with Cressey in 1967 as a recently minted PhD. He remembers that Cressey was convinced of the existence of a secret criminal society. The clearest indication of Cressey's conviction that his book presented an accurate portrayal of organised crime can be found in his Preface to *Theft of the Nation*, where he writes:

> Upon being invited to work for the [President's] Commission, I was not at all sure that a nationwide organization of criminals exists. Discussions with my friends and colleagues indicated, and continue to indicate, that this scepticism is widely shared. I changed my mind. I am certain that no rational man could read the evidence that I have read and still come to the conclusion that an organization variously called 'the Mafia', 'Cosa Nostra', and 'the syndicate' does not exist.
>
> (1969: x)

There is no question that Cressey's study on organised crime was a landmark text within criminology. While writing *Theft of the Nation* he was well aware that he was taking the first step in the development of scholarly literature on organised crime: 'To me, "starting" or "creating" a literature meant producing pages that would be accepted as scholarship by academicians. I decided to take a stab at making the study of organized crime academically respectable' (Cressey 1987: 1). His study was also a testament to his courage. He wrote on the existence of the Mafia during a period when the Mafia was dismissed as a fanciful creation of the media or an exaggerated threat fostered by law enforcers. On publication the book met with a surprising degree of resistance, but Cressey was unconcerned; he knew this criticism would help to establish a literature (Cressey 1987: 11). Cressey also drew inspiration from his critics and several years later, in 1972, he wrote a second book on the subject (*Criminal Organisation: Its Elementary Forms*) in order to further clarify and develop his position in light of his detractors.

Cressey will live on in history as the criminologist who developed a model of organised crime that attempts to make rationality and bureaucratic structure its major distinguishing features. Since then, Cressey's understanding of the (bureaucratic) structure of criminal cooperatives has been superseded by more contemporary research that argues that criminal organisations are much better understood as social networks.

His legacy also lives on in his former students, such as James W. Coleman, David Luckenbill and Sheldon Messinger. He was also responsible for enticing former undergraduates such as Joseph Albini, Egon Bittner, **William Chambliss**, and Aaron Cicourel (to name but a few) into the sociology of deviance. As well as augmenting and refining Sutherland's theory of differential association, he also undertook a veritable mass of empirical criminological research which has lost little of its meaning and relevance to our times. But Cressey wanted more: he also wanted to ensure that decisions with regard to criminal law were evidence-based; that is, based on the findings of thoroughgoing criminological research. He once wrote that his principal objective in writing *Theft of the Nation* had been to teach lawyers, legislators, and law-enforcement personnel that organisations, not people, are the important variable in organised-crime operations. People are replaceable or interchangeable; therefore, crime fighting should focus on dealing with the organisation (Cressey 1987: 5). In this way he hoped to change the cops-and-robbers character that predominated thinking about organised crime.

By the time of his death in 1987, Cressey was a celebrated criminologist, widely appreciated for his many contributions to criminology and the administration of criminal justice in the USA. However, looking back twenty years later, there is no denying that Cressey's academic career was also tinged with sadness. He devoted much of his life's work to improving differential association theory, but his achievements primarily helped solidify Sutherland's reputation, leaving Cressey permanently in the shadow of his teacher. Likewise, it is a great irony that Cressey's magnum opus, *Theft of the Nation,* was based on classified, highly sensitive sources that were off limits to other researchers at the time. When faced with criticism, Cressey, who was known to enjoy academic debate, had no option but to defend himself and his theories with one hand tied behind his back. Certainly, it is a cruel irony that these things had to happen to a man who from childhood had been so sensitive to personal injustice.

Major works

Cressey, D. (1953) *Other People's Money: A Study in the Social Psychology of Embezzlement.* Glencoe: Free Press.

—— (1969) *Theft of the Nation: The Structure and Operations of Organized Crime in America.* New York: Harper and Row.

—— (1972) *Criminal Organization: Its Elementary Forms.* London: Heinemann.

Sutherland, E. and D. Cressey (1966) *Principles of Criminology* (seventh edition). Philadelphia, Pennsylvania: Lippincott Company.

Further reading

Akers, R. and R. Matsueda (1989) 'Donald R. Cressey: An Intellectual Portrait of a Criminologist', *Sociological Inquiry,* 59(4): 423–38.

Albini, J. (1988) 'Donald Cressey's Contribution to the Study of Organized Crime', *Crime and Delinquency,* 34(3): 338–54.

Cressey, D. (1987) 'Squeezing the Accordion into the Academy', *The Criminologist. Official Newsletter of the American Society of Criminology* (May–June).

—— (1990) 'Learning and Living', in B.M. Burger (ed.) *Authors of Their Own Lives. Intellectual Autobiographies by Twenty American Sociologists.* Berkeley, California: University of California Press.

HENK VAN DE BUNT

WALTER B. MILLER (1920–2004)

American criminological theories of the 1950s seemed to be in relative agreement that middle-class values governed the behaviour of everyone. That is to say, major theories saw criminal and delinquent behaviour either as an undesirable product of a societal overemphasis on middle-class goals or as a direct reaction to failed attempts to achieve those goals. It is also probably safe to say that the public's image of delinquents during this time was similar to that portrayed in the musical play *West Side Story,* with its tale of youth gangs posturing and threatening each other on stage. **Albert Cohen**'s (1955) sub-culture theory, for example, described a middle-class value system that disadvantaged lower-class children even though they strove to gain status through it. As they entered the school system, these children were simply not sufficiently prepared to compete well with middle-class students. When the frustration of losing status became too much for these children, in defence they set about turning those values around in order to develop easier ways to gain status. This, for Cohen, was the essence of the delinquent subculture. Similarly, **Richard Cloward** and Lloyd Ohlin (1960) agreed with **Robert Merton** that middle-class goals governed society, even though they posited that an illegitimate opportunity system was more available to the lower class than the Mertonian legitimate one. Cloward and Ohlin's proposed solution to increase lower-class juveniles' access to legitimate opportunities became the basis of the Kennedy and Johnson presidential administrations' Great Society programmes of the 1960s (e.g. Peace Corps, Jobs Corps, Head Start).

Into this consensus of theorists came Walter Benson Miller with an approach that seemed not only to ignore the perspective of the decade but essentially declare that it was immaterial. As he argued in his 1958 article 'Lower Class Culture as a Generating Milieu of Gang Delinquency', lower-class street-corner delinquency was the result of juveniles pursuing values *common to their cultural surroundings,* not the pursuit of middle-class values. In fact, he argued that it was the common cultural values of lower-class areas (in particular what he referred to as 'hard-core' lower-class areas) that governed life in them, not the middle-class values of the larger society. How can such a stark difference in perspective be explained? One possibility is that Miller was simply echoing the Chicago School position of culture conflict and norm conflict. However, even a superficial reading of his work shows that not to be the case. Perhaps it was the nascent return of conflict perspectives in American sociology after the McCarthy years that influenced Miller? Again, the article neither recognises, nor references, any of the aforementioned classic sociological conflict perspectives of the 1950s. It seems that Miller's difference lies in the fact that he was thinking outside of the parameters of existing criminological tradition.

Miller's emphasis on the effect of cultural values led him to postulate that some of these lower-class values were so important that they commanded persistent attention and concern – in other words, they were 'focal concerns'. For juveniles these concerns reflected the utilitarian importance of smartness, trouble, toughness, fate, autonomy and excitement, which Miller reasoned were the focal concerns underlying what the larger culture defined as delinquent behaviour. *Trouble* represented a commitment to law-violating behaviour or being noticed as a problem to others. *Toughness* was a machismo aura of bravery, fearlessness and daring. To be *smart* was to avoid detection when committing crimes and getting one over on others, particularly adults in authority. *Excitement* meant experiencing thrills, doing dangerous and respected feats; while *fate and luck* are part of life in low-income areas where getting ahead is a long-shot and opportunities are rare. *Autonomy* signifies independence and not having to rely on others which means never being indebted and possibly viewed as weak.

Emphasis on these lower-class focal concerns placed the young male in direct conflict with the larger society. Thus, the one-sex peer group, Miller rationalised, was important for reinforcing the realistic attitudes and behaviours needed for success within their own subculture. The peer group had both the capacity and motivation to be selective in membership and to enforce its contextual norms. Exclusion, the most serious sanction that could be levied, compelled adherence to the standards of conduct expected. Miller theorised that lower-income households were typically female-dominated, often consisting of several related females of child-bearing age. The practice of serial monogamy meant that older men rotated in and out of the home too quickly to form significant mentoring relationships or to serve as role models for the younger boys. Thus, it was frequently left to the gang to provide the sex-role identification and authority needed. Time with the group served as an opportunity to practise approved masculine roles and values (the focal concerns) as well as gain status and a sense of belonging.

Miller's educational background provides some useful clues for understanding the development of this theoretical position. He was born in 1920 in Philadelphia, Pennsylvania, where he grew up. His alternative views on delinquency, however, stem from his postgraduate training. He went to the University of Chicago to study anthropology, ultimately receiving an M.A. (Phi Beta Kappa) from the University in 1950. His early fieldwork project was a study of the Fox Indian Tribe, a group of Native Americans located in Iowa. That project, directed by Clyde Kluckhohn, one of the giants of cultural anthropology and champions of the effect of values on behaviour, lasted through Miller's Master's degree studies until 1953. The experience gave Miller a perspective on the cultural ways of smaller groups in larger societies that he used for the rest of his life: these groups adapt their values and concerns to create behaviour most disposed to facilitating life in their own circumstances. Obviously, Kluckhohn's influence on Miller was important in developing his approach to cultural values but, in addition, there is a direct connection with sociological gang researchers. Kluckhohn's spouse, Florence, wrote with Fred Strodtbeck who, with James F. Short Jr., authored some of the seminal gang literature in the late 1950s and 1960s. Miller was thus exposed to the concept of gang values at about the same time as he was writing up his own research.

Miller continued his studies by enrolling in the top-ranked anthropology programme at Harvard and was awarded a PhD in 1954. As a result of this, he developed an interest in cultural theory that was based in the reality of its own setting. Subsequently, Miller joined a gang project and devoted the remainder of his life to explaining delinquent subcultures and the policies that would moderate their effects. The fact that his graduate academic training was entirely in anthropology gave him a view of gangs, subcultures and lower-class life that few others in the criminological field could attain. In particular, he saw that subcultures often existed in an uneasy peace with the population surrounding them. Thus, it was not that they acted or thought in reflection of the larger society, as Albert Cohen suggested, but that beneficial life practices for those subcultures were sometimes in conflict with larger society.

Further experiences after receiving his PhD allowed Miller to firm up his thinking. He helped to implement the Roxbury Gang Delinquency Research Project for the National Institute of Mental Health in 1955 and served as its director from 1957 to 1964. Drawing on the interventions of a small group of social workers in the field, Miller attempted to change the attitudes and activities of corner-group youth in the Boston area and, by his own admission, was somewhat effective in lowering rates of delinquency as well as reducing hostility towards law enforcement officials. When Miller began his work, inner city gangs in the Boston area were predominantly Irish. Using ethnographic traditions he attempted to characterise the richness and complexity of the lifestyles of these lower-class youths. Throughout this period, Miller continued to view gang violence as relatively rare. While fights and aggression within the group were to be expected, the major criminal enterprise for these boys was theft. This meant that Miller rejected competing gang theories that were conflict (or aggression) based and he was confident that there was a strong utilitarian motivation to the thefts reported in the neighbourhoods he studied.

It would be wrong to give the impression that Miller's 'focal concern' theory was without its critics. Charles Valentine, for instance, challenged the anthropological concept of culture and even the fieldwork behind the theory. While some criticism of the merits of the theory was deserved, much of it was not, and actually stems from reasons unrelated to actual merit: the sociological hegemony in criminology, the emerging dominance of those in American sociology who favoured an abstract-structural focus as 'proper' sociology, and the unquestioned importance of middle-class values. From the early 1920s, American sociology had fought to bring the study of crime completely under the sociological umbrella and, by the early 1950s, they had succeeded. Miller's 'outsider' status as an anthropologist was a threat to that hegemony. Moreover, Miller's ethnographic research style was more closely akin to the 'old' Chicago-School-style of sociology than the new abstract-structural sociology. The tendency was to mistake Miller's observation-based comments as abstract theoretical pronouncements with no good sociological evidence to back them up. Some even mistakenly lumped focal concern theory in with sociological culture conflict theories specifically linked to immigration – such as Cloward and Ohlin's critique in *Delinquency and Opportunity* – and others combined it with 'masculine-identity' theories. Both camps thus criticise something of a straw man. Finally, Miller had posited a perspective that, other than requiring an outside reaction, did not define behaviour in terms of middle-class values. Worse yet, from the perspective of a dominant sociology adhering to the importance of middle-class values, his observations gave credence to *a core lower-class culture as a separate and legitimate entity*. On the whole, one could hardly have committed more flagrant transgressions in 1950s' theoretical criminology. For these reasons, it is likely that Miller's theory would have passed with little further acknowledgement if not for a boost it received from the emergence of labelling and conflict theories in the 1960s as a challenge to mainstream American sociology. On its merits, focal concern theory may be challenged as having overstated the existence of a hard-core lower-class culture (which Miller put at about 15% of American society) with corresponding focal concerns. It may also be that Miller's direct observations of lower-class life in Roxbury, Massachusetts were limited in scope, or even perhaps overstated. Unfortunately, the abstract-structural dominance in American criminology resulted in the ascendance of scholars who, in Mark Hamm's words, were 'tree-top fliers' – those who fly above the trees and make observations based on what they think is under the trees. Thus, criminologists who actually went into lower-class areas and directly studied people became a rarity, making it difficult to bring pertinent evidence to bear on Miller's observations.

From 1974 to 1980, Miller directed the National Youth Gang Survey which was sponsored by the Justice Department and Harvard University. The Survey was one of the first large-scale efforts to track gang membership and migration alongside gang activity. At this point in time, shifting population trends and the changing culture and politics of the 1960s and 1970s meant that disadvantaged neighbourhoods and gang concerns were viewed as primarily African American and Hispanic 'problems'. This fact had major implications for both the way gangs were to be viewed by much of society, by criminologists and by criminal justice system agents. In 1976, Miller conducted a study of the status of gangs in 12 major cities in the United States funded by the Law Enforcement Assistance Administration. While others seemed convinced that gangs would decrease with the decline of the baby boom, Miller predicted growth in the number of youth gangs and in their increasing violence. While he never directly made a connection with the changing times, he clearly saw emerging conflict being generated by the new spreading subcultures and less focus by gangs on theft. New York was identified as the city with the most street gangs, while Detroit, Chicago, and Los Angeles were also experiencing increased levels of gang violence. Miller indicated that the level and sophistication of weaponry was increasing and he pointed out that about one half of gang members now had guns, where in the past less than ten per cent would have been armed, a fact that escalated the level of conflict. He also noted evidence that gangs were firmly entrenched in public schools, extorting money from younger, weaker youths and carrying out 'lunch money shakedowns'. Miller argued that, although most violence was gang-on-gang, there was an alarming and unprecedented trend toward attacking community residents, including younger children. He also mentioned the presence of female gangs and more violent female behaviour but cautioned that they posed far less of a threat than males. His estimates were that there were conservatively 2,700 different gangs with over 81,000 members in the six largest US cities. Police Departments, it seems, were eager to concur with Miller's findings. Most used the opportunity to point out that they were underfunded and understaffed to stem the rising tide of street violence.

Within ten years, Miller would suggest that Chicago and Los Angeles had become the points of origin of much of the new gang development in smaller cities. Graffiti and tattoo images from Vice Lords and Disciples were tracked in cities in Tennessee and Mississippi. In later interviews, he would argue that gangs were becoming more organised and that what appeared to be lulls in gang activity were instead more likely to be lulls in publicity or coverage. At this point Miller had modified his original focus on using the perspective of lower-class culture to understand behaviour to using the perspective of observers to define community gang problems. His last major report, *The Growth of Youth Gang Problems in the United States: 1970–98* (which he referred to as his 'book on crime by youth gangs') was a comprehensive chronicle of thirty years of researching the American gang. Using baseline data from some of his original studies, the report is not only a summary of Miller's changing perspective on gangs but also a documentation of the changes in larger American culture and gangs themselves. Within his lifetime, he was instrumental in moving gang research toward more sophisticated models with multi-site data collections and helping to shift the focus from understanding juveniles to understanding citizen and law enforcement perceptions of gangs and attributions of community problems related to gangs. His final major product was a document that seemed to mirror a criminologist's rather than an anthropologist's inquiry – using as the unit of analysis not the gang itself, but the location or jurisdiction reported as having a problem with gangs.

Contrary to the common stereotype of the academic, Miller was an active participant in life. He was an avid bicyclist and in-line skater, only curtailing his activity because of a concussion two years before his death. He loved to travel, which is perhaps not surprising for an anthropologist. He also played jazz trumpet, touring with the Blue Horizon Jazz Band throughout the New England area and recording several records. He used these pursuits to connect with kids in street-level interactions – a guy on skates who could blow a mean trumpet was certainly something you don't see everyday!

Major works

Miller, W. (1958) 'Lower Class Culture as a Generating Milieu of Gang Delinquency', *Journal of Social Issues*, 14(3): 5–19.
—— (2001) *The Growth of Youth Gang Problems in the United States: 1970 – 98*. Washington, DC: Office of Juvenile Justice and Delinquency Prevention.

Further reading

Miller, W. (1959a) 'Preventive Work with Street-Corner Groups: Boston Delinquency Project', *The Annals of the American Academy of Political and Social Science*, 322(March): 97–106.

—— (1959b) 'Implications of Lower Class Culture for Social Work', *Social Service Review*, 33: 219–36.

—— (1962) 'The Impact of a Total-Community Delinquency Control Project', *Social Problems*, 10: 168–91.

Miller, Walter B. (1967) 'Theft Behavior in City Gangs', in Malcolm W. Klein (ed.) *Juvenile Gangs in Context: Theory, Research and Action*. Englewood Cliffs, New Jersey: Prentice-Hall.

MARILYN D. MCSHANE AND FRANK P. WILLIAMS III

ERVING GOFFMAN (1922–82)

Anyone wishing to understand human behaviour in social situations and especially the way we 'manage' our selves in our personal and public interactions will inevitably need to engage with the work of Erving Goffman. In eleven books and numerous essays he set out a framework of 'behavioural materials' that mark him out as one of the most influential social scientists of the twentieth century.

Often regarded by his peers as a maverick, Goffman was a detached and cynical observer of social encounters, whose unique brand of sociology closely mirrored his own unwillingness to conform to social conventions and the standard 'rules' of human interaction. For example, in *Goffman Unbound!* (2006), the social theorist and former Goffman student, Thomas Scheff, documents how Goffman would not only frequently highlight behaviour that, normally, would go unnoticed or 'politely' ignored, but that he was also extremely fond of testing people in everyday conversation in order to judge their reactions. Although it was apparently possible to pass Goffman's tests by 'trading insult for insult', Scheff knew he did not have the confidence to constantly stand up to his mentor and as a consequence always felt like he was being challenged. The many accounts of Goffman's 'bizarre' interpersonal behaviour suggest he was always 'working'; a state of being that, as students, colleagues and friends have testified, was in equal parts unsettling and fascinating.

This attention to the micro detail of human practice was much apparent in his writing. Goffman was renowned for his insightful observational skills and remarkable ability to highlight taken-for-granted aspects of our everyday lives – often drawing attention to things we might prefer not to notice. In this respect, reading his work can be a rewarding, if somewhat demanding, experience. It is hardly surprising, then, that academic opinion is divided over Goffman's unconventional sociology. Sympathetic commentators maintain that his work provides an insightful and inventive vocabulary for understanding our social encounters. Critics counter that Goffman's unconventional style of analysis – involving numerous overlapping concepts and asides – is frustratingly 'unsystematic' (see e.g. Manning 1992). However one views Goffman's legacy, though, there is little doubt that he offered a distinctive analytical approach. Subsequent generations of researchers in fields such as the sociology of emotions (see Hochschild 1983) and 'performativity' (see Brissett and Edgley 1990) owe a particular debt to Goffman. Moreover, whether explicitly acknowledged or not, his insightful and sensitive work on the self, emotions, civility and resistance continues to infuse contemporary theoretical debates across the social sciences.

Erving Manual Goffman was born in Alberta, Canada on 11 June 1922. He graduated from St. John's Technical High School in Dauphin in 1939 and entered the University of Manitoba the same year to study Chemistry. Like many students, his academic interests gradually shifted and in 1943 Goffman decided to leave Manitoba and move to Toronto where he worked for the National Film Board of Canada. This was a turning point, as it was here that he met the sociologist Dennis Wrong. Wrong urged him to return to his studies but to switch to Sociology. By 1945, he had obtained the necessary credits and graduated with a BA degree from the University of Toronto. His teachers at Toronto included C.W.M. Hart and Ray Birdwhistell who first inspired him to explore the interconnections between cultural anthropology and sociology.

By the autumn of that year, Goffman had moved from Toronto and enrolled as a graduate student at the University of Chicago's famed Department of Sociology. Here he was taught by notable figures such as Everett C. Hughes and Herbert Blumer, both of whom would influence Goffman's subsequent work. After completing his M.A. thesis, Goffman upgraded to doctoral research. His original intention had been to conduct an ethnographic investigation of a farming community and he was sent by his thesis advisor W. Lloyd Warner to the Shetland Isles. Goffman's PhD research resulted in a remarkable study of the social interactions that took place between locals and visitors on the remote island of Unst. He completed his dissertation in 1953 and by 1956 his research was published as a monograph, *The Presentation of Self in Everyday Life*. This fascinating and extremely influential book became the foundation of Goffman's entire project – the sociological study of face-to-face interaction, or what he termed, the interaction order.

In 1958 Goffman moved to Berkeley to take up a new appointment as Assistant Professor in the Department of Sociology at the University of California. This turned out to be an extremely productive period in Goffman's career. The 1959 revised and expanded edition of *The Presentation of Self …* won the 1961 MacIver Award for the best book on American sociology and Goffman's reputation was sealed. This success was followed by the publication of *Asylums* (1961), *Encounters* (1961), *Behavior in Public Places* (1963) and *Stigma* (1963). Together, these five volumes consolidated Goffman's international profile, ensuring his promotion to Professor.

In 1968 Goffman accepted the Benjamin Franklin Chair in Anthropology and Sociology at the University of Pennsylvania, and by the end of the decade his success was such that he was profiled in *Time* magazine. Goffman's popularity outside the narrow confines of academia clearly failed to distract him from his research. Aside from *Interaction Ritual* (1967), published shortly before leaving Berkeley, Goffman also wrote *Strategic Interaction* (1969) and *Relations in Public* (1971), together with *Frame Analysis* (1974), which might be considered his magnum opus. Furthermore, his close contact with the Annenberg School of Communication and the Department of Linguistics at Pennsylvania inspired Goffman to incorporate new dimensions into his work. His last two books *Gender Advertisements* (1979) and *Forms of Talk* (1981) reflected his interest in gender issues and sociolinguistics, theoretical concerns that were unfortunately short-lived. Goffman died from stomach cancer in November 1982, the same year that he served as President of the American Sociological Association. By the time of his death, Goffman had become one of the most widely read sociologists of his generation.

A central theme of Goffman's sociology is how we attempt to maintain a stable self-image in the presence of others. In *The Presentation of Self …* Goffman uses the theatrical stage as a metaphor to explain the context and method of human identity construction. For Goffman, all of social life is like a play in which each of us are actors and those around us are our audience. Whenever we are with others we are 'on show' and – with differing degrees of intention and purpose – therefore, 'put on a performance'. Goffman coined the term 'dramaturgy' to describe the rule-bound active maintenance of a general consensus around how different social encounters and situations should be negotiated. Goffman saw individuals and groups as having significant opportunity to shape the impressions they convey to others, through choice of words, style of speech, mannerisms, posture, personal grooming and choice of clothing, etc. Goffman referred to this form of self-conscious presentation as 'impression management'.

Goffman's dramaturgical model has proved especially fruitful in exploring the public face of justice, through the 'staging' and enactment of trials and punishments. Law 'in action' is often highly ritualised and rule-bound, with courtrooms and trial participants all playing pre-defined roles in a production that is highly structured and controlled. In staging the trial, court staff and legal professionals seek to produce and maintain 'formality' through the use of complex and technical language, the relative placing and elevation of participants, strict control of time, and the adoption of ceremonial attire and forms of address.

Goffman makes an important distinction between what he calls the front and back regions of everyday life. The front region is a place where the performance is given and where individuals must conform to the particular roles that are expected of them. The courtroom drama is a perfect example of a social situation where we feel we have to put on a good 'show', presenting ourselves in a certain way. The back region or backstage is where we prepare ourselves, or go to relax after, or between, performances. This is also where individuals can hide from their audience and conceal aspects of their selves that may contradict or threaten their credibility. For example, an alcoholic judge would be unwise to swig from a bottle of whisky whilst presiding over a trial. This would not be an acceptable part of his professional persona and would seriously jeopardise his legal career. However, the judge may decide to have a drink in his office before the trial, away from court staff and members of the public, and then disguise his breath with strong mints to avoid suspicion. This is an extreme example, but the theatrical analogy applies to all of the social roles we are expected to play. Regardless of whether we are judges, politicians, police officers, lecturers, or students, we all develop skills of impression management to conceal aspects of our selves that are incompatible with our front-stage performances.

In *Encounters* (1961), *Behavior in Public Places* (1963), *Interaction Ritual* (1967), and *Relations in Public* (1971) Goffman turned his attention to the minutiae of human interaction between strangers in public space. Goffman used the concept of 'face work' to describe how social actors usually attempt to project an impression of themselves which has positive social value. This projection is referred to as the *face* he or she presents to the world. Criminologists have found this concept helpful in analysing the immediacies of interpersonal conflict, particularly as they involve the face-to-face negotiation of identity, through the contested accomplishment of 'reputation' and 'respect'. Paying respect to others often involves consciously avoiding the imposition of oneself, whilst not ignoring their needs and concerns. Thus, issues such as eye contact, personal hygiene, and awareness of others' personal space are intrinsic to notions of everyday civility. They become especially important in crowded and anonymous situations such as the urban 'rush hour'. For example, a current London Transport poster campaign requests that customers refrain from using noisy electronic devices and eating 'smelly food' during their journey, out of respect for fellow passengers. Inspired by Goffman and other symbolic interactionist writings, criminologist Martin Innes has coined the term 'signal disorder' to describe how certain activities, such as the public consumption of alcohol, are widely understood as threatening, being construed as a signifier of the potential for more serious problems to occur. Consumption of alcohol on the London Underground has recently been banned, presumably as a measure to assuage public fears, as much as to prevent crime.

Some of Goffman's most popular writings concerned psychiatric patients and social deviance. Through the publication of *Asylums: Essays on the Social Situation of Mental Patients and Other Inmates* (1961) and *Stigma: Notes on the Management of Spoiled Identity* (1963), his work came to be allied with the anti-psychiatry movement and labelling theories of deviance (see **Howard Becker**). A key concern was to document the processes and effects of everyday restraint upon the freedom of the individual. Goffman's thought may therefore be located within a historical moment within Western liberalism – the mid–late 1960s – in which the critique of institutionalised bureaucracy became an important cultural and political force (see **Michel Foucault**). This was reflected in the events of 1968, the Civil Rights Movement, the retreat of colonialism and anti-Vietnam War campaigns. For Goffman, social restraints may be applied by state institutions and other bureaucratic organisations, but always with a human face.

In researching *Asylums*, Goffman served as a 'visiting scientist' to the National Institute of Mental Health in Bethesda, Maryland. The inmates of St. Elizabeth's Hospital, where Goffman carried out ethnographic research, were considered by the psychiatrists to display distasteful and unusual behaviour precisely because they failed to conform to the 'normal' rules governing face-to-face interaction. However, *Asylums* offered a penetrating analysis of the way in which such 'total institutions' – which might also include educational, penal, and military establishments – actively produced and exacerbated social 'deviance' due to the bureaucratic nature of their regimes.

Once removed from everyday life and placed in a 'people-processing' institution, the inmate would experience 'civil death'. Their usual means of supporting and expressing personal identity through possessions, grooming, autonomy of movement, privacy, and so on, would greatly diminish. Institutional life would subject them to a series of 'abasements, degradations, humiliations, and profanations' that constituted a form of psychological assault. An incremental process would be set in motion, in which the inmate's previous identity was systematically 'mortified' and reconstructed in accordance with a new set of circumstances and power relations. Goffman used the concept of 'moral career' to analyse the sequence of changes in an inmate's notion of self and in his or her framework of imagery for judging self and others that this process involved.

With their 'former selves' stripped away, inmates would adopt a 'story or line' to neutralise the social stigma of their predicament. Informal norms and codes would emerge among inmates allowing access to sources of mutual support and the development of practices of resistance. Goffman showed these 'coping strategies' to involve rational adaptations to the changing circumstances of life; new routines, new pressures and concerns. Ironically, however, the strategies of resistance used by inmates to preserve a sense of their own agency were interpreted by staff as 'situational improprieties' which confirmed the institution's initial diagnosis of mental illness.

This Goffmanesque power play was perfectly captured in Ken Kesey's 1962 book (and Milos Forman's subsequent 1975 film), *One Flew Over the Cuckoo's Nest*, regarding the character Randle P. McMurphy, a misbehaving convict who shirks authority and finds himself in an asylum after faking insanity to get out of work detail in prison. Like Goffman, Kesey is careful not to present the inmates as passive; although 'the system' brings intensive pressures and disciplines to bear, individuals retain various capacities to resist and subvert the impositions of their 'carers'/captors.

Goffman's work found a receptive audience amongst prison researchers from an early stage, with essays that would later appear in *Asylums* ... being included in **Donald Cressey**'s 1961 collection, *The Prison*. Although some have questioned the degree to which Goffman may have overstated the coercive power of institutional regimes, his writings remain an essential starting point for criminologists concerned to explore the social dynamics of prison life.

Goffman's sympathetic account of the inmate world challenged his readers to consider the coercive and stigmatising effects of ostensibly caring and curative regimes. In sum, having – often forcefully – banished people from society, should we be surprised if their behaviour no longer appears 'normal'? Moreover, should we further condemn them for it? Goffman's sensitive observational skills demonstrated how our responses to 'odd' behaviour reveal a great deal about mundane interaction and the social costs of non-conformity.

Although some of the social rituals Goffman describes now appear archaic and particular to mid-twentieth-century North America, many are strikingly contemporary and universal. In revealing the rule-bound nature of human communication, both verbal and non-verbal, and its role in the construction of social success, credibility, and respect – but also stigma, embarrassment, and degradation – Goffman's observations were intriguingly perceptive and often darkly humorous. Thus, he remains a thoroughly good read; like the best drama or fiction, his work reveals, with wit and pathos, the frail artifice of identity construction and its relations to our emotional life. It is little wonder that Goffman continues to fire the criminological imagination.

Major works

Goffman, E. (1959) *The Presentation of Self in Everyday Life*. Harmondsworth: Penguin.

—— (1961) *Asylums: Essays on the Social Situation of Mental Patients and Other Inmates*. Harmondsworth: Penguin.

—— (1963) *Stigma: Notes on the Management of Spoiled Identity*. Englewood Cliffs, New Jersey: Prentice-Hall.

—— (1974) *Frame Analysis: An Essay on the Organization of Experience*. Harmondsworth: Penguin.

Further reading

Brissett, D. and Edgley, C. (eds) (1990) *Life as Theater: A Dramaturgical Sourcebook* (second edition). New York: Aldine de Gruyter.

Hochschild, A.R. (1983) *The Managed Heart: Commercialization of Human Feeling*. Berkeley, California: University of California Press.

Manning, P. (1992) *Erving Goffman and Modern Sociology*. Cambridge: Polity.

Scheff, T.J. (2006) *Goffman Unbound!: A New Paradigm for Social Science*. Boulder, Colorado: Paradigm Publishers.

Smith, G. (2006) *Erving Goffman*. Abingdon: Routledge.

PHILLIP HADFIELD AND JAMES HARDIE-BICK

GRESHAM SYKES (1922–)

Reflecting on his work towards the end of his career, Gresham Sykes described the state of criminology at the time when he was first assigned to teach it, forty years earlier. A sociologist, born in 1922 in a suburban town near New York City, Sykes had been 'appalled' to find that the textbooks of the discipline lacked material on 'basic issues such as varying conceptions of crime, how and why society defined some behaviour criminal, and the meaning of crime from the viewpoint of the offender' (Sykes 1995: 77). His subsequent contributions to criminology did much to fill some of these gaps, entailing a distinctly sociological approach to the study of prisons and delinquency, among other topics.

Sykes was a bookish child, whose father, a lawyer, encouraged his children to take a broad interest in the arts, sciences and humanities. Regular visits in his youth to the Museum of Natural History in New York led to early enthusiasms for palaeontology and both physical and cultural anthropology. Sykes began an undergraduate degree at Princeton in 1940, but dropped out after a few months and worked in the oil fields of the American Midwest for almost a year, before enlisting in the army where he served for the remainder of World War II. Sykes then resumed his Bachelor's Degree, and completed a Doctorate at Northwestern University in 1953. By this time, he had returned to Princeton to teach criminology and penology, and had begun to develop a friendship with the warden of a local prison who had invited him to bring his students into the establishment for a first-hand view of its workings.

Sykes is best known for his magisterial analysis of the social world of this prison, published as *The Society of Captives* (1958). In line with the dominant structural-functionalist approach of the period, and influenced by **Merton** and Parsons, Sykes sought to examine the prison as a self-contained social system. The point was to explore both how its constituent parts inter-related and how they contributed to the everyday functioning and stabilisation of an institution that might be expected to rise up or break down rather than persist through time. In fact, the early 1950s had seen a number of riots in American prisons, making issues of penal order especially pressing. The study was also informed by a sensitivity to the malign potential of dominative institutions. Writing in the temporal shadow of the Nazi concentration camps and Soviet labour colonies, Sykes characterised the prison as an organisation in essence concerned to exercise 'total social control'. Investigating the prison was a way of assessing the limit points and consequences of 'the new leviathan': its inherent weaknesses, its psychological effects, and the values, norms and behaviours that it allowed and promoted. Penology was at this time a rather marginal topic, located principally within social philosophy but offering an outlet for wider thinking.

By placing power at the forefront of his project, Sykes was able to move beyond existing descriptions of the everyday world of the prison towards a theory of the roots and functions of prisoner culture. His aim was to account for the roles and values of inmate society, rather than merely assume their existence and discuss the processes by which prisoners were socialised into them ('prisonisation'). Sykes thus noted the presence of a distinctive set of norms and relationships in prisoner communities across the penal system, arguing that the striking consistency of this social structure related to some essential qualities of incarceration. Influenced by work by Abraham Maslow (1947) and Bruno Bettelheim (1947), and keen to emphasise the essential painfulness of confinement, he highlighted the onslaught on the self that imprisonment entailed. Physical brutality and neglect were no longer central to penal practice, at least not officially. Yet the residual pains of imprisonment represented profound (and often unseen) threats to self-identity and psychological well-being. These pains extended far beyond the loss of liberty, comprising deprivations of security, goods and services, autonomy and heterosexual relations.

Sykes argued that these deleterious consequences of penal power provided the 'energy' for the prison social system and set the terms for social behaviour. The value system among prisoners – put simply, don't grass or interfere, stay calm, don't exploit other prisoners, don't be weak, and don't side with staff – was a problem-solving mechanism: a collective response to the intrinsic problems of the environment, enabling men in captivity to deflect moral condemnation, alleviate their fears, mitigate material scarcity and stave off the practical and psychological threats that were inherent to incarceration. Prisoners were bonded, at least partially, by their shared predicament, and almost all of them pledged public allegiance to these norms. Yet the majority of prisoners did not conform to their own stated values. (Sykes did not suggest that the prisoner community was characterised by actual solidarity, as is often claimed.) Most adopted individualistic rather than co-operative responses to their situation, exploiting scarce resources and capitalising on the needs of their peers to advance personal interests and gain influence. In this respect, all social roles within the prisoner society were structured by the rigours and limitations of the prison. Status was likewise derived from these properties, with admiration given to the few men who embodied the ideals that most prisoners breached.

These prisoner leaders – 'real men' – played a vital role in securing institutional stability. Here, Sykes put forward a theory of order that foregrounded the norms and dynamics of the prisoner society and highlighted the in-built 'defects' of 'total power'. For the almost total power that prison custodians seemed to possess was in reality highly compromised. Prisoners had little sense of duty to comply; coercive techniques were dangerous and inefficient; and punishments and incentives were weak and ineffective. Prisoners also had considerably more power over staff than at first appeared, for they could create significant problems for guards if they withheld their goodwill or labour. The result, according to Sykes, was a culture of mutual dependence and a tendency towards informal compromise between captor and captive: 'in effect, the guard buys compliance or obedience in certain areas at the cost of tolerating disobedience elsewhere' (Sykes 1958: 57).

This negotiated equilibrium functioned *through* the inmate hierarchy. By dispensing illicit privileges among the prisoner community and promoting the code of mutual aid and stoicism, inmate leaders contributed both materially and culturally to institutional order. They kept in check both the frustrations of the prisoner community and its more aggressive elements. This theorisation raised a number of ironies. First, a value system that emphasised hostility to the institution also seemed to contribute to maintaining peace. Second, disorder was likely to occur through over- rather than under-enforcement of the rules. Third, for the institution, there were dangers in challenging the prisoner power structure and eroding its stabilising effect.

The Society of Captives is widely considered the foundational text of prison sociology. This is perhaps unfair, given that Clemmer's *The Prison Community* was published almost two decades earlier and covered a range of important topics, such as friendship and social groupings, which are barely mentioned in *The Society of Captives*. That Sykes's text has been more influential reflects its theoretical coherence and originality, as well as the clarity and elegance of its writing. It established the 'deprivation' or 'indigenous' approach to the analysis of prison life (extended most famously in his colleague **Erving Goffman**'s (1961) *Asylums*, which drew explicitly on Sykes's work), which presupposed the primacy of institutional power and practices in determining the possibilities of prisoner behaviour and interaction. The prison was considered a relatively autonomous domain, cut off from the outside world, whose brutalising effects bound prisoners to a common identity, displaced their prior identities, and socialised them almost irresistibly into roles and values that would remain consistent whoever entered the milieu. Notably, Sykes had fought in World War II, and his army experiences had shaped a belief that people 'became whatever they were assigned' (1995: 78), regardless of proclivities and personalities. Later research disputed this assumption, arguing that prisoner behaviour was consistent with identities and norms that inmates 'imported' from their pre-prison lives. By the 1970s, studies showed that the prisoner social world – its hierarchies and internal relationships – was a fairly direct reflection of the social structures, values and dynamics of the criminal and street cultures of the outside community. External rivalries and sources of identity permeated the prison walls and fractured the shared identity of 'the prisoner'. More recent writings on the prison have argued that it is not only the case that prison culture is shaped by the norms of the urban ghetto, but that street culture has itself become deeply imprinted by the norms of the prison. Meanwhile, the influence of prison culture can be seen in various areas of mainstream culture, such as fashion, tattooing and music.

The Society of Captives has also been influential in the world of practice. Sykes's argument that complete enforcement of the rules was impossible in a prison, and that order relied on some degree of prisoner self-government and a *quid pro quo* compromise between officials and captives, was accepted in US prison management for many years. More recently, such claims have been challenged empirically, and the idea that the prisoner community should be enlisted in the project of institutional stability has been criticised as a reckless, illegitimate form of appeasement. In the UK, Sykes's work has been influential in informing attempts by prison administrators to use official privilege and incentive schemes to diminish the pains of imprisonment and at the same time limit the informal power structure. In return for individual compliance, the establishment provides ways of alleviating its own deprivations. Meanwhile, it reduces the need for prisoners to turn to each other to resolve or take out their frustrations via trade, coercion and fraud.

Sykes is also known for his work on delinquency, in particular the two classic articles 'Techniques of neutralization' and 'Juvenile delinquency and subterranean values', both written with **David Matza**, a student and mentee. Building on **Edwin Sutherland**'s theory of differential association, these articles took for granted that criminality was not a matter of biology or personal pathology, but had to be learnt or justified through social interaction. Both challenged notions that there existed a discrete 'delinquent subculture' and that delinquents held values that stood in clear opposition to conventional norms. 'Techniques of neutralization' argued that delinquents recognised, at least partially and theoretically, the 'moral validity of the dominant normative system' (Sykes and Matza 1957: 665). They felt guilt, they seemed to admire some law-abiding people, they did not victimise universally, and they were unlikely to be insulated from the pressures of conformist standards. Delinquency therefore required that self-disapproval and social control mechanisms were somehow 'neutralized'. The term was significant, for Sykes and Matza claimed that techniques of denial, excuse and disavowal *enabled* deviant acts rather than justified them after their occurrence (a claim that has attracted considerable criticism). These were also modes of thinking – 'no-one got hurt', 'I was protecting someone else', 'they deserved it', etc. – that were common in society at large. 'Juvenile delinquency and subterranean values' (Matza and Sykes 1961) pursued a similar point, outlining the similarities between supposedly delinquent values and those of the leisure class, and noting that thrill-seeking, machismo, disdain for work, and aspirations of conspicuous consumption were attitudes that were prized in certain circumstances across the class spectrum.

There are discernible links between Sykes's research on imprisonment and his writings on delinquency. Neither prisoners nor delinquents should be seen as a different class of person, either in terms of personality or basic moral structure. In the prison, norms were situational, a product of the demands of the environment. In the community, distinctions between the normal and the deviant were likewise a matter of context and degree. In both areas, Sykes sought to account for discrepancies between publicly expressed views and personal behaviour, and to explain how individuals negotiated social sanctions and maintained personal integrity while breaching accepted norms. In this respect, and in his discussion of the threats to identity and masculinity that imprisonment entailed, Sykes can be seen as a symbolic interactionist of sorts, working within a functionalist climate. Having worked in a post-war climate of vibrant and vigorous intellectual debate, alongside colleagues and mentors such as Sheldon Messinger, **Donald Cressey**, Aaron Cicourel, Erving Goffman and **Albert Cohen**, it is no surprise that Sykes's approach is not easy to categorise.

Inspired by George Orwell and by his own father's commitment to clarity of expression, Sykes's prose was deliberately free of jargon and academic pretension. He was un-judgmental and humanistic, keen to document the world from the perspective of the lawbreaker. As a prison researcher, he stressed the ubiquity and centrality of pain to the experience of imprisonment. But he was also an unsentimental pragmatist, who pointed out the difficulties of pursuing rehabilitative goals within an authoritarian community yet recommended trying to change the nature of the prison rather than fight fruitlessly to abolish it (for more on penal abolitionism see **Louk Hulsman** and **Nils Christie**). In his later years, reflecting on mass imprisonment in the United States, his optimism about the potential of social science to shape the terms of criminal justice appeared to have diminished considerably. As other commentators have noted (Simon 2000), shifts in political, penal and intellectual culture have made it much more difficult for researchers to produce and promote the kind of analysis for which Sykes remains known. He retired from the University of Virginia in 1987, and has worked since as an artist.

Major works

Matza, D. and Sykes, G.M. (1961) 'Juvenile Delinquency and Subterranean Values', *American Sociological Review*, 26(5): 721–19.

Sykes, G. (1958) *The Society of Captives: A Study of a Maximum-Security Prison*. Princeton, New Jersey: Princeton University Press.

Sykes, G. and Matza, D. (1957) 'Techniques of Neutralization', *American Sociological Review*, 22(December): 664–70.

Further reading

Bettelheim, B. (1947) 'Individual and Mass Behavior in Extreme Situations', in T.M. Newcomb and E.L. Hartley (eds) *Readings in Social Psychology*. New York: Henry Holt and Company.

Goffman, E. (1961) *Asylums: Essays on the Social Situation of Mental Patients and Other Inmates*. Harmondsworth: Penguin.

Maslow, A.H. (1947) 'Deprivation, Threat and Frustration', in T.M. Newcomb and E.L. Hartley (eds) *Readings in Social Psychology*. New York: Henry Holt and Company.

Simon, J. (2000) 'The "Society of Captives" in the Era of Hyper-Incarceration', *Theoretical Criminology*, 4(3): 285–308.

Sykes, G. (1995) 'The Structural-Functional Perspective on Imprisonment', in T. Blomberg and S. Cohen (eds) *Essays in Honor of Sheldon L. Messinger*. New York: Aldine de Gruyter.

BEN CREWE

LOUK HULSMAN (1923–2009)

Louk Hulsman was an internationally known penal abolitionist. In criminology, abolitionism stands for the movement of scholars and activists who reject the way social problems are approached as 'crimes' and who propose to do away with the penal system – and in some cases even with criminal justice more broadly (Van Swaaningen 1997: 116–34). Other representatives of this movement are the Norwegian scholars **Nils Christie** and **Thomas Mathiesen** and the Dutchman Herman Bianchi. In his home country, the Netherlands, Hulsman was, however, primarily known as an influential legal scholar and activist, who sat on many governmental advisory committees – he was, for example, one of the architects of the Dutch 'policy of toler-ance' towards soft drugs and a pioneer of restorative justice. In the early 1970s, he was also the driving force behind the establishment of the Dutch league of penal reform. Next to a 'public criminologist' *avant la letter*, Hulsman was also very much a teacher. In 1970, he was one of the architects of the alternative, sociologically informed curri-culum for law students at Erasmus University, Rotterdam; and in 1984, when few were contemplating the international student exchanges, he established (along with his Italian colleagues Alessandro Baratta and Massimo Pavarini) an international 'common study pro-gramme on criminal justice and critical criminology' that was based on 'a bottom up' teaching philosophy that would only become popular in the new millennium. For more than two decades after his retirement as a professor of criminal law and criminology, and right up until his death on 29 January 2009, he continued to travel the world, mainly to South America, where a revival of penal abolitionism is currently underway. In his obituary in the national newspaper *NRC Handelsblad* (3 February 2009) Hulsman was characterised as an 'anarchist who was averse to punishing'.

Hulsman was born on 8 March 1923 in the Netherlands' Catholic South, near the German border. He described his childhood in a strict Roman Catholic boarding school and his later imprisonment (and flight from) a concentration camp during World War II as determin-ing factors in his later fight against 'repressive systems'. Hulsman was arrested by the *Dutch* police for failing to fulfil his obligation to work in the German industries (the so-called *Arbeitseinsatz*). Interned in a concentration camp, Hulsman was appalled by the way the Dutch state apparatus functioned under German occupation almost as if nothing had changed. From that moment on, the State lost its moral credibility for Hulsman.

Hulsman wryly commented that his three-month imprisonment was less arduous than his years at boarding school. This may seem strange, but, as Hulsman argued, 'the political prisoner loses neither his self-respect nor the respect of his peers. He suffers in many dif-ferent ways; but he remains a man who can look the world in the eye. He is not rejected. That experience has taught me how crucial the acceptance or rejection of stigmas is in the experience of exclusion and violence' (Hulsman and Bernat de Célis 1982: 16, 25, translated by author).

After studying law in Leiden, Hulsman worked for a brief period at that university's Institute for Criminal Law and Criminology, but his career really started at the Dutch Ministry of Defence where, during a two-year stay in Paris, he was involved in the preparation of the European Defence Community. Such activities may seem out of step with his abolitionist conviction, but Hulsman maintained that his goal during this period was to make a repressive system a little less repressive. In 1955 he moved to the Dutch Ministry of Justice. Here he continued to work on international themes: he was involved in the development of the Benelux convention and later presided at the Council of Europe's Committee on Crime Problems that drew up a detailed agenda for decriminalisation (Council of Europe 1980; Blad et al. 1987: 5–6).

As an experienced civil servant he understood the realities of policy making, and took this experience with him into academia where he subsequently challenged the system's internal bureaucratic logic. This critical, yet down to earth, approach is apparent in one of his first academic publications: his inaugural lecture to the chair of criminal law and criminology at Erasmus University in 1964, *Handhaving van recht* (Enforcing law). Here he argues that criminal law is not the embodiment of a socioethical code, but *a* means of social control amongst many others – of which administrative and private law are the most closely related (Hulsman 1965). Hulsman holds a functionalist vision of criminal justice – the optimal sanction would be a minimal one. He rejects any 'metaphysical legitimation of punishment', such as retribution. The purpose of sanctioning primarily lies in the possibility of influencing undesirable behaviour. The limits of intervention are set by ethical justifications as well as by practical possibilities (Hulsman 1969).

Influenced by the spirit of the times – particularly the 'student revolution' of 1968 – Hulsman adopted a more activist approach towards the end of the 1960s. In 1969 law students from all over the country started to organise conferences that criticised the prevailing criminal justice system (CJS). These joint student initiatives led in 1971 to the establishment of the Dutch penal reform league: the Coornhert Liga (Van Swaaningen 1997: 155–63; Smits, 2008). Hulsman was one of their major sources of inspiration. According to founding student-members of the league, Hulsman had convinced a wide spectrum of scholars and practitioners that criminal justice was counter-productive. Even cabinet ministers and high civil servants were susceptible to his critique of criminal justice. While there were internal differences of opinion within the Coornhert Liga – most notably between Hulsman's abolitionist orientation and the strong focus on legal guarantees as espoused by the so-called neo-Utrecht school of Toon Peters – Hulsman claims that, when it came to the actual political work of the league, the contradictions were usually set aside. Certainly, as a former civil servant, Hulsman was skilled at working together with people whom he may have disagreed with (Smits 2008: 29).

Hulsman always stressed the high hidden crime figure of criminalisible 'events' that never reach the CJS. Whereas this is a matter of concern for many law enforcers, for Hulsman it was a cause for optimism. Since society is still not in decay, the prevalence of a high hidden crime figure implies that most problems are apparently dealt with quite effectively by informal, self-regulatory mechanisms of social control in the community. Thus, as far as crime control is concerned, criminal justice turns out to be a rather *unimportant* instrument. This belief forced Hulsman to reconsider the legitimacy of the CJS.

The development of criteria for legitimate penal intervention was the central theme of Hulsman's work during the 1970s. As absolute criteria against penalisation, Hulsman (1972) outlined the following tendencies: to a) impose moral convictions, and b) to use criminal law as a stick behind the door for social work interventions. He also rejected the legitimacy of penal intervention when c) the frequency of the acts implies that the system's capacity will be exceeded, or d) when it does not contribute to social welfare, dispute-settlement or redress. Hulsman also stressed the more relative issue about the problem of using penal or law enforcement interventions to deal with acts that are concentrated in socioeconomically deprived settings. As an implicit response to the typical Marxist position on this point, Hulsman argues that we do not need to wait for radical political reform or structural analyses of criminalisation in order to start with decriminalisation: coercion needs to be legitimised, giving up on coercion does not.

According to Hulsman, sociocultural changes should also lead to legislatory innovations; the legal concept of unlawfulness should correspond as much as possible with what society holds as undesirable. Social welfare can be advanced by the prevention of dysfunctional conflicts. This contention implies that the level of tolerance towards relatively innocent forms of deviance should be increased, that disputes over the actual content of norms and values should be possible, and that the justice system should *manage* normative conflicts rather than declaring one vision 'right' and others 'wrong'. In order to overcome the fact that criminal law lags behind with developments in society Hulsman (1967) argues for a stronger orientation at policy level – rather than legislation. In the progressive spirit of those times, Hulsman's position on this point may be understandable, but in today's so-called 'culture of control' one might *wish*, however, that the law would lag behind societal developments a bit more.

The shift from Hulsman's earlier legal work, via his influence on the Council of Europe's 1980 *Report on Decriminalisation*, to his final abolitionist perspective should be seen as a gradual one. Next to a full, *de iure* decriminalisation (taking certain acts out of the criminal code), Hulsman advocates a *de facto* decriminalisation (certain acts will formally remain illegal, but they will no longer be prosecuted). This orientation is in keeping with Hulsman's earlier argument for an expansion of the policy discretions of the prosecution. In the Council of Europe's report three rationales behind decriminalisation are distinguished:

- Type A decriminalisation means that certain behaviour is no longer considered to imply something wrong.
- Type B refers to norms that are not shared by a large proportion of the population, but it is neither considered to be a task of the state to determine right and wrong in this respect.
- Type C decriminalisation involves cases that are still considered to be wrong, undesirable or socially harmful, but there are other means of social control more effective and less stigmatising than criminal justice.

Over the years Hulsman lost faith that fundamental penal reform can be realised within the prevailing legal system. There is, however, a continuum in Hulsman's transition from lawyer to anti-lawyer. John Blad (1996) analyses the change from Hulsman's perspective of criminal justice as problem-solving institution of 1977 to his vision of criminal justice as a social problem of 1979 as follows: Hulsman's observations *as such* did not so much change, but rather the meaning he gave to these observations. He saw the CJS as more closed and autopoietic (i.e. only able to reproduce its own internal rationale) than before. His aim to achieve a fundamental change of the penal system as a means to increase social welfare necessitates a change from an internal to an external perspective. The main change lies in a transformation from a top-down to a bottom-up vision of penal reform. The stiffened penal climate of the 1980s requires a more fundamental critique. Now repressive and expansionist orientations prevail, and criminal justice policy is no longer oriented at social welfare, Hulsman concluded that the CJS exists for other than rational reasons, and therefore should be abolished. In the late 1990s, he strongly criticised the gradual transformation of the Ministry of Justice into a Ministry of (neo-conservative) norms and values and drew up an alternative value system in which Republican ideals (*egalité, fraternité, liberté*) and respect for diversity set the tone (Hulsman 1998).

Hulsman rejected the idea that crime is an ontological reality; 'crimes' only differ from non-criminalised social problems because of their labelling as such. Because 'crime' is an inadequate social construction, Hulsman (1986) advocated the decriminalisation of criminology. His abolitionism therefore does not focus on 'alternatives' at the end of the 'penal tube', but on not labelling social problems as 'crimes' in the first place. In Hulsman's abolitionism, semantic questions are important: other definitions, other categorisations can lead to other solutions. As a social and cultural organisation, criminal law is a daughter of scholasticism; it witnesses the same Manichaean vision of morality and a comparable monolithic and absolutist point of orientation, leading to one last judgement. A trial has a fundamentally non-communicative structure; it does not give an account of what has really happened, but categorises concrete experiences in standard ideological terms. In a legal procedure like tort, parties are better able to express themselves than in a criminal law suit. In Hulsman's view, the police, judiciary and probation service can in a new 'post-penal' setting perform a socially more useful role, because they can – once they are no longer hindered by the pressure of further prosecution – contribute to finding creative solutions oriented at peoples' daily life-world.

This shows the strong influence of social constructionism on Hulsman's work. Hulsman gave a rather free interpretation of Habermas' idea of the colonisation of the life-world by a system-rationality. Hulsman spoke of two different worlds: the world of systems, which is ruled by hegemonic discourse; and the informally structured life-world, which functions independently from discursive developments. The life-world's potential as a problem-solving web would, according to Hulsman, increase if it were 'freed' from bureaucratic regulations from the world of systems. Following **Michel Foucault**, Hulsman also criticised the authoritarian pretensions of so-called 'experts' in this respect (Hulsman 1989). He did not see social control as the dominion of the state – as many critical criminologists do: he rejects the top-down, repressive, punitive and inflexible character of penal control, but advocates bottom-up, integrative and informal modes of social control.

A key assumption in Hulsman's thought is that everyday phenomena would be more real than theoretical second-order constructions. In his view, the (albeit partially) structural determination of such life-world knowledge remains out of focus; the structural economical and political determination of the particular way social problems are dealt with has hardly any place in his work. It is (partly therefore) often argued that abolitionism would be a frivolous, post-modern perspective in criminology. Certainly, in respect to its rejection of the 'grand narrative' of law and its 'replacement discourse' of smaller narratives of dispute-settlement in the life-world, Hulsman was also a post-modern criminologist *avant la lettre*. He may also have been post-modern as far as his theoretical eclecticism and semantic primate was concerned. However, in his insistence on rational critiques of the penal system, he is quintessentially modern.

Ultimately, the abolitionist critique of the penal system is for many people a problematic one. Hulsman's trust in the self-regulating mechanisms at life-world level and in people's capacities to settle conflicts rationally seems in a way unrealistic. It is quite probable that people will *not* always come to an agreement on solutions and that, eventually, someone will have to be overruled. This raises the yet unanswered question of who is going to do this, according to which standards, and how a solution can be advanced without coercion. While rightly criticising the CJS's ritualistic character and punitive symbolism, Hulsman seemed to ignore the desire for public affirmation of norms a bit too easily. While it remains questionable whether people can realistically expect penal solutions to solve their concrete problems, the question as such leaves the subjective need for a public acknowledgement of their claims untouched.

Hulsman also focused on quite traditional forms of crime, with identifiable offenders and victims. In this way, he reduced social problems to individual concerns, thereby reinforcing a major analytical problem of criminal law, rather than offering any alternative to it. Another argument against abolitionism is that with the abolition of criminal law, legal safeguards against the state will decrease as well, and that the road towards increasing arbitrariness is opened because no other (legal) system has yet been designed that can potentially offer better, or indeed equal, protection. Current local security policies that permit highly intrusive interventions in people's lives without clear regulation are illustrative in this respect.

In 2009, in recognition of his many life-time achievements, Louk Hulsman was posthumously honoured with the W.A. Bonger Prize by the board of the Dutch Society of Criminology at the 50th

Anniversary of the *Dutch Journal of Criminology.* For even though Hulsman did not have all the answers to present-day problems in criminal justice, he was certainly one of the Netherlands' most creative and influential thinkers in criminology, and his intriguing questions constantly challenged the implicit criminological notions 'we' hold to be true without really knowing why.

Moreover, whilst Hulsman became far more sceptical of the possibilities to influence penal developments in any critical manner, he always remained an optimist. He maintained an unremitting enthusiasm for the world of knowledge, describing life as an ever-continuing voyage of discovery (Hulsman 1989: 127). Given the current era of managerialism combined with penal populism that voice is needed as much now as it ever was.

Major works

Hulsman, L. (1965) *Handhaving van recht.* Deventer: Kluwer.

—— (1969) 'Straftoemeting', in Enschedé, Ch.J., Hulsman, L.H.C. and Langemeijer, G.E. (eds) *Straf,* pp. 61–119. Baarn: Bosch & Keunig.

—— (1972) 'Kriteria voor strafbaarstelling', in *Strafrecht terecht? Over dekriminalisering en depenalisering.* Baarn: Anthos.

—— (1986) 'Critical Criminology and the Concept of Crime', in Herman Bianchi and René van Swaaningen (eds) *Abolitionism: Towards a Nonrepressive Approach to Crime.* Amsterdam: Free University Press

—— (1989) 'De sociale en culturele integratie van het strafrecht, de gevaren van collaboratie en literatuur als bron van verzet', *Tijdschrift voor Criminologie,* 31(2): 121–8.

—— (1998) 'Vier jaar paars in de justitiële sector: discours en praktijk', in John Blad et al. (eds) *Crimineel Jaarboek Coornhert Liga 1998.* Nijmegen: Ars Aequi Libri.

Hulsman, L. and Bernat de Célis, J. (1982) *Peines Perdues; le système penal en question.* Paris: Le Centurion.

Hulsman, L.H.C. (1967) Frustratie en justitie, in *Overheid en frustratie,* pp. 63–77. Deventer: Kluwer.

Further reading

Blad, J. (1996) *Abolitionisme als strafrechtstheorie; theoretische beschouwingen over het abolitionisme van L.H.C. Hulsman.* Arnhem: Gouda Quint.

Blad, J., Mastrigt, H. van and Uildriks, N. (eds) (1987) *The Criminal Justice System as a Social Problem: An Abolitionist Perspective; liber amicorum Louk Hulsman part I & II.* Rotterdam: Jur.Inst.EUR.

Council of Europe (1980) *Report on Decriminalisation.* Strasbourg: Council of Europe.

Smits, H. (2008) *Strafrechthervormers en hemelbestormers: opkomst en teloorgang van de Coornhert Liga*. Amsterdam: Aksant.

Swaaningen, R. van (1997) *Critical Criminology: Visions from Europe*. London: Sage.

RENÉ VAN SWAANINGEN

RICHARD CLOWARD (1926–2001)

Richard Cloward is one of the most cited criminologists and political sociologists in the world. Formerly a leading member of the Social Work faculty at Columbia University in New York City (he joined the faculty in 1954 and taught there for 47 years), Cloward is renowned for his groundbreaking work on urban delinquency, social movements and poverty. Cloward died in 2001 at the age of 74, leaving behind a rich legacy of scholarly achievement along with a life-long commitment to social and political activism (see e.g. Piven and Cloward 1977, 1988). For Cloward the development of knowledge and the struggles of society's have-nots were always intertwined. He recognised very early in his career that just being a 'desk-based' academic would not suffice. In an interview shortly before he died, he told me that, after only a couple of years as a student at Columbia in the early 1950s, 'I could see what they did. They taught and they wrote and they did research. Well, it wasn't activist enough for me' (Brotherton and Vrettos 2000).

Cloward was born on Christmas Day in Auburn, a small town in upstate New York, the son of a radical Baptist minister and a feminist/artist mother. His father, a Norman Thomas socialist, had been opposed to World War I, but like a lot of conscientious objectors was still pressed into service as an ambulance driver on the front lines in France where he was wounded. Cloward's mother, on graduating from Bucknell University, went to work in Washington, DC and 'typed the first draft of the ERA (Equal Rights Amendment) as a secretary'. At school, Cloward wanted to be an engineer but after graduating he was drafted into the US Navy at 17 years old, sent to officer cadet school at the University of Rochester, and then dispatched overseas. After two years of service he returned to the University of Rochester where he switched to Sociology, 'You could say, I suppose, that family history was asserting itself' (ibid).

Despite an indifferent relationship with undergraduate education – 'I never really went to college' he would say – Cloward was advised to pursue a PhD in Sociology. Cloward eventually finished his course-work in both Sociology and Social Work and was called up during the Korean War, becoming a first lieutenant in the US army and the director of social work (1951–54) at a medium security military prison in Pennsylvania. While there, he started to empirically test **Robert K. Merton**'s anomie theory and concluded that the great sociologist had gotten it only 'half right'. Cloward wrote to Merton, telling him that, while he had correctly explained the pressures on lower-class youth to commit delinquency, he had not accounted for either the range of delinquent subcultures available to such youth or the rationale for choosing one over the other. In other words, just as youth had different access to legitimate means to achieving mainstream goals they also had different access to illegitimate means to achieve the same goals. The key to understanding this 'choice' of the putative delinquent lay in the social context and what he later called 'the structuring variables' (Cloward 1959) (i.e. the cumulative interaction of sociological and historical forces and conditions which constitute the lived environment). Merton's response was immediate, inviting Cloward to New York for a meeting. Merton acknowledged that his theory was incomplete and could and should be developed in light of some of Cloward's insights. Cloward, looking for a subject for his dissertation, proceeded to write a study of inmate culture under Merton that became the precursor to what is still one of the staples of any criminological undergraduate course, 'the theory of differential opportunity systems' (Cloward and Ohlin 1960: x). 'Like everything else in my life,' Cloward stated, 'my introduction to criminology was serendipitous. I didn't have any interest in the subject, never thought about it'.

For most criminologists, Cloward is probably best remembered for *Delinquency and Opportunity: A Theory of Delinquent Gangs*, co-authored with Lloyd Ohlin in 1960. As suggested, the book emerged from Cloward's dissertation and combined **Emile Durkheim** and Merton's view of anomie with the insights of **Edwin Sutherland** on differential association and Henry McKay and **Clifford Shaw** on cultural deviance. Cloward's intervention was not only a major development of Mertonian sociology but with its emphasis on rational consciousness it contrasted sharply with both the more pathological readings of delinquency offered by **Albert Cohen,** and the more conservative treatment of **Walter Miller**. (For the former, delinquent behaviour had a somewhat irrational quality, as lower-class youth developed a reaction formation by expressively negating in an 'abnormal' and 'exaggerated' fashion all middle-class values. Thus delinquents eschewed values such as delayed gratification and respect for private property in response to the frustration, rejection and humiliation experienced in middle-class institutions, particularly schools. Miller meanwhile, in contrast to Cohen, saw delinquency not as the result of a conflict of class values or as a disjunction between means and ends (since lower-class youth within their subcultures had their own independent values). Instead, Miller was interested in what he called 'focal concerns' which promoted trouble, toughness, smartness, excitement, fate and autonomy.) In conventional criminology the work of Merton, Cloward and Cohen is often assembled under the umbrella term 'strain theory', that is, the lived contradictions between means (e.g. race, class and gender location) and ends (e.g. ideology) in modern 'democratic' societies and the ways youth – primarily those of the lower-class – 'adjust' to this structural blockage, often through finding 'subcultural solutions'.

This work, however, is but one small part of Cloward's contribution to the field. As noted earlier, Cloward was a scholar-activist and was uninterested in producing knowledge if it did not change the world: 'I'm a home-grown, American Populist Radical' he would say. Thus, while writing his dissertation he and Ohlin were recruited by the Henry Street Settlement on the Lower East Side of Manhattan to provide the social scientific rationale for a programme called 'Mobilization for Youth'. Together with other agency members they mapped out a 'social experiment' (Empey and Stafford 1991) to curb social problems associated with poverty in a 600-page tome entitled *Proposal for the Prevention and Control of Delinquency by Extending Opportunities*. The report emphasised the need for significant increases in public investment by improving education at all levels, expanding jobs for youth, organising the unorganised through neighbourhood associations, and providing specialised services to the marginalised, particularly those in gangs. As Cloward remembered it 'we rewrote their proposal, added a lot of social science gobbledy-gook and basically put in *Delinquency and Opportunity*'.

The proposal found enormous foundational and political support and became the basis for humanistic programmes nationwide that sought to combat delinquency and respond to the needs of lower class youth under the 'New Frontier' presidency of John F. Kennedy. In May 1962 both Cloward and Ohlin were invited to the White House (only Ohlin went) for a ceremony to launch the Mobilization for Youth programme nationwide. By 1963, the programme had morphed into one of the most ambitious US social policies of the twentieth century – the War on Poverty (later continued by the Johnson Administration after Kennedy's assassination). What explained his programme's extraordinary appeal? Cloward analysed it as follows:

The reason it got funded was Kennedy got elected. They had a problem. They got a huge Black vote and they were gonna come under increasing pressure to do things for the black community ... But in the '61–62 period they were shying away from civil rights because they didn't want to alienate the southern congressmen who chaired all the committees in Congress and who could bottle up Kennedy's legislative program.

(Brotherton and Vrettos 2000)

Despite the political support for this programme and the widespread appeal of Cloward and Ohlin's theories there was major opposition from the more conservative sector of US society, presaging perhaps the punitive turn in crime control policies that America has experienced during the last few decades. In 1964, Cloward's New York branch of the Mobilization for Youth programme became the subject of a witch-hunt and fodder for the ultra-right wing presidential campaign of Barry Goldwater. As Cloward remembers, following a muck-raking story in the *New York Daily News* alleging 'Red' infiltration of the programme 'the New York City Department of Investigations rolled trucks up to our front door with subpoenas and rolled out all our files ... Then they began calling in staff members and interrogating them' (ibid). The impact on Cloward of this red-baiting was devastating both psychologically and academically. His career at Columbia almost came to a halt as he encountered serious problems in getting tenure, especially after his former mentor, Robert Merton, refused to write a letter in his defense which would have secured his position. 'To this day I have no idea why he ditched me like that. He had been my advisor throughout my dissertation, we had had a close relationship' (ibid).

Within a few years this extraordinary 'social experiment' was ended and the brief window of opportunity to address some of the most intractable problems that come with the maldistribution of power and wealth in American society was firmly closed. Much of the critique of Cloward and Ohlin's programme was summed up in Daniel Moynihan's infamous attack on anti-poverty activism (see Moynihan 1969). Citing the problems of bureaucratic mismanagement, inter-agency competition and an unyielding academic attachment to functionalist theory, Moynihan placed the blame squarely on policies that sought to end conditions of powerlessness, much as Frederick Douglas had advocated a hundred years prior. For Moynihan, like many on the Republican and Democratic right, poverty was a consequence of cultural pathology, what became known as 'blaming the victim' – the very antithesis of Cloward's sociological and criminological worldview.

The rest of Cloward's academic life was devoted to developing his political collaboration with his partner Frances Fox Piven (see e.g. Cloward and Piven 1962, 1989 and Piven and Cloward 1971, 1977), and co-founding both the National Welfare Rights Organization in 1966 and Human SERVE (Service Employees Registration and Voter Education) in 1982. Perhaps, in his mind, he had gone as far as he could within the criminological field: 'I lost interest in criminology and I never went back to it', he said. 'The sixties started and I got interested in social movements and poverty. So what's your next question?' (Brotherton and Vrettos 2000).

Together Cloward and Piven fought both intellectually and organisationally against the rightist turn in US politics whose policies under both Democratic and Republican administrations have led to the criminalisation of vast sections of the population, exemplified today by the phenomenon of the prison-industrial complex and the 2.5 million now 'in the system'. In many respects, Cloward's views on delinquency, inseparable from his approach to both poverty and democratic politics, were victims of their own success. He believed that no social problems could be addressed without mobilising those who were most directly affected, be they gang members, tenants, the homeless, or the unemployed. Thus it was and is inevitable that the success of such a mobilisation always involves a struggle against entrenched institutional powers whose agents will never stop conspiring to restore the status quo, ensuring that the activist Cloward, despite his fame, could never be totally at home in the academy.

Major works

Cloward, R.A. (1988) *Why Americans Don't Vote: And Why Politicians Want it That Way*. New York: Beacon.

Cloward, R.A. and Ohlin, L.E. (1960) *Delinquency and Opportunity: A Theory of Delinquent Gangs*. New York: The Free Press.

Piven, Frances Fox and Richard A. Cloward (1971) *Regulating the Poor: The Functions of Public Welfare*. New York: Vintage.

—— (1977) *Poor People's Movements: Why they Succeed, How they Fail*. New York: Pantheon.

Further reading

Brotherton, D.C. and J. Vrettos (2000) Unpublished interview with Richard Cloward on 17 May 2000.

Cloward, R.A. (1959) 'The Structure of Deviant Behavior', Unpublished Manuscript, Department of Sociology. New York: Columbia University.

Cloward, R.A. and Frances Fox Piven (1962) 'The Weight of the Poor: A Strategy to End Poverty', *The Nation*, 2 May.
—— (1989) *Democracy Thwarted: The Demobilization of the American Electorate.* New York: Pantheon.
Empey, L.T. and M.C. Stafford (1991) *American Delinquency: Its Meaning and Construction* (third edition). Belmont, California: Wadsworth.
Moynihan, D. (1969) *Maximum Feasible Misunderstanding: Community Action in the War on Poverty.* New York: Free Press.

DAVID BROTHERTON

MICHEL FOUCAULT (1926–84)

Michel Foucault was a rebel with a cause. Famous for his shaved head, his open homosexuality and his rumoured experimentation with S& M practices, he was an incisive 'historian of the present' who challenged the apparent objectivity of our relationship to criminality (*Discipline and Punish*), to madness (*History of Madness, Psychiatric Power*) and to sexuality (*Abnormal, History of Sexuality*). Neither a conformist nor a revolutionary, Foucault offered – and still does – a rigorous and intelligent critical alternative to traditional left-wing perspectives. Indeed, and unlike most contemporary French intellectuals, Foucault was not satisfied with the theoretical premises of Marxism, and only joined the Communist Party briefly (1950–52), under the influence of Marxist philosopher Louis Althusser.

Beyond the cool factor of his looks and politics, the sheer range of Foucault's writings also singled him out in a country where, in the twentieth century, there was no shortage of intellectual talent. Foucault wrote on everything that interested him, not confining himself to any particular academic discipline, domain or line of enquiry. Beneath the dizzying polyvalence of his interests – Foucault wrote on literature, medicine, psychology, psychiatry, psychoanalysis, and madness, on the prison, the asylum, abnormality, perversion and sexuality, on religion, technologies of government and political economy, on ethics and politics, on method and substance, on Ancient Greece and current affairs – we perceive Foucault's formidable desire to transform completely his, and so our, understanding of the modern world. Unlike most of those inhabited with such a desire, Foucault has actually been rather successful, and in many a field of study his work has altered both the methods and the substance of the research carried out there. Criminology is one such discipline.

Foucault was born in 1926 in Poitiers in a well-to-do Catholic family, the descendant of several generations of medical doctors on both sides. Foucault's father was an eminent surgeon and professor of anatomy at the local School of Medicine – so was his mother's father. From an early age, his life bore the mark of contemporary history. In 1936 he encountered the children of Spanish refugees. From 1940 Poitiers was under the yoke of the Nazi occupation, and Foucault prepared for his entry exam to the *Ecole Normale Supérieure* under Allied bombardments. During his preparatory classes at the prestigious Henri-IV school in Paris and subsequently at the *ENS*, Foucault was taught by some of France's finest philosophers: Jean Hyppolite, Maurice Merleau-Ponty and George Canguilhem. Foucault once wrote that he 'owed everything' to Hyppolite, perhaps the most remarkable proponent of the French Hegelian tradition, in which philosophy is not dissociable from history. And Foucault's own work is something of a philosophical history. So Foucault grew up in chaotic times, an experience he structured through philosophy as the organising discourse.

As a young man Foucault also had to deal with the fact that he was a homosexual in post-war France, a moralising and puritanical environment. The question of his own madness was also very present in his early life: those who knew him at the *ENS* thought him to be 'half-mad', to have 'walked side by side with madness during his whole life'. He was very aggressive towards fellow students, deprecatingly ironic, and displayed a marked tendency toward megalomania. In addition to this asocial behaviour, one day he was found lying on the ground, having lacerated his own chest with a razor. Another time he was spotted pursuing a student with a knife in the deep of the night. When he attempted suicide in 1948, nobody was overly surprised, as many thought him to be psychologically fragile (Éribon 1991).

It is therefore probably not by coincidence that Foucault chose 'madness' as his first, and privileged, object of inquiry. After his suicide attempt Foucault developed a keen interest in psychology and psychiatry, obtaining a number of qualifications in the former (a Bachelor's Degree in 1947, and diplomas in psychopathology in 1952, and experimental psychology in 1953). Foucault also spent quite a bit of time in psychiatric hospitals, witnessing among other things the neuroleptic revolution. He also met the pioneer of existential psychology, Ludwig Binswanger, the great Swiss psychiatrist and colleague of Freud.

It is perhaps Foucault's passion for thought, nourished by numerous friendships with stimulating intellectuals (Louis Althusser, historian Paul

Veyne and sociologist Pierre Bourdieu among others) which sustained him and allowed him to get over the difficult phase which culminated in his suicide attempt. One of Foucault's biographers, Didier Éribon, notes that by 1953 Foucault seemed less fragile, and that he was able to engage in a relatively long-term relationship. For the next few years Foucault taught French literature in Sweden then Poland as he wrote his doctoral thesis (recently published in English under the title *History of Madness*). When he returned to France in 1960 to defend his thesis and to start teaching psychology at Clermont-Ferrand University, Foucault met his life-long partner, Daniel Defert. After a couple of years spent teaching philosophy in Tunisia and then at Vincennes – the experimental university born out of the May 1968 revolution – Foucault succeeded in being appointed at France's most prestigious institution, the *Collège de France*, in 1970. Foucault taught there until his death, each year introducing his audience – the *Collège's* lectures are open to the public – to whatever theme occupied his personal research at the time. Alongside the public lectures, he also convened a series of smaller more intimate seminars with prominent intellectuals, including Colin Gordon, Pasquale Pasquino, Jacques Donzelot and Robert Castel, all of whom have gone on to influence criminology (see Burchell et al. 1991).

From the 1970s Foucault was very active politically. His reputation was growing fast and he was invited to speak all over the world. He was also very militant. Thus in February 1971, on Defert's suggestion, Foucault announced the creation of the *Groupement d'Information sur les Prisons*. The main objective of the GIP was to give a voice to prisoners so they could speak of their experience and formulate complaints about their conditions of detention. The GIP was soon dissolved to give way to structures entirely controlled by inmates. Foucault also intervened repeatedly against the irregularities committed by the government in the name of security, publicly denouncing the violence and injustice perpetrated against Algerians, journalists, political militants and terrorists. He also spoke for the right to abortion, took a position against the death penalty on several occasions and pleaded the cause of the Vietnamese boat-people. Finally, Foucault visited Iran just before the 1979 revolution (which resulted in the overthrowing of the Shah) and wrote passionately on the uprising of the Iranian people, enthused by this example of resistance to oppression. Despite his support for all forms of resistance to power, Foucault's political actions always took place within the confines of legality and he never supported terrorism as a legitimate mode of political action. Some have even suggested that there lies the cause of his falling out with Gilles Deleuze, who was more inclined to support direct action such as terrorism (Éribon 1991).

In the last few years of his life, Foucault proposed the ethics of the self as the true source of political resistance, and turned his ever-inquisitive mind to the question of how, in the Western tradition, we become subjects. Foucault notably looked to the Ancient Greek tradition of ascetics. He died young, of AIDS, in a Paris hospital in 1984, after a relatively short but extremely influential life.

As must be obvious by now, Foucault's work eschews the traditional boundaries of academic disciplines: drawing from philosophy, historiography and social sciences, his written work is a series of radical analyses of the fabric of our present, exposing the omnipresence of power in all social situations. One thing, however, is certain: Foucault was never a criminologist, yet these days it is hardly possible to open a criminology book without encountering his name.

If Foucault has become a key reference in criminology, it is for three main reasons. First, Foucault showed an unwavering interest in the power exercised over individuals through specific institutions rather than by the State. It is in this respect that he departed from the classic Marxist critique of political power that prevailed at the time. His study of the power exercised through institutions resulted in histories of the psychiatric hospital and of the prison, two areas of paramount importance to criminology. In these analyses Foucault demonstrates that there can be no power without knowledge. To put it simply, if a psychiatrist exercises power over a patient (to section, prescribe treatment, etc.) it is because the psychiatrist possesses a knowledge of 'mental illness'. The radical element in Foucault's intervention consists in arguing that 'mental illness' is not a given, a natural object. What we mean by 'mental illness' changes over time, according to the shifts in discourses contributing to the definition of mental illness: medicine, psychiatry, criminology, forensic science, etc. The study of these shifts is therefore crucial to any analysis of the social, since the latter is *discursively constructed*.

Foucault's analyses of these institutions also contributed to demonstrating that power is distinct from violence: '[...] what defines a relationship of power is that it is a mode of action which does not act directly and immediately on others. Instead it acts upon their actions: an action upon an action, on existing actions or on those which may arise in the present or the future' (Foucault 1982b: 220). Ultimately, Foucault will conclude that strategies of power are historically contingent ways of 'conducting the conduct' of populations, and will seek to characterise the strategies of governance that were successively employed in the West.

Foucault's second contribution to criminology is methodological. His intellectual formation occurred at a time when France was basically split into two main traditions: Marxism and phenomenology. Broadly speaking, Foucault found both approaches problematic: for him, there is neither an a-temporal object (e.g. the insane) to be known by a historicised subject (e.g. the subject of capitalism), as in Marxism; nor an a-temporal subject knowing a historicised object, as in phenomenology. Neither objects nor subjects stand outside history. Take the human body of today's medicine: it bears little relation to the human body of nineteenth-century doctors. What we know of something, and how we conceptualise it, is always an interpretation: things have no essence.

If things have no essence, it means that the subject (e.g. the criminologist), the object (e.g. the high-rate offender) and the field of discursive and non-discursive practices (e.g. criminal justice discourses and technologies of power, such as risk-assessment methods, selective incapacitation or imprisonment) are co-emergent. Since object, subject and practice are co-emergent, Foucault suggests we analyse their relations in order to identify the logic at play in a given domain. Further, because it is impossible to think objectively about something (e.g. we can't think of a criminal justice system where the prison is not the staple of punishment because we are co-emergent with what Foucault calls a 'penality of detention'), Foucault proposes we think about it *historically*: how did an institution come about? What were its conditions of possibility? What kinds of discourses were prevalent at the time? What technologies of power were available?

Foucault calls his method 'genealogy', after the philosopher Friedrich Nietzsche. The genealogical method requires a micro-analysis of the archival minutiae pertaining to the birth of an institution or a practice in order to reveal the contingent character of what may seem a natural feature of our present. Whereas classic history sets out to explain the past from the vantage point of the present, a genealogical analysis will demonstrate that the present came about more or less haphazardly, through a conjunction of circumstantial factors which, taken together, constitute its conditions of possibility.

Strategically, what is the point of writing a genealogy? A 'history of the present' of institutions such as the prison (or practices of video surveillance, restorative justice, etc.) demonstrates that the institution under scrutiny is not a necessary part of the criminal justice system, since its emergence is conjunctural. In the words of **David Garland**, 'the point of his history is to cast light on a contemporary issue or institution by investigating those historical conditions that brought it about' in order to 'problematize and destabilize the present' (Garland 1986: 851). For example, Foucault's analysis of the birth of the prison in *Discipline and Punish* picks up, among other things, on the fact that we have only been using imprisonment as a sentence in itself since the turn of the eighteenth century. This observation leads Foucault to wonder what the conditions of possibility for the birth of the prison were, and so to elicit affinities between a 'penality of detention' and contemporary strategies of power.

Thirdly, Foucault progressively constructed a threefold periodisation of the strategies of government adopted in the West in the course of history. This characterisation is very useful to isolate paradigmatic shifts in criminal law. These three rationalities of power are *sovereign, disciplinary* and *biopolitical*. In the *sovereign* rationality the medium of power is law, which applies to the subject. Transgression is prohibited, and punishment is of the order of a 'deduction': 'a subtraction mechanism, a right to appropriate a portion of the wealth, a tax of products, goods and services, labour and blood, levied on the subjects' (Foucault 1978: 136). Classic criminal law (as defined by, for example **Cesare Beccaria**) fits with this rationality of power. In the *disciplinary* rationality the medium of power is the norm and power is applied to individualised bodies. Institutions seek to normalise individuals through spatial-temporal arrangements such as exhaustive timetabling, solitary confinement, etc. Penal welfarism, which seeks to rehabilitate and therefore normalise offenders, can be seen as an emanation of disciplinary power. In the *biopolitical* rationality power is implemented via regulations and security mechanisms aiming to manage populations by acting on statistically configured trends. The main objective of government is actuarial. Contemporary strategies of risk management come to mind, with the offender defined in terms of the risks he poses to society, for example, as a high-rate or high-risk offender – a statistical being. These three rationalities are not mutually exclusive of one another, though today the biopolitical rationality prevails.

Foucault's later work on biopolitics gave rise to 'governmentality studies', an intellectual movement regrouping criminologists, sociologists, economists and political scientists (see Burchell et al. 1991). This movement focuses on practices of government in liberal societies, building on Foucault's (2007) idea that liberalism operates through the tension introduced by the paradoxical yet paradigmatic demand for liberty and security. In other words, populations are free to govern themselves as they see fit, though security mechanisms (such as health and safety measures, for example) will be in place to prevent identifiable risks from materialising. Foucault's analysis of the different modes of governance helps us to understand the risk-management practices of criminal justice as the corollary to liberalism as a mode of government. Conversely, however, the minute analysis of a given technology of power, and of the discourses associated with it, exposes the logic of government – as 'conduct of conducts', and so of the way in which populations are governed – in operation at a given time in its purest, or to use a Foucauldian expression, *diagrammatic* form.

Foucault's life may have been short, it may have been spent in the shadow of madness, but his unique vision has irretrievably transformed ours. After Foucault, it is clear that true political resistance can only occur against the very grain of what we believe to be natural or take to be true.

Major works

Foucault, M. (1970) *The Order of Things*. New York: Pantheon.
—— (1972) *The Archaeology of Knowledge*. London: Tavistock.
—— (1973) *Madness and Civilization*. New York: Vintage.
—— (1977) *Discipline and Punish: The Birth of the Prison*. London: Penguin.
—— (1978) *The History of Sexuality vol. 1*. London: Penguin.
—— (1982a) *I, Pierre Rivière, Having Slaughtered My Mother, My Sister and My Brother ... a Case of Parricide in the 19th Century*. Lincoln, Nebraska: University of Nebraska Press.
—— (1982b) 'The Subject and Power', in A. Dreyfus and P. Rabinow (eds) *Michel Foucault: Beyond Structuralism and Hermeneutics*. Chicago, Illinois: Chicago University Press.
—— (1988) *Power/Knowledge: Selected Interviews and Other Writings 1972–77*. New York: Random House.
—— (2003) *Abnormal*. London: Verso.
—— (2006a) *Psychiatric Power*. New York: Palgrave.
—— (2006b) *History of Madness*. London: Routledge.
—— (2007) *Security, Territory, Population: Lectures at the Collège de France 1977–1978*. New York: Palgrave.

Further reading

Burchell, G., Gordon, C. and Miller, P. (eds) (1991) *The Foucault Effect*. Hemel Hempstead: Harvester Wheatsheaf.
Éribon, D. (1991) *Michel Foucault*. Cambridge, Massachusetts: Harvard University Press.
Garland, D. (1986) 'Foucault's *Discipline and Punish*: An Exposition and Critique', *American Bar Foundation Research Journal*, 847–80.
Macey, D. (1993) *The Lives of Michel Foucault*. London: Hutchinson.

VÉRONIQUE VORUZ

JULIA SCHWENDINGER (1926–) AND HERMAN SCHWENDINGER (1926–)

Partners in scholarship and marriage for over five decades, Julia and Herman Schwendinger have coauthored numerous publications that have significantly shaped contemporary critical theory and practice in sociology, social work, criminology, criminal justice, and gender studies. Their critical works on adolescent subcultures and delinquency, crimes against women, and crimes against humanity have garnered recognition from the American Sociological Association, the Society for the Study of Social Problems in the United States, the Western Society of Criminology, and from the Women's and Critical Divisions of the American Society of Criminology. At the core of their legacy is the call for a humanistic definition of crime, a call that revitalised earlier debates by **Thorsten Sellin**, Paul Tappan and **Edwin Sutherland** over the relationships among criminology, law and the State. In perhaps their best-known article, 'Defenders of Order or Guardians of Human Rights?' (1970), the Schwendingers' close analysis of state crimes against humanity yields a scathing critique of the prevailing legalistic definition of crime. Rather than proposing a corrective definition, however, the Schwendingers sought to provide 'useful points of departure' from which to explore alternative definitions of crime and their implications for social justice. Their mutual commitment to this endeavour resonates throughout their ongoing collaborative and individual contributions.

A native of Rockaway Beach, New York, Julia Schwendinger has applied her academic training to community service in a number of creative ways. Her credentials include a BA in Sociology (Queen's College, 1947), an MS in Social Work (Columbia University, 1950), and a Doctorate in Criminology (University of California, Berkeley, 1975). Listed in *Who's Who of American Women,* she co-found the first anti-rape crisis group in the United States in the early 1970s. She has also served as a Deputy Parole Commissioner and Director of the Women's Resource Center for San Francisco Jails, and as a private investigator and pre-sentencing consultant. Her early experience as a social worker serving teenagers in low-income neighbourhoods combined with Herman's social work with street gangs – as well as his personal background – to inform their ethnographic research from the 1960s onward.

Growing up in a poor, rough area of New York City profoundly influenced the trajectory of Herman Schwendinger's academic career. He holds a BS in Psychology (College of the City of New York,

1948), an MS in Social Work (Columbia University, 1957), and a PhD in Sociology (University of California, Los Angeles, 1963); but he traces his appreciation for the importance of research methodology to his Science and Engineering studies at Stuyvesant High School in the late 1940s. By the time he engaged in fieldwork as a Psychology student, he already understood the limitations of conventional survey and interview methods. For deeper, more nuanced analyses, his innovative research strategies also employed field observations and small-group experiments, as well as sociometric and various other social-psychological procedures. For his doctoral research on gangs, Herman developed methods for quantifying subcultural identities and tools for 'mapping' complex networks among thousands of youths; with the subsequent sophistication and accessibility of computers, such techniques would become commonplace in mainstream social sciences. For his many outstanding contributions through the years, Herman has been widely honored; he was elected to the New York Academy of Sciences, for example, and was granted the prestigious State University of New York Excellence Award.

Of their many collaborative efforts – aside from raising their daughter Leni and son Joseph – the Schwendingers fondly remember their participant-observer research on youth subcultures in the mid-1960s as particularly gratifying. An extension of Herman's doctoral research, this study redressed the failure of prevailing theories of juvenile delinquency to account for its incidence in middle-class populations, as well as in the lower classes. Instead of categorising their subjects in terms of socioeconomic status, the Schwendingers identified them as members of distinct peer groups, that is, intellectuals, greasers, jocks, homeboys and preppies, that cut across class distinctions. Whereas conventional delinquency researchers focused on personality disorders and social control, the Schwendingers opened up the field of inquiry to include the wide variety of adolescent social identities and dynamic peer networks generated by the uniquely American system of advanced consumer capitalism. After pondering delinquency from the inside out, so to speak, for two decades, they published their groundbreaking findings in *Adolescent Subcultures and Delinquency* (1984).

Similarly, in *Rape and Inequality* (1983), a project stemming from Julia's doctoral research, the Schwendingers demonstrate that the incidence of violence against women corresponds with the degree of sexual inequality in a given social context; furthermore, they indict corporate capitalism in the United States for its devastating toll in this regard. Indeed, the mode of production's centrality to the social construction of virtually all cultural phenomena – even Sociology itself – has been an overriding theme of the Schwendingers' scholarship since 1974, when they published *The Sociologists of the Chair: A Radical Analysis of the Formative Years of North American Sociology (1883–1922)*. Bringing radical insight to the early history of the discipline, they explain how it developed in response to shifting socioeconomic conditions and their ideological implications, rather than according to romantic notions about Sociology's liberating force. Moreover, they demonstrate that elements of liberal reformism and state instrumentalism still persist in contemporary Sociology/Criminology.

Decidedly 'out of the armchair', the Schwendingers have held research and teaching appointments at several academic institutions in the United States and abroad – despite Herman having been blacklisted for two years along the way. Currently affiliated with the Department of Criminology at the University of South Florida, they once jointly directed a half-million-dollar field study on adolescent subcultures in Los Angeles in the mid-1960s, and later worked as Research Associates at the Institute for the Study of Social Change at the University of California, Berkeley. Both have taught at the State University of New York, New Paltz – from which Herman retired in 1999 as a Professor Emeritus – and as exchange scholars in Berlin, St Petersburg and Moscow. In addition, Julia has taught at Vassar and at the University of Nevada, Las Vegas. Herman has also taught at the University of California, Berkeley, where he was denied tenure in the School of Criminology and subsequently blacklisted for his Marxist orientation. During events leading up to his departure, Herman emerged as a key strategist in efforts to prevent the elimination of the newly radicalised School itself.

When Herman assumed his teaching position at Berkeley in 1967, varied civil rights demonstrations and anti-Vietnam War protests were energising and enlightening students and faculty on campuses across the nation. As long-held cultural assumptions and values were increasingly called into question, disciplinary conventions and traditional hierarchies within the Academy were challenged by a growing number of New Left scholars. The resulting reactionary purge of radical professors took a high toll across the Berkeley campus; and the School of Criminology was no exception. The School had a four-decade tradition of community service; but when activist Criminology students and faculty took up such controversial causes as prisoners' rights, for example, and the Black Panther Party's campaign for community-based policing, worried University officials took notice.

By the early 1970s, with Herman Schwendinger, Paul Takagi and Anthony Platt in residence, the Berkeley School of Criminology was home to *the* west coast enclave of radical criminology. The Union of Radical Criminologists, a faculty-student organisation, was formed to address various campus and community issues. In this context, Herman became known as savvy political advisor, as well as a brilliant scholar and gifted teacher; Julia distinguished herself as 'a player' among the graduate students. As the number of Left-leaning professors in other departments dwindled, students who hungered for courses taught from a critical perspective somehow found their way to Criminology – an unlikely port in the political storm, considering its popular association with law enforcement and the students' general disdain for police. Yet in the fall of 1972, no fewer than a thousand students sought enrolments in an introductory Criminology course taught by Takagi, Platt and Barry Krisberg from the humanist perspective they shared with the Schwendingers.

Meanwhile, the more conservative criminologists were finding it difficult to fill their classes; many grew envious and resentful of the 'celebrity radicals'. At the same time, pressure was exerted from above to restore conservative control of the School; when efforts to that end failed, University Regents embarked on a strategy to close the School permanently. Despite unanimous faculty support, Platt was denied tenure in 1974; the following year, Herman suffered a similar fate. Takagi, who was already tenured, was relegated to a non-teaching desk job. Notwithstanding the rousing, well-organised protests of faculty and students alike, the Berkeley School of Criminology offered its final class in 1976. Radical criminologists might liken Herman to a heroic martyr for academic freedom; but having been callously mischaracterised as a reckless, Left-wing agitator, he would be unable to secure a teaching appointment for the next two years.

The feisty Schwendingers came through that crisis with their professional and personal lives intact, however, and are currently revisiting their Berkeley years in their second eBook, entitled *Who Killed the School of Criminology? Round Up the Usual Suspects!* Their first eBook, *Big Brother is Looking at You, Kid! Is Homeland Fascism Possible?* (2008), is already available online for free (see www.homelandfascism101.com). In it they examine the insidious rise of Neo-Fascism since 9/11, and expose the structural forces behind the US government's criminal abuse of civil and human rights in the name of national security. These welcome contributions are unlikely to be their last, given the Schwendingers' apparently boundless intellectual curiosity and abiding commitment to the struggle for social transformation. Pioneers of radical criminology in America, Julia and Herman Schwendinger continue to enrich its field of knowledge and invigorate its driving spirit.

Major works

Schwendinger, H. and Schwendinger, J. (1970) 'Defenders of Order or Guardians of Human Rights?' *Issues in Criminology*, 5: 123–57.

—— (1974) *The Sociologists of the Chair: A Radical Analysis of the Formative Years of North American Sociology (1883–1922)*. New York: Basic Books.

—— (1985) *Adolescent Subcultures and Delinquency*. New York: Praeger.

Schwendinger, J. and Schwendinger, H. (1983) *Rape and Inequality*. Beverly Hills, California: Sage.

Further reading

Crime and Social Justice Collective (1976) 'Editorial: Berkeley's School of Criminology, 1950–76', *Crime and Social Justice*, 6: 1–3.

Henry, S. and Lanier, M. (eds) (2000) Introduction to 'Defenders of Order and Guardians of Human Rights', in *What is Crime?: Controversy Over the Nature of Crime and What to Do About It*. Boulder, Colorado: Rowman and Littlefield.

GREGG BARAK AND CHARLOTTE PAGNI

HOWARD BECKER (1928–)

Howard Becker, a reluctant giant of criminology, is principally associated with the labelling perspective of deviance, and in particular the 'moral entrepreneurs' who seek to construct certain groups' behaviours as deviant or criminal. Despite the fact that Becker at no point viewed himself as a criminologist, his classic work, *Outsiders: Studies in the Sociology of Deviance* (1963) revolutionised criminological thinking about the processes and practices of deviant behaviour, and changed forever the way many critical criminologists went about researching and understanding crime.

Becker was born in Chicago, Illinois on 18 April 1928. His mother was a homemaker, his father a partner in a three-person advertising firm specialising in copywriting. From a very early age, Howie Becker was fascinated by the heterogeneous social worlds that characterised his native Chicago. With packed lunches in hand, Howie and his school friends would ride the El (elevated transit system) to all corners of the city. They never grew tired of their explorations, taking great delight in unearthing clues about the lives of the disparate Chicagoans they observed. Reflecting on this period Becker commented: 'What did we see? We saw people of different racial and ethnic groups as they got on and off the train, and learned who lived where [and] we were very good at reading ethnicity from small clues, including listening to the languages spoken, styles of clothing, even the smell of the food people carried' (see www.home.earthlink.net/~hsbecker/).

This was in the late 1930s and early 1940s, when racial segregation in the United States was still legal, and anti-Semitism in some neighbourhoods was rampant. If ever there was a time when it would have been safer to reside in your own neighbourhood and associate with your own kind, it was then – but Becker had other plans.

As he grew older his love of piano and jazz enabled him to discover even more of the city. When he was 14 or 15 he started playing piano in various bands that played the high school dances, parties and Bar Mitzvahs around Chicago. As his playing improved, he eventually became a professional musician, playing jazz and other types of dance music in taverns, bars and strip clubs. In his 20s and throughout his graduate training, Becker hung out with a bunch of hepcats that played jazz when they could, and what they called 'commercial music' for less refined audiences when they had to. He never met jazz legends like Monk, Miles or Bird, but he did run with a few famous musicians, including his music teacher, Lennie Tristano, an innovator in improvisational style; Leo Konitz, an alto-sax man who played on Miles Davis's classic album, *The Birth of Cool*; and Junior Mance, who played piano with greats like Charlie Parker and Lester Young.

In 1949, on the advice of his father, Becker entered graduate school at the illustrious Sociology Department, University of Chicago. He was soon captivated by the tradition of interactionism, bequeathed to him by his Chicago School teachers, Ernest Burgess, Herbert Blumer and his mentor, C. Everett Hughes. It was this largely ethnographic training that further sharpened his observation of complex social worlds.

During the late 1940s and early 1950s Becker spent his nights playing piano in bars and dance clubs, often until three or four in the morning. For many young scholars, this would have been something of a distraction, but for Becker it was an inspiration. In the same year he completed his PhD dissertation on Chicago schoolteachers, he also published his first article on a subject much closer to his heart – music. His article 'The Professional Dance Musician and His Audience' appeared in the September, 1951 issue of the *American Journal of Sociology*. Howard Becker was just 23 years old.

As rock music eclipsed jazz, and television sets replaced live music in bars and clubs, Becker found fewer opportunities to play out. Instead, he channeled his energy into his sociology. However, his experiences as a jazz musician would greatly influence the rest of his career, shaping his subsequent thinking on the learned activity of marijuana use, the social construction of deviance, and latterly the sociology of art and performance. While Becker's research interests have always been creditably broad (see also Becker 1961), few would argue that his influence has been greatest within the sociology of deviance. Becker came to understand that deviance was a matter of interpretation and degree. For example, among his jazz peers, marijuana was an enjoyable, socially acceptable experience. This, of course, sharply contradicted the standard view held in 1960s American society where it was commonly believed that reefer induced 'madness' and other forms of mental trauma. It was this type of disjuncture – married with his former tutor Everett Hughes' insistence that, 'everything is somebody's work' – that led Becker to focus his criminological lens not simply on the actors themselves but on all the parties involved in the process of defining deviance. As Becker himself told me: 'I just knew, from the places I'd worked and the people I'd known, that conventional theories of deviance were nonsense and based on insufficient knowledge of what was going on, especially with respect to the generation of the sources of the data criminologists and mental health experts used to evaluate their theories' (personal communication 2008).

In his 1963 book *Outsiders*, Becker focused on the culture of deviant groups rather than attempting to explain why certain individuals deviate from the norms of the larger society. Importantly, he suggested that behaviour does not necessarily have to be criminal to be labelled deviant or delinquent. His study of jazz musicians is a case in point. He writes: 'Though their activities are formally within the law, their culture and way of life are sufficiently bizarre and unconventional for them to be labeled as outsiders by more conventional members of the community' (1963: 79).

One of the most significant aspects of Becker's work is the idea that deviance is not a quality of the act itself but rather a function of being labelled as such. As he famously stated: 'The deviant is one to whom that label has been successfully applied; deviant behavior is behavior that people so label' (1963: 9). This means that no behaviours are intrinsically deviant.

It is this aspect of the labelling theory that troubles many social scientists, primarily because it fails to provide a causal explanation as to why people actually engage in deviant activity (i.e. structural factors, individual psychosis, improper socialisation, etc.) – or even what constitutes deviance per se. Rather, labelling theory explains a process whereby the behaviours of certain groups are labelled deviant, and those deviants are then treated as outsiders.

Becker's labelling theory does not apply to specific cultural forms; it cannot, for example, explain why some use drugs while others gamble or illegally race cars. Although he is often misunderstood, Becker does not believe that being labelled an outsider causes one to engage in deviant activity. We are all engaged in various conformist and non-conformist behaviour, and some groups' non-conformity, like smoking marijuana, is labelled deviant, whilst other activities, like drinking martinis at a business luncheon, are not.

Augmenting earlier labelling perspective studies (see **Edwin Lemert**), Becker's legacy within criminology is closely associated with the particular concept of the 'moral entrepreneur'. Becker coined this term to refer to those groups of people involved in creating and enforcing society's rules. He writes: 'Rules are the products of someone's initiative and we can think of the people who exhibit such enterprise as *moral entrepreneurs*' (1963: 147). Here Becker is describing the type of crusading reformer who feels that the existing rules of society have failed to address some pressing evil. Becker shows that social, political and economic power is the key to understanding which social groups are likely to engage in moral entrepreneurship and which groups are more likely to have their behaviours constructed as deviant. There are people who construct certain behaviours, like listening to rock music, or dating someone of a different race, as deviant evils that must be rooted out to cleanse society, yet it should also be noted that these entrepreneurs frequently profit from their campaigns. The careers of Tipper Gore of the Parents Music Resource Center, and The Reverend Calvin Butts, are but two examples of moralising figures who came to national prominence in the United States in early 1990s through their efforts to defend American youth from what they believed were satanic and violent lyrics in rock and rap music.

The idea of the moral entrepreneur greatly influenced British scholars like **Stanley Cohen**, **Stuart Hall**, and Tony Jefferson, and later provided one of the key foundations for cultural criminology. Today, 'Broken Windows' and 'Quality of Life' campaigns are the rhetorical strategies used by modern moral entrepreneurs to create public approval to utilise resources against those who are unable to defend themselves, most often, the young, the poor and people of colour.

While Becker has been criticised for failing to address the root causes, structural inadequacies, and individual forms of psychosis that produce deviance, he has articulated a set of social processes that we continue to see repeated in the criminal justice system today. Becker reminds us that the relationship between the rule makers and the rule breakers is far more complicated and symbiotic than most conventional thinkers would like to believe. For some, this idea that anything and nothing can be deviant is all too relativistic, perhaps even Zen – if a deviant commits a crime in the forest and no one is around to witness it, is it really deviant? But for those who are interested in understanding the sociology of deviance, and especially the way that crime is socially constructed within society, it is essential.

While Becker is important for his ideas, much of his legacy and continued appeal to students stems from his refreshingly clear approach to writing. Even forty-plus years after its publication, students are still attracted to *Outsiders* for its refreshing refusal to replicate abstruse academic language. Whether writing about marijuana use, the practice of ethnography, or performance art, Becker is able to express complex ideas with simple, lucid prose. For example, he opens *Outsiders* with this line, 'All social groups make rules and attempt at some times, and under some circumstances to enforce them.' He then goes on to say that people who consistently break the rules come to be known as 'outsiders' (1963: 1).

Becker, like a lot of researchers today, is very suspicious of how much of the data surrounding crime and criminality are produced and disseminated. He feels, rightly, that this in part stems from an increasing reluctance to study the everyday lives of deviant and criminal subcultures. Lots of crime theorisation comes instead from faulty statistics, recycled surveys, or data gained in jailhouse confessions or from trusted police informants. As a result it is frequently skewed or corrupted. In contrast, Becker insists that in order to understand deviant/criminal social groups you have to spend some time with them: 'The researcher, therefore, must participate intensively and continuously with the deviants he wants to study so that they will get to know him well enough to be able to make some assessment of whether his activities will adversely affect theirs' (1963: 168).

This is one of the enduring lessons of Becker's work that is currently being encouraged in various social science disciplines, including the emerging field of cultural criminology. Methodologically, some cultural criminologists believe that, in order to fully understand the production of certain forms of criminal activity, it is necessary to actually participate in criminal subcultures – a process that, on occasion, may even include law breaking itself. Cultural criminologists, therefore, not only recognise that moral entrepreneurs exist, but seek to expose the politics of crime and the mediated practices and techniques of anti-crime campaigns, by participating in the everyday life worlds of criminal subcultures.

The rest of Becker's illustrious career, which thankfully is still unfolding, would focus on the collective process of art making (Becker

1982) in addition to the books he wrote for graduate students on writing and thinking about social science (Becker 1998). It is interesting to note that, aside from a pair of articles on the way people get clues about the internal experience of drugs from social cues, Becker only returned to the topic of deviance once more in his career, and that was to address his critics in the second edition of *Outsiders*. In 'Labeling Theory Revisited' Becker accepts some criticisms, notably that his idea of 'secret deviance' is contradictory to the notion of constructed deviance, but in all he makes a cogent defense of his understanding of deviance as social process rather than individual practice.

For these reasons, as well as for his considerable personal charms as a teacher and as a lecturer, Howard Becker is essential, not only for students of interactionist sociology and criminology, but for those interested in deep thinking and the pursuit of anti-pretentious intellectualism in general.

Major works

Becker, H. (1961) *Boys in White: Student Culture in Medical School*. New York: Macmillan.
—— (1963) *Outsiders: Studies in the Sociology of Deviance*. New York: The Free Press.
—— (1973) 'Consciousness, Power and Drug Effects', *Society*, 10(May): 26–31.
—— (1982) *Art Worlds*. Berkeley and Los Angeles, California: University of California Press.
—— (1998) *Tricks of the Trade: How to Think About Your Research While You're Doing It*. Chicago, Illinois: University of Chicago Press.
—— (2007) *Telling About Society*. Chicago, Illinois: University of Chicago Press.

Further reading

Debro, J. (1970) 'Dialogue with Howard S. Becker', *Issues in Criminology*, 5 (Summer): 159–79.
Plummer, K. 'Continuity and Change in Howard S. Becker's Work', *Sociological Perspectives*, 46: 21–39.

GREGORY J. SNYDER

NILS CHRISTIE (1928–)

Nils Christie's work represents a constant reminder of the visionary potential of criminology. His ideas have left a lasting mark on criminological scholarship and find an echo in numerous contemporary criminological perspectives, from the burgeoning field of restorative justice, studies of penal punitiveness and commercial security, to comparative criminology and penal philosophy.

By his own account, Christie did not enjoy school. In fact, whilst, he saw the onset of World War II as tragic, he also viewed it as a welcome break from the exams and tedious routines of his school years. Decades later, this uneasy relationship with the institution of the school resulted in Christie's 1971 Norwegian publication *If School Did Not Exist*, which argues that the primary function of the school was to keep young people away from the lives of adults (a characteristic which they also happen to share with prisons).

Despite this somewhat bumpy start, Christie's educational career thrived when he entered university. At the time, he saw the university as a space of freedom compared to the over-regulated, exam-driven school schedule. He studied sociology at the University of Oslo but soon turned his attention to issues of punishment and social control. His 1952 Master's thesis was a study of guards in concentration camps for Serbian prisoners of war in Northern Norway. Christie was interested in what drove seemingly normal people to commit atrocities – an issue of continuous importance today with the tragedies of Abu Ghraib freshly in mind. After in-depth interviews, he concluded that, those who had perpetrated atrocities within the camp, far from being monsters, were simply different from the other guards in that they were younger and, due to various circumstances, had failed to view their victims as full human beings. Reflecting on these findings four decades later, Christie concluded, with characteristic honesty and self-reflection, that he felt far from certain which group he would have ended up in at the age of 17 (1999: vi).

Anticipating the findings from related later studies, such as those by Stanley Milgram and Philip Zimbardo, the concentration camp study marked the beginning of Christie's theorising about the relationship between social distance and the capability of inflicting pain on others. In fact, the question of which social conditions encourage 'pain delivery' became a life-time preoccupation. Likewise, the conclusion of the study, that there are no 'monsters' among us, has been a guiding theme in Christie's work. He has emphasised that definitions of criminality essentially depend on types of social settings and relations between those involved in the process; that crime is not a given, but rather is constituted – as revealed in the title of his last book *A Suitable Amount of Crime*. Here, in a radical statement, he concludes: 'Crime does not exist. Only acts exist, acts often given different meanings within various social frameworks. Acts, and the meaning given them, are our data. Our challenge is to follow the destiny of acts through the universe of meanings. Particularly, what are the social conditions that encourage or prevent giving the acts the meaning of being crime' (2004: 3).

Working in the same pioneering, intellectual tradition as his Norwegian counterpart **Thomas Mathiesen**, Christie has been a fierce critic of imprisonment and of the state's power to discipline, punish and institutionalise its maladjusted citizens. His critique of imprisonment and punitiveness is beautifully summarised in the title of his 1981 book *Limits to Pain*. Here he argues that delivery of pain is the core element of punishment and that 'imposing punishment within the institution of law means the inflicting of pain, intended as pain' (1981: 5). He was strongly critical of using punishment as a means of social reform. However, instead of proposing straight-out abolition of prisons (see **Louk Hulsman**), Christie opted for a minimalist argument where '*If* pain is to be applied, it has to be pain without a manipulative purpose and in a social form resembling that which is used when people are in deep sorrow' (ibid).

A strong critic of modern criminal justice systems and their growing appetites and ambitions, Christie has written extensively on Western drug policies, describing drug addicts as 'suitable enemies'. His 1994 book *Crime Control as Industry* focused on the extraordinary trends in the US incarceration rates, which he labelled as 'gulags Western style'. He suggested that crime control has become an industry with an almost unlimited supply of products, which are increasingly delivered by private security providers. This seminal work anticipated a wealth of studies about privatisation of social control and security, and raised a vital question: what is the proper role of the state and how much commodification of crime control and security can a society take?

Christie is critical not only of penal institutions and social and political developments, but also of criminology itself. When asked to hold a lecture at the opening ceremony of the Centre for Criminological Studies in Sheffield in 1976, he suggested – with his customary combination of charm and critical edge – that universities, rather than opening criminological centres, should instead be closing them. His objection was directed at the institutional treatment and monopolisation of the crime problem and social conflicts by professionals, including criminologists. The critique was later published as an article, 'Conflict as Property' (1977), where Christie argued that, rather than there being too much internal conflict within highly industrialised societies, there is in fact too little! He outlined a need for a system where conflicts are not monopolised by various professionals and where participants, particularly victims, have rights to their own conflicts.

Christie's critique became a seminal contribution to the restorative justice movement in Norway and worldwide, and is developed further in the work of authors such as **John Braithwaite** and Clifford Shearing.

Christie's work bears trace of several academic influences, particularly authors such as Ivan Illich and the de-institutionalisation movement. Likewise, Christie's book *Beyond Loneliness and Institutions* came out at a time when writers such as **Michel Foucault** were criticising institutions and questioning the legitimacy and superiority of professional and expert knowledge. However, Christie – both then and now – has never been satisfied with intellectual critique alone. Instead, he strives to find real-life alternatives to the problems he raises. For example, he has been a life-long supporter of villages for people with mental disabilities, whom he prefers to call 'extraordinary'. There are six such villages in Norway and several in other parts of Europe. An essential feature of these villages is that they are a free haven from the competitiveness of the outside world, and they have, as Christie (2004) observes, broken the connection between work and money.

This yearning for a simpler, even pre-modern existence – with 'a place for all', where people can live rounded, multi-dimensional lives – as opposed to a world dictated by the material rhythms of late modernity – has been a recurring theme in Nils Christie's writing. All of his books make a strong argument for maintaining 'tightly knit' societies, rich in social interaction (1973/1982). These are, according to Christie, also the least punitive societies, where crime is less likely to exist, because people are perceived as multidimensional beings rather than simply as categories of criminals and monsters. Speaking provocatively, yet with a trace of seriousness, he has argued that he would not wish to live in a society without corruption, because such would be a society without trust and social capital. However, his reading of pre-modern society is open to the criticism that it is naive and unrealistic and Christie himself has, tellingly, never lived in the idealised small society. He was raised, though, at a time when Norwegian society was still relatively poor, austere and egalitarian. He has frequently remarked that his country's recent oil fortune has been a tragedy due to the dangerous material affluence which brought with it other forms of social poverty. Christie has attempted to move against the grain of our time, which tends to measure success in economic terms and increasingly rewards intellectual brilliance with monetary benefits. And unlike many of his successful contemporaries, he has frequently argued that his salary should be lower rather than higher.

Not an intellectuals' intellectual, Christie always consciously seeks to reach broader audiences. His work is characterised by a unique style of writing through which he aims to be understood not only by his academic peers and the most diligent of students, but also by the general public. He frequently advises his colleagues and students that one should always have one's favourite aunt in mind when writing – a style that has given his books a unique clarity and appeal. That clarity of expression, as well as his proneness to surprise and shock, can perhaps be attributed to his early training as a journalist. However, this aspect of his writing is also a result of a conscious effort to simplify the complex. His style is far from the often mystifying jargon that characterises much academic writing; something which might explain his strong dislike of his own PhD, a statistical analysis of registered offenders in Norway. Seeing criminologists more as poets than as technicians and administrators, he is wary of the dangers of quantification and state-imposed statistical categories which can function as 'a block against insight' (1997).

A truly 'public criminologist', Christie's view is always 'If I want to participate in the running of my country, and I do, I have to write for a general audience' (1999: xi). His prolific lecturing activity has taken him to almost every corner of the world, where he always strives to speak to a variety of audiences, from teachers to prison officers, policemen to psychiatrists. He has been engaged in a constant and lively dialogue with the public, policy makers, professionals and politicians – a considerable achievement at a time when academic criminology finds itself increasingly marginalised in public policy debates. This public activity has been marked by an attempt to create a delicate balance in working 'close, but not too close to power' (ibid) – aiming to reform but preserving an independent, critical voice. And the success of this balancing act has been largely due to his uncompromisingly critical, yet open and engaging, style, which encourages dialogue rather than militant confrontation, and although always provocative is never disrespectful.

Through his work, Nils Christie stands not only as a fierce proponent of inclusive societies, but also as a proponent of an *inclusive criminology* – one whose style and ideas about social justice are accessible, open to everyone, and guided, as he puts it, by a deep democratic 'conviction that I have nothing of importance to say that cannot be understood by most people' (1999: xii).

Major works

Christie, N. (1977) 'Conflicts as Property', *The British Journal of Criminology*, 1: 1–15.
—— (1981) *Limits to Pain*. Oxford: Martin Robertson.

—— (1993/2000) *Crime Control as Industry: Towards Gulags, Western Style.* London: Routledge.
—— (2004) *A Suitable Amount of Crime.* London: Routledge.

Further reading

Christie, N. (1971) *Hvis skolen ikke fantes.* Oslo/Copenhagen: Universitetsforlaget/Christian Ejlers' Forlag.
—— (1973/1982) *Hvor tett et samfunn?/How tightly knit a society?* Oslo/Copenhagen, 1982 edition: Universitetsforlaget-Ejlers forlag.
—— (1989) *Beyond Loneliness and Institutions: Communities for Extraordinary People.* Oslo: Scandinavian University Press.
—— (1997) 'Four Blocks Against Insight: Notes on the Oversocialization of Criminologists', *Theoretical Criminology*, 1(1): 13–23.
—— (1999) 'Roots of a Perspective', in S. Sundbo (ed.) *Nils Christie: En kronologisk bibliografi over forfatterskapet 1945–1999.* Oslo: Nasjonalbiblioteket. Also available online at: http://folk.uio.no/christie/dokumenter/roots_of_a_perspective.htm (accessed 1 July 2009).

KATJA FRANKO AAS

JOHN IRWIN (1929–)

Over the past four decades, John Irwin has been among the most important voices on the subject of prisons and punishment in criminology. His perspective is uniquely valuable, because not only is his scholarship and research internationally recognised as pioneering and exemplary, but he is also a former prisoner himself. Since 1997, John Irwin has been a core member of a movement known as 'Convict Criminology' consisting of ex-prisoners involved in academic criminology and their supporters (see Ross and Richards 2003). At Convict Criminology panels, John helps to draw a large audience, as his published work spans three decades, his criticism of state penology is legendary, and he has mentored and advised numerous authors who attempt to understand this distant world where men and women live in cages. Every year, at conferences and events, before and after Convict Criminology sessions, John meets with new ex-prisoner graduate students struggling to complete their degrees, and concerned about their futures. John helps them to prepare for their 'coming out', where they introduce themselves to the audience by relating their criminal activity, convictions and prison time, to their research. Once they step out of the closet they are members of the Convict Criminology Group.

John takes them aside, engages them in conversation, and gives each one personal attention. He is very straightforward, as he tests their transparency, their courage to retain their own identity, despite the stigma they suffer, and the temptation to conceal their past. Irwin understands that most felons prefer not to talk about their crimes, convictions and time in prison, especially in public. The problem is the charade may become an elaborate subterfuge; the ex-convict slides into respectability, and then becomes a prisoner again of the secrets they keep. Their professional lie becomes a performance that inhibits their work and limits their ability to write about the subject they are determined to bury. How do you teach and write about prison without telling your audience what you learned inside? A core tenet of 'convict criminology' is that a former prisoner who wants to be a professor must not conceal their criminal past.

John Irwin, a former prisoner who has never hidden his past, has dedicated his life's work to helping men and women deal with the problems of prison. Most of the work he does in the community he does quietly, as he seeks no recognition. Most of the recipients of his assistance do not even know his name, or appreciate his background or reputation.

While Irwin has contributed to many community programmes over the years, he is best known for creating Project Rebound at San Francisco State University (SFSU) in 1967. Project Rebound is a programme that provides comprehensive support for ex-convicts to enter and complete degrees at SFSU. Over the last 40 years, many Project Rebound students have obtained BA, MA and PhD degrees in various disciplines.

Irwin's life began as the child of a middle-class family in California's San Fernando Valley during the Great Depression. Smart, although less than interested in attending school, he slipped into deviant activities that led to a conviction for armed robbery and five years in state prison. Irwin wrote: 'My prison experiences – five years at Soledad, a medium-security California prison, after several years of living the life of a thief and drug addict – as well as my post-prison years not only determined my academic career path but also shaped my sociological perspective in definite and profound ways.' In prison he discovered that deviants and convicts were mostly ordinary human beings. This insight, not entirely appreciated by many academics that study crime and criminals, guided all of his subsequent academic and political activities (2005: ix).

In 1957, he got out of prison and attended SFSU, graduating from UCLA in 1961, and then completed his PhD in Sociology at UC Berkeley in 1968. As a professor at SFSU for 27 years, now emeritus, his books include: *The Felon* (1970), *Scenes* (1977), *Prisons in Turmoil*

(1980), *The Jail* (1985), *It's About Time* (1994), *The Rogue* (unfinished memoir), and *The Warehouse Prison* (2005). He was also a major contributor to *Struggle for Justice* (1971).

His works on 'the prison' have traced, through a convict's eyes, developments from the 1950s to the turn of the century. The main themes have been to explore developments in convict culture, prisoner typologies, convict perspectives on how they are treated, conditions of confinement, political manipulation of the public's fear of crime to expand the reach of the criminal justice system, and the unintentional creation of a felon underclass in the United States. Beginning work on *The Felon* in 1966, he argued that felons have careers that are based on contact and identity with one or more deviant or criminal behaviour systems. This career is structured by the meanings, definitions and understandings learned on the street as well as in prison. Prisoners are subjected to routines and experiences that greatly increase their punishment, make reentry more difficult, and produce profound alienation as they are treated as less than human. Later in *Prisons in Turmoil* he would document how the social organisation of the prison had changed from a 'Big House' based on both formal and informal routines to the modern correctional institution and penitentiary dominated by racial divisions and violence, a result of failed correctional policies and changing demographics.

In *The Jail* (1985), Irwin departed from prison research to examine how US jails are used to both socially create and then manage 'rabble'. Updating his earlier typology of convicts in *The Felon* (thief, hustler, dope fiend, head, disorganised criminal, state-raised youth, man in the lower class, and square john) he describes categories of arrestees, or types of disreputables (petty hustlers, derelicts, junkies, crazies, cornerboys, lowriders, aliens, gays, and square johns). His attention to how social structures can build and destroy individual identity, demonstrates how the jail contributes to disintegration, disorientation, degradation, and then preparation of a permanent underclass he terms the 'rabble'. As a result of being jailed, people lose their jobs, homes, families, and after repeated trips to jail their membership in conventional society.

A further departure from exclusive focus on 'the prison' appears in *It's About Time* (1994). For the first time, Irwin looks not only inside the penal machinery, but outside at the way politicians manipulate the public fear of crime as diversion and a means of creating a 'vindictive society'. The analysis also focuses on the academic community's role in producing government-funded studies to justify 'voodoo criminology' and the growing correctional-industrial complex based on profiteering on prisons system designed to fail.

Together, Irwin and Austin merge different methodologies and evidence to make their case that 'America has created a lower class culture designed to produce new cohorts of street criminals each generation'. Poor inner-city neighbourhoods provide a steady stream of recruits for jails and then prisons. The combination of poverty and the harsh penalties of the War on Drugs supply police with easy arrests, courts with guilty pleas and an 'imprisonment binge' with no end.

Irwin's latest book *The Warehouse Prison* revisits many of the themes he introduced in previous books, as a means to bracket or frame his primary analytical focus on one medium-security prison in California (Solano State Prison). He begins by discussing the history of prisons and how they have changed over the years. This quick overview of the last three hundred years of capital punishment, torture, transportation to colonies, and the first prisons illustrates how England and then the United States attempted to contain and control the 'dangerous classes'. The twenty-first century has witnessed the expanded use of imprisonment with the construction of two new types of prisons. Irwin discusses the new warehouse correctional institutions and supermax penitentiaries. Prisoners who fail to conform to the warehouse are transferred to the supermax. Irwin (2005: 59) describes the warehouses thus, 'The new prisons are monocolored, plain, large, compounds. Without the gun towers and double fences, they could easily be mistaken for industrial warehouses sitting out in rural sites, where most of these prisons are located.' These prisons were designed to be secure, efficient, and economical, and to hold as many as 5,000 prisoners. In California they may be built in groups, one next to another, or across the road, like warehouses in an industrial park.

In *The Warehouse Prison*, Irwin takes us inside Solano State Prison, one of 22 California penal institutions built in the late 1980s and 1990s to house medium-security male inmates. As in previous books, Irwin (2005: 73) pays attention to what the prisoners experience day to day. 'The food is ordinary institutional fare – better than county jails, worse than hospitals.' Education and vocational programmes have few funds and resources; for example, there are no college courses, and vocational programmes are poorly supported. Even voluntary programmes are limited. Irwin (2005: 76) writes that the only programmes permitted operate under the idea that 'the prisoner is a moral inferior, pathological or disreputable being who is in need of redemption, reformation, or salvation'. Despite the lack of rehabilitation programming, this prison is relatively calm, with little violence, because of physical design, management of prisoners including quick response to prisoner disturbances, and threat of transfer to supermax prisons.

Irwin reminds us that prisoners have social agency: 'Prisoners do not simply comply with the regimens imposed on them. They actively conspire to survive, to reduce their state of deprivation, to ease their moral condemnation, and to pursue their own self-interests' (Irwin 2005: 9). Like all people in any given society, convicts adapt to their environment in unique and logical ways. Convict codes and culture rules enable prisoners to live day to day despite the torture of imprisonment. Inside or outside, prison life goes on.

In all of Irwin's books he writes about people: the folks you meet in prison (see also Terry 2002). In *The Rogue* (unfinished memoir) he wrote about his own experience in prison as a convict in the 1950s:

> First of all I had to deal with the world of convicts. This was different than entering high school or moving to a new town or neighborhood, even different than going to jail. In fact it is different than any other world. It contains a distinct and distorted sample of the general population. More than anything else, more than an asylum for criminals, it is a receptacle for society's most bothersome misfits.

He proceeds to write about unskilled, disorganised poor slobs, '33rd degree weirdo's', 'hoosiers' (hicks), and other social trash, and then balances this by discussing intelligent, creative men, who while admirable, have such intense energy (and perhaps warped behaviour) that conventional people want them locked up.

His analytical invention of prisoner typologies began with his own incarceration and became more refined in each book. In *The Warehouse Prison*, this rogue's gallery includes gangbangers, outlaws, state-raised prisoners, cornerboys, dope fiends, derelicts, crazies, sex offenders, and square johns. These men are locked up under 'mandatory minimums' and so called 'truth in sentencing' guidelines that guarantee they will spend a large piece of their young adult lives in prison. Little attention is paid to what they might be like when they finally emerge from prison to return home. Irwin writes, 'The fact remains that imprisonment does considerable harm to prisoners in obvious and subtle ways and makes it more difficult for them to achieve viability, satisfaction, and respect when they are released from prison' (2005: 149).

In effect, felons apply what they learned on the streets to survival in prison (Importation Model). Conversely, their prison experience may influence how they think and behave when they return to the community. Codes of the street and Convict Codes merge and reinforce one another. After many years in prison, or several trips to prison, a person may become alienated from civil society. This process spawns an army of zombies that walk the streets, stand on corners, and sleep under bridges, waiting to be recycled back to the warehouse.

The Warehouse Prison concludes with an Afterword by Barbara Owen, once a student of Irwin, on the gendered harm women suffer in prison. Owen summarises the problems and difficulties experienced by women as they enter prison, survive inside, and then exit to return home. She discusses 'pathways to imprisonment', the 'war on drugs as war on women', 'the mix', and how women are both the same and different from men in how they respond to the harm of imprisonment.

Irwin's work is quintessentially American and particularly focused on California; the state with the largest prison system, the one he knows best, the place where he 'did time'. In the United States, there are many prison systems, each with its own unique history and social organisation. Convict Criminologist research professors are now using many of Irwin's ideas in their research writing, which has served to open many new prisons to analytical penetration. Convict Criminologists follow Irwin inside to sit and chat with convicts, record their pain and frustrations, and give them a voice. They would agree with Irwin and Austin's concluding remark in *It's About Time*, 'For these reasons, we believe the single most direct solution that would have an immediate and dramatic impact on prison crowding and would not affect public safety is to shorten prison terms.'

Major works

Irwin, J. (1970) *The Felon.* Englewood Cliffs, New Jersey: Prentice-Hall.
—— (1980) *Prisons in Turmoil.* Boston, Massachusetts: Little, Brown.
—— (1985) *The Jail.* Berkeley, California: University of California Press.
—— (2005) *The Warehouse Prison: Disposal of the New Dangerous Class.* Los Angeles, California: Roxbury.
Irwin, John and James Austin (1994) *It's About Time: America's Imprisonment Binge.* Belmont, California: Wadsworth.
Irwin, J. and R. Cressey (1962) 'Thieves, Convicts, and the Inmate Culture', *Social Problems,* 10: 142–55.

Further reading

Ross, J.I. and Richards, S.C. (2002) *Behind Bars: Surviving Prison.* New York: Alpha/Penguin.
—— (2003) *Convict Criminology.* Belmont, California: Wadsworth.
Terry, C.M. (2002) *The Fellas: Overcoming Prison and Addiction.* Belmont, California: Wadsworth.

STEPHEN C. RICHARDS

JOAN MCCORD (1930–2004)

Joan McCord was a brilliant pioneer in criminology. Her best-known, most influential, and greatest contributions to knowledge arose from her pioneering work on the Cambridge-Somerville Youth Study, which was the first large-scale longitudinal-experimental study ever carried out in the history of criminology. As the name suggests, longitudinal-experimental studies combine two of the most important methods used in criminology, by conducting a randomised experiment within a prospective longitudinal survey. Because they are prospective longitudinal surveys, these studies provide information about the natural history of development of offending and about the effects of early risk factors on later offending. Because they are randomised experiments, these studies provide information about the impact of interventions on offending.

Joan McCord's most important papers (selected by herself before she died) and a list of all her publications are published in a volume entitled *Crime and Family* edited by her son Geoffrey Sayre-McCord (2007). In this short chapter there is only space to highlight two of Joan's major scholarly contributions – on the results of an intervention experiment and on the effects of child-rearing.

In the Cambridge-Somerville Youth Study, schools, welfare agencies, churches and police recommended both 'difficult' and 'average' boys to the programme, in Cambridge and Somerville, Massachusetts (parts of the Greater Boston metropolitan area). Each boy was rated on his likelihood of becoming delinquent, and 325 pairs of boys were matched on this and on age, intelligence, family background and home environment. By the toss of a coin, one member of each pair was randomly assigned to the treatment group and the other was randomly assigned to the control group. This was the first large-scale randomised experiment in the history of criminology.

The treatment programme began in 1939 when the boys were aged 10 on average. Except for those dropped from the programme because of a counsellor shortage in 1941, treatment continued for an average of 5 years, consisting mainly of individual counselling and frequent home visits. The counsellors gave well-meaning, friendly advice to the boys and their families, took them on trips and to recreational activities, tutored them in reading and arithmetic, encouraged them to participate in the YMCA and summer camps, played games with them at the project's centre, encouraged them to attend church, kept in close touch with the police, and generally gave support to the boys and their families.

The first results of the Cambridge-Somerville Youth Study were published in the 1951 book by Powers and Witmer entitled *An Experiment in the Prevention of Delinquency*. Joan McCord's great achievement was to follow up the males to age 45–50. This long-term follow-up produced sensational results. 'A thirty-year follow-up of treatment effects' (McCord 1978) was a landmark paper and is perhaps the most famous article that Joan McCord ever wrote. As the name suggests, it describes a thirty-year follow-up of the treated and control males. In 1975 and 1976, attempts were made to trace the 253 experimental men who were still in the treatment programme in 1942, together with their 253 matched controls. Criminal, mental hospital, and other records were searched, and questionnaires were mailed to the men.

The findings were shocking. While equal numbers of treated and control males were convicted as juveniles and as adults, slightly more treated men committed serious crimes, and significantly more treated men committed two or more crimes. The treated men were significantly more likely to die early, to be diagnosed as seriously mentally ill, to have stress-related diseases, and to show symptoms of alcoholism on a screening test. Significantly fewer treated men were in high-status jobs, and fewer of them (but not significantly so) were married.

This was one of the first criminological intervention projects to demonstrate harmful effects of a well-meaning prevention programme. Why these effects were found is not entirely clear, but Joan McCord (1978) speculated that the intervention might have created some dependency on outside assistance, which in turn might have led to resentment when the assistance was withdrawn. Alternatively, the treatment programme might have generated high expectations that subsequently led to feelings of deprivation when these expectations were not met. Another possibility was that the treated group might have justified the treatment they received by perceiving themselves as being in need of welfare help. Whatever the true reason, Joan McCord's 1978 paper, published in the very widely distributed house journal of the American Psychological Association (mailed to over 100,000 psychologists), was extremely influential in demonstrating that a welfare-oriented counselling programme could end up damaging the clients.

Joan McCord continued to publish articles on her follow-up of the Cambridge-Somerville Youth Study for the rest of her life. One of the most important was published in a landmark book containing the results of major developmental prevention experiments that she jointly edited (McCord and Tremblay 1992). This chapter concluded that significantly more of the treated men had an 'undesirable' outcome: convicted for an index crime, treated for psychosis or alcoholism, or died before age 35. Interestingly, in her 1989 Presidential Address to the American Society of Criminology, entitled 'Crime in Moral and Social Contexts', McCord reported that the boys who received more intensive treatment showed more adverse effects.

Her last article on the Cambridge-Somerville Youth Study ('Cures that Harm: Unanticipated Outcomes of Crime Prevention Programs'; McCord 2003) described the harmful effects in some detail and placed them in the context of other well-meaning programmes that had harmful effects. She reported that the adverse effects increased with the increased intensity and duration of treatment, and that they occurred only among males whose families had cooperated with the programme. This article was important because it was published in a showcase of papers presented by the influential Campbell Collaboration Crime and Justice Group, which aims to complete systematic reviews of evidence on the effectiveness of criminological interventions.

As a longitudinal-experimental study, the Cambridge-Somerville Youth Study also provided a great deal of information about the childhood antecedents of adult criminal behaviour. The methods of measuring family factors, such as parental attitudes, discipline and supervision, used by Joan and her first husband William McCord were very influential in the Cambridge Study in Delinquent Development. Donald West told me that, when he was starting the study in 1960, he wrote to both the McCords and **the Gluecks** to ask them about their methods of measuring these family factors. Donald considered that the Gluecks' coding system was very subjective, but the McCords sent a very detailed coding system with numerous examples, and Donald carefully followed this in measuring family factors in the Cambridge Study in 1961–62 in his attempt to be as objective and consistent as possible. Therefore, the original Cambridge Study in Delinquent Development measures were very much inspired by those used by the McCords in *Origins of Crime* (W. McCord, J. McCord and Zola, 1959), and we were able to replicate many of their findings on the ability of family factors to predict later delinquency and crime.

Undoubtedly Joan McCord's most influential and best-known article on child-rearing and criminal behaviour was 'Some Child-rearing Antecedents of Criminal Behavior in Adult Men' (McCord 1979). This reported on the subsequent criminal histories of the treated males. She found that poor parental supervision and the mother's lack of confidence significantly predicted later property and violent crimes committed by the males. In addition, low maternal affection and paternal deviance (criminality or alcoholism) predicted later property crimes, and parental conflict and parental aggression (including punitive discipline) predicted later violent crimes. This paper was crucial in demonstrating that early family and child-rearing factors predicted later offending up to thirty years later.

'A Longitudinal View of the Relationship between Paternal Absence and Crime' (McCord 1982) was, if anything, even more interesting. This article again investigated the later criminal histories of the treated boys, focusing on boys from homes broken by loss of the biological father. McCord found that the prevalence of serious offending was high for males from broken homes without affectionate mothers (62%), and for males from unbroken homes characterised by parental conflict (52%), irrespective of whether they had affectionate mothers. The prevalence of serious offending was low for males from unbroken homes without conflict (26%) and – importantly – equally low for males from broken homes with affectionate mothers (22%).

This article challenged the prevailing wisdom that broken homes were criminogenic. It showed that the number of parents in a family was less important than features of family functioning such as parental conflict and maternal affection. It also suggested that a loving mother might be able to compensate for the loss of a father. Since Joan spent many years as a single parent, at a time when single parents were stigmatised, she was very happy to report these results.

I now turn from McCord's scholarly contributions to her career. Joan was born in 1930 and graduated in Philosophy from Stanford University in 1952 with great distinction. She had a life-long enthusiasm for philosophy. She then worked as a teacher to support her first husband William ('Bud') McCord while he was studying for his PhD with the Gluecks at Harvard University. It is interesting to see the intellectual continuity at Harvard in the 1950s from the Gluecks to the McCords. After Bud obtained his PhD, Joan worked as a researcher at Harvard and, in 1957, began analysing the effects of the Cambridge-Somerville Youth Study on crime. This led to the landmark book on *Origins of Crime* (McCord et al. 1959). In the late 1950s, Joan and Bud moved back to Stanford when Bud became Assistant Dean of Humanities and Sciences.

However, the early 1960s were a very difficult time for Joan, as she got divorced from Bud and lost financial support from the Stanford Philosophy department. Fortunately, she received an NIMH Fellowship and completed her PhD in Sociology at Stanford in 1968. However, she then encountered problems in getting an academic position until she was appointed as an Assistant Professor at Drexel

University in Philadelphia, which was a far cry from the likes of Harvard and Stanford. In 1970, she married her second husband Carl Silver, who was a psychologist.

Joan's career began to take off again in the 1970s, when she managed to obtain an NIMH grant to follow up the participants in the Cambridge-Somerville Youth Study. As mentioned above, her results showed that the treatment programme had been harmful, and consequently she had considerable difficulty in getting them published. However, publication of the results in the *American Psychologist* in 1978 was a watershed event for Joan and she never looked back from then onwards.

I first met Joan at the American Society of Criminology meeting in Dallas in 1978 and had frequent contacts with her from then until her death in February 2004. From the first time I met her, I was struck by her infectious enthusiasm for research questions, which was really inspiring, and which she retained throughout her life. Her intellectual curiosity and energy appeared boundless. Coupled with her intellectual brilliance, this was a formidable combination.

In 1981, my family and I stayed at Joan's house outside Philadelphia. Joan and Carl were remarkably welcoming and tolerant of our three small children who rampaged around. Joan's house was an Aladdin's cave containing many books and journals on criminology and longitudinal studies. She kept a lot of Cambridge-Somerville data in filing cabinets in her basement. Also in her basement was a table tennis table, and she took great delight in thrashing me mercilessly at ping-pong. Joan was charming but also determined and competitive, and this is why she managed to overcome so many difficulties and have such a successful career. I was very proud to receive the Joan McCord Award of the Academy of Experimental Criminology in 2005, and paid fulsome praise to her work in my paper on key longitudinal-experimental studies in criminology.

From 1978 onwards, Joan's fame increased and she became a central figure in American – and world – criminology. She received many honours. It gave her particular pleasure to be the first woman president of the American Society of Criminology (1988–89), followed by her term as Chair of the American Sociological Association Section on Crime, Law, and Deviance (1989–90). She was always particularly keen to encourage the careers of women scholars. She was also a recipient of the American Society of Criminology's prestigious Sutherland and Bloch awards.

Joan contributed mightily to the International Society of Criminology (ISC), being a Vice-President and member of the Board of Directors for nearly 15 years, and receiving the Durkheim Prize of the ISC. She also contributed enormously to the Campbell Collaboration Crime and Justice Group and was President of the Academy of Experimental Criminology at the time of her death. She also served as Vice-Chair of the National Academy of Sciences Committee on Law and Justice and Co-Chair of the NAS panel on juvenile crime and juvenile justice (McCord et al. 2001).

Almost up to the time of her death, Joan retained her incredible energy and amazing enthusiasm. As proof of this, I have a photo of her dancing with me at the ASC Minority Scholarship Dance in Denver in November 2003. Her travel schedule would have exhausted most people. In Carl's final years, she travelled the world pushing Carl in a wheelchair. After Carl died in 1998, she travelled even more and seemed to be constantly criss-crossing the world.

It has been a great privilege for me to know Joan McCord. She was one of the most brilliant, inspiring, and enthusiastic researchers that criminology has ever seen.

Major works

McCord, J. (1978) 'A Thirty-Year Follow-Up of Treatment Effects', *American Psychologist*, 33: 284–89.

—— (1979) 'Some Child-Rearing Antecedents of Criminal Behavior in Adult Men', *Journal of Personality and Social Psychology*, 37: 1477–86.

—— (1982) 'A Longitudinal View of the Relationship between Paternal Absence and Crime', in J. Gunn and D.P. Farrington (eds) *Abnormal Offenders, Delinquency and the Criminal Justice System*, pp. 113–28. Chichester, England: Wiley.

—— (1983) 'A Forty-Year Perspective on Effects of Child Abuse and Neglect', *Child Abuse and Neglect*, 7: 265–70.

—— (2002) 'Learning How to Learn and its Sequelae', in G. Geis and M. Dodge (eds) *Lessons of Criminology*, pp. 95–108. Cincinnati, Ohio: Anderson.

—— (2003) 'Cures that Harm: Unanticipated Outcomes of Crime Prevention Programs', *Annals of the American Academy of Political and Social Science*, 587: 16–30.

Further reading

McCord, J. and Tremblay, R.E. (eds) (1992) *Preventing Antisocial Behavior: Interventions from Birth Through Adolescence*. New York: Guilford.

McCord, J., Widom, C.S. and Crowell, N.A. (eds) (2001) *Juvenile Crime, Juvenile Justice*. Washington, DC: National Academy Press.

McCord, W., McCord, J. and Zola, I.K. (1959) *Origins of Crime*. New York: Columbia University Press.

Sayre-McCord, G. (ed.) (2007) *Crime and Family: Selected Essays of Joan McCord*. Philadelphia, Pennsylvania: Temple University Press.

DAVID P. FARRINGTON

DAVID MATZA (1930–)

The work of Berkeley criminologist David Matza remains hugely popular in criminology. He has had a profound influence on the study of delinquency, deviance and poverty, and his books are considered foundational texts within the phenomenological school of sociology and critical criminology. In many ways, however, he is remembered as the perfect criminologist for the 1960s, skilfully capturing the turbulent nature of the times with his challenges to academic orthodoxy and efforts to understand and appreciate the deviant. Matza earned his undergraduate degree from the College of the City of New York (CCNY) which is now the City University of New York and was awarded his doctorate from Princeton University's Department of Economics and Sociology in 1959. Between 1957 and 1959, he was an instructor at Temple University and in 1960–61 he completed a post-doctoral fellowship in the Behavioral Science and Law programme at the University of Chicago Law School. Yet, he will always be associated with the University of California, Berkeley, where he was hired in 1962 and remained until he retired with emeritus status.

Matza was born to Morris and Esther Matza on 1 May 1930. His father was born in Turkey in 1885 and his mother in Greece in 1900. Morris Matza first migrated to Egypt, and then came to the United States around 1906. Esther arrived in the United States in 1921. Their common language was Greek; neither of them spoke a great deal of English and both were illiterate. His father worked as a short-order cook and sometimes as a waiter. However, throughout most of the Great Depression he was unemployed. During the late 1930s, his father worked for a couple of years for the Works Progress Administration, which provided jobs and income for the unemployed during the Depression. In that capacity he helped build the New York World's Fair. David was their youngest child; he had a brother, Abraham, who was six years older, and a sister, Stella, who was three years his senior. Sadly, Abraham was to die in military action in early January 1945, near the end of World War II at the Battle of the Bulge. Stella married and settled with her husband, Irving, in New York City.

The family lived in Harlem (between 117th and 118th Street), uptown Manhattan in New York City until 1941, moving to the East Bronx on the day Germany invaded the Soviet Union.

Matza attended Public School 103 in Harlem and Hebrew School at the Institutional Synagogue. Although his parents knew little about scholarship and higher education, his brother and sister were enthusiastic and encouraged the academically gifted Matza to pursue his studies. He registered at the Downtown campus of CCNY but then decided to drop out, taking jobs as a delivery boy and mailroom clerk for a couple of years. He returned to CCNY Uptown campus in 1949. By that time, he was developing an ambition to become a writer.

While at CCNY, Matza lived in the East Bronx. He married his first wife, Cynthia Becker, around the time he finished his studies there. Shortly after, he earned admission to Princeton University. Thanks to his love of sports – in particular basketball, football and softball – and his work as a camp counselor at the East Bronx Young Men and Women's Hebrew Association, Matza had established a wide network of neighbourhood and school friends. However, at Princeton he was exposed to a whole new set of people and influences. Fellow graduate students, researchers and junior faculty all encouraged Matza to read widely in fields such as economics, politics, literature, philosophy and religion. He was heavily influenced by Dostoyevsky, **Durkheim**, **Marx**, Plato, Veblen and Weber.

Matza's original plan was to become a social worker – although secretly he never stopped dreaming of becoming a novelist (a longing that, as Matza admits today, has never really gone away, even at the age of 79!). However, his mentor at CCNY, Charles Page persuaded him to go into sociology. This pathway was further cemented at Princeton when **Gresham Sykes** persuaded him to do his dissertation on juvenile delinquency instead of working on labour movements, an interest he had developed whilst in graduate school.

Matza had met Cynthia in 1951, when working at a summer camp, Camp Bronx House, where they were both employed as counselors. Early on in their marriage they moved to Princeton, New Jersey where he took a job at Temple University in 1957. He was still working on his doctoral dissertation during this period. His first daughter, Naomi, was born in 1956; his younger daughter, Karen, was born in 1959. Cynthia became a social worker and went on to enjoy a very successful career. His daughters married and had children. Today, holidays are special to Matza, being a time to get together with his family that now includes his son in laws, Jay and Bill, and his grandchildren, Rosa, Miles, Katie and Molly. His daughters, Karen Kelekian

and Naomi Bondy, became schoolteachers in Oakland and San
Francisco, California. He and Cynthia divorced in 1971. Matza met
his second wife, Clair Brown, in 1974 at a yoga class they were both
attending. They married that same year and had a son, Daniel, who
was born in 1980. Clair became a professor of economics at the
University of California, Berkeley. They divorced in 1984 but remain
close friends. Daniel Matza-Brown is now a lawyer working in New
York City.

At the time of Matza's appointment at Berkeley the United States
was in significant turmoil. The 1960s ushered in social movements
associated with the New Left that included new initiatives to constrain
corporate power and concerted opposition to conventional approaches
to foreign policy. Added to these were efforts to eliminate poverty,
reduce gender inequality, expand civil rights, and eliminate racism. By
the mid-1970s the efforts at social reform had begun to address the
juridical apparatus, largely because the government had used the criminal justice system and law to manage much of the crisis that grew out
of attempts at social reform. Matza was at the right place to address
some of these problems attendant to the social milieu and mood of the
time. For one thing, Herbert Blumer had joined the Berkeley faculty in
1952 after eleven years at the University of Chicago and was influential
in developing the Berkeley School of Sociology through modifying the
naturalistic approaches of the Chicago tradition. Blumer assembled an
exceptional group of interpretive scholars that included Robert
Blauner, Troy Duster and Matza himself; their work together culminated in the founding of the Institute for the Study of Social Change in
1976 with Duster as director.

In 1964, Matza published *Delinquency and Drift* where he initiated
the conversation about how delinquency is constituted. The book
received the American Sociological Association's C. Wright Mills
Award. It served to address the philosophical, theoretical and empirical
problems and contested prevailing explanations of delinquency at that
time. Matza took naturalism as his philosophical stance in the explanation of delinquency. In short, naturalistic theories are concerned
with explaining the lived experiences of people from the meanings
they construct. Thus, to understand delinquency it is necessary to see
the world from the view of the delinquents and follow their rationales
for choosing specific and patterned lines of actions. Naturalism was a
central focus of the emerging Berkeley School of Sociology, and
Blumer was keen to develop new modes of symbolic interactionism
grounded in the work of George Herbert Mead, the Chicago School
of Sociology and Max Weber's concept of *verstehen*. By adopting this

philosophical stance, with its implications for method, Matza was able to revisit the positivist explanations of crime and crucially modify that philosophical tradition in order to explain delinquency. That is to reject the positivist notion of absolute 'hard' determinism and to focus instead on the notion that delinquent action is freely willed, albeit in ways which were only sketchily and simplistically depicted in the classicism of **Beccaria** and **Bentham**.

Central to Matza's analysis was the distinction between the 'natural' and the 'positive' delinquent. The positive delinquent was, *and remains*, the typical way that criminologists explain delinquency. In Matza's view the positivists objectify delinquents, treating them as things rather than human subjects. Therefore, delinquents are thought to be unable to control themselves and their actions. Furthermore, the positive perspective is correctionalist in that it only views delinquents from the perspective of individuals who have to be controlled – as people suffering from an individual or sociological pathology. Naturalistic theories, by contrast, seek a faithful interpretation of the phenomena they describe; they are in this sense *appreciative of deviant action*. This was an important distinction for Matza, since thinking in terms of aetiology and pathology, as do positivist theories, would foreclose the idea of variation in conduct. In contrast, naturalist theories view variation in outcome as always a reasonable possibility. The subversive implication of this stance is that the rationality of deviance could be understood and celebrated as a condition of oppression and the definitions and meanings imposed by those in power could become contested. Put simply, the moral complexity suggested by naturalist theories fits well with theories of conflict and change.

As pointed out earlier, Matza's critique emerged at a time of considerable social unrest, particularly associated with the New Left. In the 1950s, the United States and the rest of the Western world were attempting to rebuild after World War II whilst also responding to the emergence of the Cold War. These conditions gave rise to pervasive social forces that demanded adherence to convention and intolerance of diversity. But with the rise of New Left politics of the 1960s, contestation and conflict became unusually intense. The University of California became a major site for the focus of that contestation and the State's attempts to manage the crisis (see **The Schwendingers**). In this context, Matza's criminology should be considered an early form of public sociology.

In *Delinquency and Drift*, Matza argued that the subculture of delinquency placed the delinquent in a moral situation of strain. On the one hand, the delinquent desired to follow social rules and laws and on the other hand the delinquent was *impelled* by the permissive conditions of delinquency. Matza analysed this relationship between the delinquent and the law. In doing so he employed a comparative legal theory where he examined primitive 'law' vis-à-vis Western juridical concepts. The language of Western law, he argues, is concise and exacting yet tends to objectify humans. And in the process of objectification, subject positions are dichotomised in contradistinction to the natural condition of humans. Matza makes this clear when he tells the reader his reason for writing *Delinquency and Drift*: 'My purpose in writing a book of this sort is that the pictures of delinquency that thus far have been drawn do not remind me and many others of the real things which they purport to explain' (1969: 2). Matza continues, '[I]n distorting reality, current pictures seem to lose what is essential in the character of the deviant enterprise'. And while, for example, his colleague, Blumer, had warned about the problem with treating attitudes and beliefs as if they were synonymous with action or the likelihood for action, Matza views delinquency as 'fundamentally' the transformation of beliefs into action (ibid: 19). These transformations are based on the commitments of the delinquents. For Matza argued that delinquents (like everyone else in society) have a moral commitment to the law. And since delinquents usually follow the law in their lives, it is when the bind between an individual and the law becomes weak that there occurs an opportunity for the individual to *drift* into delinquent actions. This would be the case with any citizen, since people range between total freedom and total constraint – they drift through life continually moving between these two poles.

The process by which Matza and his colleague **Gresham Sykes** explained how delinquents dissolve the moral bonds of law is called the 'techniques of neutralisation'. Since, like other citizens, delinquents are committed to the laws, morals, and values of the society, when delinquents violate the social norms they feel guilt. The management of such feelings is achieved through a series of rationalisations that *neutralise* this sense of guilt. In this process, the delinquent suspends commitment to societal values and this provides the freedom to commit delinquent acts. Matza pointed out that there may be many possible rationalisations to neutralise; however, he listed five salient *techniques* of neutralisation: 1) denial of responsibility, 2) denial of injury, 3) denial of a victim, 4) condemnation of condemners, and 5) an appeal to higher loyalties.

The *denial of responsibility* is a claim by a delinquent that they are the victim of a circumstance that caused them to be pushed or pulled into conditions that are beyond their control. Therefore, the delinquent will reason that it was not their fault. *Denial of injury* is a technique used to rationalise that the delinquency did not hurt anyone. Thus, if the delinquent carried out a property crime, the delinquent would reason that the victim could afford the loss. *Denial of the victim* is where the delinquent reasons that the act is not wrong; that the victim deserves the injury. Or, alternatively, that there was no victim in the delinquent act. For example, the delinquent would maintain that the victim had it coming for some imagined transgression. *Condemnation of the victim* is a technique where the delinquent claims that those that condemn delinquency are hypocrites. As such, the delinquent might assert that the condemners do the same thing; or, that they have done worst things in their life. *Appealing to higher loyalties* is where the delinquent would argue that they had to perform the delinquent act because of some higher social or spiritual values. Thus, the delinquent might suggest that it was necessary to steal to feed family members; or, to lie about witnessing a crime to protect peers.

Matza and Sykes's theory of neutralisation challenged **Albert K. Cohen**'s delinquency subculture thesis in his study *Delinquent Boys: The Culture of the Gang* (1955). Natural delinquents do not adhere to a different (subcultural) set of norms, they argued; they remain committed to conventional norms while believing in rationalisations for their delinquent transgressions; that is, they negate responsibility for their delinquency. The theory has remained one of the most influential arguments in criminology over the past 50 years (see Maruna and Copes 2005).

In 1969, Matza published *Becoming Deviant* which was written during a sabbatical year taken at the London School of Economics and Political Science (LSE); this work once again insisted on the importance of the naturalistic approach for understanding infraction. For him, there are three major contributions to the development of the naturalist approach: The Chicago School of Sociology, functionalism, and the Neo-Chicago School of Sociology. These foundations make it possible to see the world from the viewpoint of the subjects, to see the functions of deviant organisations, and to see how social control in part perpetuates the stability and emergence of new deviant organisations. In *Becoming Deviant*, major attention is paid to how naturalistic theories explain the cause of deviance. Three salient themes are critically examined by Matza: affinity, affiliation, and signification. Affinity theories are concerned with how individuals are inclined to become deviants. For example, some may reason that poverty is a major cause for turning to deviance. Matza points out that such reasoning fails because human beings are turned into objects from the perspective of such conceptual frameworks. In contrast, Matza argues that humans are active subjects. Affiliation theories stress that individuals engage in deviance through association with deviant others. Matza argues that this view precludes recognising that individuals have a *will* through which they make *choices*. Rather than thinking of deviance as spread by contagion, he stresses the necessity of realising that individuals have a choice to try something different by establishing affinity with actions, beliefs and groups. Moreover, individuals may do so continuously or intermittently; that is, they may make the choice in each situation where such options are presented. Signification theories, on the other hand, deal with the relationship between the state and its lawmaking (prohibiting) functions. Related to this is the situation of apprehension. Once a deviant is apprehended, they are stigmatised by authority and their identity is more intensely spoiled since apprehension reaffirms collective representations and the hegemony of the state. In brief, Matza reminds the reader that the study of deviance requires that the researcher appreciate the philosophical inner-life of the subject; to see the world the way the subject sees it, and to interpret the world the way the subject would interpret it.

Matza's work influenced both his contemporaries and future generations of criminologists and sociologists. It offered support for aspects of the norm erosion thesis and containment theory. In a larger sense, his work served as a form of theoretical mediation for the social change that was mentioned above. For this reason, Matza's theoretical intervention functioned as a public sociology that later became a feature of the Berkeley tradition. Matza's work also provided an opening for a greater consideration of social reaction in the process of becoming deviant. Ultimately, the political aspects of deviance become increasingly apparent. Matza's work is essential for these discourses.

Major works

Matza, D. (1964) *Delinquency and Drift*. New Brunswick, New Jersey: Transaction Publishers.
—— (1969) *Becoming Deviant*. Englewood Cliffs, New Jersey: Prentice-Hall.
Matza, D. and G.M. Sykes (1961) 'Juvenile Delinquency and Subterranean Values', *American Sociological Review*, 26(5): 712–19.
Sykes, G.M. and D. Matza (1957) 'Techniques of Neutralization: A Theory of Delinquency', *American Sociological Review*, 22(6): 664–70.

Further reading

Cohen, S. (2001) *States of Denial: Knowing About Atrocities and Suffering.* Cambridge: Polity.

Maruna, S. and Copes, H. (2005) 'What Have We Learned in Five Decades of Neutralization Research?' *Crime and Justice: A Review of Research*, 32: 221–320.

Matza, D. and Morgan, P. (1995) 'Controlling Drug Use: The Great Prohibition', in Thomas Blomberg and Stanley Cohen (eds) *Punishment and Social Control*. Chicago, Illinois: Aldine De Gruyter.

Weiss, J.G. (1970) 'Dialogue with David Matza', *Issues in Criminology*, 6: 33–53.

ANTHONY J. LEMELLE, JR.

JAMES Q. WILSON (1931–)

Post-World War II academic criminology was widely perceived to be a predominantly liberal enterprise. Most theories of crime and delinquency are sociological in origin and focus on specific social conditions – anomie, bad friends, bad neighbourhoods, bad labels, poverty, family strife – that push, it is believed, otherwise innocent people into trouble. Almost always, criminology focuses on environmental concerns and the ways these supra-individual factors mold purportedly powerless individuals. It is the environment and social conditions that cause crime – rarely individuals themselves.

Emerging at the height of this progressive consensus in criminology in the 1960s, James Q. Wilson's scholarship stands in stark contrast to this belief system and is a major reason why he is such a controversial figure in the intellectual history of criminology. Consider Lawrence Cohen's review of Wilson (and Herrnstein's) *Crime and Human Nature*:

> This book replaces the liberal biases of much contemporary criminology with the conservative ideology that has come to be associated with the authors. ... American sociologists tend to take a proprietary interest in criminology and to think of the leading theories about crime as 'sociological' ... [it] may startle numerous sociologists, and those who suffer from high blood pressure should be cautious in reading it.
>
> (1987: 202)

James Q. Wilson is not a sociologist; he does not skirt using the individual as a unit of analysis to explain a phenomenon like crime; and he does not shy away from the uglier realities about human nature, morality and immorality, vice, crime, and violence. Additionally, Wilson is interested and has been heavily involved in public policies to prevent and reduce crime (for instance, he served on a number of national commissions including The White House Task Force on Crime in 1966, the National Advisory Commission on Drug Abuse Prevention in 1972–73, Attorney General's Task Force on Violent Crime in 1981, and the President's Foreign Intelligence Advisory Board from 1985 to 1991, and was awarded the Presidential Medal of Freedom from President George W. Bush in 2003). This entry explores how his career in criminology has been paradoxical in that Wilson has been tremendously influential while also being maligned for his conservatism.

James Q. Wilson was born in Denver, Colorado in 1931 and was educated at the University of Redlands (AB, 1952) and the University of Chicago (PhD, 1959). For over thirty years, Wilson was a professor at Harvard University (later at UCLA and his current home at Pepperdine University). Wilson's early research focused on the interplay between cities, their bureaucratic and political structure, and policing. From 1963 to 1966, Wilson was the Director of the Joint Center for Urban Studies of the Massachusetts Institute of Technology and Harvard University. In 1966, Wilson was the Chair of the White House Task Force on Crime and was an early commentator on the growing political role that crime and its control would play in the United States. His definitive early work is *Varieties of Police Behavior* (1968), a detailed examination of politics, community structure, and policing in Upstate New York, suburban Illinois, and the urban center of Oakland, California. In this work, Wilson developed the classic typology of police patrolman styles: 1) the watchman style and its emphasis on maintaining order; 2) the legalistic style and its emphasis on the full enforcement stance of the letter of the law; and 3) the service style with its focus on community empowerment, help and social assistance to residents.

These and several other findings from *Varieties of Police Behavior* flew in the face of the prevailing belief that the police and the public were irreconcilable enemies. It stressed that the majority of police time is spent either gathering information, maintaining order, or providing mundane services – not enforcing the law; that due to organisational constraints, the police actually under-enforce the law; and that officer discretion is multifaceted and influenced by the nature of the criminal situation, whether the police or a citizen invoked police action, organisational structure and politics.

Wilson also noted significant differences in criminal conduct that varied by age, race and social class. He also wrote honestly about the occasional brutality of police work and the plain and obvious anti-social behaviours of some criminal offenders. According to Wilson (1968: 36), the police see people when they are 'dirty, angry, rowdy,

obscene, dazed, savage, or bloodied … they are not in these circumstances "equal," they are *different*. … "Decent people" and "bums"
are not equal.' In this work, Wilson also takes direct aim at the
sociological worldview that pervaded the increasingly critical assessments of the police during the late 1960s. He suggested that those
who did not believe the correlates of crime (or that crime was disproportionately committed by males, youths, nonwhites and the
poor) were delusional or 'still suffering from a romantic or Marxist
illusion that the proletariat was untouched by original sin or else they
were raised in a glass jar' (ibid: 41).

Throughout his career, Wilson published in periodicals outside
of refereed journal articles and reached a wider audience. He has written
on a range of topics including drug abuse, culture and crime, capital
punishment, marriage, religion, and the role of ideology in criminology
among others. Many of these essays would culminate in arguably his
most influential work, *Thinking About Crime* in 1975. Frustrated with
what appeared to Wilson to be politically motivated, academic nonsense, the treatise sought to utilise a 'clear and sober understanding of the
nature of man' to study crime sensibly. Wilson believed some criminologists were 'demagogues who would either deny what were among the
plainest of facts of everyday experience or claim that crime could best be
prevented by reconstituting the Supreme Court' (1975: 4). By ignoring
or refusing to acknowledge the true nature of crime, Wilson argued,
such academics were turning criminology into a misguided enterprise.

Thinking About Crime offered five overarching critiques of mainstream criminology (see DeLisi 2003). First, Wilson argued that the
view that 'society' induces individuals to commit crime is erroneous,
as is the policy impulse to address the root causes of crime. Wilson
buttressed this argument by noting the contemporaneous explosion of
crime with the proliferation of domestic spending associated with The
Great Society. Social spending toward a redistribution of resources, he
argued, is costly, unfair, and will do little to reduce crime. Instead,
Wilson suggested that the individual unit of analysis is the appropriate
one and would lead to more effective criminal justice policy.

Second, Wilson accused the criminological majority (sociologists) of
speaking out of ideology instead of empirical facts. Third, Wilson suggested that white-collar crime is simply not the equivalent of street
crime, despite the claims of criminologists who are more concerned
with the former. In addition to the more visceral victimisation that
violence inflicts, white-collar crimes like corporate fraud do not shatter
the social contract in the manner that conventional crimes like murder
and rape do.

Fourth, Wilson has continually sought to remind sociologists about something that **Emile Durkheim**, the founder of sociology, adamantly believed: crime is a moral phenomenon. According to Wilson, 'to destigmatize crime would be to lift from it the weight of moral judgment and to make crime simply a particular occupation or avocation which society has chosen to reward less ... if there is no stigma attached to an activity, then society has no business making it a crime' (1975: 253).

Finally, Wilson simply declared that 'wicked people exist', a claim that still generates discussion. Surely it is common knowledge that from an early age certain individuals consistently demonstrate troubling, antisocial behaviour. The disturbing profile of the career criminal has become a staple of academic criminology and has clear support in empirical research (e.g. Moffitt 1993). Wilson does not argue that such criminals are the products of moral panics. Instead, he contends that wicked people need to be controlled in potentially grim ways including capital punishment. In this sense, his writing is pragmatic and seeks achievable if controversial solutions.

Nowhere did this pragmatism reach greater fruition than with his 'broken windows' theory with George Kelling in 1982. Broken windows suggested that neighbourhood physical disorder engenders an environment whereby nuisance offending and vice are tolerated. If broken windows are left unattended, a message is sent to community residents that criminal transgressions will also be tolerated. In many urban areas, disorder and neighbourhood deterioration were commonplace. Graffiti, overt prostitution, open-air drug sales, burnt-out buildings, vagrancy, and related behaviours were tolerated by police and ignored by a desensitised public. This did not have to be the case. Wilson and Kelling argue that tolerating nuisance and other low-level criminal behaviours facilitated more serious crime. Conversely, vigorous enforcement of all laws, not just for those proscribing serious offenses, could change a community's environment and subsequently reduce crime.

Proponents credit the application of broken windows theory with the remarkable reductions in crime in many of America's former crime capitols (Giacopassi and Forde 2000; Sampson and Raudenbush 2001). In New York City, police practised such relentless social control that they helped to change community norms. Zero-tolerance policies for social disorder, however minor it seemed, resulted in a dramatically safer, cleaner, and more humane city. In theory, the offenders that engaged in minor delinquent acts such as jumping subway turnstiles, loitering on street corners, and participating in the drug trade, were the same ones committing more serious acts such as robbery and assault.

Of course, it is important to note that other major cities worldwide also experienced crime declines without zero-tolerance policing suggesting that multiple factors were responsible (see Harcourt 2001).

In *Crime and Human Nature* (published in 1985 with Richard Herrnstein), Wilson reviewed research from an array of disciplines to answer the question, 'What biological, developmental, situational, and adaptive processes give rise to individual characteristics that predict crime?' *Crime and Human Nature* is a call for criminologists to quit denying that individual-level constitutional variables (temper, intelligence, impulsivity, self-discipline, character, etc.) are meaningful and to embrace them as powerful explanations for all behaviours. The consideration of *both* constitutional and environmental factors will help to develop believable rationales for why some persons choose to violate the social contract and why most persons behave lawfully. This nature and nurture approach is increasingly relevant today.

In recent years, Wilson has written on more general topics such as the moral bases of human behaviour, the aetiology of morality, American politics and government, and many others. He has not produced a major criminological work in recent years. He does not need to. On a variety of levels, James Q. Wilson's influence continues to endure. Although he is still primarily thought of as a conservative criminologist, the overt ideological concern about Wilson's work has faded. Decades later, criminology has come to terms with many of the issues first raised in *Thinking About Crime*. More pronounced is the impact of the multidisciplinary perspective of *Crime and Human Nature*. In 1985, criminology was becoming theoretically boring and arguably mired in a structural sociological malaise (see also Bennett et al. 1996). Today, some of the most vibrant areas of study in criminology are the life-course and criminal careers, topical areas that incorporate genetics, psychiatry, psychology, paediatrics and cutting-edge genome-era technology. Although few criminologists today would endorse the idea that 'wicked people exist', it could be argued that everyone knows about them anyway (despite changes in nomenclature) (see e.g. DeLisi 2005). Indeed, 'career criminals' or 'life course persistent offenders' have become a central focus of theoretical, empirical and policy criminology. This change in the criminological landscape can be attributed at least partially to the contributions of James Q. Wilson.

Major works

Wilson, J.Q. (1968) *Varieties of Police Behavior: The Management of Law and Order in Eight Communities.* Cambridge, Massachusetts: Harvard University Press.

—— (1975) *Thinking About Crime*. New York: Basic Books.

—— (1993) *The Moral Sense*. New York: The Free Press.

Wilson, J.Q. and Herrnstein, R.J. (1985) *Crime and Human Nature: The Definitive Study of the Causes of Crime*. New York: Simon & Schuster.

Wilson, J.Q. and Kelling, G.L. (1982) 'Broken Windows: The Police and Neighborhood Safety', *Atlantic Monthly*, 249: 29–38.

Further reading

Bennett, W.J., DiIulio, J.J. and Walters, J.P. (1996) *Body Count: Moral Poverty … and How to Win America's War Against Crime and Drugs*. New York: Simon and Schuster.

Cohen, L.E. (1987) 'Social Control, Deviance, and the Law: Throwing Down the Gauntlet: a Challenge to the Relevance of Sociology for the Etiology of Criminal Behavior', *Contemporary Sociology*, 16: 202–5.

DeLisi, M. (2003) 'Conservatism and Common Sense: The Criminological Career of James Q. Wilson', *Justice Quarterly*, 20: 661–74.

—— (2005) *Career Criminals in Society*. Thousand Oaks, California: Sage.

Giacopassi, D., and Forde, D.R. (2000) 'Broken Windows, Crumpled Fenders, and Crime', *Journal of Criminal Justice*, 28: 397–405.

Harcourt, B.E. (2001) *Illusion of Order: The False Promise of Broken Windows Policing*. Cambridge, Massachusetts: Harvard University Press.

Kelling, G.L. and Coles, C.M. (1996) *Fixing Broken Windows: Restoring Order and Reducing Crime in Our Communities*. New York: The Free Press.

Moffitt, T.E. (1993) 'Adolescence-Limited and Life-Course-Persistent Antisocial Behavior: A Developmental Taxonomy', *Psychological Review*, 100: 674–701.

Sampson, R.J. and Raudenbush, S.W. (2001) *Disorder in Urban Neighborhoods: Does it Lead to Crime?* Washington, DC: National Institute of Justice.

MATT DELISI

STUART HALL (1932–)

Born in Kingston, Jamaica, and educated at Merton College, Oxford as a Rhodes Scholar, Stuart Hall belongs to a generation of intellectuals of British colonial origin that shed a new, uncompromising light on the nature of 'Englishness' in post-war, post-colonial British society. While the likes of Paul Gilroy, Tariq Ali and others all exerted a tremendous influence on British sociology, Hall is arguably the most significant figure among this group. His contributions to critical thought in the social sciences, cultural studies and the humanities have been immense. As a cultural and political theorist of the British state, of black Britain and of the changing landscape of British identity and popular culture in the post-war period, his work remains unsurpassed. As founding editor of the journal *New Left Review*, Hall created an important forum of independent socialist theoretical debate, shorn of the insular, dogmatic and mechanistic aspects of Marxism traditionally associated with the English Left. He was also to instigate a debate about the role that immigration and racism played in shoring up the floundering legitimacy of the British state.

In 1962 Hall resigned his editorship of *New Left Review* to teach media, film and popular culture at Chelsea College, University of London – a post unique in Britain at the time. In 1964 he was appointed Research Fellow at the newly established Centre for Contemporary Cultural Studies (CCCS) at Birmingham University. Founded by Richard Hoggart, the Centre offered the first Cultural Studies programme at a British University. Hall acted as Director of the Centre from 1968 to 1979 (when he left to become Professor of Sociology at The Open University). Under his stewardship the Centre explored many new and unorthodox directions, in turn challenging many aspects of the traditional British University system. However, its survival was always precarious, and despite its world renown, the Centre was eventually closed by the University in 2003 amid much acrimony.

Hall described his formative years as ones of estrangement, displacement and exile. His opposition to the stratification system of class and complex gradations of colour in Jamaican society, and his subsequent experience of migration to Britain, were seminal. The son of middle-class, upwardly mobile, conservative parents, family estrangement compounded his sense of social and racial injustice. Describing himself as a 'cultural hybrid' and 'the blackest member of [his light-skinned] family' (cited in Rojek 2003: 49), Hall's subsequent intellectual preoccupations with power, position and difference at least in part reflected these early experiences and sensitivities. After a privileged schooling in Jamaica, Hall left for Oxford in 1951, where he was a victim of racism and snobbery. His only refuge was the company of other black students. From this point on, he unequivocally identified with Black Nationalism against established elites, expressing solidarity with the most oppressed elements in Jamaican society. After embarking on a PhD, he quit Oxford in 1957 and worked as a supply teacher in South London. In the same year he co-founded and co-edited the *Universities and Left Review*, one of the precursors to the *New Left Review (NLR)*.

Alongside the renewal in socialist thought represented by *NLR*, Hall drew on a wide range of thinkers including structuralists such as Louis

Althusser, Claude Lévi-Strauss and **Karl Marx**, Antonio Gramsci's Humanist Marxism and Ernesto Laclau's poststructuralism. Although initially Hall distanced himself from poststructuralist and postmodernist thought, these theories were to exert an increasing influence on his later writing on culture, politics and difference. Perhaps most significantly, Hall was greatly influenced by the Italian Marxist, Antonio Gramsci (1891–1937). Gramsci contrasted what he called the 'organic intellectual' with the figure of the remote, aloof and elitist 'traditional intellectual'. Whereas traditional intellectuals tended to reflect dominant ruling ideals, organic intellectuals emerged from within subordinate groups and were active in giving voice to the interests and concerns of the less vaunted groups. As such, organic intellectuals were much closer to the everyday, to 'common sense' knowledge and popular culture than their traditional counterparts. This enabled them to point out sources of resistance to the authority of dominant groups found in popular culture, while at the same time demystifying the ways in which popular culture is appropriated and recuperated by powerful groups to win and maintain consent and subordination to their rule. As an 'organic', or in modern parlance, a 'public intellectual', Hall eschewed the traditional role of intellectuals as upholding elite values in favour of an active engagement with ordinary people's cultural expression. It was this passion and interest in cultural expression that led Hall to analyse the complex and contradictory meanings found in everyday popular culture. As a public intellectual, Hall defended black young people and gave voice to their experiences of pervasive racism in 1970s and 1980s Britain. In defiance of popular opinion his public broadcasts and popular writings celebrated the birth of a new black British identity, rooted in defiance of racism and marginality.

Although Hall's work in cultural studies is extremely wide ranging, the main focus here is his specific contribution to criminological thought. As one of the main founders of the academic study of popular culture, Hall unsettled the distinction between 'high' and popular culture. It is his idea of popular culture as contested that informs much contemporary critical criminology – in particular the role that popular culture plays as a source of representation, ideological mobilisation and control of the 'crime problem'. Building on such ideas, Hall produced two collaborative texts that were to prove profoundly influential within critical criminology.

In the first collection, *Resistance through Rituals* (1976, 2006) Hall and his collaborators focused on the burgeoning (predominantly) white youth subcultures of the 1970s. Drawing on the ideas of the French Marxist, Louis Althusser, the collection of essays shows how changes in popular culture and the emergence of a new consumer culture gave the appearance of freedom of choice and 'classlessness' that hid real relations of class and power. Althusser (and Hall) argue that ideologies (images or ideas) work unconsciously through our belief that they are addressing us individually rather than as a member of a group, and are felt to be freely chosen, deemed 'natural' and as 'common-sense'. Hall links Althusser's notion of ideology to Gramsci's concept of 'hegemony', describing the active process by which dominant ideas are established by consent and leadership rather than coercion and rule. In this second sense of how ideologies work, hegemony is maintained by partially accommodating or incorporating subordinate groups through popular culture. Yet as *Resistance through Rituals* demonstrates, popular culture and representations are also sites of struggle and contestation.

The second book, *Policing the Crisis* (1978), again draws on Gramsci. This time Hall and his co-authors analyse the state, focusing particular attention on the racism faced by young black people as they go about their daily rounds. Like the earlier collection, Hall continued to try and unravel the relationship between ideology and representations of crime and deviance.

As contemporaneous accounts of social, cultural and economic change in 1970s Britain, both *Resistance* and *Policing* deserve our full attention, not least because this epoch-making decade changed the nature of the British state and forms of crime control. Indeed *Policing* fully anticipated and predicted 'Thatcherism', the politico-economic form of governance ushered in by the election of Margaret Thatcher the year after the publication of *Policing*. Hall subsequently wrote and edited some of the most trenchant critiques of Thatcherism and its particular brand of 'authoritarian populism' (Hall and Jacques 1983; Hall 1988). Both *Resistance* and *Policing* begin with an analysis of the reasons behind the escalation of moral panics and heightened social control in the 1970s. The former emphasised the reappearance of class conflict partly displaced onto youthful subcultural responses to change; whereas, the latter emphasised a crisis of state authority displaced partly onto black people and their resistance and supposed criminality. Hall and colleagues argued that the consequent construction of folk-devils – of white and black working-class young people – was in fact a displacement of deeper anxieties about social disorder and change. The 'drift to a law and order society' saw a shift from a political culture based on consensus and consent to one increasingly based on coercion, control and crisis; and the greatly expanded use of the law and increasingly authoritarian policing. In retrospect it can be seen that this 'drift', beginning in the 1970s, became a core fixture of how the British state has ruled ever since. The 'crisis' to which *Policing* refers was that of the ways the British state governed in the context of changes in the class structure, community and the economy.

Under these new conditions, young people's transitions and experiences of social mobility found cultural expression in often opposed and contradictory youth styles – Ted, Mod, Skinhead and Hippy. Unfashionable by today's standards, *Resistance* was firmly rooted in a class analysis of youth subcultures, arguing that subcultures expressed 'imaginary solutions' to disruptions of class-based youth transitions brought on by rapid social change. It was *Policing*, however, that best captured the 1970s as a pivotal decade. Starting with a case study of the media's treatment of an interracial 'mugging gone wrong', *Policing* widened the analysis to incorporate the active role of the media, police and judiciary in amplifying the threat to society that mugging was said to pose. Eventually, the mugging panic – which linked race, youth and crime – was added to by an ever widening, escalating and converging series of moral panics about violence, law and disorder. The authors showed that the 'problem of crime and disorder' had become *the* metaphorical and symbolic touchstone for all that was 'wrong' with British society and its governance. The creation of a general 'law and order campaign' set the ideological tone for all subsequent official discussion by framing what the crime problem was. In these senses, *Policing* was prescient and influenced subsequent and recent analysis. For example, in Hall's work, one can find early echoes of processes such as *'governing through crime'* (Simon 2007) wherein governments are said to purposefully create a culture of fear, and the counter-productive and deleterious consequences of the criminalisation of poor black men (Western 2006). Today, it is a criminological axiom that democratic states routinely use the 'the crime problem' as a way of shoring up their authority and legitimacy. Hall et al.'s analysis of the wageless experiences of alienated and disaffected working-class black young people in the 1970s, and their systematic racist marginalisation and criminalisation by authority, appeared even more prescient when, only three years after the publication of *Policing*, a whirlwind of race-related violence and rioting erupted in several British cities during the summer of 1981.

Turning to Hall's writings on media representations, ideology and difference it can be seen how they have influenced debates within cultural and critical criminology and further afield. In relation to media-induced discourse about crime there are several aspects of Hall's (1980) writing that are of interest. Hall argued that the media message sent is seldom the one received. This 'lack of fit' between sender and audience – between the production of the message ('Encoding') and its reception ('Decoding') – occurs because meanings are not fixed and are received in different ways. Often, the encoding and decoding of messages are unstable; at other times their ideological presuppositions help shape everyday perceptions of reality and operate to reproduce hegemony. In placing a particular gloss on social reality the media 'effect' is to construct some meanings, about crime and deviance for example, as 'obvious' or 'natural' at the expense of others. The ways in which messages are constructed by producers and assimilated and 'read' by audiences depends on 'preferred' not fixed 'readings'. Preferred readings may involve the audience's suspension of critical reflection; rhetoric of impartiality and objectivity favoured by media professionals; or dismissal, inversion or opposition to media messages. Thus there are tensions between the mass media seen as a one-sided purveyor of dominant ideology and the active, unstable reception of media messages by differently placed audiences.

Hall's (1996) recent writing addresses what has been said to have been a profound cultural change in which it is no longer tenable to hold onto older notions of stability in areas such as identity, ethnicity, race and nation. His advocacy of the new politics of hyphenated identity, hybridity and difference and the rise of multiethnic Britain are well known; as is his intervention in the discursive policy shift from multiculturalism to social cohesion as ways of governing multi-ethnic relations in Britain (Parekh Report 2000). Finally, this shift from an earlier emphasis on ethnic and class identity to questions of cultural diversity and cultural relativism in Hall's studies of popular culture, points to the unresolved issues of how difference might be reconciled with solidarity and social cohesion, as well as competition over, and unequal access to, scarce material and cultural resources.

Major works

Hall, S. (1980) 'Encoding/Decoding', in Hall, S., Hobson, D., Lowe, A. and Willis, P. *Culture, Media, Language: Working Papers in Cultural Studies*, pp. 128–38. London: Hutchinson.

—— (1988) *The Hard Road to Renewal: Thatcherism and the Crisis of the Left*. London: Verso.

—— (1996, first published 1988) 'New ethnicities', in Morley, D. and Chen, K. (eds) *Stuart Hall: Critical Dialogues in Cultural Studies*, pp. 441–9. London: Routledge.

Hall, S., Critcher, C., Jefferson, T., Clarke, J. and Roberts, B. (1978) *Policing the Crisis: Mugging, the State, and Law and Order*. London: Macmillan.

Hall, S. and Jacques, M. (ed.) (1983) *The Politics of Thatcherism*. London: Lawrence and Wishart.

Hall, S. and Jefferson, T. (ed.) (2006) *Resistance Through Rituals: Youth Subcultures in Post-war Britain* (second edition). London: Routledge.

Further reading

Morley, D. and Chen, K. (ed.) (1996) *Stuart Hall: Critical Dialogues in Cultural Studies*. London: Routledge.

Parekh Report (2000) *The Future of Multi-Ethnic Britain*. London: Runnymede Trust.

Proctor, J. (2004) *Stuart Hall*. London: Routledge.

Rojek, C. (2003) *Stuart Hall*. Cambridge: Polity.

Simon, J. (2007) *Governing Through Crime: How the War on Crime Transformed American Democracy and Created a Culture of Fear*. Oxford: Oxford University Press.

Western, B. (2006) *Punishment and Inequality in America*. New York: Russell Sage Foundation.

COLIN WEBSTER

WILLIAM J. CHAMBLISS (1933–)

Even amongst the great figures in criminology, William Chambliss stands out as a creative scholar and dedicated researcher who has helped to shape the agenda of modern criminology. Throughout his fascinating career, Chambliss has been a renegade scholar, a courageous researcher of 'outsider populations', a social activist, and a caring mentor to young scholars and students. Parts of his life read almost like a movie screenplay – he has been threatened with both bodily harm and legal sanctions for his research into power and corruption; he has befriended thieves in an attempt to get an inside look at their lives and careers; and his personal story combines intrigue, morality and social ideals. In many ways it is fair to say that his has been a career unlike any other in the pantheon of criminology.

While analyses of law and power provide the theoretical framework that grounds much of his work, Chambliss's research offers a well-rounded and meticulously investigated glimpse into the big picture of crime and politics while also carefully highlighting the human details of his research subjects. The scope of his work is impressive, ranging from historical analyses of piracy, smuggling, and vagrancy laws, to the labelling process and its disparate impact on two groups of high school boys, from the life history of a professional safecracker, to an investigation into a web of corruption that wove its way through Seattle across the globe to Thailand and Turkey.

Chambliss claims he 'came into criminology quite by accident' (Chambliss 1987: 1). He was born in New York and attended high school in East Los Angeles where he was a member of the 'Solons' gang. After his junior year, he and his best friend travelled north and ended up working in the fields in Walla Walla, Washington alongside inmates from the state penitentiary; it was then that he began wondering, what are prisons for? Chambliss began college thinking he would become a prison warden; he studied at UCLA, where he majored in psychology and English and met and was mentored by **Donald Cressey**.

After graduating from UCLA, Chambliss was drafted by the army and sent to Korea with the Counter Intelligence Corps. In Korea he first began to question the connection between American policies and crime (Chambliss 1987: 5–6). On Cressey's advice, Chambliss went to graduate school at Indiana University to study sociology and law with legendary criminologists **Edwin Sutherland** and **Albert Cohen** (Cohen cites Chambliss's Master's thesis on the deterrent effect of parking tickets in his classic essay 'The Sociology of the Deviant Act: Anomie Theory and Beyond'). His first academic job was at the University of Washington in Seattle where he began the research on corruption that would become the basis for his book, *On the Take*.

Chambliss is considered to be one of the early critical criminologists and he has been recognised for his lifetime achievements in the field. He served as President of both the American Society of Criminology and the Society for the Study of Social Problems, and has received the Sutherland Award for Outstanding Contributions to Criminology, the Lifetime Achievement Award for Contributions in Criminal Justice from the Academy of Criminal Justice Sciences, and the Lifetime Achievement Award from the Sociology of Law Section of the American Sociological Association. His work was some of the first to identify the symbiotic relationship between crime and politics and to bring together interdisciplinary perspectives on the study of law. His early books, *Crime and the Legal Process* and *Law, Order, and Power* helped to focus attention on the sociology of law and its larger contexts, including the emergence of legal norms, the administration of criminal law, and the impact of legal sanctions (Chambliss 1969: vii–viii). His Presidential address to the American Society of Criminology on 'State Organized Crime' (Chambliss 1989) inspired new research on a topic which to that point had largely been unrecognised or ignored by criminologists.

Chambliss and Seidman (1971) describe the law and its institutions as 'the single most important force shaping the structure of society' (p. 507). They argue that we must look at the law in action to begin to understand how control of the legal process is used by the dominant group to shape the society according to its own interests. Following his own advice, in 'A Sociological Analysis of the Law of Vagrancy' Chambliss traced vagrancy laws and their implementation from the 1300s in England to the United States in the twentieth century, arguing that the impact of such laws has remained strikingly consistent: 'The lack of change in the vagrancy statutes, then can be seen as a reflection of the society's perception of a continuing need to control some of its "suspicious" or "undesirable" members' (1964: 75).

Perhaps the piece that has introduced most criminology students to William Chambliss's work is his study on 'The Roughnecks and the Saints' (1973), which although written several decades ago still reverberates today. Chambliss spent two years 'hanging out' with two different groups of high school boys – the upper-middle class 'Saints' and the working-class 'Roughnecks'. While the two groups of boys were fairly similar in their brushes with delinquency, the community's reactions were quite different. Chambliss explains that the Saints were constantly involved in truancy, drinking, vandalism and petty theft, yet they were never officially arrested for any of their delinquent behaviour. The Roughnecks, by contrast, committed about the same amount of delinquency as the Saints but were constantly in trouble with the police and the community.

By keeping in touch with the Saints and the Roughnecks through early adulthood, Chambliss was able to document the power of labels and community expectations. As community sentiment might have predicted, most of the Saints went on to college and outwardly successful conforming careers. Two of the Roughnecks earned athletic scholarships and were able to attend college, but others never finished high school and served time in prison.

Reflecting on the Saints and the Roughnecks for this entry, Chambliss shared that there were several major surprises while studying the two groups of boys:

(1) how serious were the crimes of the Saints and how inconsequential were the crimes of the Roughnecks. (2) How readily the boys in each group accepted the labels attached to them even though the labels were incompatible with their actual behavior and (3) how easily some of them (the two football players) changed their self image, their behavior and their lives.

While the Saints and Roughnecks offer a glimpse into how differential power affects individuals, Chambliss's book with Harry King provides a first-hand and very personal account of the life of a professional thief. King was a thief who specialised in safecracking for nearly fifty years, from approximately 1910 through 1960. Chambliss befriended Harry at the end of his career, and they spent years working on a book together about his life. The book offers insight into the norms and practices of a criminal occupation normally hidden from mainstream society. Chambliss writes in the introduction to *Harry King: A Professional Thief's Journey*:

> Here then is Harry's story. It is a vital documentary of the life of a man – a man I grew to love and whose friendship I cherished. A man who suffered as we all do from inconsistencies and contradictions. A man who struggled against oppressive forces and who made his way in the face of obstacles and with an occasional flash of luck. A man who enjoyed parts of life, suffered from others and lived with dignity. A man who was a professional thief.
>
> (1984: 3)

Another of Chambliss's seminal works is his book *On the Take*. Here Chambliss explored illegal business in Seattle, Washington and argued that crime is structurally based and is a product of the political economy. He demonstrates that organised crime is quite different from the portrayal it receives in popular culture. Instead of a mafia or unified group of private citizens running illicit businesses, Chambliss found 'that organized crime really consists of a coalition of politicians, law-enforcement people, businessmen, union leaders, and (in some ways least important of all) racketeers'. Of these groups, it was the 'politicians who for many years have had the ultimate and most important practical control of organized crime' (1988: 9).

Researching this book was a risky venture. Stakeholders in the profitable network of organised crime obviously did not want their illicit dealings and relationships to be exposed and *On the Take* did just that. Chambliss explained: 'During the research for *On the Take* I was threatened with harm to myself and my family. After publication I was threatened with a subpoena if I did not reveal my sources (I refused and the subpoena was never sent). I continued to be threatened with bodily harm and law suits after leaving Seattle but nothing ever came of it' (personal communication 2008).

The research on organised crime would take Chambliss around the world as he conducted hundreds of interviews over several years. The analysis began in Seattle with a focus on bookmakers, pawnbrokers, pimps, drug dealers, prostitutes, thieves and cops, and eventually led him across the globe to Thailand, Hong Kong, Africa, Sweden, Norway, England and Cuba. Reflecting on the journey and the resulting book, Chambliss shared: 'On the Take took me into the field and required me to make theoretical sense out of a mass of seemingly unconnected data. To the degree that I succeeded in doing that, I am pleased with the outcome.'

Equally at home in a library, in a classroom, in local bars, or in the opium fields in Thailand and Burma, Chambliss is a versatile researcher and scholar. He explained his motivation as follows: 'On a day to day basis, the love of digging through archives (for historical documents on law and piracy for example) combined with an equal love of being on the street to meet "outsiders" and figure out why the world is constructed the way it is has driven my choice or particular researches. I find the world, its people and its institutions incredibly fascinating and curious.'

While always deeply engaged with his subjects and research, Chambliss paid a high personal price for acting on his ideals in his daily life as a university professor. He says that one of his biggest professional disappointments stemmed from his political activism at University of California, Santa Barbara supporting the anti-war movement and the Black Student Union. As he explained, his activism made him 'a Pariah' and alienated him from a number of colleagues whom he admired. 'I learned the price of being politically active against the inherent conservatism of faculties and universities. But it is a price I paid and would pay again' (personal communication 2008).

In offering advice to young criminologists, Chambliss highlighted three key points. First, in recognising that his own years of teaching and researching organised crime in Nigeria, Thailand and Zambia were invaluable for his intellectual and personal growth, his most important suggestion is to: 'GO OVERSEAS. Africa, Latin America, Asia: the more different the culture, the better'. Second, Chambliss suggested that young criminologists 'Forget about research grants. You will never be able to do groundbreaking field research if you wait for grants. I made my mind up early on that part of my salary had to be spent on research and it still is.' Finally, Chambliss offered this insight: 'Realize that people love to talk about their work, even if their work is killing people or stealing from the public.'

Listening to Chambliss talk about his own work is certainly an experience in itself. His insight, work ethic and compassion have made him an exemplary researcher and teacher; he is a model for generations of scholars working to contribute to our understanding of the impacts of social inequality and the promise of social justice.

Major works

Chambliss, W.J. (1964) 'A Sociological Analysis of the Law of Vagrancy', *Social Problems*, 12: 67–77.

—— (1969) *Crime and the Legal Process*. New York: McGraw-Hill Book Company.

—— (1973) 'The Roughnecks and the Saints', *Society*, November/ December: 24–31.

—— (1978/1988) *On the Take: From Petty Crooks to Presidents* (second edition). Bloomington, Indiana: Indiana University Press.

—— (1989) 'State-Organized Crime—The American Society of Criminology, 1988 Presidential Address', *Criminology*, 27(2): 183–208.

Chambliss, W.J. and R.B. Seidman (1971) *Law, Order, and Power*. Reading, Massachusetts: Addison-Wesley Publishing Company.

King, H. and W.J. Chambliss (1984) *Harry King: A Professional Thief's Journey*. New York: John Wiley & Sons.

Further reading

Chambliss, W.J. (1987) 'I Wish I Didn't Know Now What I Didn't Know Then', *The Criminologist*, 12(6): 1, 5–7, 9.

—— (2001) *Power, Politics and Crime* (second edition). Boulder, Colorado: Westview Press.

Moyer, I.L. (2001) 'Conflict/Radical/Marxist Theory', in *Criminological Theories: Traditional and Nontraditional Voices and Themes*. Thousand Oaks, California: Sage.

MICHELLE INDERBITZIN AND HEATHER BOYD

THOMAS MATHIESEN (1933–)

Critical, reflexive, autobiographical elements are always interweaved in academic research and writing, even if one has to look hard for them. Intertwined with theoretical stances are subjective positions, political choices, social responsibilities and self-disclosures of an intensely personal kind. In the work of Thomas Mathiesen, these elements are closer to the surface than in most criminological scholarship. But what can we learn about Mathiesen's work from his young and early adult life? He was born in 1933 into a middle-class family living in the suburbs of Oslo, Norway. His mother and father were first cousins and their courtship and marriage, while not illegal, was subject to considerable disapproval from the rest of the family. The relationship was strong, though, even surviving over three years of forced separation while his mother studied in the United States and his father remained in Norway. Thomas's childhood was happy, stable and relatively comfortable. Even during the wartime German occupation of Norway when basic commodities became so scarce that there were concerns about famine, the family were not unduly affected. Most Norwegians turned their hands to growing crops and keeping livestock and Thomas, who was seven years old when the Germans arrived, remembers it as a time when his family grew potatoes and tobacco and kept chickens and rabbits. Like many of his countrymen, Thomas's father took part in passive resistance efforts, circulating an illegal newspaper but, for the most part, Thomas grew up during the military occupation without experiencing significant risk or danger.

Aside from his close-knit family, one of the primary reasons for Thomas's early feelings of security, and an ongoing defining characteristic in his life is that his mother was born in the United States. The love for America that she instilled in her son was augmented by the second 'occupation' of Norway by American GIs, who had come to Norway through Italy during the gruesome Italian campaign where thousands of Americans were slaughtered during fierce German resistance. A small group of GIs befriended the family and won the awe and admiration of the young Thomas. His later decision to study at the University of Wisconsin – the state in which his 'American family' lived – is therefore unsurprising. More remarkable is that he turned his back on his intended path which was to study music (despite fearing at the time that he was not good enough to be a professional musician, Mathiesen is a gifted pianist and continues to indulge his passion on a Schimmel grand piano). He decided instead to study sociology. Like many of us, it was a series of chance encounters that decided his fate: meeting fellow students studying sociology who impressed him; finding at the University of Wisconsin a vibrant sociology and anthropology department that had recently seen Hans H. Gerth and C. Wright Mills pass through; and signing up for a course in 'American Society' which whetted his appetite for more. Having made the decision to become a sociologist, he found himself studying under the tutelage of Professor Howard Becker (that is, Howard Paul Becker, author of *Through Values to Social Interpretation*, not **Howard Saul Becker** of *Outsiders* fame). Becker's approach was qualitative, interpretive and phenomenological; he himself had been mentored by **Robert E. Park** and was steeped in the Chicago School as well as classic European sociology. Such was Becker's towering influence that other great sociologists of the time, among them Talcott Parsons, barely registered on the intellectual development of Mathiesen and his peers, other than as someone who took the joy, passion and fun out of sociology and was therefore to be avoided if at all possible!

An equally pervasive series of events which shaped his intellectual and political leanings was McCarthyism. Wisconsin was Senator Joseph McCarthy's state and during Thomas's time there the McCarthy hearings took place. Tellingly, the author who, half a century later, would pen *Silently Silenced* writes of his University days that 'McCarthy's shadow was all over the campus, silencing people' (see http://folk.uio. no/thomasm/biography.html). However, despite (or, more likely, because of) the fervent political climate, a liberal and critical spirit prevailed at the University of Wisconsin and Mathiesen flourished.

Back in Norway in 1955, Mathiesen registered at the University of Oslo's Department of Sociology where he was encouraged to pursue experimental, empirical research on small-group dynamics; studies that he found a welcome and stimulating diversion from the rather conservative, structural-functionalism that dominated sociology in the 1950s. In Norway, Talcott Parsons was simply unavoidable; his influence on the social sciences was, as Mathiesen reflected later, 'part of an American cultural conquest of post-war Europe' and the primary reason why his time as a student of sociology at Oslo was one of the unhappiest periods of his life (a year later Mathiesen visited Salzberg in Austria for a month-long seminar and heard Talcott Parsons speak. He found him more interesting in person than his books had indicated). His opposition to this sociological hegemony went unvoiced, however, much to his later chagrin. He reflects 'I … remained silent. I was too weak and probably too conformist and didn't have the guts to protest' (ibid).

After seven years of studying, Mathiesen's professional career began on 1 January 1959 at the Institute for Social Research in Oslo, an independent research centre where he was to remain, in various capacities, for 20 years. Funded by the Norwegian Research Council for Science and the Humanities, he found himself in a very different academic environment to that of the University's Department of Sociology. Here he became part of a creative, communicative, critical, interdisciplinary and politically active team who imbued their work with a sense of optimism and vitality. It was also here – against a backdrop of the Vietnam War and growing political and civil rights protests in the United States – that his love affair with America finally and irrevocably crumbled.

Reflecting on a career that has spanned six decades and is still going strong, it seems fruitless to try and categorise a body of work as conceptually innovative, theoretically nuanced and politically demanding as that produced by Thomas Mathiesen. However, it is convenient for our present purposes to think of his scholarly output in three main areas: prisons, media, and surveillance.

It was at the Institute for Social Research that Mathiesen first came into contact with prisons. He received funding to spend two years of participant observation at a prison in Oslo; his first major empirical project. Written up as *The Defences of the Weak* he claims that at this time he was still United States-oriented and that the book was geared towards American prison research. Yet it stands apart from his American contemporaries' work, particularly the enduring **Gresham Sykes**' (1958) *Society of Captives*. While they share the view that imprisonment is a painful and disabling experience Mathiesen contradicts Sykes in his assessment of how prisoners adapt to life inside. The latter argued that the pressures of confinement are substantially mitigated by social interaction, solidarity and by the taking on of stylised subcultural roles; a finding that spawned dozens of studies throwing up ever more complicated typologies of inmate adaptation. Mathiesen, however, found little evidence of the degree of social solidarity which Sykes describes. His themes bear some similarities to those of Sykes – loyalty, fairness, manhood and privacy – but he claims that in the dog-eat-dog environment of the prison (which, in Mathiesen's work constitutes a much more 'disrupted' society than that which Sykes writes about) prisoners are essentially weak and lonely individuals, subject to an enforced dependency on their custodians.

The convergence of Mathiesen's prison research with his growing political maturity and disaffection with American cultural and military hegemony in Europe led to his involvement in establishing and chairing KROM, the Norwegian Association for Penal Reform. No longer 'conformist' or prepared to remain silent, Mathiesen was instrumental in setting KROM's agenda which was guided by four sets of ideas (see www.krom.no). First, there was a recognition among several prominent intellectuals and practitioners in Norway that prisons were inhumane and did not work, and a shared feeling that something had to be done about this situation. Second, there was a commitment to involving prisoners themselves in political action. While such grass roots involvement is more common now, at the time it was viewed as radical and alarming, especially by the media of the day. Third, and again a cause for sensationalised reporting by the media, KROM swiftly moved its agenda from prison reform to prison abolition and was instrumental in the abolition of major parts of the Norwegian penal system, including the youth prison system in 1975. Fourth, the early members of KROM viewed their work as a learning experience and their mistakes and setbacks as useful lessons to guide future actions. Their emphasis has always been on 'action research' which is ongoing and which constitutes 'unfinished business' (Mathiesen 1974). Given the upward trend in prison population numbers in Norway as in most European countries in the last two decades, KROM's unfinished business has, of necessity, been switched to reducing further expansion of the penal system, and making prisons more humane, although Mathiesen still regularly speaks and writes about the importance of not diminishing or abandoning the principles of abolition in favour of the easier and more politically attractive goals of 'alternatives' to imprisonment and prison reform. Forty years after its inception, KROM still holds a three-day annual conference in a Norwegian mountain resort, attracting lawyers, social scientists, policy makers, politicians (including from the Ministry of Justice) and prisoners who obtain special release to attend.

Throughout much of his published work, Mathiesen has explored the phenomenon of public acquiescence towards the prison which, he believes, is partly organised around a process of political silencing. By this he means 'the attitudinal and behavioural subordination to political standpoints which are regarded as authoritative ... so that acquiescence follows and given standpoints are accepted without protest' (Mathiesen 2004: 9). He is further interested in the role that television has played in making prison population growth acceptable to – or at least unquestioned by – the public at large. Mathiesen outlines three developments which he says are interwoven with the development of television: the commodification of penal policy; unprincipled and opportunistic attempts at legitimation; and changes in the nature of public debate which is now framed by the sensationalised, sound-bite culture of TV talkshows (Mathiesen 2001). His response to these processes is to call for the development of an alternative public space that can compete with the superficiality of the mass media's output and facilitate intellectualism and principled thinking. The conferences and other meetings organised by KROM are a manifestation of Mathiesen's personal sense of responsibility to create such a space.

Another contribution that Mathiesen has made to debates about media influence is to argue that **Michel Foucault**'s interpretation of the Panopticon must – within the context of the 'total system of the mass media' (ibid: 219) – be supplemented by the Synopticon. In other words, in modern surveillance-rich and media-saturated societies, panopticism is intimately fused with synopticism in a process that simultaneously permits both top-down scrutiny by authority figures and bottom-up observation by the masses. 'Reality TV' shows combine the panoptic and synoptic, being designed to allow the few to see the many (the programme producers in the studio gallery who observe the activities of contestants 24 hours a day), while simultaneously and synoptically allowing millions of viewers to watch both participants and, occasionally, the 'watchers' themselves. For Mathiesen, television news and the popular press also act as Synopticons, devouring crime and purging it of every detail other than that which can be easily digested by a mass audience. In both cases – *Big Brother* and news media – it is the essentialist, the sensational and the stereotypical elements of individual characteristics and behaviour that get hurled back into society to titillate, terrify and panic (Mathiesen 1997).

The threads of Thomas Mathiesen's professional life have been too many and varied to mention in anything but the briefest terms here. He became Professor of Sociology of Law in 1972 at the age of 39 and eventually landed in a merged Department of Criminology and Sociology of Law. He, along with that other colossus, **Nils Christie**, came to shape, promote, indeed, personify Norwegian criminology. He remains involved with KROM and with campaigning more widely for prison abolition, and continues writing and researching on the media. More recently he has contributed to debates about the surveillance of citizens by governments (notably in the UK) under the guise of protecting them from potential acts of terrorism, and the consequences of this for democracy. Mathiesen has received numerous honours and accolades and has inspired countless students and peers, yet he remains a modest and gentle man. Never afraid of mixing the personal and the political, throughout his long and distinguished career his work has been marked by a rare integrity, honesty and generosity of spirit.

Major works

Mathiesen, T. (1965) *The Defences of the Weak: A Sociological Study of a Norwegian Correctional Institution*. London: Tavistock.
—— (1974) *The Politics of Abolition: Essays in Political Action Theory*. London: Martin Robertson/Oslo: Universitetsforlaget.
—— (1980) *Law, Society and Political Action: Towards a Strategy under Late Capitalism*. London/New York; Academic Press.
—— (1990/2006) *Prison on Trial*. London: Sage (third edition). Winchester: Waterside.
—— (1997) 'The Viewer Society: Michel Foucault's "Panopticon" Revisited', *Theoretical Criminology*, 1(2): 215–34.

—— (2001) 'Television, Public Space and Prison Population: a Commentary on Mauer and Simon', *Punishment & Society*, 3(1): 35–42.
—— (2004) *Silently Silenced: On the Creation of Acquiescence in Modern Society*. Winchester: Waterside.

Further reading

Mathiesen, T. (2000) *An Autobiographical Note*. Available online at: http://folk.uio.no/thomasm/biography.html (accessed 23 July 2009).
Ryan, M. and Sim, J. (2007) 'Campaigning for and Campaigning Against Prisons: Excavating and Re-affirming the Case for Prison Abolition', in Y. Jewkes (ed.) *Handbook on Prisons*. Cullompton: Willan.
Sparks, R., Bottoms, A.E. and Hay, W. (1996) *Prisons and the Problem of Order*. Oxford: Clarendon Press.

YVONNE JEWKES

SUSAN BROWNMILLER (1935–)

Susan Brownmiller may be considered by some an unusual choice for inclusion in a book recognising key thinkers in criminology. But Brownmiller has been a significant contributor to criminological thought and understanding, despite never having studied or taught the subject. This is particularly evident in relation to the revolutionary influence of her ideas and writing on the crime of rape. Brownmiller's book, *Against Our Will: Men, Women and Rape*, is widely hailed as a 'classic' and serves as a touchstone for those researching and analysing sexual violence. Her book shook the ground when first published in 1975, and the shockwaves reverberate to this day.

Brownmiller was born on 15 February 1935 in Brooklyn, New York. Her parents were both in paid work – her father as a sales clerk in Macy's department store and her mother as a secretary in the Empire State building. She secured scholarships to assist in attending Cornell University and later studied at the Jefferson School of Social Sciences, all the time dreaming of becoming a Broadway actress. While studying acting in New York City she worked as a waitress and file clerk before moving into writing and editorial-type jobs. She had articles published in a range of periodicals including *Coronet*, *Newsweek* and *Village Voice*.

This was the early 1960s, an era of protests, demonstrations and campaigns for civil rights. Brownmiller was in the thick of it. Her involvement started when she participated in a sit-in to end lunch counter segregation – the practice of having 'Whites Only' seating areas at restaurants in the Southern states of the United States. She joined the Congress of Racial Equality (CORE) and began what was to become a life of political and social activism. In 1964, while working as a researcher for *Newsweek* magazine, she took time out to be one of a thousand white volunteers participating in the Freedom Summer in Mississippi to register black voters. Marches against the war in Vietnam followed, and in 1968 Brownmiller became a co-founder of the New York Radical Feminists. The following year she wrote a piece for the *New York Times Magazine* on Shirley Chisholm, the first black woman elected to the US Congress. The children's division of publishing company Doubleday asked if she could extend this piece into a short book on Chisholm's life aimed at young readers – Brownmiller says she gasped when reaching page 50, having never previously written anything longer than a magazine article.

Brownmiller reflected on this period of her life in her 1999 book *In Our Time: Memoir of a Revolution* – a work still recognised for its candid, insider account of the history of radical feminism in the United States. *In Our Time* notes the parallels between the development of the contemporary Women's Liberation Movement and the suffrage movement of the nineteenth century. Women who had initially joined the struggle against slavery began to see parallels with their own oppression and started campaigning for the vote. Likewise, in the 1960s, many of the women who joined the civil rights struggle went on to play key roles in the Women's Liberation Movement.

Brownmiller's memoir also records how it was within the context of her participation in a consciousness-raising group in New York in 1970 that she began engaging with rape theory. This was a time when women lived with the daily humiliation of sexual harassment; only now, some of these women decided to fight back. She describes how the 'Ogle-In' became a popular tactic, where a group of women would gather on the street with the aim of turning the tables on men. On one occasion, for instance, a newspaper reported that male employees from the stock exchange had begun a 'fun' morning ritual in which they lay in wait watching for a particularly large-breasted secretary to exit the subway station. The feminists responded by organising an Ogle-In on Wall Street. Brownmiller observes: 'It was incredibly liberating to reverse the wolf whistles, animal noises, and body parts appraisals that customarily flowed in our direction' (Brownmiller 1999: 196).

Despite such actions, when a member of her consciousness-raising group suggested that rape was an important issue for feminists to consider, Brownmiller says she was initially not convinced. She adhered to the prevailing view that 'rape was a murky, deviant crime any alert woman could avoid' (ibid: 197). However, after listening to another group member's account of group rape, she began to change her mind. She and other members of the New York Radical Feminists decided to organise a public speak-out on rape, to be followed by a conference several months later, under the slogan 'Rape is a Political Crime Against Women'.

Initially there was trepidation as to whether anyone would turn up, let alone speak out. The organisers need not have worried. On a Sunday afternoon in January 1971, a church hall filled to overflowing with over 300 women and a handful of men (it was agreed the latter could be admitted if they paid two dollars and were accompanied by a woman). Thirty women shared their stories of being raped, and women's consciousness was indeed raised: 'Sexual assault was a crime of power that crossed all lines of age, race, and class; women feared they would be killed; resistance was possible: the police were dismissive. All of us were reeling from the new knowledge' (ibid: 200–1).

As planning for the conference progressed, Brownmiller began outlining the different aspects she felt should be covered. These included workshops addressing the psychology of rape offending, the impacts on victims, marital rape, and rape during times of war. She realised that this conference on its own would be insufficient to produce the analysis of rape that was needed – a book was required and she wanted to be the one to write it.

Meanwhile the conference needed planning and promoting. One day Brownmiller and a friend were out on the street distributing flyers when a guy 'goosed' (bottom-pinched) her. Brownmiller's response was swift. Unsure whether to blame years of accumulated anger or inspiration gleaned from watching Emma Peel on *The Avengers*, she set off in pursuit of her attacker and attempted to high-kick him on the backside. The result was a severely sprained ankle that forced her to attend the conference on crutches. This in no way subdued the excitement she felt following social worker Florence Rush's analysis of child sexual abuse, an analysis that made explicit the connections between male dominance over women, the socialisation of girls, and sexual abuse. Brownmiller saw rape for what it was and told a reporter for *Good Housekeeping*: 'Rape is to women as lynching was to blacks. It's a conscious process of intimidation that keeps all women in a state of fear' (ibid: 204). By the end of that weekend she had drafted a proposal for a book on rape, and soon secured a publishing contract from Simon and Schuster. She expected it would take a year to write – in fact it took four.

Against Our Will: Men, Women and Rape was published in 1975. By now other feminist writers had also begun addressing the issue of rape and Women Against Rape groups were springing up in various cities across North America. The climate was right for a strong and clear analysis exposing the ways in which rape was not an isolated act committed by a few social deviants but a mechanism by which men exerted control over women. Brownmiller's book hit the mark. As she later described it: 'Writing "Against Our Will" felt like shooting an arrow into a bull's-eye in very slow motion. Few people are lucky enough to be in on the creation of a new cause, and then to publish a book on the subject five years down the line, when a large mainstream audience is ready to receive it' (ibid: 244).

The book quickly became a controversial bestseller, significant in bringing the arguments of radical feminism into everyday, mainstream society. Brownmiller confronted head-on the dominant psychological conception of rape as a lust-motivated crime, exposing the political utility of rape as a means of enforcing patriarchy. Rape was not committed by a few deviant men but a culturally condoned tool of oppression, an established means by which men could assert their masculinity and dominance.

This was one of the first histories of rape to be written, exploring its role in society from Old Testament times until today. Brownmiller approached this task in a interdisciplinary manner, drawing on an eclectic mix of literary sources, sociology, psychoanalysis, law and mythology. She demonstrated the impossibility of understanding rape without reference to the historical development of laws and attitudes reflecting women as the property of men. Her research illustrated how when rape was first made a crime, it was a crime between men – one man had violated another man's property. The impact on the woman was not even acknowledged – it was inconsequential, because women themselves were of no consequence.

Today the notion of rape being about power is widely accepted. Yet when Brownmiller penned *Against Our Will*, this was not the case. She discussed previously seldom acknowledged occurrences such as prison rape and gay rape, drawing attention to the centrality of notions of power and control underlying such issues. As she described it:

> [R]ape became not only a male prerogative, but man's basic weapon of force against woman, the principal agent of his will and her fear. His forcible entry into her body, despite her physical protestations and struggle, became the vehicle of his victorious conquest over her being, the ultimate test of his superior strength, the triumph of his manhood. ... [Rape] is nothing more

or less than a conscious process of intimidation by which *all men* keep *all women* in a state of fear.

(Brownmiller 1975: 14–15, emphasis in original)

The response to this book catapulted Brownmiller overnight into national prominence. She was sent on a six-week tour of twenty-one cities to publicise the book, and appeared on numerous talk shows, being named as one of *Time* magazine's twelve women of the year in 1975.

The book was not without its critics, though, and illustrating the principle of 'divide and rule', some of the most vitriolic attacks came from other women of the activist left. One fiercely debated issue arose from Brownmiller's discussion of the 'Scottsboro Nine', a group of young black men sentenced to death in the 1930s for the rape of two white women on a train. A subsequent campaign led by the Communist party exposed the ways in which the 'victims' had been pressured by a group of white men into making the allegations, and committed perjury in the process. Her efforts to draw attention to the sexism involved saw her criticised for defending the women's false allegations, with black feminist leader Angela Davis being one of those who labelled Brownmiller 'racist' as a result (Barrett and McIntosh 1985).

Against Our Will has also been criticised for reflecting a position of biological essentialism. The early pages of the book assert: 'By anatomical fiat – the inescapable construction of their genital organs – the human male was a natural predator and the human female served as his natural prey' (Brownmiller 1975: 16).

Brownmiller has also been criticised for promoting a polarised perspective of men as predators versus women as victims, and for emphasising that rape is violence to such an extent that the sexual element is obscured (MacKinnon 1989). The subsequent development of feminist theory acknowledges the importance of recognising the differences among women and among men, rather than simply between women and men. The complex connections between rape and sex are also more widely appreciated now, with it being better understood as to why some men choose to assert their power through the act of rape, and how power and sex are often fused in the crime of rape. Greater attention is also given today to the prevalence of marital and acquaintance rape, and the 'ordinariness' of rape, rather than the book's emphasis on such aspects as gang and prison rape. However, Brownmiller needs to be remembered for her pioneering role in this field and for her courage in challenging the established orthodoxy of the time – rape was no longer the crime that could not be named.

Since its initial publication, *Against Our Will* has been published in more than sixteen foreign-language editions. Brownmiller herself has stayed actively involved within the feminist movement, writing challenging books and articles. These included a paper in which she expressed her views against pornography entitled, 'Let's Put Pornography Back in the Closet' (originally published in *Newsday* in 1979), and an exploration of *Femininity*, published in 1984. She also wrote a novel, *Waverly Place*, taking only four months to complete it after being provoked by the murder of a child in her neighbourhood, Greenwich Village. A reporting assignment for the magazine *Travel and Leisure* led to her publishing the book, *Seeing Vietnam: Encounters of the Road and Heart*, in 1994. Today she still teaches feminist courses in New York, including one at Pace University on great tragic novels written by twentieth-century women, and a writing course at New York University. She also has a website on which more recent writings appear, including her reflections post-9/11. When asked by an interviewer for *Book Reporter* in 2000 who influenced her specifically as a writer, her responses included an eclectic mix of authors such as Virginia Woolf, Emile Durkheim and James Michener.

Brownmiller's analysis of rape remains the publication for which she is most known. It is difficult to assess the immense significance this book has had on the development of criminology. Before it was written, we were in the 'dark ages' of understanding violence against women generally, and sexual violence in particular. She conducted the research necessary to inform an examination of rape that transformed the ways in which this crime was viewed and explained. Her analysis provided a platform that subsequent theorists could build on, as evidenced in the works of later feminist researchers such as Liz Kelly and Betsy Stanko. Susan Brownmiller's work has helped us understand why rape happens and continues to inspire us to do everything possible to end rape now.

Major works

Brownmiller, S. (1975) *Against Our Will: Men, Women and Rape*. New York: Simon and Schuster.
—— (1999) *In Our Time: Memoir of a Revolution*. New York: Dial Press, Random House.

Further reading

Barrett, M. and McIntosh, M. (1985) 'Ethnocentrism and Socialist-Feminist Theory', *Feminist Review*, 20: 23–47.

MacKinnon, C.A. (1989) 'Sexuality, Pornography, and Method: Pleasure Under Patriarchy', *Ethics*, 99(2): 314–46.

Miller, S. www.susanbrownmiller.com (accessed 21 July 2009).

Stanko, B. (1985) *Intimate Intrusions: Women's Experience of Male Violence*. London: Routledge & Kegan Paul.

The Book Reporter. www.bookreporter.com/authors/au-brownmiller-susan.asp (accessed 21 July 2009).

JAN JORDAN

TRAVIS HIRSCHI (1935–)

For many, Travis Hirschi is the quintessential North American (US) criminologist. His writing is urbane, succinct and engaging. Primarily associated with two versions of 'control theory' (association or social bond and self-control), Hirschi's work, either alone or co-authored, almost unfailingly presents a master class in running together substantive concerns, theory and data analysis. Regarded as the most cited criminologist of the late twentieth century and early twenty-first, his work is methodologically infused and structured so that whatever claims are made appear easily traced to data and backed by an underlying architecture that makes visible the objective concerns, originating assumptions, collected data and the interpretations derived.

It is also on reflection, particularly to those not from the United States, perplexing: something seems to be missing, but what exactly? This is a pressing question, for on a quantifiable analysis, the majority of 'criminological' works published in the twentieth century were from the United States. This vast output of work was made possible by the institutional strength of the university sector in the 'liberal', democratic, constitutional, social order (the United States) that became the dominant political, cultural and military power in the world. As we come to the waning of US power in what is now termed a multi-polar world, a re-evaluation of US criminology, and the central role it has played in constituting the criminological imagination globally, is due.

There are opposing ways of asking a foundational question for criminology: 'why do (some) people commit crime'? Or 'why do (all) people not commit crime'? This opposition has a universal applicability (for example, in genocide studies). Addressing the first question, we seek to explain something about 'them'; in the other question we look to explain something that *could* have involved 'us' and *did* involve people who shared a great deal of 'our' characteristics, desires and fears.

All of Hirschi's work is predicated on the choice of the second question. He seeks not to explain crime as the product of 'them', or to look for the characteristics of the offending cohort as if that was the key to criminological knowledge. Instead crime is to be explained as something that some of us chose in particular situations; or we did because we failed to calculate; or we did because of characteristics all of us have but some of us do not exercise appropriately in a range of situations or those characteristics do not act upon us in a preventive fashion. His first major work *Causes of Delinquency* (1969) considered factors such as our attachment to our peer group or parents; our commitment to our life projects (or more mundanely, our investment in time and effort in the range of conventional activities we are immersed in); our involvement in mainstream activities (such as sport or church); our belief in the social values of friendship, family, loyalty, honour and so forth. He moved on to ask what is it that we all have in common, but may have in varying degrees that can match the data on crime offending; in his last major work (*A General Theory of Crime*, 1990), that answer was self-control.

His other choice we may call ethical: Hirschi believes passionately that the theory that a theorist backs may initially be chosen for a variety of reasons but *must* face testing against the available data in the area and its results *should* be replicable. A theory that does not match data, or that is not replicable is to be treated as a person's political belief, not a theory. Theories, not people, should be placed in engagement: the human theorist is the vehicle through which ideas are expressed and the agent that works methodologies. But to try and use knowledge of the identity of the theorist, or of his or her personal history, as an explanation for the resulting work is greeted by the repost that 'such explanation is unnecessarily complex and largely unrewarding' (Hirschi, Foreword, in Laub 1983: ix).

What then of Hirschi's biographical data? Is it of any value or relevance to understanding his work? Can it help explain the feeling that something is missing? From the few published essays on his life and work (e.g. Laub's 2002 interview), it is clear that Hirschi's own answer would be no. Hirschi quotes A.E. Housman: 'My ... philosophy is founded on my observation of the world, not on anything so trivial and irrelevant as personal history.' By contrast, the black, female, US legal scholar Patricia Williams argues that observation and interpretation of the world is a factor of one's 'subject position'. In her book *The Alchemy of Race and Rights: Diary of a Law Professor*,

Williams tries to express her 'personal voice' in an attempt to gain truth: since 'much of what is spoken in so-called objective, unmediated voices is in fact mired in hidden subjectivities and unexamined claims'. For Williams, white and black US experiences have provided wholly different existential histories and identities: the black experience has been a 'confrontation with the utter powerlessness of status' – a sense of illegitimacy flowing from the fact that they have not been recognised by the law as citizens, but mere property.

Hirschi explains that his grandfather had been a rancher and cowboy and his father viewed that as the ideal way of life. But his father was instead a transit man on highway survey crews in Utah and Idaho, experiencing an existential tension: 'He hated wage labour, but it was always his major source of income. His generation were caught in the transition from the free range to the more orderly form of existence. Many of them did not adjust all that well to this new way of life' (Laub 2002: xii). This description of the American experience as moving from the unconstrained to the settled is of course in line with the national narratives of the white institutional majority; however, the range was free only because it had been gained from the native inhabitants of those lands. Following Williams, Hirschi's background from white settler heritage may provide an unconscious wherein the institutional structures of contemporary America need not be examined for their justice, for their normativity, but can be taken for granted and accepted as institutional fact.

Growing up, Hirschi had assumed he would become a civil engineer, continuing the process of building roads, of 'laying asphalt', as his father had. He married young (aged 20) and he and his fiancée decided on other things: '[I] decided on sociology and an academic career from the first day I arrived at the University of Utah. I was going to study crime and race relations – and get a teaching certificate on the side just in case' (ibid).

Hirschi's institutional career – apart from a two-year stint in the army (1958–60) where he was involved in data analysis interpreting surveys on army morale – was conditioned by spending a considerable and very fruitful time as a graduate student. In 1957–58, he gained a Master's in Sociology and Educational Psychology from the University of Utah and upon release from the army began Doctoral studies in sociology at Berkeley (from 1963 funded by a National Institute of Mental Health pre-doctoral fellowship, and 1966–67 as an acting assistant professor), before moving to the Department of Sociology at the University of Washington Seattle. His only trip 'east' on the job market had been a shock: 'The ideas I found exciting and obviously consistent with available data had been treated as contrary to fact, passé, and even appalling. The only way to remedy this situation ... was to show the ability of the ideas to account for a single body of relevant data.' The chance of a large data set came when Alan Wilson who was beginning the Richmond Youth Project allowed Hirschi to add questions to the survey in return for working on the project. Hirschi thus had a data set for his dissertation to 'test' the more fashionable recent 'sociological' theories of delinquency (such as 'strain') against the 'tradition' of social control theory. The resultant work, *Causes of Delinquency* (1969), became a modern sociological classic, arguing for the victory of social control theory.

That attribution of a classic is certainly correct: not only was Hirschi now established as the spokesperson for control theory (Kornhauser 1978), but this work laid out a template for the testing of theory by engagement with data and clarity of methodology that was to influence judgements as to what was a successful criminological study. Having also published *Delinquency Research* (co-authored with Hanan Selvin) 1967 and taken on a professorship in the Department of Sociology at the University of California at Davis, an established career path in sociology would have seemed apt. But Hirschi now realised he 'was a fish out of water in sociology' and moved to a professorship in the School of Criminal Justice at the University at Albany, State University of New York, and later in the 1980s went on to the University of Arizona, where he remained until his retirement.

Throughout his career, his work has remained labelled as 'sociology' but we can see under analysis that this is a misattribution. Hirschi locates his work with reference to the European classical rational choice theorists beginning with 'the English philosopher' Thomas Hobbes (1651) and the sociology of **Emile Durkheim**. For all its methodological prowess, Hirschi's work is best conceived as criminological rather than sociological theorising.

Hirschi works from the premise of a methodological individualism that allows him to read Durkheim as providing an argument whereby 'behaviour is a function of one's connection to society. Those inside society are controlled by it; those outside society are free to follow their own impulses' (Laub 2002: xiv). This opposition fits many of our ordinary or everyday ways of interpreting ourselves, yet for a committed sociologist no 'individual' can stand outside of society. For a sociologist, individuality is a social product, whereas in Hobbesian social philosophy individuality is a pre-social assumption of the natural state of humans. Hirschi, however, runs together Durkheim and Hobbes as if they worked with the same operating assumptions and concepts. Yet, the legacy of Hobbes is to work with our everyday understandings of ourselves as individuals, while for Durkheim the 'social', no matter how evasive, elusive and even mysterious, is the inescapable milieu.

Consider his first, classic work (*Causes of Delinquency*, 1969). This first version of control theory, often termed social bond theory, was structured in terms of controlling or restraining forces at work that prevent criminal behaviour. 'Individuals' bonded to social groups of family, school and church would be less likely to engage in criminal behaviour: 'Control theories assume that delinquent acts result when an individual's bond to society is weak or broken.' In Hirschi's neo-Hobbesian reading, society buys conformity from its individual members. The social bond develops as the individual accumulates rewards by following social rules. Failing this reward structure, society would be forced to rely on coercion alone and the greater a person is tied to conventional society in any of these ways the more closely he is likely to be tied in the other ways. Compared to **Robert Merton**'s use of anomie giving rise to strain theory (which appeared not to fit the available, discernable data), Hirschi's argument appeared plausible and measurable. Not only did strain theory appear to predict much greater crime than there actually was amongst the poor, it also seemed unable to fit into a replicable data set. Yet from the vantage point of European social science, one needs to distinguish a theoretical-political issue from a theoretical-methodological issue. Strain comes about in the problem that modernity's promise of social emancipation remains unfulfilled. The 'social', attempted by Durkheim to be captured in time, space and movement is a place of frustration arising from the tension between regulation and emancipation. For a European criminologist, such as **Jock Young**, the fact that the concept and the reality of 'relative deprivation', for example, is difficult to capture in a data set does not make it any less real. Hirschi's data-driven pragmatism, in this sense, is distinctly North American.

At Albany in the 1980s, Hirschi collaborated with other acclaimed methodologists like Michael Hindelang (see e.g. Hirschi and Hindelang 1977) and Michael Gottfredson (Hirschi and Gottfredson 1983). The long-term and fruitful partnership with Gottfredson was to culminate in *A General Theory of Crime*, a work as ambitious as its title that sought to explain 'all crime at all times' (1990: 117). This work tried to combine the classical and positivist strands in criminology by distinguishing and separately analysing the logical structure of 'crime' and the (positivist) conception of criminality. 'Crime' is derived from a classical conception (acts of force or fraud undertaken in pursuit of self-interest) and their analysis brings out the short-term immediate nature of the motive for 'standard' crimes. 'Criminality', is defined not in terms of something that only 'they' would have but something that we all share but in varying amounts: 'self-control'. Criminality and self-control are linked together in various ways. Persons with low self-control tend to be indifferent, self-centred and insensitive to the needs of others although not necessarily antisocial.

What are the policy implications of this theory of crime and related social problems? While we have a criminological concern for individual accountability and the self as an active agent, government cannot successfully act as the primary means of structuring choice, since the major difference in propensity to engage in crime is the amount of self-discipline that comes about by means of proper parenting. Self-control must be taught; it requires careful, deliberate efforts to monitor children's behavior, recognise wrongful behaviour, and punish that wrongful behaviour. Two-parent households with one or two children have more success instilling self-control than households with three or more children and single-parent households who simply have less time for supervision. The law is not an instrument to make people behave; children who grow up in households where self-discipline is not taught, or where parents demonstrate their own lack of self-control by engaging in crime, are likely to engage in behaviour that will bring in the criminal justice system. Yet, this legal response is unlikely to be effective. Other than responsible parenting, schools have the best chance of teaching self-control, according to the theory.

In a later edited collection (*The Generality of Deviance*, 1994), Hirschi and Gottfredson argue that all forms of deviant, criminal, reckless and sinful behaviour have one thing in common: the tendency to pursue immediate benefits without concern for long-term costs. A wide range of behaviour, including smoking, auto accidents, burglary, and rape were presented as having similar structural features in that they all involve disregard for their inevitable consequences: poor health, injury, loss of freedom, shame or disrepute. This similarity lies in self-management dependent upon levels of self-control. Thus the theory fits a particular image of social organisation and a view of the self as an entity to be managed and directed through life's challenges.

But is this world of observable facts that Hirschi and Gottfredson seek to be faithful to, a result of their subject-position? Could a theory of self-control fit equally acts like people smuggling, piracy, genocide or state-sponsored massacres? Reading accounts of the bureaucrats who played their part in the mass murder of six million Jews, one suspects not. Hirschi and Gottfredson did state that a general theory of crime would require a theory of the entire social order; this they did not provide. Instead the 'crime' they explain is very much the staple subject of mainstream US criminology, the everyday 'street' crimes internal to developed modern Western society. The justice of that society, or the role of the state as a criminogenic agent, or the context of that society in global processes is no part of the general theory. If the theory really wanted to be a 'general theory', a much wider world of crime and normative tensions would need to be observed. This is what many European readers find missing in Hirschi's entire body of work.

Still, Hirschi's lifelong commitment to framing the question of explaining crime not as 'why do they do it?', but as 'why do we not?' remains a transformative contribution to criminology and gives all his work an appeal beyond any particular study.

Major works

Gottfredson, M. and Hirschi, T. (1990) *A General Theory of Crime*. Stanford, California: Stanford University Press.

Hirschi, T. (1969) *Causes of Delinquency*. Berkeley, California: University of California Press.

—— (1983) 'Foreword', in Laub, J. (ed.) *Criminology in the Making*. Boston, Massachusetts: Northeastern University Press.

Hirschi, T. and M. Gottfredson (1983) 'Age and the Explanation of Crime', *American Journal of Sociology*, 89: 552–84.

—— (eds) (1994) *The Generality of Deviance*. New Brunswick, New Jersey: Transaction publishers.

Hirschi, T. and Selvin, H.C. (1967) *Delinquency Research: An Appraisal of Analytic Methods*. New York: The Free Press.

Further reading

Hirschi, T. (2002) *The Craft of Criminology*. New Brunswick, New Jersey: Transaction publishers.

Hirschi, T. and Hindelang, M.J. (1977) 'Intelligence and Delinquency: A Revisionist Review', *American Sociological Review*, 42: 571–87.

Kornhauser, R.R. (1978) *Social Sources of Delinquency*. Chicago, Illinois: University of Chicago Press.

Laub, John H. (2002) 'Introduction', in Hirschi, T. (ed.) *The Craft of Criminology*. New Brunswick, New Jersey: Transaction Publishers.

Pratt, T.C. and F. Cullen (2000) 'The Empirical Status of Gottfredson and Hirschi's General Theory of Crime: A Meta-Analysis', *Criminology*, 38: 931–64.

WAYNE MORRISON

ANTHONY E. BOTTOMS (1939–)

Anthony Bottoms is an eminent British criminologist whose work is widely known in international circles. As former Director of the Institute of Criminology at the University of Cambridge (1984–98), and worthy successor to previous directors Professor Sir Leon Radzinowicz (1959–72), Professor Nigel Walker CBE (1973–81) and Professor Donald West (1981–84) he has made significant contributions to the development of criminology. There have been major works on *inter alia* housing policy and crime, environmental criminology more generally, defendants in the criminal process, social inquiry reports, intermediate treatment, 'order' and compliance within the prison setting, and general deterrence. More recently, the Economic and Social Research Council-funded 'Sheffield Pathways Out of Crime Study' (SPOOCS) on desistance, has captured his intellectual energies. All are testament to his theoretically informed and sophisticated analyses of both the patterns of crime, and the validity of constructs which have determined the shape of responses to crime, whether this be in the courts, community or prisons.

Bottoms's father was a medical missionary who worked in a hospital near Chittagong (in what is now Bangladesh). There was no adequate schooling there, so from the age of eight, Tony (as he is always called) attended Eltham College in London (1947–58) as a boarder. Eltham was a school originally founded to provide boarding education for sons of missionaries, but by the 1940s it had become mostly a grammar school for day-boys from the local area, with some missionary-boarders. In an era before regular jet travel, finance precluded summer trips to Bangladesh, so holidays were spent with an aunt and uncle in Yorkshire. (Bottoms' parents returned to Britain for just one year in every six.) In many ways this unusual childhood – which combined strong Christian roots, some social marginality and an excellent formal education – has shaped his life's work both in terms of public service, and in terms of an interest in 'other lives', social welfare and social justice.

From 1958 to 1961 Anthony Bottoms studied for a BA in Law at Corpus Christi College, University of Oxford, followed by the Postgraduate Diploma in Criminology at the Institute of Criminology, University of Cambridge – in fact, he was on the very first intake for this course in 1961. He did not write a conventional PhD, but was awarded that degree on the basis of published work in the 1970s. More recently, he has received many honours and awards, including in 1996, the Thorsten Sellin and Sheldon and Eleanor Glueck Award from the American Society of Criminology for international contributions to criminology. In 1997 he was elected a Fellow of the British Academy, and in 2001 was appointed Knight Bachelor in the Queen's Birthday Honours List, 'for services to the criminal justice system' (the second of only two such honours, the first having been awarded to Professor Sir Leon Radzinowicz, founder of the Institute of Criminology in Cambridge). An honorary degree (Doctor of Laws) was given by The Queen's University of Belfast in 2003 – acknowledging among other things his work as a Specialist Advisor to the House of Commons Select Committee on Northern Ireland Affairs for its post-1997 inquiries on Northern Ireland Prisons.

Unusually, perhaps, for a modern-day criminologist, Anthony E. Bottoms spent a two-year period at the beginning of his career as a Probation Officer. It was clearly an important experience and served to shape later interests in the 'real lives' of offenders and desistance. He was then a Research Officer at the Institute of Criminology in Cambridge between 1964 and 1968 – conducting an action-research study of a borstal (young offenders' institution) under his criminological mentor F. H. ('Derick') McClintock. This was followed by a lectureship, senior lectureship, and personal chair at Sheffield University (1968–84). In 1984 Bottoms left Sheffield to take up the Wolfson Chair in Criminology and Directorship at the Institute of Criminology, Cambridge. The Directorship was surrendered in 1998, the Wolfson Chair upon retirement in 2006. But he remains active as an Emeritus Professor at Cambridge and an Honorary Professor at Sheffield.

Bottoms' work characteristically links theory, policy and practice. This is perhaps epitomised in a guided criminological and theological exploration of the implications of the 'collapse of the rehabilitative ideal' which had informed so much policy and practice in the 1960s. With a penal crisis looming, a group of criminologists and penal practitioners met to discuss the relevance of Christian theology to issues of crime and punishment (Bottoms and Preston 1980). Bottoms took a leading role in this early collaborative venture and it marks his remarkable ability to cross not just disciplinary boundaries, but the boundaries between intellectual and practical pursuits too.

Bottoms' work is also characteristically well grounded in detailed empirical analysis. An early (1970s) example of this revolves around analysis of recorded crime in Sheffield relating to the Census and other social data as well as attention to local authority housing areas (Baldwin and Bottoms 1976). This interest in environmental criminology was developed in analysis of nine contrasting small areas of Sheffield to ascertain to what extent differential recorded crime and offender rates were the product of differential policing or differential public reporting. A further phase of the study involved an attempt to explain differential crime rates in terms of the operation of the housing market (Bottoms and Wiles 1986). Elements of the studies were repeated in the 1980s and inform what has become perhaps the definitive chapter on environmental criminology in the various editions of the *Oxford Handbook of Criminology* (see Bottoms 2007a).

A further example of sophisticated empirical analysis revolves around analysis of two dispersal prisons, Albany and Long Lartin, carried out in the late 1980s. The researchers (guided by Bottoms as the senior academic) drew upon a wealth of data, interviews with both staff and inmates and hundreds of hours of patient observation, in order to explore and illustrate some of the abiding problems of creating an ordered environment amongst men in long-term captivity (Sparks et al. 1996). The comparison of these two prisons with different reputations, disciplinary profiles, histories of conflict, and indeed styles of approach to handling disorder, is widely perceived to have helped to provide the key to an understanding of prisons as complex institutions in which different ways of creating order emerge in response to different environments. Central to this empirical study is a detailed analysis of the processes which lead to the breakdown of order and to the processes which constitute 'order'. The reference to wider sociological and political discourses again is characteristic of Bottoms' work, in this instance in relation to the conception and exercise of power and the legitimacy accorded to institutions and social processes. The depiction of control through 'situational' strategies of control (through locks and bolts and other similar constraint-based approaches) and 'social' (normative) methods of achieving compliance and analysis of what prisoners experience as 'just' and 'legitimate' through this study thus adds to broader social and penological interests in why people obey the law and the perceived legitimacy of the law, as well as offering a critique of the prison service policy and practice at the time.

Bottoms' conceptual work relating to order and compliance was advanced in later work on community penalties (Bottoms 2001) where he sets out an instructive outline of the principal basic mechanisms underpinning legally compliant behaviour. Bottoms also elaborated upon his theoretical understandings of compliance in work on 'Criminology and the Normative', arguing, for example, that criminologists have perhaps neglected the moral (normative) dimensions of their subject (Bottoms 2002). Indeed, Bottoms' collective works do much to promote the importance of the individual subject. This is never more evident than in recent work (relating to desistance) which links normative compliance to differential social circumstances (Bottoms 2006). Drawing on social theory and philosophy Bottoms' lead in this research reflects the importance of social bonds and social context in patterns of desistance, whilst at the same time offering insightful and careful reflections on the theorisation of human agency. The empirical work on a sample of male non-occasional offenders (with a starting age of about twenty) has yet to be concluded, but this study, which Bottoms claims will be his last empirical project, promises rich analysis and development of existing theory.

It is also important to mention Bottoms' direction of a major evaluation of 'intermediate treatment' (funded by the then Department of Health and Social Security, 1984–94) (Bottoms et al. 1990). Given that 'intermediate treatment' was itself a new concept – developed to extend the range of alternatives to custody, Bottoms' analysis of effectiveness in four local authority areas, using both custodial and supervision order control groups, was important research. In typically thorough fashion, the study involved both processual dimensions (e.g. magistrates' perceptions of intermediate treatment) and outcome measures (e.g. sentencing patterns) (Bottoms 1995). This comprehensive approach applied to the task of evaluation has served as a model for other researchers.

Any overview of Bottoms' contributions would also not be complete without reference to work in which he has reflected on the relationship between theory and empirical observations in criminology (Bottoms 2007b). This aspect of his work offers some important reflections on the need to maintain a continuing dialogue between theory and empirical data-gathering and analysis, having consistently demonstrated this within his own work.

Professor Sir Anthony Bottoms' contributions to academic criminology are distinctive beyond doubt. There has also been notable contribution to criminal justice policy making at a national level, with repeated invitations from Government telling of his distinction and influence. But beyond all the honours and awards it is important to return to Bottoms' route into criminology, particularly his experiences of working as a probation officer which have given him an enduring interest in criminal justice practice and in people. It is arguably this kind of direct experience of the criminal justice system which inspired him to develop specially designed Master's degree courses for senior police, prison and probation staff as Director of the Cambridge Institute, drawing the worlds of theory and research and practice closer together. Indeed, the influence of missionary parents is seen in Bottoms' service to teaching as well as to research and policy making.

One is as likely to come across Bottoms talking to an undergraduate about criminological matters as to a government official. Generous with time given to students and colleagues alike, there are successive generations of criminologists who know what it is like to have had essays, papers or chapters 'Tonyfied', made subject to careful and thorough scrutiny, and a red pen. And all agree that the comments were worth waiting for. Thus Anthony E. Bottoms, the internationally renowned scholar, the empirical researcher, the theorist, the facilitator of links between academic criminology and practice, is also the immensely patient and inspiring teacher, advisor and mentor.

Major works

Baldwin, J. and Bottoms, A. E. (1976) *The Urban Criminal: A Study in Sheffield*. London: Tavistock Publications.

Bottoms, A.E. (1995) *Intensive Community Supervision for Young Offenders: Outcomes, Process and Cost*. Cambridge: University of Cambridge, Institute of Criminology.

—— (2006) 'Desistance, Social Bonds and Human Agency: A Theoretical Exploration', in P.-O. Wikstrom and R. Sampson (eds) *The Explanation of Crime: Context, Mechanisms and Development*. Cambridge: Cambridge University Press.

Bottoms, A.E., Brown, P., McWilliams, B., McWilliams, W. and Nellis, M. in collaboration with John Pratt (1990) *Intermediate Treatment and Juvenile Justice: Key Findings and Implications from a National Survey of Intermediate Treatment Policy and Practice*. London: HMSO.

Bottoms, A.E. and McClean, J.D. (1976) *Defendants in the Criminal Process*. London: Routledge and Kegan Paul.

Bottoms, A.E. and McLintock, F.H. (1973) *Criminals Coming of Age: A Study of Institutional Adaptation in the Treatment of Adolescent Offenders*. London: Heinemann Educational Books.

Bottoms, A.E. and Preston, R.H. (eds) (1980) *The Coming Penal Crisis: A Criminological and Theological Exploration*. Edinburgh: Scottish Academic Press.

Bottoms, A.E. and Wiles, P. (1986) 'Housing Tenure and Residential Community Crime Careers in Britain', in A.J. Reiss, Jr. and M. Tonry (eds) *Crime and Justice: A Review of Research*. Vol 8. Chicago: University of Chicago Press.

Sparks, R., Bottoms, A.E. and Hay, W. (1996) *Prisons and the Problem of Order*. Oxford: Clarendon Press.

Further reading

Bottoms, A.E. (2001) 'Compliance and Community Penalties', in A.E. Bottoms, L.R. Gelsthorpe and S. Rex (eds) *Community Penalties: Change and Challenges*. Devon: Willan Publishing.

—— (2002) 'Morality, Crime, Compliance and Public Policy', in A.E. Bottoms and M. Tonry (eds) *Ideology, Crime and Criminal Justice. A Symposium in Honour of Sir Leon Radzinowicz*. Devon: Willan Publishing.

—— (2007a) 'Place, Space, Crime and Disorder', in M. Maguire, R. Morgan and R. Reiner (eds) *The Oxford Handbook of Criminology*. Oxford: Oxford University Press.

—— (2007b) 'The Relationship between Theory and Empirical Observations in Criminology', in R. King and E. Wincup (eds) *Doing Research in Crime and Justice* (second edition). Oxford: Oxford University Press.

LORAINE GELSTHORPE

PAT CARLEN (1939–)

Pat Carlen, one of Britain's most imaginative and innovative sociologists, has often been called a 'feminist criminologist' though maybe that is something of a misnomer since she always insists that she never has employed any body of feminist theory when doing sociological analysis. Nor does she think of herself as a criminologist but rather as someone who engages in sociological work. She describes herself as 'a knowledge worker ... whose creative and theoretical work is about objects of knowledge'. Her interest in criminology is not for its own sake but rather as a dimension of sociology in general and social exclusion in particular. As a 'thinker', one of her greatest characteristics is her refusal to be pigeonholed; she does not belong to any particular 'school' of thought nor is she any sort of 'ist'. Nonetheless, her writings have exerted distinctive and important influences on feminist, critical and abolitionist perspectives and on criminology more generally. The primary sources of inspiration for her own work come from social theory (Durkheim and Marx), and from literature (Virginia Woolf). These influences shine through in Carlen's concern with the morality of punishment, in the way she situates crime-related and penal questions in terms of their sociological and political connections and surrounding economic conditions, and in her engagement with feminism. Though best known for her two classic works, *Magistrates' Justice* (1976) and *Women's Imprisonment: A Study in Social Control* (1983), Carlen's prolific and always vital writing stretches to eighteen books and many articles, some of which have been translated into Dutch, Spanish, Norwegian, Portuguese and Japanese.

Carlen was born in Norwich in 1939 to working-class parents who were active Labour Party members and she is still proud of the Old

Labour values she grew up with. Her parents were delighted when she won a place at the local grammar school and her lifelong love of reading, theatre and National Trust historic houses began in those school years – her love of travel and playing mah-jong came later as did her love of Virginia Woolf and Alan Bennett for their exemplary sociological writing. Although she did well at grammar school, she managed to antagonise the headmistress who refused to engage in the customary handshake with her when she left school and, more disastrously, refused to give her a reference for University. After attending a teacher training college in Lincoln, Carlen went on to teach English to secondary school children in London's Bermondsey docklands. Then, after marrying and having two children – who are the love of her life and, she claims, her greatest achievements – she took a degree in Sociology at Bedford College, London University, graduating in 1971 with first class honours. Carlen wanted to do a PhD that combined her main sociological interests: sociology of deviance, industrial and organisational sociology and social theory. She chose to focus on the courts where she could also explore an enduring interest in varieties of social rules and social rule-usage. Carlen was awarded her PhD from the University of London in 1974 for her doctoral thesis which subsequently became her first major published work, *Magistrates' Justice*, regarded by many as the best sociological book on English magistrates' courts.

Magistrates' Justice, which analyses the production of justice in the metropolitan magistrates' courts in London, gave birth to Carlen's distinctive approach and creative style. Here she analyses how the rituals, relationships and language of professionalism articulate to form the coercive structures necessary to the speedy production of justice in over-burdened courts and how mundane interaction within court settings reinforces the exercise of social control. The book's sophisticated theoretical analysis, fully grounded in sensitive ethnography, is characteristic of Carlen's work, all of which moves elegantly from an analysis of a particular empirical project – be it magistrates' justice, official discourse, youth homelessness, women's imprisonment, women lawbreakers, penal regimes or penal policy – into a broader account of the political, economic and ideological conditions that generate particular constellations of power and inequality in the area of criminal justice and punishment. *Magistrates' Justice* also signifies a theme that runs through Carlen's work – that particular forms and types of social and criminal injustices occur not through the malevolent intent of individual agents of social control, be they magistrates, prison officers, governors, politicians or other social actors, but through the routine workings of organisations and social processes, often driven by political expediency. At the time of publication, the style and whole approach of *Magistrates' Justice* were unique. The book cut through the well-worn arguments in the established literature and was very influential in changing academic perspectives on what happened in the courts.

Official Discourse similarly broke new ground when published in 1979 and it remains a significant text for scholars engaged in deconstruction and critical examination. Burton and Carlen shared theoretical interests in relation to 'knowledge' at the time and their analysis of the structures and processes in official reports on law and order, and the ways in which this official discourse produces knowledge, is characterised by both theoretical tightness and ideological intensity. It played – and continues to play (Gilligan and Pratt 2004) – an important role in encouraging a reflexive and critical approach amongst scholars to the 'conventional wisdom', or what is now called 'evidence', in official statements that claim to pass for knowledge in penal policy and the criminal processing system. Carlen's concern with the production of knowledge in *Official Discourse* runs through all her work. And this fascination, together with a large measure of sociological imagination and curiosity – in her own words, 'nosiness' – define her always innovative research projects including her now classic 1981 study of women's imprisonment centred on Cornton Vale, the Scottish woman's prison.

Carlen's interest in studying women's imprisonment can be traced to her concern as an early member of the Preservation of the Rights of Prisoners – the prisoners' rights organisation founded in the UK in the 1970s – that there seemed to be little interest in women's imprisonment at that time. The publication of *Women's Imprisonment* in 1983, generally regarded as Carlen's most influential and important contribution to criminology, established her as an international scholar and stimulated studies of the treatment of women lawbreakers across the world. In identifying the modes of discipline specific to the carceral control of women, *Women's Imprisonment* was the first theoretically informed empirical study that did not reduce the conditions of existence for women lawbreakers either to their gender alone or to their status as 'victims' of capitalism, or patriarchy, or individual men. Instead it left the space open for the reader to appreciate that the women in the study made choices, but not in conditions of their own choosing. At the time the book was unique and opened up a whole new field in showing how wider social, political, ideological and economic conditions as well as class and gender shaped those choices.

Carlen's research for *Women's Imprisonment* also motivated her co-founding of the English campaigning organisation Women in Prison in 1985. Her commitment to moral penal practice and social justice for imprisoned women, combined with the creative theorising in *Women's Imprisonment*, proved to be inspirational for a generation of students and academics throughout the UK and internationally. Her later books on the social or 'anti-social control' of women lawbreakers (1988, 1990, 1998; Carlen et al. 1985; Carlen and Worrall 1988, 2004) and on 'carceral clawback' (2002) are all logical extensions of her original work in *Women's Imprisonment*. The book remains a major reference for scholarship on the social control of women lawbreakers, including Carlen's own subsequent cross-national studies of reconfigurations in penality in women's imprisonment.

Jigsaw: A Political Criminology of Youth Homelessness, published in 1996, is also concerned with social control but this time with the social control (through criminalisation) of young people outwith family, work, training and education, and with the implications of the phenomenon of youth homelessness for a politics of youth citizenship. Carlen was motivated to study youth homelessness because so many people in prison were homeless, and the Thatcher governments were exacerbating this by selling off public housing and implementing welfare cuts. Like her earlier work, *Jigsaw* does not reduce youth homelessness either to structure or to individual choices, motivations and personalities but rather to both/and. Her penetrating politico-economic and sociological analysis, which draws on her ethnographic work with homeless young people in England during the 1990s, reveals the historical, economic and political conditions that coalesced to produce youth homelessness as a 'distinctly 20th-century phenomenon, caught up in the tensions between late-modern systems of welfare and regulation, postmodern creativities of identity, risk and reflexivity, and premodern fears about the wanderer, the traveller, and the mendicant'. In addition, *Jigsaw's* innovative theorisation of 'survivalism as subculture' in analysing how homeless young adults survive and repair their shattered lives augments subcultural theory and has been influential in the development of cultural criminology.

Carlen's latest book, *Imaginary Penalities* (2008), derives from her longstanding interest in how people make sense of and then cope with contradictory demands on them. *Imaginary Penalities*, which is about contemporary ideological and political struggles over the manufacture and policy-harnessing of crime, risk and security knowledges, is characteristically deeply creative in its theorisation of the concept of 'imaginary penality' and resonates with her scholarship over the previous three decades. The book's theoretical focus, influenced by the perspective on 'the imaginary' set out by Burton and Carlen in *Official Discourse*, is on questions of ideology, knowledge and critique. In particular, *Imaginary Penalities* emphasises the necessary tension between 'imagination', defined as a never-ending quest for new knowledge, and 'imaginary', defined as the process and product of ideological structures attempting either to suppress or incorporate new knowledge. The empirical focus of the book provides rich analytic descriptions of how global trends and national policies are realised in imaginary form at local level and how these imaginary penalities have deleterious effects not only on crime control but also on the quality of justice nationally and internationally. Carlen's theorisation of imaginary penalty is a major contribution to understanding what is going on in late modern times in relation to crime and punishment.

Carlen's significance as a thinker extends well beyond her writings. In the early 1990s she was responsible for establishing criminology as a separate and subsequently internationally renowned department at the University of Keele in England (where she worked from 1976 to 1996). She was responsible also for instigating Keele's undergraduate criminology degree programme in 1991, the first in the UK. In this, and in many other respects, her qualities as an academic trailblazer are legendary. Carlen's sense of integrity, collegiality and professionalism are widely recognised as exemplary. She is held in very high regard by ex-students and colleagues alike who testify to her superb qualities as a doctoral supervisor and as a promoter of junior colleagues. As a PhD supervisor, through making her own ethical and methodological craft criteria explicit, students learned how to set high standards for themselves in creating new knowledge and to do this in a principled way. Currently, as Editor-in-Chief of the *British Journal of Criminology*, one of the leading international criminology journals, Carlen's dedication to promote the best work of new generations of scholars continues.

Throughout her career Carlen has talked to practitioners and policy makers in the UK and internationally about the implications of her analyses for programmes of reform and change in responses to lawbreaking and other social harms. In 1998, for example, she held a British Council secondment to the Office of the Ombudsman in Peru to advise on research into women's imprisonment there. She has given major public lectures in the Irish Republic, Australia, New Zealand, Peru, South Africa, USA, Canada, Israel, Spain, Netherlands (Annual Bonger Lecture 1993), Portugal, Austria and Hungary. She has held visiting fellowships at universities across the world and has conducted original empirical research in many countries. For example, she was an

Exxon Fellow at Stanford University in 1987 and studied women's jails in California. In 1996 in Australia and New Zealand she investigated alternatives to women's imprisonment; in Israel in 2000 she conducted a study of the Israeli Rehabilitation Authority's Mothers and Children's Projects; and from 2003 to 2005 she was Co-Director of the English research team engaged in an European Union-funded six-nation study of the rehabilitation of women ex-prisoners.

The breadth, depth and originality of Pat Carlen's research and writings are awesome. When dealing with someone who has been a major contributor to criminological thinking for over thirty years and who has been honoured widely by her peers (for example, by the award of the Sellin-Glueck Prize from the American Society of Criminology in 1997 for Outstanding International Contributions to Criminology), it has been necessary to be selective. Above all, however, Carlen's work, which reveals the impossibility of criminal justice in a class society, is rooted in her concern with the relationships between social and criminal justice and her belief in 'the old abolitionist adage that there is *no way* that primarily *penal* methods can address primarily *social* injustices'.

Major works

Burton, F. and Carlen, P. (1979) *Official Discourse*. London: Routledge & Kegan Paul.
Carlen, P. (1976) *Magistrates' Justice*. London: Martin Robertson.
—— (1983) *Women's Imprisonment: A Study in Social Control*. Oxford: Blackwell.
—— (1996) *Jigsaw – A Political Criminology of Youth Homelessness*. Milton Keynes: Open University Press.
—— (ed.) (2008) *Imaginary Penalities*. Cullompton: Willan.

Further reading

Carlen, P. (1988) *Women, Crime and Poverty*. Milton Keynes: Open University Press.
—— (1990) *Alternatives to Women's Imprisonment*. Milton Keynes: Open University Press.
—— (1998) *Sledgehammer: Women's Imprisonment at the Millennium*. London: Macmillan.
—— (ed.) (2002) *Women and Punishment: The Struggle for Justice*. Cullompton: Willan.
Carlen, P., Christina, D., Hicks, J., O'Dwyer, J. and Tchaikovsky, C. (1985) *Criminal Women*. Cambridge: Polity Press.
Carlen, P. and Worrall, A. (eds) (1988) *Gender, Crime and Justice*. Milton Keynes: Open University Press.

—— (2004) *Analysing Women's Imprisonment.* Cullompton: Willan.

Gilligan, G.P. and Pratt, J. (eds) (2004) *Crime, Truth and Justice: Official Inquiry, Discourse, Knowledge.* Cullompton: Willan.

JACQUELINE TOMBS

RONALD CLARKE (1941–)

Ronald Victor Gemuseus Clarke's research has made significant conceptual and policy contributions across the globe. He has led the British Home Office Research and Planning Unit (i.e. the UK government's criminological research department), worked as a university professor in the United States and mentored numerous students, some of whom have become leading criminologists in their own right. The name 'Clarke' has become synonymous with rational choice theory, situational crime prevention, environmental criminology, problem solving, crime science, and evaluation research. Along with Derek Cornish, Clarke played a leading role in revitalising the classical school of criminology (see **Beccaria**) by developing rational choice theory. This approach assumes that offenders have agency/free will and decide to commit a crime because in their view (limited though it may be) it benefits them to do so.

Clarke also led the research team that pioneered situational crime prevention (SCP). Unlike most criminologies that focus on 'why' people commit crimes and that assume offenders differ from conformists, SCP focuses on why certain crimes happen and why they concentrate in time and space. The goal is to understand 'how' the crimes are successfully completed so as to find ways to prevent their occurrence. Dr Clarke's ideas have led to an entire area of study. Most criminology textbooks include a chapter on rational choice theory. Today there are academic journals and annual conferences devoted to SCP and it has become a central part of UK crime prevention policy. Clarke founded *Crime Prevention Studies*, a peer-reviewed edited book series with twenty-five volumes published to date. He helped found the annual Environmental Criminology and Crime Analysis conference that began in 1992 and focuses on crime analysis and prevention. In addition, the American Society of Criminology and other professional associations have entire sessions devoted to rational choice theory and SCP at their annual conferences. Clarke was a founding member of the board of the Jill Dando Institute in England, and co-founded the World Criminal Justice Library Network that has held bi-annual meetings since 1991.

Ronald Clarke was born in Tanganyika during World War II to a German mother and English father who worked as a civil engineer. He learned Swahili as an infant and attended a boarding school in Tanganyika from age six to ten, which required a five-day journey to reach from his home. He went to England at the age of eleven with his mother and two siblings (one brother and one sister) to attend a selective day school. Life in post-war England with food rationing and other deprivations was a shock for someone reared in colonial luxury, but he looked forward each week to his candy ration and Saturday morning pictures at the movie theater. He also developed a keen interest in model airplanes. Clarke completed a BA (1962) in Psychology and Philosophy at the University of Bristol, but his real interest was psychology which he decided to pursue in graduate school. In 1965, Clarke completed an MA in Clinical Psychology, and a PhD (1968) in Psychology at the prestigious Maudsley Institute (made famous by Hans Eysenk among others) at the University of London. While at the Maudsley, Clarke met his wife, Sheelagh, a dedicated teacher who now directs a preschool in their home town of Millburn, New Jersey.

Upon completing his PhD, Clarke took a job with the British Home Office Research and Planning Unit because he wanted to do research that had an impact on policy. He worked there for sixteen years, and was the Director from 1983 to 1984. While at the Home Office, Clarke played a key role in developing the British Crime Survey in 1982. This survey is a nationally representative sample and is now repeated every year. Dr Clarke greatly enjoyed working at the Home Office, he liked the pressure and the variety of the work and he liked working in small teams of dedicated researchers. Eventually, however, he became frustrated by interference in research by politicians. He also wanted to pursue his research agenda on situational crime prevention, which his increasing administrative duties at the Home Office made impossible. He was encouraged to move to the United States by Leslie Wilkins, who had also left the Home Office for the United States many years previously. In fact, Wilkins arranged for Clarke to have a visiting position at SUNY Albany in 1981/82, where he met Graeme Newman with whom he has worked ever since.

Clarke's wife was also from a colonial family and was used to moving around the world. They both thought that the United States would offer their children greater career opportunities. (Henry their elder son is now an orthopaedic surgeon at the Mayo Clinic, George is a research economist at the World Bank, and their daughter, Marianne, is a middle school speech therapist.) In 1984, Clarke became a professor of criminal justice at Temple University, and in 1987 he was appointed as the dean of the school of criminal justice, at Rutgers, the State University of New Jersey. Clarke served as Dean at Rutgers for eleven years, much longer than most deans. It is widely agreed that he helped make the school one of the top criminal justice PhD programmes in the United States. During his tenure internationally recognised crime prevention scholars George Kelling and Marcus Felson joined the Rutgers faculty. Clarke stepped down to become a University Professor in 1998, which is his current position. Since then he has published an average of six books/papers per year.

Clarke's interest in situational factors, opportunity and crime prevention began while he was studying for his PhD. At that time, he also worked as the research officer at the Kingswood Training School, a residential school for delinquent boys. His PhD was an examination of why some boys ran away ('absconded') from the schools. At that time, most frameworks assumed that deep-seated psychological factors could explain absconding, but Clarke's analysis of absconding records found that situational factors such as daylight hours and sunshine influenced the opportunity structure (longer periods of darkness provided youths more opportunities to escape unseen from school) and were related to absconding. Clarke published these results in the *British Journal of Criminology* in 1967.

Clarke often describes his job at the training school as the best one he ever had. He was left completely alone for four years to do research of his own choosing so long as he could demonstrate its relevance to the mission of the training schools. Not only did he undertake work on absconding, but with Derek Cornish, he undertook a randomised controlled trial of a therapeutic regime in one school. This study left him skeptical about the value of such trials in evaluating complex problems and about the ability of treatment to modify criminal dispositions. Clarke extended these ideas when he was at the Home Office and led the team that created SCP. This approach analyses a specific crime type to uncover the situational factors that facilitate the crime's commission. Intervention techniques are then devised to manipulate the situational factors to reduce crime. SCP is a dynamic framework and the number/type of intervention techniques has steadily increased over the years. There are currently five general strategies that encompass twenty-five techniques that are used to prevent crime. The techniques range from 'hard' approaches that incapacitate targets and make it impossible for the crime to be committed to 'soft' techniques that reduce situational prompts/cues that increase a person's motivation to commit a crime during that specific event.

To date, dozens of empirical studies (encompassing case studies, experiments and other quantitative tests) have evaluated situational interventions. These studies are highly supportive of SCP and find that most situational interventions lead to crime reductions. Importantly, most studies also found little support for the 'crime displacement' critique of SCP, that is, that an offender thwarted in one situation will simply commit the same crime somewhere else, or turn to another type of crime. But the empirical tests of SCP find that displacement either does not occur, or if it does, there is still an overall crime reduction. In fact, Dr Clarke (with Pat Mayhew) published a seminal piece in 1988 that demonstrated the fallacy of displacement claims. This study showed that the number of suicides in England and Wales fell from over 5,700 people in 1963 to almost 3,700 people in 1975. In the early 1960s gas suicides accounted for over forty per cent of suicides each year. The progressive removal of carbon monoxide from the public gas supply, in other words, led to the almost complete elimination of gas suicide. Clarke and Mayhew explained that when the gas was available in people's homes it was easy to use, deadly and painless. However, other forms of suicide lacked these benefits and thus most motivated gas 'suicide seekers' did not displace when the easy opportunity (the poisonous public gas supply) was removed. Accordingly, the British suicide rate fell by forty per cent.

Clarke is undoubtedly one of the leading figures in criminology. He has published over 220 books, monographs and articles. These works span many subjects and include the psychology of crime, suicide, terrorism, burglary, vandalism, robbery, vehicle theft, police effectiveness, crime prevention, institutional regimes, evaluation methodology, and policy-relevant research. Currently, Clarke is Associate Director of the Problem Oriented Policing (POP) Center, funded by the US Office of Community Oriented Policing Services. The POP Center is composed of affiliated police practitioners, researchers, and universities and it promotes problem-oriented policing by disseminating information about how the police can reduce specific crime and disorder problems.

Importantly, Clarke's work is ongoing and his future plans include further developing the SCP approach. It is an approach that keeps evolving in response to new ideas and findings. Clarke believes that SCP's strength is that it is oriented to action, prevention, getting results, and having an impact. It is also a linchpin between criminological research and policing, something that most theories of crime rarely engage or care to do so. Finally, in addition to his criminological interests Clarke also enjoys photographing wild birds, which he has done all over the world, sometimes when invited to give key note addresses in foreign countries.

Ron Clarke is a practical thinker who wants to make and see changes, which he believes should be the main objective of criminological study. This is what makes many young people want to follow in his footsteps.

Major works

Clarke, R.V.G. (1967) 'Seasonal and Other Environmental Aspects of Absconding by Approved School Boys', *British Journal of Criminology*, 7: 195–202.

—— (1972) *The Controlled Trial in Institutional Research*, with D.B. Cornish. *Home Office Research Studies No. 15*. London: HMSO.

—— (1980) 'Situational Crime Prevention: Theory and Practice', *British Journal of Criminology*, 20: 136–47.

—— (1982) 'Situational Crime Prevention: Its Theoretical Basis and Practical Scope', in Tonry, M. and Morris, N. (eds) *Crime and Justice, Vol. 4*. Chicago, Illinois: University of Chicago Press.

—— (1986) *The Reasoning Criminal*, edited with D.B. Cornish. New York: Springer-Verlag.

—— (1987) 'Understanding Crime-Displacement: An Application of Rational Choice Theory', with D.B. Cornish, *Criminology*, 25: 933–47.

—— (ed.) (1997) *Situational Crime Prevention: Successful Case Studies* (second edition). Albany, New York: Harrow & Heston. Available online at: www.popcenter.org (accessed 2 July 2009).

—— (2005) *Crime Analysis for Problem Solvers. In 60 Small Steps*, with J. Eck. Office of Community Oriented Policing Services. Washington, DC: US Department of Justice.

—— (2006) *Outsmarting the Terrorists*, with G. Newman. Portsmouth, New Hampshire: Praeger Security International.

Further reading

Sullivan, R.R. (2000) *Liberalism and Crime: The British Experience*. Lanham, Maryland: Lexington Books.

Tilley, N. (2004) 'Karl Popper: A Philosopher for Ronald Clarke's Situational Crime Prevention?' *Israel Studies in Criminology*, 8: 39–56.

JOSHUA D. FREILICH AND MANGAI NATARAJAN

STANLEY COHEN (1942–)

Stan Cohen's work is always ahead of the pack, but at the same time deeply grounded in the very best theoretical foundations of social inquiry. What distinguishes Cohen's rich scholarship is its capacity to traverse the disparate disciplines underpinning criminology while maintaining irreverence for their routinisation and loss of critical edge. Cohen writes widely on social control, criminological theory, mass media, juvenile delinquency, criminal justice policy, prisons, political violence and human rights violations. The thread that joins these interests is an abiding and personal commitment to the struggle for social justice.

The experience of growing up in apartheid South Africa never left him; that inner sense of a state's capacity for justifying oppression combined with his Jewish family background to heighten his insight into marginality, deviance and control. This personal history fuelled a steely scepticism towards received accounts which was to inform his life's work. It also proved the source of a biting wit and inspiring teaching.

Cohen completed undergraduate study at the University of Witwatersrand before moving to London in 1963. He worked as a psychiatric social worker for a year, before enrolling to do a PhD in Sociology at the London School of Economics (LSE) under the supervision of Terence Morris. He took up a lectureship at the University of Durham in 1967 (before accepting a professorship at the University of Essex in 1972), and in 1968 was a founding member of the National Deviancy Conference and the movement it began.

Those old enough to remember will know the National Deviancy Conference as, in many respects, the genesis of critical criminology in the UK. Contemporary criminologists tend to take as given the critical tradition, but in the early 1970s, when Stan Cohen edited *Images of Deviance* (1971) the struggle was to contain the therapeutic model, and to politicise and socially locate an instrumentalist criminology captured inside a crumbling welfare state. That Cohen should have, in this collection, introduced the 'New Criminologists' reveals his pre-eminent place in the emergent radicalism.

Cohen's first major work, *Folk Devils and Moral Panics* (1972) set a totally new agenda for interactive criminology. Linking the work of Leslie Wilkins's *Social Deviance* to that of the emergent labelling perspective in the USA (**Howard Becker**'s *Outsiders* in particular), Cohen theorised deviancy amplification in the context of media distortion as generating a counter-productive moral panic. The book has been extraordinarily influential, extending well beyond the discourse of European criminology. In terms of the development of criminology as a sophisticated critique of interventionist social policy in developed urban cultures, and beyond the limitations of the social defence perspective of the 1950s, it is impossible to overestimate the impact and influence of *Folk Devils*. The concepts popularised in the work have become such common features of the lexicon that we no longer reflect on Cohen's amazing achievement to extend the tentacles of academic analysis so far across the broader public domain.

Quite simply, the language of 'moral panics' is now part of commonsense understanding. In the ground-breaking work *Policing the Crisis: Mugging the State, and Law and Order*, **Stuart Hall** (1978: 17) and his collaborators recognised Cohen's work on moral panics as 'a major shift of focus from conventional studies of crime ... [that] alters the nature of the "object" or phenomenon which needs to be explained'. Cohen's work translated the rich history of American subcultural scholarship (such as that of **Albert Cohen**) into a distinctly politicised and symbolic form 'through which the sub-ordinate group negotiates its position' in transitional cultures (Cohen 1980: v). No 'tortuous sociology of knowledge' for Stan Cohen, but rather a breath-taking engagement with 'culture/style/solution' – and all long before it was fashionable and anticipated in the sons and daughters of labelling theory. The book's conclusion is no less applicable today than when it was first published, thirty years ago: 'More moral panics will be generated and other, as yet nameless, folk devils will be created ... our society as presently structured will continue to generate problems for some if its members ... and then condemn whatever solution these groups find.' In his new introduction to the third edition, Cohen reviews recent sociological theory and criticism about the concept of 'moral panics' and discusses the moral panics generated around the 'folk devils' of today: ecstasy and designer drugs; the murder of the English toddler James Bulger; the 'name and shame' campaign against suspected paedophiles; and the vilification of 'bogus' asylum seekers.

In the 1970s, Cohen's research and writing returned to environments of control. In many respects this work was the fore-runner to **Michel Foucault**'s considerations of punishment and **David Garland**'s reflections on control in the late modern world. In *Psychological Survival: The Experience of Long Term Imprisonment* (1972, with Laurie Taylor), Cohen gave voice to the long-term incarcerated. The prisoner's fear of psychological deterioration was juxtaposed in the discussions with Cohen and Taylor against human and contextual adaptation, to preserve personal identity. The book is a moving account of the struggle of those we would otherwise place out of sight and out of mind.

Cohen and Taylor's interest in and commitment to the socially excluded were further expanded in *Escape Attempts: The Theory and Practice of Resistance to Everyday Life* (1976). Here, though, the men and women in these pages are not escaping from the cramped cells and barred windows of a prison; they are fleeing from the demands of everyday life, from the suffocating pressure of routine and ritual, from the despair of the breakfast table and the office. Their search is for meaning, novelty, progress, and a sense of identity. *Escape Attempts* chronicles the multitude of free spaces which we construct as refuges from the daily routine. It focuses on the amazing variety of devices we employ in order to persuade ourselves and others that we are truly individual, that we are capable of creating distance between ourselves and the world. It is also about the precariousness of these escape attempts, the danger that they will drift into obsessions and madness, become undermined by self-consciousness, or lose their potency by being rendered banal or commercially co-opted. The book is a warning about society's strengths – but at the same time it is a homage to the self, a celebration of the daily struggle to rise above social destiny.

Such a warning was next directed against the excesses of state power for social control, in *Crime, Social Control and the State* (1986). Of this redirection in Cohen's thinking, Andrew Scull recently commented; 'that book ... helped establish the research agenda in the field for the next decade or more' (Downes 2007: 238).

As far back as *Social Control and the State* (1983) Stan pre-empted the critique of control fascinations in the late modern world (see Garland 2001). It was this indictment of state failure, and Cohen's implication in the 'net-widening' of criminal justice post-rehabilitation, that led almost seamlessly to Cohen's interrogation of crime, control and community. Arguably his most influential book, *Visions of Social Control* (1985) set out to introduce the work of Foucault and Rothman on control, while also producing an entirely original synthesis of empirical literature and theoretical terrain, against the paradox of 'the quest for community'. This is a massive intellectual vision which, the legal scholar Richard Abel observed, represented a 'combination of comprehensiveness and depth, passion and fairness, concern with theory and rich descriptions of concrete social institutions' (Cohen 1985 (blurb)). Having the privilege to know Stan as a friend, it is as if Abel was describing the man as well as the product.

Before cultural criminology entered into some contested vogue, Stan Cohen's *Visions of Social Control* flagged the dangers in an uncritical reversion from the 'failure theory' of state intervention to a culturally dislocated reliance on pastoral notions of community justice.

> Each one of the destructuring ideologies (of justice decarceration, diversion, decentralisation and the rest) and their implied or actual

preferences (community control, informalism, re-integration etc.) are sustained by, and owe their public appeal to, the rhetorical quest for community. It would be difficult to exaggerate how this ideology – or more accurately, this single word – has come to dominate Western crime control discourse in the last few decades.

(1985: 116)

The critique that followed about what 'community control' actually meant, would have been well heeded by the restorative justice explosion in the dying days of the last century. **John Braithwaite** in *Crime Shame and Reintegration* (1989) identified the intellectual debt owed to Cohen for conceptualising re-integrative shaming, and he conceded that Cohen 'correctly pointed out that the symbolic emptiness of the inclusionary writings of the sixties left the field open for conservative law-and-order politics. It also did this because it was instrumentally empty; to counsel no more than tolerance and acceptance of deviants by the community … ' (1989: 156).

But in charting this retreat, *Visions of Social Control* did not shirk from facing the critical consequences of crime on the streets, both in terms of political and popular cultures. Cohen argued this was the consequence of distracted and expansive community justice strategies which failed 'to confront the moral issues of guilt, wrong-doing, punishment and responsibility and the empirical issues of harm, danger and fear raised by the problem of crime' (1985: 268). *Visions of Social Control* marked a shift in focus away from the neutralisation of criminal responsibility to the pain of crime and victimisation. As the critical mirror to debates between so-called realists and idealists, the book's argument represented a cathartic moment for criminology, where selective criminalisation faced off against the needs of real victims.

In his next major work, *Against Criminology* (1988), Cohen had the courage to lay out fifteen years of reflecting on the debates that shook (or shot past) criminology as an emerging, and for him underachieving discourse. The essays confront the research achievements (and failings) of British criminology but do not stop there. With refreshing distance and good humour, Cohen also turned his eye to the foundations and fumblings of American criminology and thereby sought a transatlantic perspective for a sociology of deviance where methodologies were shared, orthodoxies common, and prevailing challenges for criminology frustratingly distant. The frank critique of *Against Criminology* provided the insights behind a sustainable project for criminology set out in *Visions of Social Control* and the work to follow.

While railing against the prostitution of social control research for the purposes of capacity building (both in terms of state legitimacy and academic reputation), Stan Cohen could never be accused of disengagement: the personal and the political are deeply interwoven in his life. Significant among his reasons for moving to Israel in 1980, and taking over the Institute of Criminology at the Hebrew University in Jerusalem, was to immerse his scholarship in the daily realities of political violence and state repression. Cohen was criticised, at the time, for apparent compromise and partiality against a personally-held research question; 'whose side are we on?' In answering this challenge Cohen came down firmly on the side of individual human rights against state excess. This translated into hands-on engagement with Amnesty and other human rights organisations mediating the Israel–Palestinian conflict. Throughout this period, indeed throughout her life, he was greatly supported by his wife Ruth, herself an active member of the Israeli feminist peace movement 'Women in Black'.

In 1994, he returned to the LSE as a Visiting Professor, and two years later was appointed Professor of Sociology. His most recent book *States of Denial: Knowing about Atrocities and Suffering* (2001) launches a new direction – critiquing public reaction to images and appeals about inhumanity and rights violations. The book grows out of his practical endeavour to position human rights and political violence squarely within a social control agenda. Such a commitment is the criminological challenge of the risk and security age where too much research energy is directed at modifying, rather than confronting, the excesses of neo-conservative retributivism.

No doubt with a commitment to continue the realistic examination of communitarian justice, Cohen's recent research interests focus on 'Truth Commissions' and the creation of collective memory. The work has an obvious genesis in *Visions of Social Control* and its 'stories of change'. Prophetic of the developments in international/ communitarian criminal justice, Cohen observed in *Visions*, that the 'symbolic evocation of a lost world' should not substitute for culturally specific control initiatives.

> The most immediate problem (for control) lies in the ideological flaw of trying to base a social-control ideology on visions derived from other societies. In the first place the content of the visions themselves is often historical or anthropological nonsense ... but even the authentic features of the vision ... simply cannot be recreated mimetically in another society,

reproduced intact like the lifelike exhibits in a historical or folk museum.

(1985: 121–22)

Rather than providing a justification away from comparative contextual analysis, Cohen in his later work is searching for interdisciplinary opportunity in a climate of public outreach where inhumanity cuts across social location, but its imagining is intensely dependent on its active social location.

In recognition of a career, beginning with commitments to understanding the sociology of deviance, and progressing to engage the complex rights challenges posed through violence and control in wide comparative and cross-disciplinary forms, Stan Cohen was elected to the British Academy, received the American Society of Criminology's Sellin-Glueck Award and the 2009 British Society of Criminology Outstanding Achievement Award. Far beyond these recognitions, Cohen's work remains inspirational for generations of researchers and research students across numerous disciplines. As Noam Chomsky comments in the foreword to a recent feschrift: 'The hope for the future is that others will take up the cause that Stanley Cohen has followed with courage, dedication and penetrating honesty' (Downes et al. 2007).

Major works

Cohen, S. (ed.) (1971) *Images of Deviance*. Harmondsworth: Penguin.
—— (1980) *Folk Devils and Moral Panics* (second edition). New York: St Martins Press.
—— (1985) *Visions of Social Control: Crime, Punishment and Classification*. Polity Press.
—— (1988) *Against Criminology*. New Brunswick, New Jersey: Transaction.
—— (2001) *States of Denial: Knowing About Atrocities and Suffering*. Cambridge: Polity.
Cohen, S. and Skull, A. (1983) *Social Control and the State*. London: Palgrave Macmillan.
Cohen, S. and Taylor, L. (1976) *Escape Attempts: The Theory and Practice of Resistance to Everyday Life*. London: Routledge.
Garland, D. (2001) *The Culture of Control*. Chicago, Illinois: University of Chicago.
Taylor, L. and Cohen, S. (1972) *Psychological Survival: The Experience of Long Term Imprisonment*. Harmondsworth: Penguin.

Further reading

Cohen, S. (1979) 'The Punitive City: Notes on the Dispersal of Social Control', *Contemporary Crises*, 3(4): 341–63.

—— (1981) 'Footprints on the Sand: A Further Report on Criminology and the Sociology of Deviance in Britain', in Fitzgerald, M. et al. (eds) *Crime and Society*. London: Routledge and Kegan Paul.

Downes, D., Rock, P., Chinkin, C. and Gearty, C. (eds) (2007) *Crime, Social Control and Human Rights: From Moral Panics to States of Denial; Essays in Honour of Stanley Cohen*. Cullompton: Willan.

MARK FINDLAY

ELLIOTT CURRIE (1942–)

The turning point in Elliott Currie's life came when he was 11 years old and his family moved to an integrated neighbourhood in Chicago. Other children who lived there were from varying backgrounds – minorities, poor whites, and, as in his own case, the children of parents who taught at the University of Chicago. It may sound like a cliché, but Currie considers this move the event that led him to sociology and criminology. He saw at first hand various inequalities in society, and knew that he wanted to be part of change. For example, in Chicago he saw differences in the way different groups were treated. Even when he himself was involved in delinquency in high school, it was immediately obvious that he was treated differently from his working-class peers. He began to notice how elements of labelling worked: when he was in trouble, his parents came in and made the problem 'go away'. Others were not so lucky.

After high school, Currie spent two years at the University of Chicago during the 1960s civil rights movement. However, much of his time was spent participating in activist causes, and he left university to enter the workforce before declaring a major. Currie worked a series of temporary factory jobs, as well as several months in a steel mill. He may not have been in college, but he found factory labour an education in and of itself. There he began noticing things about the job, such as broken liquor and beer bottles in the parking lot, workers drinking immediately before and after their shifts, the danger involved in this type of work, and the fact that, as a middle-class kid, he could leave that job and have other options, but for other workers it was their complete life.

During this period, Currie continued his intellectual development through informal reading. His major influences in this period were C. Wright Mills and Michael Harrington's *The Other America*. Finally, having had enough of factory jobs, and filled with a desire to change the problems he read about and saw around him, the time finally came to return to school. This time he enrolled at Roosevelt University in downtown Chicago, where he found the most influential professor to be Helena Lopata, the daughter of the esteemed philosopher and sociologist Florian Znaniecki.

After Roosevelt University, Currie entered graduate school in Sociology at Berkeley, where he was soon drawn into the world of student activism. This was after the free-speech movement, but at the height of Vietnam War protests. After attending a peaceful protest where the police turned violent against the participants, he found that many people grew cynical and withdrew from activism in frustration. In Currie's case, such incidents only intensified his quest for social justice. At Berkeley he found a number of intellectual mentors; it was a remarkable place to be at that particular time, with experimentation going on in various approaches to doing social research. Currie credits **David Matza**, Jerome Skolnick, and Bob Blauner as important influences in teaching him how to think about being a social scientist. The faculty members at Berkeley were challenging the established theoretical perspectives, holding broad discussions, and encouraging him to think of social science as a calling, and not simply as a job. This is where, Currie claims, he learned to 'jump to the big issues, tackle them as best you can; you didn't pay much attention to disciplinary boundaries'.

Towards the end of his PhD work, he accepted a job at Yale in 1970, where he stayed for two years, but left with the feeling that academia wasn't the place for him. Again, he worked various jobs, writing for activist and left journals before returning in 1973 to teach at UC Berkeley's School of Criminology. This appointment was short-lived, however, as the school was soon to be shut down by the California State government for being too radical (see **The Schwendingers**). Junior faculty who participated in protests lost their jobs, and student demonstrations happening at the time were met with tear gas. Currie once again left academia determined to help fix the injustices that he saw occurring around him. Strongly disturbed by the conservative shift in criminology during the 1970s, he was equally frustrated that, while many of his colleagues did not agree with this shift, very few publicly spoke out. In contrast, conservative thinkers of the time took advantage of any opportunity to influence public policy.

In an attempt to speak out against the conservative shift, Currie wrote a number of essays in the policy journal *Working Papers*. These in turn were picked up by a *New York Times* columnist and quickly caught on with the public. Eventually this led to *Confronting Crime*

(1985), which not only countered the dominant conservative position, but also the prevailing liberal view that crime wasn't much of a problem. It also challenged the naïve belief that minimally funded and scattered responses to crime could overcome deep structural problems.

The problem to Currie was that, although he thought it was obvious, many readers were not clear on the basic issues and facts surrounding crime. This led him to the next major aspect of his work, an interest that continues to the present day: if social scientists write only for each other, they will not be generally and widely understood. This would be doing a huge disservice to their field and to society. *Confronting Crime* was received and sold well, especially as it was seen as providing a leftist counterpoint to the popular conservative theories of the likes of **James Q. Wilson**, which was in part one of the reasons for writing the book. Currie is still surprised that he needed to write this book because he thought that everyone already knew this information. Still, he believes that this bestseller helped to stimulate people's thinking on the subject, and more importantly, empowered some people to realise that they could provide their own critiques from the left without dire negative consequences. He feels that he at least engaged and helped to precipitate a more serious debate.

His classic *Reckoning: Drugs, the Cities, and the American Future* (1993) ran through similar themes in another major synthesis of an enormous amount of data and research to argue that the cause of drug abuse was mass social deprivation, economic marginality, and cultural and community breakdown. The solution, he felt, was not in treatment but in realistic alternatives for potential addicts.

Unfortunately, any influence from the left in public discussion did not last. Within a decade of *Confronting Crime* the incarceration rate had doubled, and American crime policy was still drifting to the right. By now, all of the figures in his book were outdated, and a whole new genre of writing had emerged to justify the rightward drift. Worse for Currie was his feeling that Americans were beginning to lose any sense that there were any differences between the two major political parties on crime and justice, particularly after the Clinton 1994 crime bill, which Currie saw as draconian. Nothing was happening to challenge the thrust of public policy, but justifications (especially econometric research) emerged to justify mass incarceration. It was time, he felt, for another book to systematically challenge the justifying literature.

By now a more confident writer, Currie felt that *Crime and Punishment in America* (1998) was more fun to write. Certainly he enjoyed being able to 'mix it up' with the right. Unfortunately, his editor and publisher told him that the book would be a failure because no one would buy any publication that far to the left. Although working with the same publishers as before, they felt that the conservatism that was beginning to emerge in 1985 had become the 'religion of the land' – the movement to the right had triumphed, and it was cemented by the abandonment of opposition from political parties. Currie insisted that his book was not too far removed from the mainstream, and indeed it turned out to have a much better reception than expected. By challenging various myths about the benefits of over-incarceration, he helped generate some scepticism of the claims about the beneficial effects of getting tough on crime. Further, the book's focus on the possibility of rehabilitation and prevention programmes as having a possible effect, spurred another debate regarding crime and communities, which had been largely dormant throughout the 1990s. The book helped convince a wider public, largely sold on individual-level explanations of crime, to see that crime could also be addressed by supporting communities and that as troubled as some neighbourhoods have become, these problems aren't beyond repair.

In *Whitewashing Race* (2003) Currie participated in a collaborative effort on a similar but much broader topic: the idea of challenging the increasingly accepted conservative view of racial issues, including race and crime. He saw a drift toward a 'blame the victim' mentality in regards to ghetto communities even in the academic literature. The authors found the arguments similar to the crime debate: 'We already tried it all and nothing worked, therefore nothing will work'. Currie's well-written broadside on the popular conservative notion that America is a colour-blind society, however, failed to reach a large audience.

His most recent book, *The Road to Whatever* (2004), emerged from students talking about their own past. The book takes a different approach than his earlier work, centring on the drug abuse, violence and despair of middle-class youth. Here Currie finds a harsh meritocracy at fault for the despair that allows suburban adolescents to engage in these acts. His solution is to engage them, and bring them back into society rather than exclude them.

Overall, the major theme of Currie's writing involves the consequences of social neglect. Simply put, if you treat people badly, neglect them and then wash your hands of them, what will emerge are terrible social problems that will not go away. His goal is not to be antiseptically neutral, but at the same time that doesn't mean one cannot be honest and honourable in scientific research. Other disciplines, like public health, do not worry about separating advocacy and research in the way that criminology does. It is not unscientific to advocate, Currie feels. Rather, criminologists should be bringing what they know into the world of social action – indeed, that should be part of the job. While some people think they can do this without taking a policy or political position, Currie disagrees. Rather, he argues that one should take the position that honest research provides and the best theoretical analysis supports – then go out and make it happen.

In sum, Currie's most important mark on criminology has been his emphasis on bringing the big issues back to the table, particularly in the 1980s, when alternative voices were being silenced. He takes great pride in not just looking at the smaller pieces of the puzzle, but rather using his best understandings as a social scientist to 'slug it out with people who I thought were just flat wrong'.

Major works

Brown, M.K., Carnoy, M., Currie, E., Duster, T., Oppenheimer, D.B., Shultz, M. and Wellman, D. (2003) *Whitewashing Race: The Myth of a Color-Blind Society*. Berkeley, California: University of California Press.
Currie, E. (1985) *Confronting Crime*. New York: Pantheon.
—— (1993) *Reckoning: Drugs, the Cities, and the American Future*. New York: Hill and Wang.
—— (1998) *Crime and Punishment in America*. New York: Metropolitan.
—— (2004) *The Road to Whatever*. New York: Metropolitan.

Further reading

Currie, E. (1997) 'Market, Crime and Community: Toward a Mid-Range Theory of Post-Industrial Violence', *Theoretical Criminology*, 1(2): 147–72.
—— (2003) 'Social Crime Prevention Strategies in a Market Society', in McLaughlin, E., Muncie, J. and Hughes, G. (eds) *Criminological Perspectives: Essential Readings*. London: Sage.
—— (2007) 'Against Marginality: Arguments for a Public Criminology', *Theoretical Criminology*, 11: 175–90.

MARTIN D. SCHWARTZ AND ASHLEY DEMYAN

FRANCES HEIDENSOHN (1942–)

In 1968 Frances Heidensohn, then a junior lecturer at the London School of Economics and Political Science (LSE), published her first article, 'The Deviance of Women: a Critique and an Enquiry', in the *British Journal of Sociology*. Whilst she has described this work as pre-feminist in its approach in the sense of lacking the vocabulary and conceptual analysis provided by modern feminism of the 1970s, it is a remarkable paper in that it addresses the major themes for the study of women and crime and provides the agenda, albeit unintentionally, for the development of a 'feminist criminology'. Thus, it critiques both the neglect and sexist treatment of women in historical and con-temporary theoretical debates on criminality and the lack of explanation given for women's consistently low crime rate. Male delinquents, Heidensohn acknowledges, were given more attention due to their greater numbers, more obvious visibility and likelihood of being seen or defined as an urgent social problem; the latter impacting on research funding.

Moreover, Heidensohn pre-empts the arguments against the 'liberation causes crime' hypothesis of Freda Adler and Rita Simon in the mid-1970s by pointing out that, despite changes in women's role within society and greater participation in public life, their crime rate has remained relatively constant over time. The general lack of effort afforded to the study of the deviance of women has meant that these are 'lonely, uncharted seas of human behaviour' (1968: 171). There was no female equivalent of **Shaw**'s *The Jack Roller* or **Sutherland**'s *The Professional Thief* and thus, what was needed was 'a crash programme of research which telescopes decades of comparable studies of males' (ibid). This research should, for example, examine the characteristics of female deviance, why it occurs or does not occur, how it is reinforced and how deviant career patterns and roles emerge. The sociological value of such work is immense for, 'greater knowledge of the sociology of female deviance would enhance our knowledge of feminine behaviour, of sex roles – their characteristics, norms and socializing processes associated with them; it would broaden our view of deviance in general' (ibid). The following year, Heidensohn went on to publish an article in *The Howard Journal of Criminal Justice* on prison for women; together these two papers are noteworthy for their coverage and prescience. But let us first place Heidensohn biographically.

Frances Doherty (Heidensohn was to come later with marriage) was born in July 1942 in Birmingham, UK during the middle of a World War II air raid. From 1940 onwards Birmingham, as a major manu-facturer of armaments and military supplies for the allied forces, had been subject to extensive bombing raids from the German Luftwaffe; that summer the attacks were especially heavy, making it the second most bombed city in England after London and a particularly worri-some period in which to have a small baby. Heidensohn's parents were Irish Catholics and had met as undergraduates at the University of Birmingham. Her father had graduated with a degree in Classics and spoke German fluently; the latter led him to be recruited as part of the war effort to counter intelligence and to the German code breaking centre at Bletchley Park. After the war he returned to Birmingham where he became a teacher and then a headmaster. Her mother, having achieved a postgraduate diploma in education, had also become a teacher. As teachers, the Dohertys, were committed to public education and spent their working lives in the state sector. Heidensohn's mother, uncommonly for the time given her class position and the prevailing social attitudes, remained in paid employment after having children. In an interview with Mary Eaton for the biographical piece, 'A Woman in Her Own Time', Heidensohn recalls that her mother was also determined that she should get the best education available and, although Catholic girls were expected to go to Catholic schools, secured permission from the Archbishop of Birmingham so she could attend The King Edward's Foundation, a prestigious and highly academic institution where 'no subjects were "off limits" to girls' (2000: 10) and it was assumed you would go on to university. At school Heidensohn was conscious of being different from her class mates due to her Catholic background, working mother and cultured family: 'my parents went to art exhibitions and came to London to the theatre. In the suburbs where I grew up people didn't do that' (ibid: 11).

This upbringing clearly instilled in Heidensohn the importance of education and a strong social conscience. In her teens she became involved in running play schemes in deprived areas of Birmingham. Thus, although her choice of studying sociology as an undergraduate at the LSE, an institution well known for its Fabian socialism, would have been seen as unusual by her school where many of the girls went to Oxford and Cambridge, Heidensohn has described it as a 'natural step' given her interest in social issues. Moreover, she saw sociology as a subject that could prepare her for a career in social work.

It was exciting to be a sociology student at the LSE in the 1960s, for as Heidensohn has put it,

> The era itself was one of excitement and change in society, the arts and politics. At that time the civil rights movement in the USA was mobilizing and in eastern Europe the Prague spring flowered for a while. A series of social issues with equality, justice and freedom as their themes were widely discussed both in public and academic debate.
>
> (1997: 10)

Furthermore, the LSE was at the forefront of developments in criminology and sociology and 'we were fortunate not only in that new ideas and opportunities opened up to us in the 1960s but also that we were in time to know criminologists from older generations' (1998: 56). Indeed Heidensohn's first job was a survey of recent research for Herman Mannheim, one of the three European refugees – Radzinowicz at Cambridge and Grunhut at Oxford – who established criminology in Britain. Mannheim was exceptional in his stress on the sociology of crime and his importation of American ideas into a British context. Such an approach was expanded upon by Alan Little and Terence Morris and the LSE was to become a major conduit of the new deviancy theory which had developed in the United States in the intensely creative decade of 1955 to 1965. In 1965 Heidensohn, who as an undergraduate was awarded the Hobhouse Memorial Prize, began her graduate studies under the supervision of Little and Morris. She was made an Assistant Lecturer in 1966 and her colleagues included David Downes and Paul Rock. She remembers the July 1968 Cambridge Criminology Conference where the idea for the National Deviancy Conference was discussed with the first symposium occurring at the University of York later that year. There was at the LSE at that time a remarkable cluster of researchers interested in the new sociology of deviance: not only Downes and Rock but fellow PhD students were **Stan Cohen**, Mike Brake and **Jock Young**. **David Matza** came for a sabbatical from 1967 to 1968, writing *Becoming Deviant* (1969) during this period.

This is the intellectual context in which Heidensohn found herself in the mid-to-late 1960s. 'The Deviance of Women: a Critique and an Enquiry' is particularly characterised by a versatile yet critical transposition of the two strands of new deviancy theory – the subcultural and labelling approaches – to the subject of women and crime. From **Albert Cohen**'s *Delinquent Boys*, she drew on the work of Talcott Parsons and the lesser known George Grosser, who pioneered the study of sex differences in delinquency. But to this Heidensohn added the work of the labelling theorists: **Becker**, **Lemert**, Scheff and Gibbs. She is thus concerned not only with differences in male/female crime rates but in the question of why have the differences been largely ignored or explored merely as a pathological 'add on' to explanations of male crime. Her explanation has echoes of both C. Wright Mills and **Matza**. Namely that criminology reflects the interests of the operators of the criminal justice system, hence because of low numbers this results in 'the almost total *exclusion* of females from the serious literature' (1968: 162) and that, 'at the very least most workers in the field tend to approach their subject with the dual purposes of investigating then eradicating what they term social "disorganization" or "pathology"' (ibid). Her answer to this, tentative at the time but rehearsing the concerns of standpoint feminism, is that one must start from the female sex role and definitions of women themselves. In doing so she drew on the important work of Rose Giallombardo and David Ward and Gene Kassebaum which had recently transformed views of women's prisons and the debate over the impact of total institutions.

Heidensohn's interest in women and offending stemmed from the observation made by Barbara Wootton in her 1963 Hamlyn lectures, 'If men behaved like women the courts would be idle and the prisons empty.' Not only, as discussed above, did she find this area to be under-researched and poorly theorised, but that 'fellow criminologists, administrators, staff and governors at penal establishments were "puzzled" and "uncomprehending"' (1994: 21) as to why anyone wished to study women. Heidensohn's first presentation on the topic, which formed the basis for 'The Deviance of Women', was at a research seminar in the LSE's Sociology Department in 1967; it was met with polite disinterest, 'really, nobody understood. They didn't think there was a problem. So women don't commit so much crime, so what's the problem?' (as told to Eaton 2000: 13). Heidensohn's main interest at this time was in studying young women in Borstal – this too was met with 'bewilderment' when she approached the Home Office for the necessary permission for the research. Indeed, despite Heidensohn's work, there was still little discussion in the late 1960s and early 1970s of women and offending or lack of offending. For example, *The New Criminology*, the classic text of radical criminology, which arose from discussions from the National Deviancy Conferences, makes much of class but ignores the sexism and gender bias of traditional and new theories.

Frances married Klaus Heidensohn, an economist, in 1965 and had two children. She found it difficult, as have so many women academics, to combine being the mother of small children and a demanding job with little institutional support and thus resigned her position. She returned to the LSE a year later on a part-time basis before leaving again in 1974 to take up a position at the Civil Service College. This latter experience was to prove invaluable and informed the direction of her later work; indeed she learnt a great deal about central government and the workings of powerful elite groups and 'became fascinated by social policy and with obstacles to ways of achieving social change' (1997: 11). She returned to the academic mainstream in 1979 taking up the position of Lecturer at Goldsmiths' College, London.

By the late 1970s modern feminism was beginning to take root within the academy. **Carol Smart**'s *Women, Crime and Criminology*, which was written from a committed feminist position, had been published in 1976 and the core themes of what has become a 'feminist criminology' or as some would prefer, 'feminist perspectives in criminology' were being discussed. In 1985 Heidensohn published *Women and Crime* which firmly established her as a major criminological thinker. In many ways this book builds on Barbara Wootton's observation and the questions posed in 'The Deviance of Women'. Thus, its aim is to explore, why it is that women do not commit crime. And, using the language of contemporary feminism, provides a focus on how patriarchal society controls women by requiring them to conform to their roles as wives and mothers.

In 1994 Heidensohn became Chair of Social Policy at Goldsmiths and still retains an affiliation with the university as an emeritus professor. She is currently Visiting Professor at the LSE, her alma mater. Heidensohn's work has over the last twenty years or so broadened out to consider international and comparative perspectives and the role of women in law enforcement. In 1995 she edited *International Feminist Perspectives in Criminology* with Nicole Hahn Rafter which brought together a number of contributors from various countries including Australia, South Africa, Britain, Italy, Poland, the United States and Canada to assess the impact of feminism on criminology through an international lens. *Women in Control? The Role of Women in Law Enforcement* (1992) is based on interviews with British and American Police Officers, exploring women's role in law enforcement in these two societies and the importance of gender in social control. Theoretically it engages with the work of **Michel Foucault** and **Stan Cohen** on social control and Raewyn Connell on masculinity. Although this book reveals a move from seeing women as controlled to an analysis of their participation in systems of control, Heidensohn notes women are still a long way from being in charge of these institutions. Heidensohn developed her interest on women and policing further in the book, *Gender and Policing* (2000), co-authored with the psychologist, Jennifer Brown. This documents the findings of her most ambitious research project to date, a worldwide and comparative study of women police officers which involved the collection of both qualitative and quantitative data and the integration of sociological and psychological approaches. It situates women's experiences both historically and in terms of their specific national contexts and considers the difficulties women experience in gaining access to work in law enforcement. It traces similarities in the experiences of the first police women and their contemporary counterparts, the levels of harassment and discrimination encountered, the impact of police occupational culture on women officers and the overall effect of women police officers on policing. Heidensohn's most recent book is *Gender and Justice: New Concepts and Approaches* (2006), an edited text that brings together key research and work on the relationship between gender and justice, serving to address many of the concerns that are evident in her own writing, such as the gender gap, levels of equality in the criminal justice system, penal institutions and how these affect women's lives. Moreover, with a sense, as she has put it, of her life coming full circle, in 2008 Heidensohn became General Editor of *The British Journal of Sociology* which had published that extraordinary first paper, 'The Deviance of Women: a Critique and and Enquiry' in 1968.

Despite all her academic achievements, Frances Heidensohn is no ivory tower intellectual; she has retained the sense of civic responsibility that was so clearly evident in her teenage years when she worked in socially deprived areas of Birmingham. She has been actively committed to the National Health Service, serving on a number of committees and chairing health authorities in some of the poorest areas of London. As part of her commitment to health care provision she has published reports on cancer treatment services, primary care and the challenge of AIDS. In the area of criminal justice, she has served as a member of the sentencing advisory panel and was commissioner for judicial appointments.

In 2004 Heidensohn received the Sellin-Glueck Award from the American Society of Criminology in recognition of her international contributions to criminology. However, she remains unsure of the practical impact of work such as hers and that of other feminists in the discipline. Whilst in *International Feminist Perspectives in Criminology*, Heidensohn and Rafter note that the feminist project in criminology is ultimately one of, 'self-obsolescence, for if the discipline were engendered and crime control policy transformed as feminists recommend, they could retire from the field' (1995: 14), they stress the immensity of the work involved. There is still much to be done. Indeed when I interviewed Frances for this piece and asked whether she thought the feminist enterprise had been successful, she shook her head: 'How can it be when we have today more women in prison than ever?'

Major works

Brown, J. and Heidensohn, F. (2000) *Gender and Policing: Comparative Perspectives*. Basingstoke: Macmillan.

Heidensohn, F. (1968) 'The Deviance of Women: A Critique and an Enquiry', *British Journal of Sociology*, XIX(2): 160–75.

—— (1969) 'Prison for Women', *The Howard Journal of Criminal Justice*, Spring: 281–8.

—— (1985) *Women and Crime*. London: Macmillan.

—— (1992) *Women in Control? The Role of Women in Law Enforcement*. Oxford: Clarendon Press.

—— (1994) 'From Being to Knowing: Some Issues in the Study of Gender in Contemporary Society', *Women and Criminal Justice*, VI(4): 13–37.

—— (2000) *Sexual Politics and Social Control*. Milton Keynes: Open University Press.

—— (eds) (2006) *Gender and Justice*. Cullompton: Willan.

Heidensohn, F. and Hahn Rafter, N. (eds) (1995) *International Feminist Perspectives in Criminology*. Milton Keynes: Open University Press.

Further reading

Eaton, M. (2000) 'A Woman in Her Own Time: Frances Heidensohn Within and Beyond Criminology', *Women and Criminal Justice*, 12(2/3): 9–28.

Heidensohn, F. (1997) 'Discovering Sociology: Further Enquiries', in Ballard, C., Gubbay, J. and Middleton, C. (eds) *The Students Companion to Sociology*. Oxford: Blackwell.

—— (1998) 'Translations and Refutations', in S. Holdaway and P. Rock (eds) *Thinking About Criminology*. London: UCL Press.

JAYNE MOONEY

JOCK YOUNG (1942–)

On the surface, the Hampshire town of Aldershot is a fairly unremarkable place; its high street and collection of ordered middle-class estates imbue it with the same deadening familiarity that characterises hundreds of non-descript English towns. There is, however, one notable difference: Aldershot is the 'Home of the British Army', and has been the site of a huge military garrison since 1854. Given the nature and focus of his work over the last four decades, perhaps it's no surprise, then, that Aldershot is also where William 'Jock' Young – one of Britain's foremost criminological thinkers – spent his formative years. For if Aldershot is defined by sedentary suburbia and military might, Young's research corpus is characterised by a long-standing opposition to middle-class cultural conformity and the ideologies associated with state power and imperialism.

Young was actually born in Midlothian, Scotland (hence the playground appellation of Jock – the standard nickname for exiled Hibernians in post-war England), his family only moving to Aldershot when he was five. If primary school was a culture shock, grammar school was literally a boot camp. So embedded was the local militarism that his school enforced mandatory attendance in a uniformed Cadet Force. The crushing regimentation and hours of 'square bashing' did not sit well with Young, who rebelled and, along with a motley group of conscientious objectors and Jehovah's Witnesses, formed an anti-Fascist/pro Campaign for Nuclear Disarmament group to oppose what they saw as the school's military institutionalisation. This was the opening exchange in a lifelong campaign against structural oppression and cultural imperialism.

Despite this rebellious streak, Young was an outstanding student, excelling particularly in the hard sciences. He was heading for University College London to read biochemistry, but during a detour at Regent Street Polytechnic, he met and was inspired by the Marxist criminologist, Steve Box. Encouraged by Box, Young switched his studies to sociology and enrolled at the London School of Economics (LSE) in 1962. To start with, Young was extremely disappointed with life at the LSE. Interviewed for this entry, he described it as 'appallingly boring, a dreadful Fabian place'. However, during the course of his PhD, things changed. The mid-to-late 1960s was an era of student protest, and it didn't take long for many at the LSE to get in step with the rhythms of radicalism. Young recalls: 'Suddenly there were sit-ins everywhere, demonstrations by Trotskyites and Situationists. The whole world seemed to be turning upside down.' The sociology faculty was also undergoing something of a transformation. Young's doctoral supervisor, Terry Morris, along with a small group of junior faculty (including subsequent luminaries of British Criminology David Downes, **Frances Heidensohn**, and Paul Rock) were busy importing American concepts such as symbolic interactionism and labelling theory into British sociology. While this work greatly influenced Young, more important still was the counter-culture revolution taking place outside the University seminar room. These were heady times: R.D. Laing was promulgating his anti-psychiatry message in public readings at the Roundhouse, and the Rolling Stones were hard at work shocking the post-war British establishment. According to Young, it was this counter-cultural sensibility that triggered the first National Deviancy Conference (NDC) in 1968. Avowedly anti-institutional, and highly critical of orthodox criminology, the NDC was a decade-long series of bi-annual (sometimes even quarterly) interdisciplinary conferences based around emerging research in 'the sociology of deviance'. Attracting the likes of Phil Cohen, **Stuart Hall**, Paul Willis and Dick Hebdige from cultural studies, and second-wave feminists like Mary McIntosh and Angela McRobbie, the NDC was an incredible outpouring of leftist and anarchist intellectual energy. It was also where Young presented his first conference paper, 'The Role of Police as Amplifiers of Deviance'. Like the NDC itself, the paper was a reflection of changes underway in British society in the 1960s; it was also the foundation stone for his first major work, *The Drugtakers* (1971).

Young had spent the best part of the 1960s living and squatting in the then Bohemian North London enclave of Notting Hill. Populated by a mix of poets and petty criminals, drug dealers and art school dropouts, Notting Hill was also home to a large Afro-Caribbean community. Young was fascinated by the way many of these groups constituted their shared identity through antagonistic encounters with the police, and in particular the Notting Hill Drug Squad. *The Drugtakers* documented the flinty social interactions that surrounded the control of drugs in his neighbourhood, paying particular attention to the extraordinary moral panics that frequently bubbled up in their wake.

For many commentators *The Drugtakers* is just another example of classic labelling theory. In a recent assessment of early British moral panic theory, **David Garland** (2008), for example, argues that what Young and others like **Stan Cohen** were engaged in was simply a hip advocacy of the counter-culture movement. Looking back on that period now, Young sees some merit in Garland's analysis: 'We saw it as our job to represent youth culture, and in that sense our work was parallel to the socialist history movement of "writing from below". The problem was that, on occasion, we overestimated the irrationality of the reaction, and underestimated the problem that provoked the reaction in the first place.' To be fair to Young, many of the weaknesses associated with the labelling perspective were actually acknowledged in *The Drugtakers* (and later dealt with in detail in a chapter – 'Working Class Criminology' – in Taylor et al. 1975). In this sense, *The Drugtakers* can be seen as a working through of some of the debates and concerns that would preoccupy Young's work in the remainder of the decade.

Thanks in part to the ongoing work of the NDC, Young became increasingly aware of the need to approach the subject of deviance from a more holistic position that included the wider structural concerns of society. At this point, Young was working closely with Ian

Taylor and the orthodox Marxist, Paul Walton. The result was *The New Criminology* (1973), a thoroughgoing critique of existing criminological theories that (re)considered crime and deviance in terms of power relationships derived from the ownership (or non-ownership) of the means of production within capitalist societies. The book was an immediate global success – much to the considerable surprise of the three authors who had compiled it largely from their teaching notes. Reflecting on the impact of the book now, Young told me: 'Whilst we saw *The New Criminology* as an extremely committed socialist book, we never intended it as a blueprint for a Marxist criminology – but in some parts of the world that is exactly what it became.'

Taylor, Walton and Young were riding the crest of a wave, and one that gathered more momentum with their follow-up publication *Critical Criminology* (1975) – an anthology of essays by radical British and American criminologists. Taken together, the two books defined the field of 1970s 'radical' or 'critical' criminology; setting the agenda for a mode of criminological analysis that both challenged the discipline's relationship to the state, and more importantly introduced a reflexive critique of the criminal justice apparatus and the related disciplinary processes of welfare capitalism (see also **William J. Chambliss** and **The Schwendingers**).

The strength of the radical criminological approach as set forth in *The New Criminology* was that it brought together the interpretivist aspects of interactionism (as exemplified by *The Drugtakers*) with the more 'structural' perspective associated with Marxist conflict theory. The weakness, of course, was that, as a result of its overriding interest in the way power and class functioned to define crime and enforce law, radical criminology failed to adequately explain individual criminal and deviant behaviour. This lack of an aetiological focus opened the door to the criticism that radical criminologists were 'romanticising criminals' as proto revolutionary actors engaged in the struggle against capitalist oppression.

Such criticisms struck a chord with Young, especially when viewed against a backdrop of rising crime rates. It also became apparent that it was the working classes who were disproportionately experiencing the spike in crime, further substantiating the view that radical criminology was 'not taking crime seriously'. All this was brought home to Young when he was approached by his local Labour council to do something about the on-the-ground realities of crime in his North London neighbourhood. Young recalls: 'I was struck at the most immediate level by the fact that none of my training was geared towards intervening in the crime problem at the practical level – when all of a sudden someone starts asking you about the criminological value of street lighting, it's something of a challenge!' The response – Left Realist criminology – formulated by Young and his Middlesex University colleagues John Lea and Roger Matthews, would send shock waves through radical criminology, opening up personal disputes and ideological cleavages that endure to this day.

Emerging during the UK Labour Party's unelectable years, left realism was a direct response to both the rise of 'the New Right' and the significant political and cultural transformations that took place during the 1980s. Although it would be crude to say that left realism was simply a way for certain radical criminologists to free themselves from the ideological constraints of Marxism, it is fair to suggest that it offers a more pragmatic, policy-oriented approach to the problem of crime than much previous critical criminology (Lea and Young 1984). Rather than the focus placed by Marxist criminologists – or left idealists, as Young now controversially chose to call them – on macro political theory, and in particular the crimes of the powerful, left realism viewed crime from both ends of the social structure. When set out in such straightforward terms, left realism appears highly attractive. Viewing crime as an 'amalgam' of many 'interacting elements' (e.g. the victim, the public, the police and other agencies of social control, the legal rules of criminal law, the criminal act, and the offender) allowed left realists to consider such issues as multiple victimisation, multi-agency co-operation, progressive crime prevention, even street lighting – all things that previously had largely been ignored by radical criminologists in favour of the over-arching goal of revolutionary sociopolitical transformation.

Young remains entirely phlegmatic about this lurch towards a more pragmatic criminology ('The policy demands really exercised us and forced us to think differently'). Yet, his role in the development of left realism has earned him more condemnation than any other aspect of his career. He was severely criticised by British radical criminologists who maintained that left realism was a major ideological step backwards; little more than a retreat to normative capitalist values and mainstream legal conceptions of crime and punishment. Young, though, has refused to be drawn into this argument. Instead, just like at other times in his career, he has shifted gears and moved on – if not perhaps in terms of his overall objective, then certainly in terms of perspective.

While Young never openly disavowed left realism, there is no doubt that in recent years he has distanced himself from its more orthodox manifestations. Young sees this retreat from realism as having much to do with the reversal of 'New Labour's' crime policy following the election of Tony Blair in 1997. Young told me:

> When Blair first made his famous, 'tough on crime, tough on the causes of crime' speech, it was in an article called 'Crime is a Socialist Issue' in *The New Statesman* magazine. However, by the time he'd set up shop in Number Ten, the 'S' word had been purged by the spin-doctors. No one was asking us about progressive crime policies anymore. No one was even interested.

Indeed, as the UK prison population continued to rise and progressive ideals were shot down by successive centre-right Labour Home Secretaries, Young knew that, not only was left realism no longer viable, but that his next work must be a substantive critique of New Labour and the wider system of neo-liberal capitalism that underpinned it.

If Young was frustrated, for example, by the way New Labour took a progressive idea like social exclusion and then hung it onto the work of Charles Murray and other right-wing conservative thinkers he was even more troubled by what he saw as a developing 'sociology of vindictiveness' and the rise of increasingly punitive mechanisms of social control. These concerns came together in his 1999 book *The Exclusive Society*, a major work of social theory that crosscuts disciplinary boundaries and continental divides with equal ease – reflecting perhaps Young's status as a global academic and his increasing fascination with the social problems of North and South America. In *The Exclusive Society* Young charts the transition from an *inclusive society* (characterised by the social stability, cultural homogeneity and high modernity of the post-war period up to the 1960s) to a late modern *exclusive society* (characterised by hyper pluralism, casino capitalism, and the unravelling of consensual politics and the traditionalities of community, family and stable employment). It is a world where the 'bulimia' of 'massive cultural inclusion' is counterbalanced by 'systematic structural exclusion'.

If *The Exclusive Society* was about cultural revolutions and economic reconfigurations, its sequel *The Vertigo of Late Modernity* (2007) was an attempt to see how all this would play out at the psychodynamic level. Here the 'slow riot of crime and violence' that pervades late modern society is an eruption of the anxieties, insecurities and tensions that 'haunt the everyday world'.

Much of the work for the latter of these two books was completed in the United States following Young's move to New York City in 2002. This was also around the time when he began to gravitate towards cultural criminology (a relationship that gathered further traction following his move to the University of Kent, UK in 2005: see e.g. Hayward and Young 2004). Young sees the move to America as affecting his thinking in two interrelated ways: first, it forced him to revisit (in context) the extraordinarily rich tradition of American sociological criminology – both its strengths and its weaknesses; and second, he was struck by how, despite all these tremendous socio-logical antecedents, American criminology had morphed into some-thing so positivistic and boring. Young explains:

> It was like criminology had developed an anti-Midas touch, an ability to take a subject that fascinated millions of people and turn it into sanitised dust! This is why the arguments being made by cultural criminologists were so timely – they continued the line of thinking that runs from the Chicago School through to Merton, but updated and revitalised it for our very interesting late modern world.
>
> (Ferrell et al. 2008)

In this sense, one can see cultural criminology as a culmination of Young's work to date: from the interactionism of *The Drugtakers* to the critique of structural inequalities in *The New Criminology*, from the desire to understand and ameliorate the everyday realities and micro harms that permeated left realism to the interest in the late modern existential insecurities and sociocultural fluctuations that constitute *The Exclusive Society* – all are central themes within the new cultural criminology.

Young continues to be fascinated by crime, society and power – a lifelong passion that shows no sign of abating. Indeed, in a recent acceptance speech following his Lifetime Achievement Award from the Critical Criminology Division of the American Society of Criminology, he wryly and resolutely declared: 'They usually hand out these gongs when someone's about to shuffle off into retirement and obscurity. I can assure you, I have no plans to entertain either of these two options!'

Major works

Lea, J. and Young, J. (1984) *What is to be Done about Law and Order?* Harmondsworth: Penguin.

Taylor, I., Walton, P. and Young, J. (1973) *The New Criminology*. London: Routledge and Kegan Paul.

—— (1975) *Critical Criminology*. London: Routledge and Kegan Paul.

Young, J. (1971) *The Drugtakers*. London: Paladin.

—— (1999) *The Exclusive Society*. London: Sage.
—— (2007) *The Vertigo of Late Modernity*. London: Sage.

Further reading

Ferrell, J., Hayward, K. and Young, J. (2008) *Cultural Criminology: An Invitation*. London: Sage.
Garland, D. (2008) 'On the Concept of Moral Panic', *Crime, Media, Culture*, 4(1): 9–31.
Hayward, K. and Young, J. (2004) 'Cultural Criminology: Some Notes on the Script', *Theoretical Criminology*, 8(3): 259–73.
Young, J. (1994) 'Incessant Chatter: Recent Paradigms in Criminology', in Maguire, M. et al. (eds) *The Oxford Handbook of Criminology* (first edition). Oxford: Oxford University Press.
—— (2002) 'Critical Criminology in the Twenty-First Century: Critique, Irony and the Always Unfinished', in Hogg, R. and Carrington, K. (eds) *Critical Criminology*. Cullompton: Willan.

KEITH J. HAYWARD

DAVID P. FARRINGTON (1944–)

Few criminologists have made the kind of contribution that has shaped the life course of the discipline. Professor David P. Farrington is one of those individuals. Having directed the Cambridge Study in Delinquent Development (CSDD), a prospective longitudinal survey of over 400 London males followed up from age eight to age forty-eight, Farrington has been involved in charting the course of developmental and life-course criminology. This particular theoretical perspective in criminology seeks to understand not only the longitudinal patterning of antisocial and criminal activity, but also the risk and protective factors associated with onset, persistence, and desistance in criminal careers.

In addition to his important role in the CSDD, Farrington also serves as co-investigator of the Pittsburgh Youth Study, a prospective longitudinal study of over 1,500 Pittsburgh males aged between seven and thirty years. While these two large-scale projects have consumed much of his time and attention, Farrington has also been involved in a large array of professional and national study groups and projects, has served as President of several major professional societies, has mentored many successful graduate students, and has accumulated a prolific and highly influential academic record, having published over 450 papers and chapters on criminological and psychological topics as well as over sixty books, monographs and government publications.

Yet, one feature of Farrington's legacy that may be overlooked by many criminologists is his archival of the Cambridge Study data. By granting criminologists access to the data that he has spent an entire career collecting (with very little extramural funding), Farrington has provided students and researchers the ability to study important criminal career issues. In short, Farrington's research on criminal careers has not only generated important information on the patterning and nature of criminal activity over the life course, but has also stimulated the development of theory, including the area known as developmental/life-course criminology. By any measure, David P. Farrington is clearly one of the most important figures in the discipline.

Originally from Lancashire, England, Farrington completed his BA, MA, and PhD degrees in Psychology at the University of Cambridge. His doctoral work, conducted in experimental psychology, focused on human learning, and was very much in the model of experimental science. Towards the end of his PhD degree, he had grown disillusioned with the field of human learning and experimental psychology because it seemed so divorced from 'real-life learning problems', which triggered an interest in social science research. At that time, there was an advertisement in the Psychological Laboratory to work with Donald West on a longitudinal study of crime and delinquency. He applied for the job, and defected from psychology to criminology. He was offered the job because of his computer and statistical skills, and knew very little about criminology when he started working with Donald West in 1969. In hindsight, Farrington observes that it was probably not a strategic move to leave psychology. He was offered two lectureships in psychology and could have continued a career in experimental psychology. His move to criminology, in a sense, made him 'burn his boats in psychology'. Moreover, there was not an abundance of jobs for psychologists in the field of criminology during that time, but he persisted and was finally offered a lectureship in criminology in 1976.

Farrington's most notable contribution to criminology is his work with the CSDD, of which he is director. While he acknowledges that it is difficult to obtain and maintain funding for longitudinal research, he has succeeded in sustaining funding for the study for over four decades. In recent years, he was successful in getting funding to study the third generation of the study, the children of the study men. To date, 336 of the third generation have been interviewed and with another year and a half of funding, Farrington estimates that another

500 could be interviewed, enabling more robust analyses on inter-generational transmission of antisocial behaviours and offending habits.

Farrington has frequently emphasised the need for prospective longitudinal studies, arguing that this research design may address various questions that cannot be addressed with cross-sectional data, particularly questions about within-individual change. However, interviewed for this entry, he also acknowledges the difficulty in obtaining funding for this type of research, and offers advice to junior researchers:

> Perhaps it is better for younger researchers to join in with existing datasets. Perhaps we should have a space shuttle model, like a crime shuttle, where we mount big projects and have lots of people linked up to it, addressing different questions. Maybe we can only have a small number of major longitudinal studies, and perhaps younger scholars would be best advised to join in with existing studies and do their own analyses. Every study is really under-analyzed.
>
> (Personal communication 2008)

The Cambridge Study has made numerous important contributions to the advancement of knowledge in the field of criminology. The study has demonstrated the predictive power of early risk factors on criminal career outcomes, as well as the effect of life events on life-course patterns of offending and patterns of continuity and discontinuity that are observed over time. The CSDD is one of the few longitudinal studies that integrates both measures of self-reported offending and official convictions. One of the key findings arising from comparisons of self-reports and official records is the relationship between a first conviction and subsequent self-reported offending; analysis of these data suggests that official sanctions may have an undesirable labelling effect (Farrington 1977; see also **Becker**, **Lemert**).

Within-individual analyses and the effects of life events are another important contribution of the Cambridge study. Farrington has often argued that studies investigating within-individual changes in offending behaviour are highly informative but have been quite scarce, and that even longitudinal data are often analysed in a cross-sectional manner. Throughout his career, he has supported the importance of collecting longitudinal data, and analysing these data to their fullest potential.

The vast amount of knowledge generated as a result of the Cambridge Study led Farrington to develop his own developmental theory of offending behaviour: the Integrated Cognitive Anti-social Potential (ICAP) Theory. In this theory, Farrington has integrated concepts and theoretical constructs from various other theories, such as social learning, labelling, routine activities, rational choice, control and strain, to provide a more comprehensive explanation of antisocial behaviour. The theory emphasises the importance of considering both individual predispositions and social context in the explanation of antisocial and offending behaviour, and more importantly the inter-action between these internal and external factors. The fundamental construct underlying ICAP theory is antisocial potential, that is, this potential to engage in antisocial behaviour. Farrington argues that the shift from antisocial potential to antisocial behaviour occurs as a result of cognitive and social processes (see Farrington 2005, for a detailed description of ICAP theory).

Looking back on his career, Farrington's fondest memories include being President of the American Society of Criminology, having papers published and advancing the state of knowledge, and obtaining grants. A particularly enjoyable memory for Farrington was his parti-cipation on the National Academy of Sciences panel with Al Blumstein in 1983–85:

> This was enjoyable because we really felt that we were develop-ing a new paradigm, the criminal career paradigm, and so we felt that we were really pushing back the frontiers of knowledge. It was really exciting to be a part of the meetings, and collaborating with Al Blumstein was great. So, the criminal career panel was definitely an enjoyable memory because of the excitement, the feeling of defining a new paradigm which became quite impor-tant in the US in the 1980s. We were developing important sci-entific studies that were going to define Criminology for the next 20 years. It was an exciting time, in the 1980s, even a golden age for American Criminology.
>
> (Personal communication 2008)

Forty years later, his passion for research persists. He still discusses his plans for further data collection in the context of the Cambridge Study (with hopes of a final data collection with the men at age sixty), and remains active in various other research endeavours that are too numerous to offer a comprehensive list. In addition to being the director of the CSDD, he is also co-investigator of the Pittsburgh Youth Study, a Fellow of the British Academy, of the Academy of Medical Sciences, of the British Psychological Society and of the American Society of Criminology, and an Honorary Life Member of the British Society of Criminology and of the Division of Forensic

Psychology of the British Psychological society. He is co-chair of the US National Institute of Justice Study Group on Transitions from Delinquency to Adult Offending, a member of the Board of Directors of the International Observatory on Violence in Schools, a member of the Campbell Collaboration Crime and Justice Group Steering Committee, a member of the Board of Directors of the International Society of Criminology, joint editor of the journal *Criminal Behaviour and Mental Health*, and a member of the editorial boards of fifteen other journals. He has served as President of the American Society of Criminology (the first non-North American to be elected to this position), President of the European Association of Psychology and Law, President of the British Society of Criminology, President of the Academy of Experimental Criminology, and Chair of the Division of Forensic Psychology of the British Psychological Society.

His awards and distinctions include the Sellin-Glueck Award of the American Society of Criminology for international contributions to criminology, the Sutherland Award of the American Society of Criminology for outstanding contributions to criminology, the Joan McCord Award of the Academy of Experimental Criminology, the Beccaria Gold Medal of the Criminology Society of German-Speaking Countries, the Senior Prize of the British Psychological Society Division of Forensic Psychology, the US Office of Juvenile Justice and Delinquency Prevention Outstanding Contributions Award, the Hermann Mannheim Prize of the International Centre for Comparative Criminology, and the prize for distinguished scholarship of the American Sociological Association Criminology Section for his book, *Understanding and Controlling Crime* (1986, with Lloyd E. Ohlin and James Q. Wilson). In 2003, he was appointed to the Order of the British Empire for his services to the field of Criminology.

David Farrington is, without question, one of the most important figures in the field of Criminology. His contributions have helped create developmental/life-course criminology, and he has been an open and willing partner in the pursuit of scientific knowledge. His genuine passion for research and intellectual curiosity have truly 'pushed back the frontiers of knowledge', and continue to do so.

Major works

Blumstein, A., Cohen, J. and Farrington, D.P. (1988) 'Criminal Career Research: Its Value for Criminology', *Criminology*, 26: 1–35.

Farrington, D.P. (1977) 'The Effects of Public Labelling', *British Journal of Criminology*, 17: 112–25. Reprinted in South, N. (ed., 1999) *Youth Crime,*

Deviance and Delinquency, vol. 2: Empirical Studies and Comparative Perspectives, pp. 145–58. Aldershot: Dartmouth.

—— (1992) 'Criminal Career Research: Lessons for Crime Prevention', *Studies on Crime and Crime Prevention*, 1: 7–29.

—— (2003) 'Developmental and Life-Course Criminology: Key Theoretical and Empirical Issues', *Criminology*, 41: 221–55.

—— (2005) 'The Integrated Cognitive Antisocial Potential (ICAP) Theory', in Farrington, D.P. (ed.) *Integrated Developmental and Life-Course Theories of Offending*, pp. 73–92. New Brunswick, New Jersey: Transaction.

West, D.J. and Farrington, D.P. (1973) *Who Becomes Delinquent?* London: Heinemann.

—— (1977) *The Delinquent Way of Life*. London: Heinemann.

Further reading

Farrington, D.P. (2004) 'Reflections on a Cross-National Criminological Career', in Winterdyk, J. and Cao, L. (eds) *Lessons from International/ Comparative Criminology/Criminal Justice*, pp. 89–105. Willowdale, Ontario: De Sitter.

Farrington, D.P., Lambert, S. and West, D.J. (1998) 'Criminal Careers of Two Generations of Family Members in the Cambridge Study in Delinquent Development', *Studies on Crime and Crime Prevention*, 7: 85–106.

Farrington, D.P., Loeber, R., Yin, Y. and Anderson, S.J. (2002) 'Are Within-Individual Causes of Delinquency the Same as Between-Individual Causes?' *Criminal Behaviour and Mental Health*, 12: 53–68.

Farrington, D.P., Ohlin, L.E. and Wilson, J.Q. (1986) *Understanding and Controlling Crime: Toward a New Research Strategy*. New York: Springer-Verlag.

Piquero, A.R. Farrington, D.P. and Blumstein, A. (2007) *Key Issues in Criminal Career Research: New Analyses of the Cambridge Study in Delinquent Development*. Cambridge, UK: Cambridge University Press.

LILA KAZEMIAN AND ALEX R. PIQUERO

MEDA CHESNEY-LIND (1947–)

By any standards, Meda Chesney-Lind's contribution to criminology has been profound. Her work is remarkable not only because it flipped the lens through which women in prison, girls in gangs, women drug users and institutionalised delinquent girls were studied and researched, but also because of the numerous personal and professional hurdles she had to surmount to become one of the world's leading feminist criminologists. It would not be an overestimation to say that her work revolutionised the study and treatment of women and girl offenders. Prior to Chesney-Lind's scholarship, when female offenders were discussed (which was rare), their characterisation and interpretation was almost exclusively corrupted by sexist, racist, and classist stereotypes. In contrast, Chesney-Lind used official data and the voices of women and girls themselves to more accurately reflect both the traumas that lead to female offending, and the powerful roles played by sexism, racism and classism in determining how they are viewed by society and the criminal justice system.

While she is best known for path-breaking work that made visible the personal experiences of women and girls charged with and incarcerated for offenses, Chesney-Lind is also widely recognised as being one of the pioneering scholars of 'pathways criminology' – the idea that early childhood traumas, particularly abuse, are strong precursors for later delinquency. Remarkably, post-war 'malestream' criminology not only ignored girls and women but also the childhood traumas of men and boys (with the exception of the frustrations of lower-class boys and their attempts to achieve middle- or upper-class status, see e.g. **Albert Cohen**). We now know that childhood abuse and trauma are prevalent among both girls and boys (although more so among girls). This important finding has tremendous implications, not just for criminological research, but also for the implementation of policy and practice. Chesney-Lind's scholarship in this area has helped improve the juvenile justice system's treatment of countless children, as well as changing specific forms of legislation (for example, the deinstitutionalising of young runaways).

In terms of academic scholarship, Chesney-Lind has published two books on female offenders: *Girls, Delinquency, and Juvenile Justice* (1992, with Randall G. Shelden) and *The Female Offender: Girls, Women and Crime* (1997). Most recently she has collaborated with Katherine Irwin to produce *Beyond Bad Girls: Gender, Violence, and Hype* (2008). Her edited work includes *Female Gangs in America* (1999, co-authored with John M. Hagedorn), *Girls, Women, and Crime: Selected Readings* (2004, with Lisa Pasko) and *Invisible Punishment* (2002, with Marc Mauer). In addition, Chesney-Lind has published over forty journal articles, thirty-eight book chapters, and four national monographs contributing to the documentation, understanding, and policy implications of female offending.

Meda Chesney was born in 1947, in the small town of Woodward, Oklahoma. At four months old she was almost killed by one of the worst tornados in US history. The tornado destroyed her home and levelled much of her neighbourhood. However, while she survived the ordeal with the help of her father (she was actually rescued on her father's shoulders), for several days she was separated from her mother, who it was thought had perished in the storm. Fortunately, this was not the case and Meda was eventually reunited with her mother. The events, however, took a toll on Chesney-Lind's father, a geologist, who was so traumatised by the experience that he left the field of geology and moved his family to Baltimore, Maryland, where Chesney-Lind – the oldest of four children – lived until she was sixteen years old.

Chesney-Lind believes her father was bipolar; he was either "fun" or "exploding" in rage (see Belknap 2004). During their time in Baltimore, her parents and her father's parents appeared plagued by disappointment and resentment that her father was unable to reclaim a successful career. Chesney-Lind's mother was additionally resentful of the limited career opportunities for women at the time. The marriage was under stress and her father's worsening drinking problem only added to the difficulties. Chesney-Lind responded to the demise of her parents' marriage by burying herself in books. However, her burgeoning intellect only served to enrage her father, who was desperate to maintain his status as the smartest member of the family. Eventually his frustration manifested itself in physical and verbal abuse against his daughter. Chesney-Lind believes it was this abusive treatment that instilled in her a lifelong passion for social justice.

According to her own account, Chesney-Lind was only saved from becoming a runaway and likely delinquent by her mother's intervention. In 1962, when Chesney-Lind was fifteen, her mother made the difficult decision to separate her children from their abusive father and move across the country to Portland, Oregon, to live with her parents. Meda's mother had not worked outside of the home since the end of World War II, and thus the struggle for financial independence from her former partner and his family was a tough one. However, once again, it proved a character-building experience for Chesney-Lind, who witnessed first hand the problems faced by single women fighting for financial independence.

Eventually, her mother returned to college to pursue a Master's in Psychology, something that impacted on Chesney-Lind in two ways. Whilst she was tremendously impressed with her mother's determination, at the same time, as the eldest child, she was forced to both run the household and take care of her three younger siblings. Despite these demands and working both as a nurse's aide and a waitress during high school, Meda Chesney-Lind graduated as the valedictorian of her high school in 1965.

From 1965 to 1969 Chesney-Lind attended Whitman College in eastern Washington State. During an internship at a school for the mentally disabled she discovered a series of problems at the institution. Unable to keep quiet about what she found, she chose to confront the senior psychologist on staff. After her concerns were ignored, she decided to go public and wrote a controversial op-ed article for the Whitman paper, documenting the injustices she had witnessed. Her growing concern with social issues during this period was also evident in her work with Latino immigrants in the Farm Workers Union, and in her protest activities against the Vietnam War. It was through her anti-war work that she met and fell in love with Ian Lind, a vocal critic of the Vietnam War and someone who risked imprisonment for his political views. This experience piqued her interest in the prison system and criminal justice more generally.

Chesney-Lind also benefitted from the skilled teaching of a number of Whitman College professors who not only supported her intellectual abilities but also her political activism. She arrived at Whitman without a chosen major, but her first sociology class was so inspiring that she chose this subject as her specialist field. Influenced by the labelling perspective, Chesney-Lind wrote her undergraduate sociology honours paper on how the anti-war movement examined and questioned laws.

Meda Chesney and Ian Lind married in the summer of 1969. After graduating from Whitman they moved to Ian's native Hawaii, where they both entered graduate school at the University of Hawaii in Honolulu. Chesney-Lind pursued her studies in sociology while Lind concentrated on political science. They made little money, with Chesney-Lind working as a nurse's aide and both of them continuing their activist work protesting the Vietnam War. Towards the end of the war, Chesney-Lind began to merge her anti-war work with her growing feminism (influenced by her involvement in the University of Hawaii's first ever 'consciousness raising' group) by organising women's protests against the war. Despite such varied and time-consuming commitments, Chesney-Lind still managed to produce a ground-breaking Master's thesis.

Chesney-Lind happened upon the data for her Master's thesis quite by accident. For some unknown reason, the Sociology Department at the University of Hawaii had in their basement boxes of juvenile court records for the years 1920 to 1954. Working her way through the files, Chesney-Lind was stunned to read about a common practice that occurred when police detained girls: *they contacted physicians to conduct vaginal examinations on the girls* to determine whether the girls were sexually active (no medical examinations were undertaken on the boys in the files). Chesney-Lind was thus the first scholar to document this incredibly invasive and highly sexist practice of criminalising girls' sexuality. She presented these findings at a gender panel at the Pacific Sociological Association meeting in 1973. The paper was incredibly well received and was subsequently published in *Issues in Criminology*. When findings from the same study were later published in the major journal *Psychology Today*, Chesney-Lind's success began to irritate some members of her faculty programme. Certain faculty simply could not believe that a student in their department, a woman no less, was being lauded in *Psychology Today* when none of them had been similarly honoured.

In her search for a doctoral dissertation topic, Chesney-Lind wanted to study how women convicted of crimes in Hawaii were forced to serve their sentences in other states. Surprisingly, the faculty in her department thought this was too close to her Master's topic (the forced vaginal examinations of delinquent girls) and urged her instead to conduct research on how women and girls made the decision to either keep their babies or have an abortion. Illustrating her lifelong commitment to both methodological approaches, she combined quantitative (Department of Health) data with intensive qualitative interviews to produce a thesis that further identified the myriad ways that sexism affects women and girls.

Chesney-Lind completed her doctorate in 1977, but rather than publish it straight away, she chose instead to respond to the troubling and sexist 'women's liberation' hypothesis being promoted by Rita Simon and Freda Adler in their respective books (both published in 1975). Put simply, this hypothesis asserted that the feminist movement would wreak havoc in society, and ultimately result in women offending at levels similar to men. Along with other feminist scholars (such as Clarice Feinman, Eileen Leonard, Ngaire Naffine, Allison Morris, **Frances Heidensohn** and **Carol Smart**), Chesney-Lind was effective in showing this was not the case.

Chesney-Lind's first teaching experience was at Honolulu Community College, where she started as a lecturer during graduate school in 1973. She loved the student population which was comprised of a diverse and less privileged group of students, including men returning from the war in Vietnam, non-traditional women students, and police officers. In the late 1970s she started teaching classes inside a prison that incarcerated both women and men. The community college and prison teaching experiences were profound: She found she loved to teach and it was rewarding to spread knowledge to individuals so eager to learn. One of the women students in her prison class, Michelle Alvey, a former prostitute, wrote a paper on incest. Alvey told Chesney-Lind that she was writing about this subject because most of her fellow women prisoners were victims of incest, something almost completely absent from the research literature at that time. Chesney-Lind learned a great deal from Alvey and dedicated her first book to her.

In the 1980s, Chesney-Lind and a group of social worker colleagues started interviewing incarcerated girls and women about their lives. They uncovered the extraordinarily high rates of sexual and physical abuse and trauma in these women's lives, which has been subsequently documented in numerous studies. Chesney-Lind was an instructor in sociology from 1973 to 1985. In 1986 she became a faculty member in Women's Studies at the University of Hawaii at Manoa, where she has remained ever since. More recently, she has turned her attention to subjects such as US mass incarceration and the prison industrial complex, whilst also devoting much of her efforts to countering the myth populated by the media and some criminological researchers that girls are becoming more violent. With respect to the latter, she has effectively identified how the media, pop psychologists, and juvenile justice system professionals, have changed how they report on and respond to girls charged with crimes. She used Center for Disease Control self-report statistics to show that the violence of girls was not rising, but that the system was processing them differently: girls were being arrested and processed for what were no more than minor scuffles, including altercations with their parents.

Chesney-Lind's many books and articles have resulted in significant policy changes, scholarly recognition, and prestigious awards (for example, she has received the Cressey Award from the National Council on Crime and Delinquency, the Michael Hindelang Award for the most Outstanding Scholarship to Criminology and was appointed as a Fellow to the American Society of Criminology). Her work has been crucial in garnering visibility for female offenders, both in terms of identifying the traumatic lives that many of them lead prior to being labelled as offenders, and the subsequent injustices they face as they proceed through the various stages of the criminal legal system.

Major works

Chesney-Lind, M. (1997) *The Female Offender: Girls, Women and Crime.* Thousand Oaks: Sage Publications (second edition with Lisa Pasko 2004).

Chesney-Lind, M. and Hagedorn, J. (eds) (1999) *Female Gangs in America: Essays on Gender, and Gangs*. Chicago, Illinois: Lakeview Press.

Chesney-Lind, M. and Irwin, K. (2008) *Beyond Bad Girls: Gender, Violence, and Hype*. New York: Routledge.

Chesney-Lind, M. and Pasko, L. (eds) (2004) *Girls, Women, and Crime: Selected Readings*. Thousand Oaks: Sage.

Chesney-Lind, M. and Shelden, R. (1992) *Girls, Delinquency and Juvenile Justice*. Pacific Grove, California: Brooks/Cole (second edition 1997, third edition 2004).

Mauer, M. and Chesney-Lind, M. (eds) (2002) *Invisible Punishment: The Collateral Consequences of Mass Imprisonment*. New York: The New Press.

Further reading

Belknap, J. (2004) 'Meda Chesney-Lind: The Mother of Feminist Criminology', *Women & Criminal Justice*, 15(2): 1–23.

JOANNE BELKNAP

CAROL SMART (1948–)

Since the late 1970s, Carol Smart's name has been inextricably linked with feminist criminology despite the fact that much of her more recent intellectual endeavour has been focused on the sociology of the family, how the law influences our personal lives, and why it is that people turn to the law to solve their personal problems. Carol Smart was brought up in London. She studied sociology at Portsmouth Polytechnic (now the University of Portsmouth) in the turbulent 1970s – just as second-wave feminism was taking a hold on academics and activists alike – before taking her Master's degree in Criminology at the University of Sheffield. She was awarded a PhD in Socio-Legal Studies at that same university in 1983 where one of her lecturers was the late Ian Taylor, one of the founders of the National Deviancy Conference, and by then a widely recognised critic of criminology. She was a lecturer then senior lecturer in sociology at the University of Warwick before taking up a Chair at the University of Leeds in 1992. She moved from there to the post that she currently holds in 2005 as the Co-Director of the Morgan Centre for the Study of Relationships and Personal Life at the University of Manchester. Smart also worked as Director of the National Council for One Parent Families. From these biographical details the reader may be forgiven for asking what her contemporary relevance to criminology might be given that her relationship with the discipline was really rather brief. However the impact of Carol Smart's work on criminology has been profound both in terms of the questions it raised about the discipline itself, and the subsequent agenda it generated.

Her first book, *Women, Crime and Criminology* (1976), written whilst she was a Master's student, raised fundamental questions about criminology that severely tested the discipline's domain assumptions about the nature of female criminality. A critical *tour de force* of criminological theory, this book details how the theoretical frameworks available at that time denied women a sense of agency, perpetually rendering them and their offending behaviour pathological, abnormal and unnatural. In particular she pointed to the way in which criminology, whilst having moved away from its Lombrosian heritage in respect of explaining male criminality (the notion that the criminal was atavistic, a throwback to some earlier biological stage of development: see **Cesare Lombroso**), nevertheless remained deeply committed to that heritage when it came to female criminality. Her argument made explicit that criminology still viewed female offenders as not only having broken the law (i.e. were atavistic by definition as a result of their criminality) but also as having offended against their very nature as females (biologically driven to conserve the species and therefore, by definition, law abiding), thus rendering the female offender 'doubly deviant'.

These deep-rooted assumptions about women in general, and female offending in particular, were for Smart exceedingly dangerous in their potential outcome. When connected to a criminal justice process driven by a desire to treat female offending as an outcome of biological difference or hormonal imbalances, these theories served to support a way of thinking that ensured that the female was kept subordinate to the male. In other words this book did much to challenge the prevailing criminological work that presumed, or tried to show, that female offenders were treated chivalrously in the criminal justice system because of their inherent 'difference'. Smart's analysis made the case that such practices, if they existed and if they worked at all in women's favour, only served to further endorse inequality between the sexes. Ultimately they supported the view that women needed the protection of men and as a consequence further damaged the position of women in general and female offenders in particular. She also pointed to the remarkable absence within criminology of any understanding of women as victims of, for the most part, male crime. Put simply Smart's challenge was that 'criminology must become more than the study of men and crime' (1976: 185).

It is widely accepted that the arguments presented in *Women, Crime and Criminology* were instrumental in generating a plethora of studies concerned with the question of 'women and crime'. The work that was produced as a result made female offending behaviour in all its diversity, and policy responses to such behaviour, much more visible within the discipline of criminology. Other books followed that took Smart's critical agenda into different areas of criminological concern. For example, it is possible to argue that the work of Allison Morris (1987) which provided a more detailed analysis of women as victims in the criminal justice system was directly linked to the impact Smart's work had on the wider concerns of the discipline. However, the move to make women visible within the discipline was not without its problems. As Beverley Brown was to observe, 'crudely, the criticism they are offering is that the more one seeks to show that male criminologists take leave of their senses when the question Woman looms on the agenda, the more one implies that they are in their right minds when they talk about male crime' (1986: 35). This problem was not lost on Carol Smart either.

A further significant intervention in the discipline came from Smart in 1990 in an essay published as part of the collection, *Feminist Perspectives in Criminology*, edited by Loraine Gelsthorpe and Allison Morris. This was entitled 'Feminist Approaches to Criminology or Postmodern Woman Meets Atavistic Man'. In this paper Smart reflects on the wide variety of activity that feminist incursions had generated in criminology since the publication of her book in 1976; to the extent that by 1990 the claim could no longer be made that there was a lack of concern with feminist-inspired questions. However, she goes on to argue that this activity had only served to revitalise a moribund discipline. For the commitment to the deep-rooted assumptions of the discipline and its modernist origins, especially reflected in its embrace of positivism (in particular to be able to differentiate and as a result pathologise the criminal from the non-criminal) and its close links with the policy arena, could not be denied – whatever the interventions left realist criminology offered to the contrary. Indeed her critique of the left realist agenda could not have been more scathing particularly in relation to its claim to have taken to heart the questions raised by feminist-inspired criminology. For the questions raised by feminism for criminology required much more than the adaptation of methodology in order to be able to count criminal victimisation more effectively: a charge made against left realism. These questions required a critical methodological rethink at a much more fundamental level. It required reflecting on such questions as, who could 'know' things and what was it that could be 'known'? Consequently it was clear to Smart that the key question now was, not what could feminism offer criminology but what could criminology offer feminism! In her view it was very little. The impact of this essay was profound. It marked a significant break for Smart herself with the discipline of criminology but also constituted an enormous challenge for those who worked within the discipline and wanted to retain their feminist credentials; that is, those who wanted to continue to make women visible in the discipline as victims, offenders and practitioners.

However, Smart's engagement with post-modernism had encouraged her to pursue the questions that such an agenda implied and specifically its claim of the impossibility to speak for 'all women'. This agenda made not only the modernist platform of criminology (tied as it was to the policy process) intellectually problematic but also challenged the discipline's embracement of positivism. This postmodernist agenda had implications for criminology as a discipline as well as for those who sought recourse to law as part of the solution to the crime problem. These dilemmas in particular led Smart to consider the gendered nature of the law and into a considerable debate with others concerned with the women and crime agenda whose approach was informed by much more pragmatic issues, like, for example, the problems faced by women in prison (qua the work of **Pat Carlen**). However, as Smart says:

> Law does not stand outside gender relations and adjudicate upon them. Law is part of these relations and is always already gendered in its principles and practices. We cannot separate out one practice – called discrimination- and for it to cease to be gendered as it would be a meaningless request. This is not to say that we cannot object to certain principles and practices but we need to think carefully before we continue to sustain a conceptual framework which either prioritises men as the norm or assumes that genderlessness (or gender blindness) is either possible or desirable.
>
> (1990: 80)

So, in her view, the law does not hold the key to women's oppression. Indeed, as her analysis illustrated, it can be used to further that oppression. This engagement with post-modernism marked her break with criminology and her return to socio-legal studies.

Smart's transition from criminology generally, and feminist criminology per se, to a more direct engagement with socio-legal studies was signalled in her book *Feminism and the Power of Law* published in 1989. As Maureen Cain comments in her Editor's Introduction to this work, it offers an analysis that focuses on 'the power of law as a discourse which disqualifies other forms of knowledge' (ibid). In this, Smart brings together a critical feminist analysis of a range of substantive issues – rape, child sexual abuse, pornography (clearly substantive concerns shared with many criminologists) – and subjects them to the power of law. From this analysis we get a very real appreciation of the gendered nature of law and of the problems and possibilities for both men and women when subjected to it as a locus of social control. Thus mapping out a critical challenge again for criminologists and feminists alike for whom recourse to the law might have appeared to be a solution to the social problem called crime.

Latterly Smart's work has remained focused on the regulatory power of the law especially in relation to people's personal lives whether that is marriage, divorce, child custody, or commitment ceremonies. Arguably it is this work, reaching back as it does to *The Ties that Bind: Law, Marriage and the Reproduction of Patriarchal Relationships* (1984), rather than her incursions within criminology, which constitutes the continuous thread of critical thought and endeavour throughout her academic career. Her current concerns notwithstanding, it is without doubt that Smart's early interventions in criminological debates did much to force the discipline to reflect upon itself and its domain assumptions. That these assumptions still retain a powerful hold in some parts of the discipline is a statement about their continued power and influence not about the legitimacy of the questions that Smart's work posed or the generation of studies that were produced as a consequence. The questions that she raised about the power of the law, and some would say the unfortunate drive to look to the law as a vehicle for change, are still as pertinent today as they were in 1989. The attrition rate evidenced in the statistics on rape stands as testimony to this issue and the inherent gendered nature and power of the law. Consequently it is without doubt that *Women, Crime and Criminology*, the essay 'Feminist Approaches to Criminology or Postmodern Woman Meets Atavistic Man', and *Feminism and the Power of Law* will continue to be not only essential reading but inspiring reading for those newly entering the discipline of criminology.

Major works

Smart, C. (1976) *Women, Crime and Criminology*. London: Routledge and Kegan Paul.

—— (1984) *The Ties That Bind: Law, Marriage and the Reproduction of Patriarchal Relations*. London: Routledge and Kegan Paul.

—— (1989) *Feminism and the Power of Law*. London: Routledge.
—— (1990) 'Feminist Approaches to Criminology or Post-Modern Woman Meets Atavistic Man', in L. Gelsthorpe and A. Morris (eds) *Feminist Perspectives in Criminology*. Buckingham: Open University Press.

Further reading

Brown, B. (1986) 'Women and Crime: the Dark Figures of Criminology', *Economy and Society*, 15(3).
Morris, A. (1987) *Women, Crime and Criminal Justice*. Oxford: Blackwell.

SANDRA WALKLATE

JOHN BRAITHWAITE (1951–)

Thomas Scheff (1990: 741) describes John Braithwaite's book *Crime, Shame and Reintegration* as possibly 'the most effective application of sociological theory to statistical data since **Durkheim**'s *Suicide*'. To underscore this point, Scheff titles the piece: 'A New Durkheim'. If such a label seems a heavy burden to carry for a scholar who was, at that time, not quite forty and who only very recently had found his first permanent academic job, then Braithwaite has done a reasonable job of living up to the hype.

In the last two decades, Braithwaite's work has been recognised with major awards from the Society for the Study of Social Problems, the American Sociological Association, the Law and Society Association, and the Socio-Legal Studies Association. His highly influential book *Global Business Regulation* (2000) with Peter Drahos was awarded the substantial Grawemeyer Award for 'Ideas for Improving World Order', and in 2006, Braithwaite was one of two criminologists awarded the first Stockholm Prize in Criminology from the Swedish Ministry of Justice. In his nomination letter for that distinction, David Bayley wrote: 'John Braithwaite has had the greatest impact of any criminologist in the last century'. (On learning that Braithwaite's alma mater, the University of Queensland, now gives out an annual 'John Braithwaite Prize' to outstanding students, the President of the Australian and New Zealand Society of Criminology joked that the Society would be establishing a new prize called the 'Award for Someone Other than John Braithwaite.')

In spite of all the prize-winning, Braithwaite is renowned for his humility, and is regarded as the very opposite of an elitist academic celebrity. On the occasion of his being awarded the American Society of Criminology's highest honour, the Edwin Sutherland Award, in 2004, Henry Pontell and Gilbert Geis (2004: 1) wrote that Braithwaite 'is a good deal more than a brilliant intellectual who has contributed some of the most solid empirical work and some of the most challenging policy recommendations to our field. He is, besides this, the most extraordinarily decent human being we have had the privilege of knowing.' This widely shared reputation is a reflection both of Braithwaite's approach to his work (he is famous for volunteering his time and talents to grassroots causes, rather than trying to make fast bucks with his expertise in the corporate sphere), but also the content of his research output with its focus on social justice, participatory democracy and sustainable social development.

Although Braithwaite's research is fundamentally criminological in its concerns with punishment and stigma, it clearly transcends the narrow confines of the field. His may be the only CV in the world that features publications in *The British Medical Journal, Michigan Law Review, The Japanese Journal of Criminal Psychology, Journal of Political Philosophy* and the *International Journal for the Study of Animal Problems.* For a scholar that now only dabbles in criminological research, Braithwaite has played a central role in at least four of the key paradigmatic debates within the discipline: the social class and crime debate; the 'just deserts' discussion; efforts to integrate criminological theories; and of course the emergence of restorative justice. Additionally, he is recognised as being among the world's experts on aged care and the nursing home industry, taxation policy, and white-collar crime, although none of these areas are what most criminologists think of as his research specialism. Yet, despite this breadth of scholarship, there is a remarkable coherence to Braithwaite's work. This is not the profile of a dabbler who follows his curiosity hither and thither, but rather that of an intellectual quest, following an almost inevitable journey from one idea to the next.

Braithwaite's journey began in Ipswich, Australia, a tight-knit coal-mining community where he was raised on a diet of rugby league and labour party activism. Although originally more interested in the former than the latter, Braithwaite grew up quickly in 1969, after spending six weeks living on the island of Bougainville, Papua New Guinea, at a time when Bougainville's tiny population was trying desperately to hold off Australian and English industrial interests seeking to exploit their land for copper mining. (Just south of the village, where Braithwaite was living, native women stood up to bulldozers trying to destroy their village to create a port for the new mine. They were forcibly and violently removed by the police.) Far from the average 'semester abroad', Braithwaite lived in a thatch hut, ate local foods, wore a 'lap-lap', worked in the garden and helped build new huts in the village.

Closer to home, he lost two school friends to accidents in Ipswich's coal mines, and in 1972, his home town was rocked by tragedy when seventeen men were killed in Box Flat Mine, one of the worst incidents in Australian mining history. The disaster at Box Flat was a turning point for Braithwaite, and he has devoted much of his life to protecting workers and consumers from exploitation and harm. Yet, his response to the tragedy surprised even himself. In the preface of *To Punish or Persuade: Enforcement of Coal Mine Safety*, Braithwaite (1985) writes: 'After Box Flat, I expected one day to write an angry book about death in the mines. This modest and dispassionate contribution hardly meets that aspiration, but I have come to the conclusion that it might ultimately benefit miners more than a book directing fire and brimstone at those responsible for mine fatalities.'

Setting out to 'find the method of punishment (defined broadly as any formal or informal sanction imposed for violations of law) that will achieve the greatest reduction of carnage in coal mines', Braithwaite reaches the conclusion (soon to become a familiar theme in his work) that stigmatising attacks on employers may do more harm than good in this regard. Fire and brimstone might feel like the right response to horrific wrongdoing, but it might not necessarily save lives.

Part of this remarkable pragmatism may have had something to do with another turning point that occurred in 1972: John and Valerie Braithwaite were married and began a lifelong dialogue and occasional research collaboration. Valerie – now a well-known social psychologist with expertise in identifying institutional practices that undermine cooperation and generate defiance – met John at age four. John says: 'She drew attention to herself by being the noisiest kid during sleep time. She got much better marks than me at school and university. This was a time when playing rugby league was rather more my obsession than politics, but she got better marks all the way through' (personal communication 2008).

Even at postgraduate level, Braithwaite's commitment to his own education was somewhat dubious. He says that he pursued a PhD purely to 'fill in time before I went into politics' (and only chose to study criminology because there was grant money available for research on the topic). Under the supervision of the criminologist Paul Wilson, he finished his dissertation in 1977, and, precisely according to plan, comfortably won a local ballot to run for a safe

Labour Party seat in Ipswich. Yet, because he was a reformist candidate seeking to clean up the Labour Party machine, his victory was overturned by the Party's central executive on a vote of 43 to 42. He sees it now as a 'lucky escape': 'I would have made a terrible politician and Val would have been a lousy politician's wife. I had to cook the stuff for her to take to the "Labour Women's afternoons". She didn't even have enough burning ambition for me to succeed in politics to cook some pikelets!'

That disaster averted, Braithwaite briefly lectured at Griffith University and Queensland, before winning a Fulbright Postdoctoral Fellowship to work for a year in the University of California-Irvine's Program in Social Ecology. There, he met Gil Geis with whom he would later collaborate on white-collar crime research, and he taught a class on corporate crime that became a catalyst for his future work in this area.

On his return to Australia from California, however, Braithwaite was, remarkably, unable to secure an academic post at the Australia National University (ANU) where Valerie had started lecturing. In retrospect, this exclusion from a traditional academic career path was probably fortuitous, as these years were crucial in shaping his thinking and approach to research. His first job was at the Australian Institute of Criminology (a research office similar to the UK's Home Office), where he co-authored ten articles with the so-called 'Godfather of Australian Criminology' David Biles. During this period, he published a series of studies on social class, disadvantage and crime, including the book *Inequality, Crime and Public Policy* (1979), based on his PhD dissertation. In 1982, he drifted even further from academia, taking up the directorship of the Australian Federation of Consumer Organizations, yet his research hardly missed a beat during these years, with two books appearing in 1983 and 1984 on corporate crime issues.

Arguably, it is these two parallel tracks in Braithwaite's work – moving back and forth from writing about poverty and street crime to a focus on the regulation of the corporate and industrial world – that has been the catalyst behind Braithwaite's considerable theoretical insights. Despite the urgings of criminologists like **Sutherland** and **Cressey**, research on corporate and white-collar offending remains largely segregated and distinct from mainstream work on 'street' offending – as if putting on a tie makes one a fundamentally different being than the offender who wears jeans and a hooded sweatshirt. The ugly racist and classist assumptions underlying this split – dating back to criminology's origins in phrenology and crude forms of evolutionary psychology – have allowed for a bifurcated approach to justice involving negotiated settlements for the rich, and banishment and medicalisation for the poor. In his book on crime in the pharmaceutical industry, for instance, Braithwaite (1984) writes that he was frequently criticised for his one-sided portrayal of the industry and his failure to point out all the good that pharmaceuticals have done for the world. He points out that he is a criminologist, his job is to study crime, and 'If a criminologist undertakes a study of mugging or murder, no one expects a "balanced" account which gives due credit to the fact that many muggers are good family men, loving fathers ... or perhaps generous people' (viii).

Braithwaite's essential trick in *Crime, Shame and Reintegration* (1989) (hereafter *CS& R*) may be to ignore such distinctions and apply his long-established research findings from work with nursing home owners, pharmaceutical companies and coal mines to the realm of personal theft and violence. He argues that low crime societies are those that shame wrong-doing, but not wrong-doers, in a reintegrative fashion: making clear their intolerance for the 'sin' but equally expressing a love for the 'sinner'. The book had a dramatic impact on the direction of criminological theory and research. For one, by talking about shame, the book re-introduced the issues of morality and emotion back into criminology which was at the time dominated by portrayals of offenders as 'rational calculators' who could be easily deterred by punitive consequences.

CS& R also demonstrated Braithwaite's considerable skills as a peace-maker. In the book, he not only argues for a 'third way' between the pendulous debates between punishment and rehabilitation or labelling and deterrence, he also reconciles a number of rival criminological theories of aetiology, bringing 'the parable of the elephant and the blind men to vivid life and breath' (Scheff 1990: 743). Prior to *CS& R*, criminological research was characterised by often acrimonious squabbles between competing theoretical paradigms. Like others, Braithwaite did not view these competitions (which typically resulted in a draw, somewhat akin to the dodo's verdict in *Alice in Wonderland*: 'Everybody has won and all must have prizes') as advancing the field. Yet, most of the 'integrative' theories that became all the rage in the 1980s had a 'kitchen sink' feel to them, arguing that crime is a product of a complex web of interrelated factors. Braithwaite's theory, on the other hand, had the benefit of being a parsimonious story based on the unifying central concept of shame (see Uggen 1993).

Finally, *CS& R* broke with criminological tradition by outlining not just an empirical theory (i.e. 'what works and why') but also a normative theory (e.g. 'what should be', 'what sort of society do we want').

In a one-two punch, Braithwaite spelled out the latter, his pioneering 'Republican Theory of Criminal Justice' in his follow-up book with Philip Pettit (Braithwaite and Pettit 1990). As a result of these contributions, Braithwaite is sometimes credited with founding or discovering restorative justice. In fact, the term, which first appeared in the late 1970s but did not gain widespread currency until the early 1990s, is never used in *CS& R*. Braithwaite did, however, provide restorative practices with a badly needed theoretical foundation, and *CS& R* has become something of a bible to many in the disparate restorative movements. Braithwaite has also been at the forefront of the move to evaluate these practices, in particular with the Reintegrative Shaming Experiment, which has become a model for rigorous programme evaluation throughout criminal justice and beyond.

Braithwaite's work is not without its critics. Many have argued that the sorts of organic reintegration rituals Braithwaite describes would not be well suited to highly populated urban settings. Although the theory is partially based on practices in the highly urban and modern setting of Japan, some have accused Braithwaite of romanticising Japanese culture. There is considerable irony to the latter critique, as Braithwaite's father had served three years in a Japanese prison camp at Sandakan, Borneo and was one of only six prisoners to survive the Borneo Death March in 1945 that resulted in over 2500 deaths. Still, a great thinker needs more than just great co-authors and colleagues, one needs great sparring partners; even as an acknowledged peacemaker, Braithwaite has engaged in some fascinating published debates with scholars ranging from Charles Tittle to Ernest van den Haag – and an even more heated, but sadly unpublished exchange with Supreme Court Justice Antonin Scalia (Pontell and Geis 2004). Additionally, Braithwaite's (1987) 'Return of the Mesomorphs' was one of the most incisive and comprehensive review essays of **James Q. Wilson** and Richard Herrnstein's effort to redirect criminology back to physiology and biology.

Yet, Braithwaite did not find his perfect counterpart until a series of public discussions with the 'just deserts' theorist Andrew von Hirsch. Beginning with the book *Not Just Deserts* by Braithwaite and Pettit, this sophisticated philosophical exchange resulted in articles with titles such as 'Not Not Just Deserts: A Response to Braithwaite and Pettit' and the reply 'Not Just Deserts, Even in Sentencing'. Some mediation has occurred, however, with Von Hirsch and colleagues' recent concession that a streamlined vision of restorative justice might be an improvement on retributive practices, albeit in a limited number of cases.

Since the publication of *Not Just Deserts*, Braithwaite has largely turned his attention back to the world of business oversight. At ANU, he co-founded the Regulatory Institutions Network, a network of institutions, practitioners and academics seeking to 'undertake regulatory research that promotes social justice, fairness, human rights and freedoms, and efficient, ecologically sustainable development'. There, he wrote influential books like *Responsive Regulation* (1992) co-authored with Ian Ayres and *Global Business Regulation* (2000) with Peter Drahos. Drawing on hundreds of interviews with international leaders in business and government, this work once again presents a 'third way' intended to 'transcend the intellectual stalemate between those who favor strong state regulation of business and those who advocate deregulation' (Ayres and Braithwaite 1992: 3). In the tour de force *Restorative Justice and Responsive Regulation* (2002), Braithwaite brings together the two parallel streams of his research. And, Braithwaite's latest book *Regulatory Capitalism* (2008), with its advice for moving beyond 'the Neoliberal fairytale', surely qualifies as his timeliest book – considering the havoc that massive deregulation of the financial market during the George W. Bush years has had on the world economy.

Yet, his planned follow-up act may be his most impressive yet. Along with Valerie and colleagues at ANU, he has embarked on a project that he says will keep him occupied for the 'remainder of his days' – a twenty-year comparative project on international peace-building efforts supported by the Australian Research Council. The goal is to identify 'what works' and, perhaps more importantly, 'what does not work' in the realm of peace-building: international interventions into war-torn areas in Asia, Europe, the Middle East, Africa, Latin America and the Pacific. Appropriately, this hugely ambitious project begins back in Bougainville where Braithwaite was first inspired to understand peacebuilding (in a 'reintegration ceremony' of sorts, Braithwaite has recently been adopted as a chief of the Naboin clan in Toretei, the village where he lived over thirty years ago). In a formidable travel schedule, Braithwaite is committed to spending six months of each of the next twenty years in the field at one of the different locations, interviewing thousands of key stakeholders in conflict-torn and post-conflict societies. The goal is that by 2021, the data collected will be combined into a single, first-of-its-kind database and utilised in the development of an evidence-based theory of international peace-building.

On first glance, the plan sounds far-fetched and overly ambitious, but somehow it seems perfectly reasonable looking at the track record of John and Valerie Braithwaite and their colleagues.

Major works

Ayres, I. and Braithwaite, J. (1992) *Responsive Regulation: Transcending the Deregulation Debate*. Oxford: Oxford University Press.
Braithwaite, J. (1979) *Inequality, Crime, and Public Policy*. Boston, Massachusetts: Routledge & Kegan Paul Books.
—— (1984) *Corporate Crime in the Pharmaceutical Industry*. London: Routledge Kegan and Paul.
—— (1985) *To punish or Persuade: Enforcement of Coal Mine Safety*. Albany, New York: State University of New York Press.
—— (1989) *Crime, Shame and Reintegration*. Cambridge: Cambridge University Press.
—— (2002) *Restorative Justice & Responsive Regulation*. Oxford: Oxford University Press.
Braithwaite, J. and Drahos, P. (2000) *Global Business Regulation*. Cambridge: Cambridge University Press.
Braithwaite, J. and Pettit, P. (1990) *Not Just Deserts: A Republican Theory of Criminal Justice*. Oxford: Oxford University Press.

Further reading

Pontell, H. and G. Geis (2004) '2004 Edwin Sutherland Award Recipient: John Braithwaite', *The Criminologist*, 29(5): 1–3.
Scheff, T. (1990) 'Review Essay: A New Durkheim', *American Journal of Sociology*, 96(3): 741–46.
Uggen, C. (1993) 'Reintegrating Braithwaite: Shame and Consensus in Criminological Theory', *Law & Social Inquiry*, 18: 481.

SHADD MARUNA

DAVID GARLAND (1955–)

David Garland is acknowledged on all sides as one of the world's leading scholars of crime and punishment, and an acute analyst of the peculiar scale and character of contemporary punishment and social control in advanced liberal societies. Like many of criminology's most influential figures Garland's work escapes easy categorisation as standing wholly 'within' criminology (whatever this might mean), still less as representative of a particular section or school of that contested and sometimes fractious discipline. The scope and reach of his work is quite well indicated by his joint appointment (from 1997) to positions in both the Law School and the Department of Sociology at New York University. Garland's work, and his choice of intellectual reference points, is expansive and wide ranging. It seems unlikely that

Garland has ever felt himself to be especially constrained by whatever fences people put up around the supposed proper field of criminology. There are good institutional reasons for this sense of freedom and these may be instructive.

David Garland grew up in Dundee, Scotland. He graduated with first class Honours in Law from the University of Edinburgh in 1977. Legal education in Scotland – then as now – centred on the 'flagship' four-year undergraduate qualification, the LLB. The first two years of that programme featured a demanding slog through all the basic required subjects. The prize for persistence in that marathon was that the final two years, by sharp contrast, offered a very wide choice of courses. In this environment the youthful Garland was exposed not just to criminology but also to legal theory, and to historical and political perspectives on Law more or less simultaneously. Following graduation Garland took an MA in Criminology at the University of Sheffield before returning to Edinburgh to undertake the PhD that eventually became his book *Punishment and Welfare* (1985), the work that secured his scholarly reputation. He took up post as Lecturer in the Faculty of Law in 1979. Criminology in Edinburgh at this time occupied a distinctive and unusually creative position. The creation in 1983 of the Centre for Criminology and the Social and Philosophical Study of Law formalised the close relationship between criminology and other fields of legal study, especially jurisprudence and sociology of law. Garland was promoted to a Personal Chair as Professor of Penology at Edinburgh in 1992. In the 1990s he made several extended visits to New York University before moving there full-time in 1997.

Garland's early published work, from about 1980 onwards, displays many of the virtues – patient exposition and a talent for close reading, a keen eye for the key point and an ability to make confident but careful and concise critical judgements – that were to become so evident in his major contributions. Garland quickly established himself as an authoritative reader, perhaps in particular of two very different authors who came to play a major role in the development of his own thinking, namely **Michel Foucault** and **Emile Durkheim** (see further below).

Given the 'chronocentrism' (the tendency to disregard anything written more than about fifteen years earlier) that Paul Rock attributes to British criminology (Rock 2005), not to mention the prominence in the sociology of punishment of Garland's later work, it is easy to forget the catalytic impact of Garland and Peter Young's edited collection *The Power to Punish* (1983) and the *succès de folie* of *Punishment and Welfare* (1985). Indeed, among the more notable aspects of *The Power to*

Punish was that it happened at all – that two relatively junior and not yet specially well known scholars managed to persuade several much more senior and established ones to write in their book in the first place. There are a number of essays of lasting value in the book, not least the editors' introduction which stands as a kind of manifesto for the very 'social analysis of penality' which Garland went on to accomplish. In other words Garland and Young advocated an approach to questions of punishment and social regulation that was not limited by the terms of a primarily 'instrumental' penology (preoccupied with pragmatic concerns with effectiveness) nor by traditional philosophical debates over normative justifications for imposing punishments, nor yet by a purely internal history of penal ideas, but rather one that addressed the whole *ensemble* of discourses and practices ranged around the penal question. The approach was intended not only to stimulate more challenging and penetrating analysis of the articulation between regimes of punishment and regulation and wider social interests, ideologies and divisions, but also to free up that analysis to look at media discourse, political rhetoric, fictions, fables and so on – in other words to open a channel between studies of punishment and control and what was to become a central operative term throughout Garland's later work: *culture*. (Twenty years later a conference in Edinburgh celebrated these achievements, whilst also providing a practical demonstration of the vitality of the field whose development *The Power to Punish* has assisted: Armstrong and McAra 2006.)

Punishment and Welfare itself remains one of the best exemplars of the social analysis of penality in action. It charts the emergence of what Garland termed the 'penal-welfare complex', especially during the last decade or so of the nineteenth century and the first years of the twentieth. The deepening complexities during these years of the 'social question' that preoccupied the governing classes (of how to secure order in a maturing capitalist industrial economy with an increasingly organised labour movement, but with persistent problems of inebriation, infirmity and 'delinquency') came together with the rising prestige of the human sciences and the emergence of new professional bodies of knowledge. The invention of the 'welfare sanction' – classically, in the British context, probation – offered many advantages over a Victorian penality centring on rational deterrence in making criminality a 'practicable object' for management, measurement and intervention. Many of the pioneering figures in the development of criminological inquiry in Britain had their professional base in the associated occupations – in psychiatry, social work, the prison chaplaincy service and so on. Very few first books are so widely praised, nor receive extended and respectful reviews from the luminaries of the field (see, for example, Messinger and Weston 1987).

Some reviewers had noted at the time of publication of *Punishment and Welfare* the irony that the penal-welfare complex that the book described, and which had largely endured in Britain throughout most of the twentieth century, was only then receiving sustained challenge, partly as a result of the ascendancy of a new and more confrontational free market ideology. *Punishment and Modern Society* opens by identifying a 'crisis of penal modernism'. It suggests, in other words, that some of the prevailing assumptions of most intellectuals and many practitioners had reached a point of exhaustion, marked by a perhaps terminal decline in prestige and political support. Here Garland's work turns for inspiration back to themes from classical social theory. For instance, in addition to the elegant expositions and critiques of these from **Marx**, Foucault, Weber and Elias in *Punishment and Modern Society*, he recovers from Durkheim the view that systems of punishment, however much they claim justification in rationality or usefulness, are under-girded by passion – anger, indignation, outrage, fear. Garland insists that he never doubts that punishment *is indeed* purposive and instrumental and organised towards sustaining social control, merely that these strategic aspects are not all that the sociology of punishment has to wrestle with. Instead Garland now emphasises that punishment may also and inherently be emotive, expressive, internally contradictory, contested. In an indicative statement from this time Garland asserts that:

> … modern punishment is a cultural as well as a strategic affair; that it is a realm for the expression of social value and emotion as well as a process for asserting control. And that for all its necessity as an institution, and despite all our attempts to make it positive and useful, it still involves a tragic and futile quality which derives from its contradictory cultural location and which ought to be recognized in analysis. Our frameworks for analysing punishment ought thus to be geared towards interpreting the conflicting social values and sentiments which are expressed and evoked in punishments as well as tracing instrumental strategies of penal control.
>
> (Garland 1990a: 4)

One of Garland's more striking extensions of our ways of looking at penal problems is his discussion in *Punishment and Modern Society* of the notion of penal 'sensibilities'. Historical changes in penal practices and institutions come about not just because of changing practical needs or requirements but also because of what influential opinion in the surrounding society feels to be appropriate, acceptable, desirable. These 'emotional configurations' exercise a 'determinative capacity' in shaping what can and cannot be done. This has implications for what we need to study and how – it demands attention to popular culture as well as official discourse, for example. It also suggests that what the cultural study of penal regimes and relations discovers will not be neat, tidy or coherent, since a penal culture is 'the loose amalgam of penological theory, stored-up experience, institutional wisdom and professional common sense' (1990b: 210).

Garland's next major statement might be seen as an attempt to put these analytic principles and methodological precautions to serious use in coming to terms with the peculiarities of the present time in the two societies with which he was most familiar, the United States and the UK. *The Culture of Control* brings up to date the suggestion of a crisis of penal modernism. What has in fact occurred in the last quarter of the twentieth century has been a transformation in penal values and practices ushered in by a yet wider set of economic, social and technological changes summarised by Garland, echoing Giddens, Bauman and others, as 'the coming of late modernity'. What this means in practice is that a new 'collective experience' of crime and insecurity combines with a new range of technical possibilities and policy devices to produce a set of 'adaptations' markedly different from those that preceded them. The old form of the penal-welfare complex is superseded by a rather different 'crime complex', one in which responsibilities for control are simultaneously both more dispersed and more intensely politicised. On one hand we as citizens and consumers are increasingly rendered responsible for the protection of our safety and property through appropriate private choices (of housing, insurance, transport and so on) whilst on the other there is a clamorous politics of vindication around criminal victimisation and the punishment of offenders. The enhanced awareness of risk and the increased salience of crime in everyday life situates the pursuit of safety as normal, pragmatic and everyday. Yet at the same time it imposes new pressures on political actors. The growth of crime sharply exposes the limits of state capacity, but as well as stimulating the whole array of pragmatic, adaptive responses this incites a more reactive, gestural penal politics as decision-makers strive to demonstrate their strength and display solidarity with victims and their angry and indignant supporters. Thus even as the inherent limits of the sovereign state become more visible, so 'the criminal justice state' also grows.

Garland's career is not distinguished by the sheer quantity of his publications – many other scholars have written more. Rather his work is marked by a confidence and clarity of purpose that has enabled him to side-step some of the distractions that hamper many academic careers and to focus intensely on his own chosen concerns. Garland's work combines a genuine sense of the past with an acute diagnostic attentiveness to what is going on now. These features are again fully in evidence in his most recent work on capital punishment in America (e.g. Garland 2005). This work, which includes the insistence that the long-term trajectory of capital punishment in the United States is towards abolition, notwithstanding many persistent institutional and cultural obstacles, might also go some way towards countering the objection of some critics that Garland's writing is marked by a certain pessimistic disengagement. Clearly Garland's recognition of a 'tragic' dimension to the problem of punishment makes it something other than a call to arms. Does this make it more commentary than critique? Garland clearly affirms in the Preface to *The Culture of Control* that his analysis of 'why things are as they are' is not to be conflated with the view that 'our world currently is as it must be'. Similarly Garland and I have jointly argued that clear and self-conscious awareness of its contemporary situation offers criminology new opportunities for relevance and 'a more critical, more public, more wide-ranging role' (Garland and Sparks 2000). Garland insists that understanding the political culture that defines its position and possibilities is a crucial step in challenging criminology to rethink, and to grasp, its responsibilities.

Major works

Garland, D. (1985) *Punishment and Welfare: A History of Penal Strategies*. Aldershot: Gower.
—— (1990a) 'Frameworks of Inquiry in the Sociology of Punishment', *British Journal of Sociology*, 41(1): 1–15.
—— (1990b) *Punishment and Modern Society*. Oxford: Clarendon.
—— (2001) *The Culture of Control: Crime and Social Order in Contemporary Society*. Oxford: Clarendon.
—— (2005) 'Capital Punishment and American Culture', *Punishment and Society*, 7(4): 347–76.
Garland, D. and R. Sparks (2000) 'Criminology, Social Theory and the Challenge of Our Times', *British Journal of Criminology*, 40: 189–214.
Garland, D. and P. Young (1983) (eds) *The Power to Punish*. London: Heinemann.

Further reading

Armstrong, S. and McAra, L. (eds) (2006) *Perspectives on Punishment: the Contours of Control*. Oxford: Oxford University Press.

Messinger, S. and Weston, N. (1987) 'Review of D. Garland Punishment and Welfare', *American Bar Foundation Research Journal*, 12(4): 791–807.

Rock, P. (2005) 'Chronocentrism and British Criminology', *British Journal of Sociology*, 56(3): 473–91.

RICHARD SPARKS

ROBERT J. SAMPSON (1956–)

Though it can be a dangerous game to assess a scholar's contribution to the field at the mid-point of their career – such a task is typically undertaken posthumously, or, upon retirement – it is entirely appropriate in the case of Rob Sampson. One might be even so bold as to predict that it will not matter when scholars collectively assess the field of criminology, now or in a hundred years hence, Sampson will easily be one of the fifty most influential thinkers. This is because Sampson's work has consistently expanded the boundaries of two main areas in criminology: crime and communities and offending over the life course. Sampson's many influential articles are among the most cited in criminology over the past decade and a half, and his award-winning collaborations with John H. Laub, notably *Crime in the Making: Pathways and Turning Points Through Life* (1993), and *Shared Beginnings, Divergent Lives: Delinquent Men at Age 70* (2003), have invigorated the study of crime over the life course in the case of the former, and redrafted the agenda for the discussion of desistance in the case of the latter.

Sampson was born and raised in the upstate New York city of Utica. Growing up in the 1960s, he witnessed the deindustrialisation of this once thriving industrial town, which he has described as a 'microcosm of the changes that had gone on in some of the larger, more famous cities in the United States' (Marino 2008). This firsthand experience of rapid social change, combined with an avowed childhood interest in maps, sowed the seeds for some of the issues that have preoccupied Sampson throughout his academic career. Sampson is concerned with how the individual is shaped by his or her context, and how social change impacts individual trajectories throughout life.

If his childhood experiences and preoccupations laid the groundwork for his later scholarly endeavours, then his university experiences, first as an undergraduate at SUNY-Buffalo and later as a graduate student at SUNY-Albany, gave a definite shape to these interests. Sampson's educational experiences equipped him with a set of intellectual tools that he has since used to expand the study of crime in

urban communities and to better specify the field of life course criminology. Sampson was introduced to psychology and sociology while
an undergraduate at Buffalo, and though he graduated with a degree in
the latter field, he has continually integrated the study of social process
with a focus on the individual actor, illustrating the mutual influence of
each approach on his own scholarly trajectory.

It is fair to say that most scholars bear the mark of their graduate
training, and Sampson is no different. At SUNY-Albany in the 1970s,
Sampson worked with **Travis Hirschi**, Michael Hindelang and Peter
Blau among others, while his fellow grad students included his later
collaborators John Laub and Casey Groves, who was also his roommate
at a farmhouse they rented outside Albany called 'the Ranch'. The
decision to study criminal justice was 'not planned', and Sampson
nearly attended Cornell to study the sociology of science. However,
on a visit to Albany he felt that there was 'something in the air there at
the time' and though he only originally intended to stay for a Master's
degree, he was 'hooked' after taking a course with Hindelang on the
nature of crime. Whilst at Albany, Sampson also immersed himself in
the work of the Chicago School of Urban Sociology. He was particularly taken by their concern with documenting processes of urban
social change and how the structures and configurations of urban life
shape individual behaviour, especially delinquency and crime. With
Hirschi, the architect of social control theory, as his dissertation advisor
and the Chicago School precepts of urban social change foremost in his
thinking, Sampson began working on a social-ecological approach to
criminology that privileged the place of social control. In this latter
regard, Sampson was at the forefront of a movement in American
criminology at the time to reinvigorate the Chicago School theory of
social disorganisation, which held that neighbourhood level characteristics affected local crime rates by altering the ability of a community to
control crime and delinquency. **Clifford Shaw** and Henry McKay had
shown that delinquency rates in certain types of neighbourhoods in
Chicago had stayed relatively high over time regardless of the types of
people that lived there. Such areas were defined by high levels of
poverty, residential mobility and by the fact that they were ethnically
heterogeneous. Shaw and McKay reasoned that the concentration of
such properties led an area to become *socially disorganised*, leading in
turn to high crime through low levels of control and an intergenerational transmission of delinquent values. Though the original formulation of social disorganisation by Shaw and McKay soon lost favour in
American criminology, several theoretical advances in the 1970s and
1980s paved the way for a reconsideration of its central ideas.

First, Ruth Kornhauser (1978) argued that the real core of social disorganisation theory should have been the focus on social control rather than the intergenerational subcultural transmission of delinquent values – Sampson describes being 'blown away' by reading Kornhauser in a seminar that Hirschi led at Albany. Second, Robert Bursik (1988) argued that the reason that social disorganisation theory was not more influential was that researchers had mistakenly characterised the neighbourhood indicators as *causes* of delinquency. This confusion led criminologists at the time to miss the crucial process through which neighbourhood-level factors could reduce the capacity of a community to control behaviour, thereby opening the door for delinquent behaviour to flourish.

The confluence of these theoretical advances was being made at a time when a number of empirical data sets were first available that would enable scholars to test some of these ideas. In the initial phases of his professorial career, Sampson, who had taken his first appointment at the University of Illinois at Urbana-Champaign, worked with several collaborators on a series of important articles using the British Crime Survey. In a ground-breaking test of social disorganisation theory, Sampson and Groves (1989) found that communities with unsupervised teens, poor or non-existent friendship networks, and low organisational participation had high crime and delinquency rates. They concluded that the variables that mattered most are the between-neighbourhood variations in social disorganisation.

It is perhaps fitting, given his intellectual fascination with process and ecology, that Sampson's next appointment was at the University of Chicago, birth place of the so-called Chicago School. During his twelve years there, his ideas and research matured as he simultaneously worked on the two major studies that would transform criminology and secure his place as a luminary in the field. The collaboration with Laub began as the result of the serendipitous discovery at Harvard University of **Sheldon and Eleanor Glueck**'s data archive of the famous, longitudinal study they completed on a matched sample of 500 delinquents and non-delinquents from the Boston area. This included data first collected in the 1940s and several waves of subsequent follow-up data tracking a sample until the subjects were thirty-two years old. The impressive reams of data were in pristine, if not computer analysable form. Sampson and Laub set about reconstructing the data set, and submitting it to the rigors of modern statistical techniques unavailable during the Gluecks' era.

In *Crime in the Making*, Sampson and Laub advance what they call an age-graded theory of informal social control that at once examines the continuity and change in offending over time for the sample in the original Glueck data. Utilising the concepts of 'pathways' and 'turning-points' borrowed from life course research, they argue that, as delinquent boys age, many experience changes in informal social control (triggered by getting married, finding stable employment or entering the military). Alone or in combination with each other, these life events can function as turning points away from criminal behaviour.

In *Shared Beginnings, Divergent Lives*, Laub and Sampson expand upon the ideas of their first book, and break new ground by analysing quantitative and qualitative data on subjects from childhood to seventy years of age. They used criminal records, death certificates and homicide cold case detectives to locate as many of the original men from the delinquent sample, ultimately conducting life-history interviews with fifty-two subjects. In so doing, they challenged many of the assumptions that form the bedrock of criminological theorising on crime and desistance. For example, they contend that it is impossible to prospectively identify life course persistent offenders using a risk factor approach because both 'kinds of people' and 'kinds of context' explanations of crime fail to adequately explain how behavioural change occurs over the life course. They argue that desistance occurs for all types of offenders at different ages, but crucially in response to turning points that set in motion a long-term behavioural change. These structural turning points include finding a steady job, a good marriage and, for some, military service. Laub and Sampson argue that the approaches that often seek to explain desistance from crime – namely maturation, development, rational choice and social learning – cannot explain change as well as a life-course approach that is sensitive to within individual change as it emerges from a particular context. They modify their age-graded theory of informal social control, formulated in *Crime in the Making*, by adding a focus on individual agency and routine activities that should be considered alongside the impact of the structural turning points emphasised in the first work. *Shared Beginnings* illustrates both the heterogeneity of adult outcomes for similarly situated juvenile offenders, and the different offending trajectories they occupy in adulthood. Because of the implications for how we think about desistance, this will be a work with a lasting and profound influence on criminology.

The second major project that Sampson has spearheaded and which has fundamentally altered the criminological landscape is the Project on Human Development in Chicago Neighborhoods (PHDCN), a large-scale, multiple-study project that has investigated the lives of children, families and their communities over the past decade and a half. The inter-related PHDCN studies include a multi-cohort accelerated longitudinal study of 6,000 children, a community survey of 9,000 residents in over 300 neighbourhoods, and the systematic social observation of 22,000 face blocks in the city. The ambitious projects have yielded an astonishing array of data and led to some of the most important findings in criminology of the past few decades, as well as some of the more promising recent breakthroughs in criminological theorising. In a seminal article published in the journal *Science* in 1997 by Sampson, Raudenbush and Earls, the authors showed that violent crime rates varied not by the level of disadvantage in a neighbourhood, but by the level of what they termed 'collective efficacy' or the willingness of community members to intervene on behalf of the common good. Collective efficacy is strong where there is social cohesion and cooperative social action. Sampson and colleagues' finding that, even in disadvantaged neighbourhoods, high levels of collective efficacy can lead to lower violent crime rates has important implications for crime policy, especially in urban areas. Other major findings from the PHDCN that bear the Sampson imprimatur are that the relationship between crime and disorder is not causal (Sampson and Raudenbush 1999), and that 'broken windows' (see **James Q. Wilson**) are socially constructed (Sampson and Raudenbush 2004) in that all race/ethnic groups perceive there to be more disorder in a neighbourhood that has an increasing number of minority and/or immigrant groups (the effect being strongest for whites). More recently, Sampson has argued in the *New York Times* that, contrary to widespread popular belief in the United States, immigrants actually commit less crime than native-born populations (Sampson 2006).

The PHDCN is now among the most utilised data sets in criminology. Yet, beyond merely providing a data set for a generation of scholars, Sampson and his collaborators have given the discipline new concepts and tools to examine crime, disorder, wellness and development. Testament to the influence of the PHDCN is that collective efficacy is now part of the mainstream criminological lexicon. Likewise, the toolkit 'ecometrics' that Sampson and colleagues developed to analyse 'collective processes at the neighborhood level' (Marino 2008: 843) is a methodological advance that will be used for decades to come. Although in some ways this 'big science' approach seems far removed from the style of research sponsored by the original Chicago School, the concern with the ecological context of behaviour and with documenting social change in its multiple positive and negative forms illustrates how the concerns of the first great American school of sociology still resonate in Sampson's work.

Sampson's contribution to modern criminology is already significant and is sure to increase. His work is theoretically and methodologically sophisticated, and he seamlessly integrates scholarship from a wide variety of disciplines into his work. He is a consummate collaborator, a clear thinker, and he was the first criminologist to be elected to the National Academy of the Sciences in 2006, which is a career-defining honour in the life of any scientist. Only members of the academy can nominate a person for membership and it is exceedingly rare for a social scientist to be nominated, never mind selected. Sampson is currently Chair of the Department of Sociology at Harvard University, having occupied the same post at the University of Chicago. He is the recipient of numerous awards, including the Michael J. Hindelang book award (twice), the Edwin H. Sutherland award from the American Society of Criminology, the Robert Park award (twice) and the Albert J. Reiss Outstanding Book Award from the American Sociological Association. Moreover, the life course of his own criminological career is only just getting started. With the sheer pace of Sampson's productivity and contributions to the discipline, it will not be long before this entry will need a substantial revision.

Major works

Laub, J.H. and R.J. Sampson (2003) *Shared Beginnings, Divergent Lives: Delinquent Boys to Age 70.* Cambridge, Massachusetts: Harvard University Press.

Sampson, R.J. and Groves, W.B. (1989) 'Community Structure and Crime: Testing Social Disorganization Theory', *American Journal of Sociology*, 94(4): 774–802.

Sampson, R.J. and Laub, J.H. (1993) *Crime in the Making: Pathways and Turning-points Through Life.* Cambridge, Massachusetts: Harvard University Press.

Sampson, R.J. and Raudenbush, S.W. (1999) 'Systematic Social Observation of Public Spaces: a New Look at Disorder in Urban Neighborhoods', *American Journal of Sociology*, 105: 603–51.

—— (2004) 'Seeing Disorder: Neighborhood Stigma and the Social Construction of Broken Windows', *Social Psychology Quarterly*, 67: 319–42.

Sampson, R.J., Raudenbush, S.W. and Earls, F. (1997) 'Neighborhoods and Violent Crime: a Multilevel Study of Collective Efficacy', *Science*, 277: 918–24.

Further reading

Bursik, R.J. (1988) 'Social Disorganization and Theories of Crime and Delinquency: Problems and Prospects', *Criminology*, 26(4): 519–51.

Kornhauser, R.R. (1978) *Social Sources of Delinquency*. Chicago, Illinois: University of Chicago Press.

Marino, M. (2008) 'Profile of Robert J. Sampson', *Proceedings of the National Academy of the Sciences*, 105(3): 842–44.

Sampson, R.J. (2006) 'Open Doors Don't Invite Criminals', *New York Times*, 11 March, A24.

PATRICK CARR

INDEX

Printed in the USA/Agawam, MA
September 25, 2012

569343.003